Critical Essays on Philip Roth

Critical Essays on Philip Roth

Sanford Pinsker

G. K. Hall & Co. • Boston, Massachusetts

Library of Congress Cataloging in Publication Data
Main entry under title:

Critical essays on Philip Roth.

  (Critical essays on American literature)
  Includes index.
  1. Roth, Philip—Criticism and interpretation—Addresses, essays,
lectures.   I. Pinsker, Sanford.
II. Series.
PS3568.0855Z64   813'.54   81–13300
ISBN 0–8161–8423–2   AACR2

This publication is printed on permanent/durable acid-free paper
MANUFACTURED IN THE UNITED STATES OF AMERICA

CRITICAL ESSAYS ON AMERICAN LITERATURE

This series seeks to publish the most important reprinted criticism on writers and topics in American literature along with, in various volumes, original essays, interviews, bibliographies, letters, manuscript sections, and other materials brought to public attention for the first time. Sanford Pinsker's volume on Philip Roth is the most comprehensive scholarly anthology ever published on this important and controversial writer. It contains, along with reprinted essays by Leslie Fiedler, Robert Alter, Alfred Kazin, and Irving Howe, among others, original articles by Daniel Walden, Joseph Voelker, Morton P. Levitt, and Howard Eiland. We are confident that this collection will make a permanent and significant contribution to American literary study.

JAMES NAGEL, GENERAL EDITOR

Northeastern University

CONTENTS

Philip Roth
Chronology of Books

INTRODUCTION

Philip Roth published his first story—"The Day It Snowed"—in the Fall 1954 issue of the *Chicago Review*.[1] He was twenty-one years old. The bonechilling despairs one associates with, first, Chicago and then the University of Chicago were less apparent than the heady promises of a big city and a prestigious university. The difficulties of *Letting Go* (1962) would come later. Roth arrived trailing the usual clouds of academic glory: he was a B.A. magna cum laude, an English major, and the former editor of Bucknell University's literary magazine. At the University of Chicago the English Department was thick with high-powered, generally neo-Aristotelian, critics. Nonetheless, Roth made an impressive start in a city where it snows hard and often.

A year later Roth published "The Contest for Aaron Gold"[2] and the rest, as they say, is history. Granted, having a story chosen for inclusion in Martha Foley's *The Best American Stories of 1956* does not a career make, but it did establish the necessary credentials for the larger success that was sure to come. With *Goodbye, Columbus* (1959), the short-awaited Success arrived—along with a notoriety that has dogged Roth's footprints ever since.

In a culture that seems bent upon making good on Andy Warhol's quip about everybody in America being famous for fifteen minutes, Roth's sheer *staying* power deserves mention—especially since he has studiously avoided becoming a talk-show pundit or, worse, a "TV personality." He remains, in a word, a writer. But that condition has been enough to sustain his reputation through two very trying decades. There are, no doubt, times when Norman Mailer must wonder how Roth did it. And, no doubt, there are those who still grit their teeth, hoping that the irreverent, satirical Mr. Roth would go away. Or at least stop writing. That, of course, seems unlikely. Ignoring him is equally unlikely, for the fact of the matter is that attention must be paid to the sort of fiction Philip Roth writes. In learning how best, how truly, to criticize his work, we learn something important about ourselves.

The process began with *Goodbye, Columbus*. Not surprisingly, the early reviews lump Roth with other voices and other rooms: William German heard echoes of Irwin Shaw, John O'Hara, J. D. Salinger, Shirley Jackson and Sholom Aleichem,[3] the *Virginia Kirkus* entry concentrated on Roth's "Salinger-like ear·for dialogue, humor and maturity of outlook,"[4] but it was Saul Bellow who probably came closest to the mark where "influences" were concerned: "Neil [Klugman] is descended from the shlimazl on the Jewish side, the clerk in Gogol's 'The Cloak' on the Russian side, and the youth of Sherwood Anderson's 'I'm a Fool' on the

1

American side."⁵ Such exercises in comparison-and-contrast are part of the ritual indignities every new fictionist is expected to endure. Later, he would be talked about on his own terms, but, for the moment, he was traveling in good literary company.

Other reviewers chose to drop the polite banter and go directly to the bottom line. Jeremy Larner accused Roth of seeking "only to cheapen the people he writes about,"⁶ while Harold Ribalow gave the objection a parochial twist: Roth is "unnecessarily caustic and looks upon his fellow Jews with a jaundiced eye."⁷ Christian critics saw this as the stuff of which Old Testament prophets were made. In *Philip Roth and Bernard Malamud: A Critical Essay*, Glenn Meeter turned the irreverent Mr. Roth into a very "religious" writer indeed.⁸ His Jew was a "Man of Faith," his "quest," a religious—"Christian"—quest, his "conversion," a matter of rejoining the fold. I suspect Roth preferred hot argument to bland sentimentality. In any event, Ribalow can claim a certain amount of credit for being the first one to use "tasteless, vulgar, anti-Semitic and over-rated" all in a single review. That Larner's remarks appeared in *Partisan Review*, while Ribalow's were in the *Chicago Jewish Forum* speaks volumes about the academic/critical marketplace. The bifurcation would continue.

Moreover, it would continue in responses to Philip Roth mounted from the pulpits of synagogues and the program lecterns of Jewish Community Centers. I have chosen the words of my last sentence carefully because the bulk of these shrill responses were not so much directed at Roth's fiction, to either its protagonists or its textures, but *ad hominem*, against Roth himself. No bibliographer could, or *should*, list this sort of unpublished finger-wagging, but it was there nonetheless, always just beneath the polite, quasi-official polemics of a spokesman like Harold Ribalow. Those who cheered him on had rougher things to say.

At an early stage in Roth's career, Irving Howe enjoyed playing a role as "defender of the literary faith." After all, enough self-protectiveness was enough. Those who dismissed Roth as a self-hating Jew cried out for instruction. In a review of *Goodbye, Columbus* he used the occasion to talk about Roth's aesthetics with one breath (Roth's stories lack "imaginative transformation,"⁹ drive "openly to moral conclusions"; nonetheless, Howe was impressed) and to take a few swipes of his own at the meretriciousness of suburban Jewry with the other. (In effect, by name-calling Roth a "self-hating Jew," the need for self-examination disappears. Howe strongly suggests it shouldn't.) Later, of course, Howe would accuse Roth of being a vulgarian, one who reduced his characters to objects of derision.¹⁰ But in 1959, Howe felt duty-bound to welcome a new, exciting voice in American-Jewish literature.

Indeed, the critical reactions to *Goodbye, Columbus* established patterns that have persisted through the Roth canon. Neutral criticism, whether the sort which collects images or discovers structures, hardly exists where Roth is concerned. His readers have strong attachments to one end or the other of the evaluative yardstick; they either love his work, or they hate it. Gray areas are rare indeed.

As if this were not enough, Roth's career has had a nasty habit of not developing in ways his admirers or, for that matter, his detractors had envisioned. Just when he seemed destined to write tightly constructed, Jamesian fictions like *Letting Go* (1962), Roth published the free-wheeling *Portnoy's Complaint* (1969); just when a constituency grew comfortable with the fabulistic experimentation of *The Breast* (1972), he published *My Life As a Man* (1974). The effects were unsettling, and reviewers, critics, and common readers alike were not shy about issuing "directives" to Roth about where his fiction ought to go. In his most recent novel, *The Ghost Writer* (1979), Roth's protagonist is a very young, very vulnerable writer named Nathan Zuckerman, who discovers that Life and Art have a strange, interpenetrating relationship. One of his stories has deeply upset his family: Artistic Truth is all well and good, but some things should remain private. Moreover, what will non-Jews think when they read such a distasteful story? The task of making Zuckerman see the light falls to Judge Leopold Wapter, a man who takes a special delight in arranging a series of questions designed to domesticate the satirist in Zuckerman and to turn Zuckerman, the literary artist, into Zuckerman, the Jewish community's Public Relations man. One suspects that Philip Roth has had to face similar questions, in and out of print, long before.

Not surprisingly, Roth responds in kind. If Auden is right about "mad Ireland" hurting William Butler Yeats into poetry, it is equally true that nagging criticism could sting Roth into self-serving prose. He launched the counter-attack with a manifesto entitled "Writing American Fiction"[11] and then followed it with a few remarks to a *Commentary* symposium on "Jewishness and the Younger Intellectuals."[12] Later, he wrote about "The New Jewish Stereotypes"[13] or about "Imagining Jews"[14] and in 1975 a collection of his articles, picked-up pieces, interviews (including one in which Roth interrogates himself) and miscellaneous prose appeared between hard covers. It was entitled *Reading Myself and Others*, and the title said it all: in talking about others (be they Saul Bellow or Bernard Malamud, Franz Kafka or Richard Nixon), Philip Roth always had his eye firmly on the main chance. This is scarcely a new phenomenon. Writers have an itch to knock off the competition or to chart out some new territory where one's peers might be afraid to tread. Roth did a little of both, but in ways that added an unusual amount of brilliance and dazzle to the process.

T.S. Eliot's essay "The Function of Criticism" comes to mind, not because Eliot's best essays were a justification of Eliot's best poetry, but because it speaks to the very heart of why criticism *per se* is attractive to certain creative writers. Eliot catalogues them as those who "have a critical activity which is not all discharged into their work" or those who "seem to require to keep their critical powers in condition for the real work by exercising them miscellaneously" or, finally, those who "on completing a work, need to continue the critical activity by commenting on it." *Reading Myself and Others* makes it clear that Roth is all three, but with an urgency Eliot could not have imagined.

For Roth, the "function of criticism" has to do with maintaining a balance between the libinal wackiness of his protagonist and the serious, even "palefaced" demeanor of Roth himself. Evidently the condition is infectious, because many of his critics suffer from the same malady. That is, they vacillate between applauding (identifying with?) the confessional candor of characters like Alexander Portnoy or David Kepesh, and finger-wagging at Philip Roth. This, too, started early. Winning a National Book Award for *Goodbye, Columbus* made it a certainty that widespread attention would be paid to his next book. It was.

Letting Go (1962) has its focus, its confusions, securely anchored in the 1950s, High Culture, graduate student ennui, and Chicago. Roth would go over the same ground a dozen years later in *My Life as a Man*, but, this time, he wore a grim, pinched face. Many of the reviewers seemed not to notice; it was as if those who missed out on *Goodbye, Columbus* felt an obligation to put their position on Roth into the public record. Predictably enough, opinion was sharply divided along what had, even then, become dreary lines: Charles Angoff accused Roth of a "peculiar artistic vulgarity"[15] which, as it turns out, meant there was too much sex and, in particular, too much *Jewish* sex. Once again, Harold Ribalow seconded the motion, adding that Roth himself is guilty of the conditions he so deplored in American life—namely, that it is infuriating, sickening and embarrassing.[16] And, once again, the country's major literary journals chimed in with lavish praise: the *Kenyon Review* called it "a masterful achievement"[17]; *Harper's* felt it was "worthy of Roth's first promise"[18]; and *Atlantic* claimed it was "probing, tentative, complex."[19]

Indeed, so much reviewers' ink was spilled about *Letting Go* that Richard A. Rand "reviewed" the reviews a year later.[20] After dismissing most of the prior commentary as fastened either to social issues or Roth's personality, Rand went on to compare the Jamesian qualities of *Letting Go* with the reflexivity of Vladimir Nabokov's *Pale Fire*. Not surprisingly, Nabokov won, but not before Rand tested out his pet theories about *Letting Go*'s aesthetic structure: Gabe, the Jamesian hero, is pitted against Paul, the would-be mensch. The result, according to Rand, is a draw because each fails to "alter the other's development." Much later Scott Donaldson would expand these Jamesian implications in an article entitled "Philip Roth: The Meanings of *Letting Go*."[21]

Those who see Jamesian footprints on Roth's work are, of course, not wrong. Echoes from a Henry James story are heard and then much pondered in *The Ghost Writer*; indeed, James is one of the "ghosts" who haunt this fiction about the making-and-responsibilities of fiction. Which is to say, Donaldson's thesis has a staying power that Roth's own imagination confirms. Nonetheless, Stanley Cooperman's reading of *Letting Go* entitled "Old Jacob's Eye With a Squint"[22] may, finally, be more penetrating and more telling. "Old Jacob's Eye" is at the very heart of why Roth's protagonist cannot "let go." It is a matter of moral judgment, however ambivalent that might be, a matter of personal commitment, however much avoided. It is, in short, the vision Paul Herz tried to achieve and Gabe Wallach tries to deny.

If it is true Roth has a habit of biting the Jewish hands that have fed him, it is also true that he can occasionally snap at Mid-Western WASPs. In a brief flirtation with the New Journalism entitled "Iowa: A Very Far Country Indeed,"[23] Roth bid a satiric farewell to that state where he had labored for two years as a member of the Iowa Writers Workshop. The exercise apparently warmed him up because four years later Roth struck at the Midwest again. This time it was called *When She Was Good* (1967) and, this time, critics—both Jewish and non-Jewish alike—had the pinched feeling of shoes being forced on the wrong feet.

Time magazine was quick to dub Lucy Nelson a "Midwestern Madame Bovary"[24] and to complain that she is just too plain nasty to sustain our interest. *Virginia Quarterly Review* also hoisted the white flag by claiming that "such unrelieved gloom and appalling hopelessness eventually wear down the reader. . . ."[25] But an equally large number of reviewers were just as convinced that when Roth was good—in his ear for the rhythms of native American speech, in his uncanny knack for realistic detail, in his capacity for moral vision, in his Jamesian nuances—he was very good indeed. For example, Jonathan Baumbach called the novel "a surprising tour de force, an accomplishment comparable to Zero Mostel doing an extended imitation of Jimmy Stewart."[26] I am not sure that readers of *Commonweal* fully understood the analogy, but there was no mistaking the high praise of others: Doris Grumbach declared it a novel of "inescapable authenticity"[27] (an assertion which, no doubt, came as something of a surprise to those, like Wilfred Sheed, who were of the opinion that Roth had merely superimposed "his own sense of social textures on his Lutheran characters, making them just like Jews only duller"[28]); in the pages of *Nation*, Shaun O'Connell insisted, unequivocally, that it was "a great book," one that "cuts to the heart of a place, a tight, right American girl and, finally, the reader. . . ."[29] Josh Greenfield was so taken with Lucy Nelson that he not only hailed *When She Was Good* as "a major work, Roth's most completely realized novel, fulfilling much of his golden promise," but also went beyond encomium to the airy realms of prophecy—the portrait of Ms. Nelson's rise-and-fall "may one day rank among the best in our fiction."[30]

A dozen years have not seen Greenfield's projection come true, nor are things likely to change very soon. Like the nursery rhyme on which its title was based, when *When She Was Good* is good, it is quite good, but when it is bad, it is horrid. Nonetheless, the novel did open up warfare on yet another continually expanding front—namely, charges and counter-charges about Roth's misogyny. The Brenda Patimkin of *Goodbye, Columbus* was the first instance, but she soon had equally bitchy company: Libby Herz from *Letting Go* and, in Midwestern drag, the shrill, plotting Lucy Nelson. In each case, there were suspicions abroad that these were the self-serving fantasies of a spoiled Jewish boy named Philip Roth.

Like the grumbling in the foyers of synagogues, much of this discontent did not see public print. In an *Atlantic* article, Alix Kates Shulman argues that the sexual war is localized, for better or worse, in the automobile backseat and that popular novels and films tend to portray the uptight forties and fifties from a male point of view. In this regard, "*When She Was Good* is a book which, though widely hailed as the definitive portrait of the Great American Bitch, seems to recognize, even to understand, the Middle-American girl's plight—and yet still manages to blame her for the awful consequences."[31] If he were not such a dazzling writer, it would, presumably, be easier to work up a good feminist mad. But even Ms. Shulman had to admit that his parking scenes were "spectacularly accurate." But all that said, the *best* way to insure that the female side of the back seat gets equal time is to write the fiction oneself. That, of course, is exactly what Ms. Shulman does. And I suspect that her reactions to a review taking *Memoirs of an Ex-Prom Queen* to task for being unfair to men, one that chastised her for laying all the blame for the heroine's unhappy consequences on men, would be both predictable, and not unlike Mr. Roth's.

In this sense, female critics have it easier. Sarah Blacher Cohen's "Philip Roth's Would-be Patriarchs and Their Shikses and Shrews"[32] can investigate Roth's misogyny and still retain certain measures of good cheer and critical disinterest. After all, the woods of American literature are filled with adolescent males; for academic types—even those who bow to nobody in their insistence on sexual equality—Roth's continuing problems with women fit snugly within the American literary tradition. After all, which American authors, with the possible exception of Henry James, did all that well when they created female characters? And who would want to swap literature, even the lopsided fiction of Philip Roth, for the bromides of Ann Landers?

Apparently, Mary Allen would. At least that is the sense one gets when reading *The Necessary Blankness*, her study of women in the contemporary American novel.[33] Her book is dedicated "To Women" and begins with a short burst of chic candor: "Women matter to me." Moreover, there is "something wrong in the way women feel about themselves" (p. 1). From that heartfelt concern to an indictment of John Barth, Ken Kesey and, of course, Philip Roth, it is but a baby step. Here, for example, is Allen on what is wrong with *Letting Go*:

> While the adoption of a child for Libby is a central issue of the novel, it is obviously only an illusion of the three main characters that this or any other form of parenthood will be a cure for her despair. Libby is delighted when she finally gets a baby, but her pleasure is demonstrated in an abnormal obsession with the child—too much running to the baby's room to see if she is still there, with the same brittle tension that is her reaction to other things. Since the truest satisfaction in Libby's life comes from wanting things, she would be better off making money than raising children. But Roth, the humanist, could hardly suggest this. Becoming a mother is surely the conventional answer to what Libby might do with her life, but it does not represent a choice that has anything to do with her understanding of or suitability for motherhood. (pp. 85–86).

Libby, in short, should be a career woman.

Lucy Nelson, on the other hand, should be simply "good" or at least better than Roth allows her to be. She is "one of the most monstrous bitches in a tradition made up of too many weak and bland women" (p. 95). Worse, she can never come up to what Roth conceives as our decade's moral standard. In a word, Philip Roth is disappointed. Not surprisingly, so is Ms. Allen:

> If woman was at one time in literature designated as man's moral guardian, for Roth she no longer has even the possibility of containing that which is moral. There is no evidence that he wishes such a condition to be true . . . and therefore in his creation of heroines he projects his enormous rage and disappointment with womankind, writing with power and conviction, but as a man who rails at the world because he has never found in it a woman who is both strong and good (p. 96).

Portnoy's Complaint (1969) changed everything—including the older charges about misogyny. Now Roth was, if anything, even worse: an ungrateful son and a mother baiter. The title of Alfred Kazin's review tells it all: "Up Against the Wall, Mama!"[34] As Kazin points out, Roth reduces his experiences to psychology, all his fictive Jews to raving hysterics. In this sense he lacks "general ideas," that touch of the intellect Kazin associates with, say, Saul Bellow's Moses Herzog. Other New York intellectuals were prone to agree. Josh Greenfield, writing in the *New York Times Book Review*, equated psychoanalytic confession with "the existentially quintessential form for any American-Jewish tale-bearing."[35]

Others were not nearly as serious-minded, either feeling that the novel did not deserve that sort of attention, or that an outrageous joke deserved an outrageous review. Thus, Anatole Broyard dubbed it the "Moby Dick of masturbation,"[36] while Guy Davenport coined "onanistic Bildungsroman"[37] as the appropriate phrase for the wacky Alex Portnoy. Only J. Mitchell Morse was convinced that this book is not worth discussing at length. And in a short review that put into practice what he preached for others, he castigated Roth as a "pimp of his particularity . . . a professional Jew-boy."[38]

Not surprisingly, non-Jewish reviewers had an easier time of it. For most of them, *Portnoy's Complaint* could be simply a funny book that one didn't especially have to defend or attack. Brendan Gil called it one of the "dirtiest and funniest books ever published"[39]; even Granville Hicks thought it "something like a masterpiece."[40] To be sure, the British novelist Kingsley Amis called it everything *but* funny—"fluent, lively, articulate, vivid, energetic"[41]—but perhaps *that* compliment is too much to ask of a fellow comic novelist.

At one point in the novel Portnoy rails against those who would label, and thus restrict, him as a Jew: "Jew Jew Jew Jew Jew Jew Jew! [Portnoy shrieks on the psychiatrist's couch] It is coming out of my ears already, the sage of the suffering Jews! . . . *I happen also to be a human being!*" Roth's reviewers, however, were not convinced. As one after another pointed out, the pains of childhood are universal. In the *Antioch Review*, Jewish reviewers were reminded—gently, but sharply—that they had overlooked "the universal elements of this wildly hilarious (and quite moving) book. Gentiles can also have Jewish mamas and Jews are not alone in the hang-ups between gentility and genitalia."[42] In the *New York Times*, Christopher Lehmann-Haupt called *Portnoy's Complaint* the greatest Jewish joke ever told, one that brings the "so-called Jewish novel to an end."[43] *In pace requiescat.*

Unlike, say, Saul Bellow's *Herzog*, this was a novel that American Jews both owned and read. Needless to say, many were shocked rather than delighted at what they found between its hard covers. The word the reviewers had missed was *shmutz*, a term of contempt that its English translation, "dirt," only approximates. The anti-Roth crusade the Rabbis began when *Goodbye, Columbus* was published turned into a full-scale, suburban war with *Portnoy's Complaint*. The phones rang off the hooks and the sounds of tsk! task! could be heard wherever defenders of Sophie Portnoy met. Granted, Marya Mannes called Portnoy "the most disagreeable bastard who ever lived"[44] and Jacqueline Susann fired off her talk-show quip about Roth being a good writer, but not the sort of person you'd like to shake hands with, but, by and large, Lois G. Gordon's measured, academic cadences are more typical:

> The theme of the book—and a significant and universal one—is . . . this dichotomy and tension between the public and private man, between consciousness and unconscious motivation, between the adult ideal one strives for and the childhood fantasy one cannot relinquish, between abstract morality with its noble dictates and the unconscious, parental, superego precipitates that are the source of morality.[45]

Mark Shechner's "Philip Roth"[46] travels over the same psychoanalytic ground, but with a greater sense of scope and less hackneyed psychoanalysis. Even before *The Ghost Writer* made it very, very clear, Shechner had pointed out that fathers-and-sons, rather than Jewish Mothers and their Nice Jewish Sons, were at the heart of Roth's best work. Manhood, of course, is a reconciliation with both, but Roth can never rail against father figures with quite the easy zeal he could *shpritz* about mothers. He needs desperately the approval of the the former. Ironically enough, it cannot be earned by devastating the latter.

Roth's Chicago friend, Theodore Solotaroff, updated his earlier piece on "Philip Roth and the Jewish Moralists"[47] with a brilliant essay entitled "The Journey of Philip Roth."[48] And there were other signs that Philip Roth was a writer to be reckoned with: an article by Melvin J. Friedman entitled "Jewish Mothers and Sons: The Expense of *Chutzpah*" appeared in a collection edited by Irving Malin.[49] The anthology also included a bibliography compiled by Jackson Bryer, one section of which was devoted to Philip Roth. Indeed, essays on Roth began to appear often between hard covers: Sheldon Grebstein's "The Comic Anatomy of *Portnoy's Complaint*"[50] continued the preoccupation with *Portnoy's Complaint*, the be-all-to-end-all American-Jewish novel, while, in *America's Humor*, Walter Blair and Hamlin Hill chose to emphasize *The Great American Novel* as the Roth work must clearly in the Great [Humorous] Tradition.[51]

Moreover, there were whole books devoted to the Roth canon. In 1974, Bernard Rodgers, Jr. expanded and updated the Bryer bibliography into a full-scale and very useful volume.[52] During the same year, John McDaniel published the first critical study of Roth's fiction from *Goodbye, Columbus* to *My Life as a Man*.[53] McDaniel investigates Roth's affinities with Franz Kafka by applying the terms of Helen Weinberg's *The New Novel in America: The Kafkan Mode in Contemporary Fiction*—especially her categories of the "activist" and "victim-hero"—to Roth's protagonists.[54] Not everyone agreed with Weinberg's notion of the "Kafkan novel" or with McDaniel's application, but it became increasingly clear that their hunches about Kafka's influence and Roth's affection were dead right. Roth's blending of fiction and literary criticism entitled "I Always Wanted You to Admire My Fasting; or, Looking at Kafka" (included in *Reading Myself and Others*) confirmed the collective suspicion.

Two other full-length studies followed relatively close on the heels, or perhaps the "wake," of McDaniel's book: my own *The Comedy That "Hoits": An Essay on the Fiction of Philip Roth*[55] and Bernard Rodgers' *Philip Roth*.[56] It will surprise nobody—including Professors McDaniel, Rodgers and myself—when other books on Philip Roth appear, no doubt thicker, smarter, and better written. This comment says as much about

Roth's continuing production as it does about the continuing critical interest in his work.

Back at the writing desk, however, the year was 1971, the War in Vietnam threatened to drag on forever and Philip Roth published the wickedly satirical *Our Gang*. Predictably, reviewers were divided. Pearl K. Bell represented one camp. She found *Our Gang* "empty of genuine wit and effective comic inspiration," that his satire had "neither the moral intensity of Swift nor the annihilating clarity of Orwell."[57] In a word, *Our Gang* was "juvenile." Like-minded souls including Murray Kempton [58] and Marvin Mudrick[59] agreed that the issue was not whether Roth's political heart was in the right place (most pundits felt it was), but whether his Swiftian satire deserved either the adjective or the noun. Their consensus was, it didn't.

Dwight MacDonald, by contrast, was willing to buy both the premise and the thin book. In his unhedging words, *Our Gang* was "tasteless, disturbing, coarse and very funny."[60] Far from being indulgent, sophomoric or shoddy goods, *Our Gang* was "a masterpiece." Ironically, the widest circulation magazines (e.g. *Newsweek*, *Atlantic*) echoed MacDonald's opinion. It was an era more notable for its critical heat than for its critical light.

Even more ironically, the last word on *Our Gang* may have been written, inadvertently, by Roth himself—in a piece entitled "Writing American Fiction" that he had published in *Commentary* a decade earlier: "American reality stupefies, it sickens, it infuriates, and finally it is even a kind of embarrassment to one's meager imagination."[61] In the last analysis, it was not the swipes from Pearl K. Bell and Crowd that did *Our Gang* in, but, rather, it was Richard Nixon who proved Roth a mere piker where the grotesque is concerned. Even Roth's fabulistic imagination was no match for Watergate. "Watergate" editions of *Our Gang* only made things sadder.

After the first wave of critics exhausted the subject of Roth's stature as a Classical Satirist, there seemed little else to say, especially since the dust settles on efforts like Barbara Garson's *MacBird* rather quickly. All this may also help to give Brom Weber's "The Mode of Black Humor" an added lustre.[62] Granted, "black humor" is a slippery term, but it is still a more useful way of approaching the vision in *Our Gang* than those which forced Roth to compete with the likes of Swift and Dryden. Moreover, *Portnoy's Complaint* had already called Roth to the attention of those people collecting evidence about black humor.

Roth's next novel—*The Breast* (1972)—confirmed a wide range of suspicions: that Roth was a Black Humorist; that he was a male, sexist pig; that he was our country's most interesting, most daring and most literary fabulist; that Ralph Nader should insist the Consumer Protection Agency stamp every copy with *Caveat emptor*. Once again, the critical opinion divided sharply, but this time, the controversy continued. Indeed, the only thing the novel's defenders and detractors shared was an obligation to make groaningly bad puns on the title. Thus, Frederick Crews—who would go on to praise the novel for its "high seriousness"—cannot quite resist the impulse to title his review "Uplift,"[63] while Margaret Drabble—who found the novel one of the "funniest to appear in a long time" and, in fact, a worthy successor to Gogol's "The Nose" and Kafka's "Metamorphosis"—cannot resist a title like "Clean Breast."[64] My own suspicion was that *The Breast* is the first volume of a projected trilogy. I even had some hunches about what the next titles might be and I wondered how the reviewers would handle them.

But puns aside, *The Breast* must be able to support itself—and, alas, it can't. As Peter S. Prescott points out, "Roth did not decide whether [the novel] was to be a buoyant farce like Gogol's story, or a dark parable like Kafka's.[65] After *Our Gang*, Roth suffered the slings and arrows of Swiftian comparison; after *The Breast*, reviewers reminded him that he was *not* Gogol, *not* Kafka. The result, according to Duncan Fallowell, reaffirms "the mediocrity of Roth's own contribution to the genre."[66] Indeed, the exercise can only be written down as "masochistic."

Other reviewers thought the proper word to describe this overpriced book was "criminal." Roger Sale is perhaps the most forthright spokesman of this disgruntled group. He skirts the whole issue of literary allusion and, instead, drives relentlessly toward *The Breast*'s bottom line: this book, Sale insists, is "stupefyingly bad; I read it through twice, surely more than Roth himself has done, just trying to fathom what could have made him write it . . . It will, and should, be read, if it all, standing up in a bookstore."[67]

For better or worse, Sale did not have the last word he had hoped for. Indeed, there were those who defended *The Breast* when it first appeared and who still regard it as breaking fresh, important fictional ground. Once again, it was Theodore Solotaroff who captained the defense, who continued the role as Explainer of Roth's Literary Faith. He talked about Roth's "transformation" from the cool, steady realist of his first three books to the blue comedian of *Portnoy's Complaint* and *Our Gang* in ways that both justified and approved of the metamorphosis. Thus, *The Breast* was "a fable of bisexual recognition in all of its strangeness, torment and possible use."[68] Moreover, it was "not only the best example yet of Roth's astonishing prowess when he is at the top of his talent and control . . . but also a permanent addition to the writer's consciousness of himself." All this from the editor of the highly influential *New American Review!*

Since the thumbs-up/thumbs-down situation in which reviewers found themselves, there have been several critical articles devoted to *The Breast* worth mentioning; Pierre Michel, who writes often about Roth, sees *The Breast* as inextricably related to the conditions of writing. His article is entitled "Philip Roth's *The Breast*: Reality Adultered and the

Plight of the Writer."[69] On the other hand, Elizabeth Sabiston views the novel as a cautionary tale for critics,[70] while Julian C. Rice reconsiders the whole question of Roth and Freudianism in "Philip Roth's *The Breast*: Cutting the Freudian Cord."[71]

Alexander Portnoy had a seemingly endless list of "complaints," but there was one turf that was uncomplicated, unencumbered, downright *pastoral*—center field:

> Thank God for center field! [Portnoy shouts] Because center field is like some observation post, a kind of control tower, where you are able to see everything and everyone, to understand what's happening the instant it happens . . . For in center field, if you can get to it, it is yours.[72]

The Great American Novel (1973) turns the baseball diamond into stage-center. The result, however, proved to be yet another installment in the shell game that Roth played with critics and critics played with Roth. From his side, there was the bravado, the Big Promise, the shameless chutzpah of his title; from theirs, the disappointment that, this time, Roth had ruined the comic parts by making them too long, rather than vice versa. Ironically enough, the same Philip Roth who had been accused of cynical exploitation in passing off a novella like *The Breast* as a hardcover book was now hectored for his overly large ambition. Thomas R. Edwards, for example, recognized *The Great American Novel*'s preoccupation with "heroic and pastoral myth" but, at the same time, Roth's determination to get in every joke he can think of about our past and present follies . . . finally is exhausting and self-defeating."[73] Moreover, the heavy doses of black humor had the look of a dead horse beating a man, especially since Edwards was convinced that the charm of that sort of humor "has seen its day."

Christopher Lehmann-Haupt felt otherwise. *The Great American Novel* was, in his words, a marvelous "bathtub book," the perfect thing to take along on a long soak. But Lehmann-Haupt's review does its particular brand of damning with high praise:

> *The Great American Novel* is a masterpiece. What hilarity! What giddiness! What fantasies! What nonsense! . . . Was ever baseball fantasy and reality so gloriously, comically and tastelessly interwoven? It made me laugh so hard that had I been where I belonged the waves would've lapped onto the floor. Why, were it not that Mr. Roth's novel is so deeply sunk in the tradition, one would almost chance the claim that he has risen above the bathtub.[74]

John Leonard was more respectful and more serious about his plaudits: "After several years of fiddling around—*Our Gang, The Breast*—Philip Roth has gotten back to serious work."[75] Granted, if the result was not quite that mythical beast known in abbreviation as the G.A.N., *The Great American Novel* was, according to Leonard, a "hugely inventive, often brilliant, very funny book that collapses into giggles and splinters two-thirds of the way through." Nevertheless, as a "baseball novel, Leonard felt it "finishes first, with Bernard Malamud's *The Natural*, Robert Coover's *The Universal Baseball Association*, and Mark Harris's *Bang the Drum Slowly* close behind."

Baseball has a way of attracting our best writers of fiction and non-fiction alike. Which is also to say, as that hearty band of critics involved with Sports & Literature continues to prosper, so will commentary about *The Great American Novel*. Robert F. Wilson, Jr.'s "An Indisputable Source for the Baseball Contest in *The Great American Novel*" is a portent of scholarly things to come.[76]

Meanwhile, more traditional modes of literary criticism continue to talk about archetypes rather than batting averages, about double-entendres rather than double plays. Ben Siegel's "The Myths of Summer: Philip Roth's *The Great American Novel*"[77] is an excellent example of the former, while Bernard Rodgers', "*The Great American Novel* and the Great American Joke"[78] is an equally impressive example of the latter.

My Life as a Man (1974) is yet another trip to the Roth confessional where, this time, his protagonist announces that he has been had by capital-L Literature. The strategy makes for what J.W. Aldridge calls "a totally solipsistic novel, which may well make it a perfect expression of the times."[79] Thus, *My Life as a Man* turns out to be an "endlessly ranting monologue," and, as Aldridge would have it, all Roth can do is "talk, talk, talk. . . ."

By contrast, P.S. Prescott, writing in the *New Yorker*, began by summing up: "This is Roth's best novel. . . ."[80] Best, because in *My Life as a Man*, Roth manages to "sustain a high decibel level, to deal with shrillness and excess, without succumbing to these conditions himself." What Aldridge bemoans as "solipsism," Prescott praises as the stuff of which aesthetic distance is made. Thus, Roth's fictions are filled with "people living on the brink of collapse, unable to function because they have overextended themselves, lacerated themselves, locked themselves into obsessions and other prisons of their own construction." For Prescott, these are "Roth's creatures whom he [Roth] treats with affection and wit. . . ."

In such a world Peter Tarnopol wants desperately to become a man. After all, if a commitment to High Art got him into trouble, perhaps the stories of his alter-ego, Nathan Zuckerman, will get him out. These "useful fictions" distance Zuckerman from Tarnopol and Tarnopol from Roth. *My Life as a Man* is an extended exercise in the reflexive mode, one that intrigued Modernists like Aldous Huxley (*Point Counter Point*) and André Gide (*The Counterfeiters*), as well as post-Modernist experimenters like John Barth (*Lost in the Funhouse, Chimera, Letters*). But, as Morris Dickstein points out, the novel merely confirms one's suspicions that "despite his superb gifts as a mimic, *tummler* and hyperbolist, Roth is only good at fantasticating materials from his own life."[81] Moreover, that life is decidedly limited, not, alas, to chronicles of his manhood, but, rather, to the milieu that dooms him to be a whining, spoiled little-Jewish boy: "As a satirist of middle-class Jewish life, he is brilliant and wicked, endowed with a perfect ear and a cold eye."

By contrast, David Monaghan's "*The Great American Novel* and *My Life as a Man*: An Assessment of Philip Roth's Achievement"[82] argues that Roth's ear for speech rhythms has been cocked elsewhere of late—toward pulp fiction and newspapers, political speeches and psychiatric jargon. He is, according to Monaghan, no longer either a disciple of Henry James or a chronicler of gilded American-Jewish ghettos. Rather, in *My Life as a Man*, he develops "the thesis that reality is a soap opera, and the novel repeatedly exposes us to the pop sensibility at work."

Roth's best characters *talk*. Alexander Portnoy "complains"; David Kepesh, *The Professor of Desire* (1977) lectures. Later, of course, he will become "The Breast" of Roth's earlier novel, but now he has all the savage energy we associate with Roth's portraits of artists as unhappy young men. In my review of the novel I tried to amplify this notion by pointing out that "young David is caught between temptation and restraint, between the impulses of exhibitionism and the aftermaths of shame."[83] Kepesh claims that "At twenty I must stop impersonating others and Become Myself, at least begin to impersonate the self I ought to be." Like Peter Tarnopol, Kepesh desires to transmogrify himself into a Serious Person. In his case, this means becoming what I call "a priest of the critical imagination":

> In short, he reads voraciously. And like other Roth protagonists, he desires . . . The result is a sybarite willing to sacrifice everything on the altar of Desire. At the same time, however, he is an incurable academic, the sort of professor who draws his lecture texts from a curious interpenetration of the great Modernists' works (e.g. Chekov, Flaubert, Kafka, *et al.*) and his own chaotic life (p. 12).

As Richard Boeth suggests, *The Professor of Desire* affords "many of the pleasures of intelligent discourse," albeit, ones drawn from a "self-absorbed and bookish person."[84] Perhaps the most representative response to the novel came from Paul Gray's comments in *Time* magazine:

> Like most writers who prove they have enough talent for the long haul of a career, Roth has found the story he will tell either until he or it is exhausted. It is a good story and, as *The Professor of Desire* proves, it gets better with each telling.[85]

Indeed, there were even hints that the wisecracking, Temper Tantrum Kid aspects of Roth's art were beginning to give way to the deeper rhythms of the human heart. In this novel, nostalgically loved fathers replace castrating mothers and the frenetic attractions of kinky sex become less important than the pastoral days with Claire Ovington which end the novel. To be sure, David Kepesh is destined to end his fictional days as a disoriented, shrieking breast, but Roth had added some important humanistic notes to his repertoire.

In his latest novel, *The Ghost Writer* (1979), he returns—in the guise of Nathan Zuckerman—to his earliest days as a fiction writer and the controversies born along with *Goodbye, Columbus*. It is an exercise in both having-it-out and making peace, in charting out that territory of the imagination which the genuine Artist must explore with honesty and asking, once again, what one's responsibilities to the American-Jewish community actually are. As Peter Prescott points out, *The Ghost Writer* is Roth's "best novel yet . . . From its rather *un*dramatic situation emerges a complex story of fathers and children, the artist's responsibility, the deceptive line between what a writer knows and what he imagines."[86] Robert Towers felt much the same way: "I had only to read two opening sentences to realize—with a long sigh of anticipated pleasure—that I was once again in the hands of a superbly endowed storyteller . . . The voice that Roth developed for his first-person narrations . . . is surely one of the most distinctive and supple in contemporary American literature."[87]

Thus, a retrospective meditation links the brash talent that produced *Goodbye, Columbus* twenty years ago with the maturing one that ponders Life & Art in *The Ghost Writer*. But, as John Leonard suggests, there is something just a bit disconcerting about a writer who keeps his anxious, non-fictional thumb forever on the pulse of his work:

> The trouble with reviewing *The Ghost Writer* a few weeks late is that Roth has already explained it for us. He is ever explaining. Like David Susskind, he can't shut up. *The Ghost Writer*, he told readers of *The New York Times*, "is about the surprises that the vocation of writing brings," just as *My Life as a Man* is "about the surprises that manhood brings" and *The Professor of Desire* is "about the surprises that desire brings." . . . This isn't Nabokov's ice-blue disdain for the academic ninnyhammers who went snorting after his truffles. Roth, instead, worries himself, as though a sick tooth needed tonguing. He is looking over his shoulder because somebody—probably Irving Howe—may be gaining on him.[88]

Leonard is correct, of course, but, then again, Philip Roth did not begin his career as either a compulsive explainer or a paranoid defender.

Well-meaning critics and well-intentioned rabbis have been hectoring him since those halcyon days when Neil Klugman held Brenda Patimkin's glasses. It would be difficult, if not downright impossible, to think of a love-hate affair in contemporary American literature that has been its equal. Meanwhile, Philip Roth is only forty-seven years old and at the top of his form. Which is also to say, I would be flabbergasted if the ripostes did not continue.

Sanford Pinsker

Notes

1. Philip Roth, "The Day It Snowed," *Chicago Review*, 8 (Fall 1954), 34–45.

2. Philip Roth, "The Contest for Aaron Gold," *Epoch*, 5–6, (Fall 1956), 37–50. Reprinted in Martha Foley, ed. *The Best American Short Stories of 1956.* (Boston: Houghton Mifflin, 1956.)

3. William German, *"Goodbye, Columbus* by Young Philip Roth," *San Francisco Chronicle.* (May 11, 1959), 37.

4. *Virginia Kirkus Reviews*, 27 (March 1, 1959), 190.

5. Saul Bellow, "The Swamp of Prosperity," *Commentary*, 28 (July 1959), 77.

6. Jeremy Larner, "The Conversion of the Jews," *Partisan Review*, 27 (Fall 1960), 761.

7. Harold Ribalow, *"Goodbye, Columbus,"* *Chicago Jewish Forum*, 18 (Summer 1960), 361.

8. Glenn Meeter, *Philip Roth and Bernard Malamud: A Critical Essay* (Grand Rapids: William B. Eerdmans, 1968).

9. Irving Howe, "The Suburbs of Babylon," *New Republic*, 140 (June 15, 1959), 17.

10. ———, "Philip Roth Reconsidered," *Commentary*, 54 (December 1972), 69–77.

11. Philip Roth, "Writing American Fiction," *Commentary*, 31 (March 1961), 223–33.

12. ———, Statement to symposium on "Jewishness and the Younger Intellectuals," *Commentary*, 31 (April 1961), 350–51.

13. ———, "The New Jewish Stereotypes," *American Judaism*, 11 (Winter 1961), 10.

14. ———, "Imagining Jews," *New York Review of Books*, 21 (October 3, 1974), 22.

15. Charles Angoff, "Caricatures of Jewish Life," *Congress Bi-Weekly*, 30 (March 4, 1963), 13.

16. Harold Ribalow, *"Letting Go,"* Chicago Jewish Forum, 21 (Summer 1963), 327.

17. Ellington White, "Throw Out the Paddle and Get a Reactor," *Kenyon Review*, 24 (Autumn 1962), 750.

18. Elizabeth Hardwick, *"Letting Go,"* Harper's, 225 (July 1962), 92.

19. William Barrett, "Let Go, Let Live," *Atlantic*, 210 (July 1962), 111.

20. Richard A. Rand, "A Late Look at *Letting Go," New Republic*, 148 (January 12, 1963), 22.

21. Scott Donaldson, "Philip Roth: The Meanings of *Letting Go," Contemporary Literature*, 11 (Winter 1970), 21–35.

22. Stanley Cooperman, "Old Jacob's Eye With a Squint," *Twentieth Century Literature*, 19 (July 1973), 203–16.

23. Philip Roth, "Iowa: A Very Far Country Indeed," *Esquire*, 58 (December 1962), 132.

24. *Time*, 89 (June 9, 1967), 120.

25. *Virginia Quarterly Review*, 43 (Summer 1967), cv.

26. Jonathan Baumbach, "What Hath Roth Got," *Commonweal*, 86 (August 11, 1967), 498.

27. Doris Grumbach, *"Letting Go," America*, 116 (June 17, 1967), 857.

28. Wilfred Sheed, "Pity the Poors Wasps," *New York Times Book Review* (June 11, 1967), 5.

29. Shaun O'Connell, "The Death of the Heart," *Nation*, 205 (July 17, 1967), 53.

30. Josh Greenfield, "The Trouble With Lucy," *Washington Post Book World* (June 4, 1967), 3.

31. Alix Kates Shulman, "The War in the Back Seat," *Atlantic*, 230 (July 1972), 50.

32. Sarah Blacher Cohen, "Philip Roth's Would-be Patriarchs and Their Shikses and Shrews," *Studies in American Jewish Literature*, 1 (Spring, 1975), 16–22.

33. Mary Allen, *The Necessary Blankness* (Urbana: University of Illinois Press, 1976). Subsequent references to Allen are to this book and pagination is included parenthetically.

34. Alfred Kazin, "Up Against the Wall, Mama!" *New York Review of Books*, 12 (February 27, 1969), 3.

35. Josh Greenfield, *"Portnoy's Complaint," New York Times Book Review* (February 23, 1969), 1.

36. Anatole Broyard, *"Portnoy's Complaint," New Republic*, 160 (March 1, 1969), 21.

37. Guy Davenport, "Cui Bono?" *National Review*, 21 (May 20, 1969), 495.

38. J. Mitchell Morse, *"Portnoy's Complaint," Hudson Review*, 22 (Summer 1969), 320.

39. Brendan Gil, "The Unfinished Man," *New Yorker*, 45 (March 8, 1969), 118.

40. Granville Hicks, *"Portnoy's Complaint," Saturday Review*, 52 (February 22, 1969), 38.

41. Kingsley Amis, "Waxing Wroth," *Harper's*, 238 (April 1969), 104.

42. *Antioch Review*, 29 (Spring 1969), 109.

43. Christopher Lehmann-Haupt, "A Portrait of the Artist as a Young Jew," *New York Times*, (February 18, 1969), 43.

44. Marya Mannes, "A Dissent from Marya Minnes," *Saturday Review*, 52 (February 22, 1960), 30.

45. Lois G. Gordon, *"Portnoy's Complaint*: Coming of Age in Jersey City," *Literature & Psychology*, 19 (Nos. 3 & 4, 1969), 57.

46. Mark Schechner, "Philip Roth," *Partisan Review*, 41 (Fall 1974), 410–27.

47. Theodore Solotaroff, "Philip Roth and the Jewish Moralists," *Chicago Review*, 13 (Winter 1959), 87–99.

48. ——, "The Journey of Philip Roth," *Atlantic*, 223 (April 1969), 64–72.

49. Melvin J. Friedman, "Jewish Mothers and Sons: The Expense of Chutzpah" in Irving Malin, ed. *Contemporary American-Jewish Literature: Critical Essays* (Bloomington: University of Indiana Press, 1973), 156–75.

50. Sheldon Grebstein, "The Comic Anatomy of *Portnoy's Complaint"* in Sarah Blacher Cohen, ed. *Comic Relief: Humor in Contemporary American Literature* (Bloomington: University of Indiana Press, 1978), 152–72.

51. Walter Blair and Hamlin Hill, *America's Humor* (New York: Oxford University Press, 1978), 472–87.

52. Bernard Rodgers, Jr., *Philip Roth: A Bibliography* (Metuchen: Scarecrow Press, 1974).

53. John McDaniel, *The Fiction of Philip Roth* (Haddonfield: Haddonfield House, 1974).

54. Helen Weinberg, *The New Novel in American: The Kafkan Mode in Contemporary Fiction* (Ithaca: Cornell University Press, 1970).

55. Sanford Pinsker, *The Comedy That "Hoits": An Essay on the Fiction of Philip Roth* (Columbia: University of Missouri Press, 1975).

56. Bernard Rodgers, *Philip Roth* (Boston: Twayne United States Authors Series, 1978).

57. Pearl K. Bell, "Waxing Roth," *New Leader*, 54 (November 29, 1971), 14.

58. Murray Kempton, "Nixon Wins," *New York Review of Books* (January 27, 1972), 20.

59. Marvin Mudrick, "*Our Gang*," *Hudson Review*, 25 (Spring 1972), 142.

60. Dwight MacDonald, "*Our Gang*," *New York Times Book Review* (November 7, 1971), 34.

61. Philip Roth, "Writing American Fiction," *Commentary*, 31 (March 1961), 224.

62. Brom Weber, "The Mode of Black Humor" in Louis D. Rubin, ed. *The Comic Imagination in American Literature* (New Brunswick: Rutgers University Press, 1973), 361–73.

63. Frederick Crews, "Uplift," *New York Review of Books* (November 16, 1972), 18.

64. Margaret Drabble, "Clean Breast," *The Listener*, 89 (March 22, 1973), 378.

65. Peter S. Prescott, "Off His Chest," *Newsweek*, 80 (September 25, 1972), 118.

66. Duncan Fallowell, "A Suitable Case of Mastectomy," *Books and Bookmen*, 18 (June 1973), 70.

67. Roger Sale, "Enemies, Foreigners, and Friends," *Hudson Review* 25 (Winter 1972/73), 701.

68. Theodore Solotaroff, "Fiction," *Esquire*, 78 (October 1972), 82.

69. Pierre Michel, "Philip Roth's *The Breast*: Reality Adultered and the Plight of the Writer," *Dutch Quarterly Review*, 5 (1975), 245–52.

70. Elizabeth Sabiston, "A New Fable for Critics: Philip Roth's The Breast," *International Fiction Review*, 2 (1975), 27–34.

71. Julian C. Rice, "Philip Roth's *The Breast*: Cutting the Freudian Cord," *Studies in Contemporary Satire*, 3 (1976), 9–16.

72. Philip Roth, *Portnoy's Complaint* (New York: Random House, 1969), 68.

73. Thomas R. Edwards, "*The Great American Novel*," *New York Times Book Review* (May 6, 1973), 27.

74. Christopher Lehmann-Haupt, "Philip Roth's Bathtub Novel," *New York Times* (May 14, 1973), 29.

75. John Leonard, "Cheever to Roth to Malamud," *Atlantic*, 231 (June 1973), 114.

76. Robert F. Wilson, Jr., "An Indisputable Source for the Baseball Contest in *The Great American Novel*," *Notes on Contemporary Literature*, 5 (1975), 12–14.

77. Ben Siegel, "The Myths of Summer: Philip Roth's *The Great American Novel*, "*Contemporary Literature*, 17 (Spring 1976), 171–91.

78. Bernard Rodgers, "*The Great American Novel* and the Great American Joke," *Critique*, 16 (Winter 1974), 12–29.

79. J. W. Aldridge, "*My Life as a Man*," *Commentary*, 58 (Spring 1974), 82.

80. P. S. Prescott, "*My Life As a Man*," *New Yorker*, 50 (June 24, 1974), 102.

81. Morris Dickstein, "*My Life As a Man*," *New York Times Book Review* (June 2 1974), 1.

82. David Monaghan's The Great American Novel and My Life as a Man: An Assessment of Philip Roth's Achievement," *International Fiction Review*, 2 (1975), 113–20.

83. Sanford Pinsker, "*The Professor of Desire*," *The Drummer*, 475 (October 18, 1977), 6, 12.

84. Richard Boeth, "*The Professor of Desire*," *New Yorker*, 53 (October 31, 1977), 162.

85. Paul Gray, "*The Professor of Desire*," *Time* (September 26, 1977), 78.

86. Peter Prescott, *"The Ghost Writer," Newsweek*, 94 (September 10, 1979), 70.

87. Robert Towers, *"The Ghost Writer," New York Times Book Review* (September 2, 1979), 1.

88. John Leonard, "Fathers and Ghosts," *New York Review of Books* (October 25, 1979), 4.

REVIEWS

The Image of Newark and the Indignities of Love: Notes on Philip Roth

Leslie Fiedler*

In recent years, I have more often gone by Newark than into it, though it is the place where I was born and brought up. Still, seeing even from the Pulaski Skyway the Public Service Building lifted above the Meadows, and imagining around it the yellow trolley buses and the crowds at the curbs, frantic and disheveled as refugees—I feel again the ennui and terror and crazy joy of my childhood. It was at once depressing and exciting to live in a place which we came slowly to realize did not exist at all for the imagination. That Newark was nowhere, no one of us could doubt, though it was all most of us knew. What history the city possessed had been played out before our parents or grandparents were a part of it, and we did not even trouble to tell ourselves that we disbelieved it. What could Robert Treat, the founding father, mean to second generation Jewish boys living on a street of two-and-a-half family houses with stone lions on the stoops? He was an embossed figure on a teaspoon, steeple-hatted and unreal: a souvenir given away at a forgotten centennial and fought over by the kids when the pot roast was taken off the table and the stewed fruit brought on.

And Newark itself, the whole living city, what was it beyond a tangle of roads defining our own neighborhood and enclosing others utterly alien? The city on whose streets we walked with schoolbooks or ice cream cones or packages from the store we could not feel for a moment as one of those magical centers whose very names were thrilling to say: Paris, London, even New Orleans or Chicago or New York—the last only ten miles away. Newark was not even a joke like Brooklyn or Oshkosh or Peoria; vaudeville performers with canned gags for everywhere on the circuit could scarcely find one able to extort a perfunctory laugh. In those days, to be sure, there were the Bears, a ball club at least, and always the airport; after a while Dutch Schultz was shot in a local tavern, and for a thrilling moment Longie Zwillman, whose mother we could watch walking our sidewalks with the diamonds he bought her, made the Public

*Reprinted from *Midstream*, 5 (Summer 1959), 96–99, by permission of the journal.

23

Enemy list! Public Enemy Number One, we liked to boast; but I have been afraid to try to verify it, uneasily aware that at best he was only third or fourth.

No, even as kids we felt really how undefined, how characterless our native place was—without a legend older than last week's *Star-Eagle*. We did not *know* its characterlessness, perhaps, but we lived it just as we lived its ugliness. Later we would know, when it was time. In the meanwhile, we prepared for the moment of knowledge by reading in that Public Library, in which, fittingly, the protagonist of Philip Roth's longest story works to put himself through college. If Newark, our Newark, had any focal point at all it was The Library; but there those of us who took books seriously learned almost first of all that poor Newark had no writer, and hence no myth to outlive its unambitious public buildings, its mean frame houses. When Bamberger's Department Store was at last closed down and the Prudential Insurance Company had crumbled away, how would anyone learn that we had ever existed? Maybe the name would survive at least on some old commutation ticket for the Hudson Tubes, petrified in coal dust.

There was, to be sure, Stephen Crane, memorialized in the classroom, but his fictional world was a small-town Gentile world called Whilomville, not his native Newark at all; and we found it as alien as most of the teachers who told us about it—or as those Newark *goyim* who are all the time passing by the centers of action of Roth's stories without ever quite impinging on them: the *shikses* in white hats, the Sunday churchgoers walking to and from scarcely conceivable services. For Newark, *our* Newark, to exist for the imagination of strangers and of our own children, Newark would have to produce a writer as vulgar, comical, subtle, pathetic and dirty as itself. He would have to be Jewish, ungenteel, emancipated from all limitations except those of memory and of the remembered city.

But by the mid-fifties, it was clearly too late for such a writer to appear. With prosperity, the city we had known, the city of *cheders* and lox, "Vote Communist" buttons and college boys working in shoestores, despair in gravel schoolyards and epiphanies in the open stacks, had long since disappeared. A prosperity more final than death had translated the very *yentes* from the brick stoops to the Beach Clubs of Livingston and even more unimaginable suburbs; had removed the sons of leatherworkers and the owners of candy stores to Bucknell or Ohio State or (God forbid!) Princeton. Those who had not lusted for the suburbs or college towns had dreamed of New York; and to each the best he could desire was granted. The houses, the lots, the hedges that had defined our Newark passed now into the possession of the Negroes, from whose midst the laureate would have to come that we had apparently not been able to bring to birth. At best, our Newark would be in the long life of the city, multiple and squalid as Troy's, the Newark *before* the Newark that had become a fact of literature; archaeologists would give us the proper number.

In Philip Roth's stories, however (how can he be only twenty-six?), my own remembered and archaic city survives, or more precisely, lives fully for the first time; I live fully for the first time the first twenty years of my life. Maybe he has only dreamed that world, reconstructed it on the basis of scraps of information recollected from conversations with cousins or older brothers or uncles; or maybe a real city only becomes a mythic one when it is already dead. No matter—he has dreamed truly. In his nightmare vision, that is, a Newark very like the one from which I still occasionally wake sweating has been rescued from history, oddly preserved. At the Little Theatre across the Park from the Museum, Hedy Lamar is still playing in *Ecstasy*, as she played for 39 weeks (or was it 79?) when I was sixteen. Through the landscape of "switchman's shacks, lumberyards, Dairy Queens, and used-car lots," Roth's characters still ascend the one hundred and eighty feet toward suburban coolness—the breath of air of which Newarkers vainly dream all summer long. For it is summer, of course, Newark's infernal season, in Mr. Roth's fictional city—and somebody's aunt and uncle are "sharing a Mounds bar in the cindery darkness of their alley, on beach chairs." It is possible to persuade oneself (though Roth does not say so) that with the proper coupon clipped from the *Newark Evening News* one could still get *three* transparent White Castle Hamburgers for a nickel.

I would not have believed I could feel nostalgia for the meager world Roth so improbably evokes, and I do not really believe it now; but there is a suspicious kind of satisfaction for me in knowing that world is fixed now forever in his gray authentic poetry. I can smell the sweat of my own lost August nights as I read *Goodbye, Columbus*, and am aware that I must be on guard lest, sentimentally and uncharacteristically (God knows!), I can go out to meet Philip Roth more than halfway. I realize that because there is more Newark in the title piece of his book—more passionate social anthropology, rich as invention, depressing as fact, witty as the joke the survivors of Newark have had to make of their lives to live so long—it is for me the most moving of Roth's fictions. But I am convinced that my reaction is more than personal and eccentric.

There is more room in his single novella than in any of his shorter stories for non-theoretical life, for the painful wonder of what is given rather than the satisfactory aptness of what is (however skillfully) contrived to substantiate a point. Random and inexhaustible, such life is, after all, more the fictionist's business than any theme, even the rewardingly ironic and surely immortal one of how hard it is to be a Jew—quite differently elaborated in "Defender of the Faith," and "Eli the Fanatic." For the first, Philip Roth has already received the young Jewish writer's initial accolade: the accusation of anti-Semitism; and both stories are effective, convincing—the second even terrible in its reflections on how these days the holiest madness is "understood" and cured. But their terror and irony alike remain a little abstract—fading into illustrations of propositions out of Riesman, or pressed hard toward some not-quite committed religious position. I should suppose that if Roth is to be as funny and as terrifying as he has the skill and insight to be, he must move out in the religious direction he has so far only indicated; but at the very least he must learn to risk a certain slovenliness, which in his short stories he evades with the nervousness of a compulsive housecleaner. Other readers, I know, are more capable than I of responding to his pace, vigor and candor without the nagging sense that they are all a little compromised by something uncomfortably close to slickness; but I cannot deny that feeling in myself.

"Goodbye, Columbus" appeals to me, therefore, precisely because it is untidier than the rest, not so soon or so certainly in *control*. And in its generous margin of inadvertence, there is room enough for a mythical Newark, truth enough for the real one. In the end, "Goodbye, Columbus" does not quite work as a novella. Its plot (satisfactorily outrageous, but a little gimmicky and eked out with echoes of Mary McCarthy) and its themes tend to fall apart. Unlike some of the short stories, it evades rather than submits to these themes, perhaps because the author is afraid to submit to the old-fashioned motif of love across class lines which struggles to become its point. But love, desperate and foredoomed, love as a betrayal which takes itself for pleasure, is the only subject adequate to the city Roth has imagined. This he knows really, and *incidentally* has exploited full even in "Goodbye, Columbus."

It is in its incidents rather than in its total structure that the novella comes alive. Its details are as vivid as its themes are inert, its properties more alive, perhaps, than its chief protagonists: the furniture which symbolizes status, refrigerators crammed absurdly with mountains of fruit, a jockstrap hung from the faucet of a bathtub, the record that gives the story its name. *Things* writhe, assert themselves, determine lives in a Dickensian frenzy. But some of the people who are possessed by them or subsist in the margins they leave free come alive, too—like Uncle Leo with his memories of the "oral love" which he learned from a girl called Hannah Schreiber at a B'nai Brith dance for servicemen, and which he exacted later from his wife, who was "up to here with Mogen David" after a Seder. "In fact, *twice* after Seders. Aachh! Everything good in my life I can count on my fingers." Here it seems to me is the profoundly atrocious pathos which is Roth's forte, his essential theme. Love in Newark! Beside it, the reminiscences of childhood, the anecdotes of peacetime army life, even the accounts of the disruption of the Jew's suburban truce with respectability come to seem of secondary importance—preludes to a main theme.

Even as the legendary city which Roth creates is one looked back to at its moment of dying, so is the love which is proper to it. In his fables, the young watch with horror and without sympathy the old yearning desperately for an idyll of sex, whose unreality the decay of their own flesh declares; or the old, sleepless, hear from their beds the zip-zip of the young making out on the downstairs couch. The latter is the subject of

"Epstein," for me the most successful of the shorter pieces despite a last-minute concession to sentimentality as banal as the required ending of a box-office movie. Urged by spring, the copulation of the young and the imminent failure of his own flesh, Epstein reaches out for romance with, naturally, the lady across the street. But he moves toward love through the drab horror of Newark whose embodiment he is, sagging, frantic, rather dreaming lust than enduring it; and he ends, as he must, convinced that he has syphilis, facing the prospect of a divorce, overtaken by a heart-attack in the very act of love. ". . . his eyes were closed, his skin grayer than his hair . . . His tongue hung over his teeth like a dead snake." And his wife looms over him with the proper advice, "You hear the doctor, Lou. All you got to do is live a normal life." It should be the end, but Roth gives it away—concludes with a promise of recovery and reconciliation. "You can clean it up? 'So it'll never come back,' the doctor said. . . ."

But maybe even this is all right. Maybe it is better because more terrible to imagine Epstein living than dead: he and his Goldie on their beach-chairs; with their Mounds bars, "in the cindery darkness of their alley"—while their nephew speeds toward a failure as complete as Epstein's, though his dream of love has been transformed from the lady across the street to the girl in Briarpath Hills.

Newark! A Florence it will never be in the minds of men, nor a Baghdad nor a Paris; but after Roth, we can hope that perhaps it will survive on library shelves ravaged by ambitious boys as another Yonville or Winesburg, Ohio—another remembered name for the "cindery darkness" which men build around themselves and in whose midst they suffer the indignities of love.

The Conversion of the Jews

Jeremy Larner*

For a writer in his late twenties, writing almost exclusively about Jewish subjects, Philip Roth has had an unusual success. Amid general acclaim, he has won a Houghton Mifflin Literary Fellowship, the 1958 Aga Khan Prize for Fiction, and, most recently, the National Book Award, which designates *Goodbye, Columbus* as the best American fiction published during 1959.

One could discredit much of this applause—the Aga Khan, for example, on the grounds that Jewishness is the latest thing in Harvard literary circles. Yet the quality of Mr. Roth's writing has been attested to

*Reprinted from *Partisan Review*, 27 (Fall 1960), 760–68. Copyright © 1960, by *Partisan Review*.

by two expert Jewish critics—Irving Howe and Alfred Kazin, and by our most highly-praised Jewish novelist, Saul Bellow.[1] Each of these knowledgeable men verifies Roth's portrait of the Jewish upper-middle class and sets forth qualified but positive claims for his merits as a novelist. I think they are mistaken on both counts, and that their mistake is grounded in a basic ignorance of the people Roth writes about.

All three of Mr. Roth's distinguished supporters correctly identify the major force behind his novel as an indictment of the Jewish upper-middle class—that large body of Jews who have made it to the top as merchants and professional men. Mr. Howe puts the matter nicely:

> The best parts of *Goodbye, Columbus*, done with a deadpan malicious accuracy, are those in which Mr. Roth sketches the manners and morals of the Patimkins. . . .
>   Mr. Roth skillfully—I suppose the word had better be, ruthlessly—charts the varieties of amiable vulgarity, *arriviste* snobbism and sheer mindlessness. . . .
>   To the uninformed reader all of this might seem to verge on caricature, but I think it is ferociously exact. . . .
>   If one is to object to these stories on non-literary grounds, out of a concern for the feelings or reputation of middle class American Jews, it can be done only by charging that, in effect, Mr. Roth is a liar. And that, I am convinced, he is not.

But Mr. Roth is, in the literary sense, a liar. I say so not out of concern for middle-class Jewry, but on the most literary grounds. Any novel is a lie unless it can tell some truth of the human heart. Roth, however, seeks only to cheapen the people he writes about. This motive is betrayed both by his selection of detail and by the kind of action that goes into his plots. The direct effect of his literary technique is to reduce the people he is describing to morons. Morons, of course, are easier to write about insofar as simple actions lend themselves most readily to moral judgment. Granted that a novelist has a right to create his own distorted world; still, we must demand of him that his distortions give us insight into the world we know. Roth is so eager to press for his judgment that his distortions are simply a matter of form and convenience—i.e., false art.

I think most of us share Mr. Roth's general conviction that the blatant materialism of the Jewish newly-rich is vulgar and destructive of human values. But to attack—even to lampoon—this materialism in terms that are convincing, the novelist is obliged to convey an accurate picture of what the Jewish upper-middle-class world is like. Roth does not come close to this accomplishment; an "informed reader" can easily correct him on many details crucial to the accuracy, and hence to the aesthetic success, of his novel. For example:

1. The central family of the novel, the Patimkins of Patimkin Sink, are passionately *athletic*. Yet, as any decent sportswriter will tell you, athletics are not a favorite vehicle of the upper-middle class, but rather of

lower classes on the move upwards. To illustrate, Jewish athletes were most prominent in the 30's and earlier, while lately more and more champions have come from the Negro population. Patimkin & family would be likely to have *cultural* affectations—they would sponsor the Newark Symphony, travel to Europe, press expensive educations on their children, and perhaps even encourage their son to become a college professor. So all the scenes in which Roth dwells upon the limitless activities and paraphernalia of the Patimkins—in tennis, basketball, golf, football, swimming, etc.—are gratuitous, and have nothing to do with the Jewishness or the wealth of the people he is describing.

2. Brenda Patimkin, who so conclusively captivates the undertrodden Neil Klugman, is made out to be a Radcliffe girl. While it is probable enough that Patimkin Sink would want to send his daughter to Radcliffe, Miss Patimkin's behavior betrays not the slightest hint of her alma mater. Radcliffe girls are usually intelligent—or at least sophisticated. Among them one could find grinds, dilettantes, bohemians, snobs, etc.—but nary a one aspiring to All-American Girlhood. And yet Brenda Patimkin is characterized as a round-the-clock athlete who is absorbed exclusively in sex and clothes and who wouldn't dream of questioning her parents' values. She might just as well be a California "wasp" attending Los Angeles Junior College. Then, at any rate, it might not be so difficult to imagine her insisting that her boyfriend run round a track with her. Apparently Radcliffe closes some symbolic circuits for Mr. Roth, but all it does for his novel is to provide Neil Klugman, when all is lost, with the desire to throw a stone through the window of Lamont Library.

3. Mrs. Patimkin, Brenda's mother, who once had "the best backhand in the state of New Jersey," is an avid member of Hadassah, an organization which draws its membership mostly from lower-middle-class Jews. A country club woman would more likely belong to the Council of Jewish Women, or—better still—the League of Women Voters, or—best of all—a Wednesday bridge club. As if to compound her incongruity, Mrs. Patimkin is made to lecture Neil on the lapsing Jewishness of the younger generation. She herself is Orthodox. This is a patent absurdity: a woman of Mrs. Patimkin's position would be lukewarm-Reform, and not only that, a rabid assimilationist. Mr. Roth has a perfect right to portray an eccentric; but to imply that the eccentric is typical is to take great liberties with the truth.

These three examples will give some notion of the general trend of Roth's distortions. Notice that in every case he simplifies his material, making the people he describes seem weaker and more ridiculous than they really are. The unfortunate truth is that Roth, while adroitly spinning an allegory of the classes, has overlooked genuine sources of drama in the lives of the people he is supposedly writing about. Although his admirers claim that he presents a fresh perspective on the Jewish social climb, Roth is terribly old-fashioned. His concern with the European theme of never-the-twain-shall-meet is inappropriate to the real problem of the children of the risen Jewry: the typically American problem of *freedom*. The twain *does* meet—poor Jewish boys *do* marry rich Jewish girls; but after the marriage they don't know what to do with themselves. While their fathers were necessarily absorbed in the struggle to raise their families above the pariah style of life which confronted immigrant minorities, the children find this problem solved, and no longer challenging. The brightest of them have no desire to enter the family business, and often the family doesn't really expect it of them. They are the ones who must achieve something important in terms of the American community-at-large. The successful Jewish family is willing to provide its children with lavish educations, send them to Europe, prod them with lessons, tutors and bribes, hoping that they will develop into scientists, doctors, engineers, or professors. The children respond to this pressure as individuals, choosing and re-choosing and not-choosing among the various pains of freedom. Not the least of their problems is that they reject the values of their parents along with their occupations, and suffer in consequence from a schizoid distrust of the very things they are accustomed to need. Sooner or later, most of them sell out to their need for material comforts; others never do. But the process makes them entirely more complicated and devious than Mr. Roth would have them—fine subjects, indeed, for a novelist of insight and compassion.

In view of the preceeding corrections, it is hard to understand Irving Howe's business about how the uninformed reader might find *Goodbye, Columbus* a caricature, but to him it is all ferociously exact. Nor Saul Bellow's exhortation to keep up the good work. Apparently Howe and Kazin and Bellow accept without question the accuracy of Roth's portraiture. But when one thinks of it, why should they know the world Roth is ostensibly describing? All of them are non-bourgeois intellectuals who have made their careers in literary and academic circles. The people I'm talking about are merely their students.

Once the setting of *Goodbye, Columbus* is seen to be artificial, the plot, too, appears contrived and trivial. Alfred Kazin, however, describes it as the story of "a romantic and credulous youth defeated in love by a brutally materialistic society, like Fitzgerald's Gatsby." The comparison is far-fetched. Gatsby's fate is moving because Gatsby is noble, fantastic, creative; Neil Klugman is only a symbol. Whereas the structure of *The Great Gatsby* is focused on the fabulous mysteries of Gatsby's personality, *Goodbye, Columbus* flounders in a vacuum; for Neil Klugman is emotionally bankrupt. The only positive sensation he is capable of is the physical pleasure of luxuriating; as for his personal relations, he despises every other character in the book. Yet Mr. Kazin is so impressed with Neil that he centers his elaboration of the action around Neil's "love" and "dignity": When Brenda, perhaps unconsciously, allows her mother to discover that she has been sleeping with Neil so that the family itself can decisively end the romance, the betrayal is felt by Neil as a betrayal not only of his love but of his dignity as a human being who comes from the slums.

This account simply doesn't tally with the book. First of all, Neil Klugman is shown to feel no "dignity as a human being who comes from the slums." As a matter of fact, he's ashamed of it. The novel's sole representative of Neil's lower class Jewish background is his Aunt Gladys, who is ridiculed every time she appears, chiefly for her obsessive dread of food spoiling in the refrigerator. (Neil's parents are his characters, he rapidly brushes a brittle surface of conveniently missing [sic]; they are asthmatic, and so, as Neil puts it, "the two of them went wheezing off to Arizona.") Furthermore, Kazin is not accurate in placing the entire blame for Mrs. Patimkin's discovery on Brenda. Mrs. Patimkin uncovers the affair through chancing upon the diaphragm which Neil himself had insisted Brenda buy. Finally, it is not the family who break up the romance; it is Neil himself who tries to force complete responsibility on Brenda, and who walks out when she won't accept it. Clearly there is more than ample evidence that Neil has a hand in his own disaster; his is not a mere "betrayal." In fact, there is nothing to betray: Neil is nothing more than the allegorical Poor Boy. He is never assigned the slightest ambition, interest or sentiment that might give him credence as a full-bodied character: he does not seem to exist outside of his frustration with the Patimkins.

Setting aside the fact that one can't care about Neil, I wonder if one is intended to? It would appear that Mr. Roth never quite decided this point for himself—the slickness of his first person style seems to cover up for an excessive identification. Mr. Howe regards Roth's choice of the first-person as a masterly bit of strategy: "Mr. Roth, to his credit, presents Neil with a matter-of-fact detachment which eliminates chances for self-pity." But it seems to me that the presentation of such a character in the first person is begging for pity on Roth's part, because it is an invitation for the reader to side with Neil and accept his point of view (which is exactly what reviewers have done). The book is put together so that the writer is never faced with the possibility of questioning the bleakness of Neil's judgments. Neil's "detached" reactions are simply equated with "reality." The comparison to Gatsby is most instructive: when Fitzgerald wished to make use of a detached observer, he placed Nick Carraway on the periphery of the action. Gatsby himself is warm and attractive—to picture him coldly telling his own story, cleverly dissecting the Buchanans in the process, is unthinkable.

The possibility of *Goodbye, Columbus* conveying any serious meaning is negated by the very techniques by which the story is told. Every time Mr. Roth chooses a detail, it is blatantly comic, as in a cartoon. In fact, *Goodbye, Columbus* is essentially nothing but a string of clever metaphors. Roth's ambiguity is purely a matter of style—wherever he has to supply personal motivation for vagueness over the troublesome spot. In place of motivation, the narrative is held together by carefully designated symbols, such as the two refrigerators, the colored boy, the swimming pool, etc. But emotional events are arbitrary and shallowly explored.

Much has been made of the fact that Philip Roth has found a "voice," which means that he has devised a personal and consistent way of arranging his materials so that his narrative flows smoothly from one sentence to the next. This is certainly true, and it is a pleasure to discover a writer whose technical equipment is so completely adequate to the demands placed upon it. Yet one could wish that the demands had been greater, even if that would entail a blurring of the voice. As it stands, the price Roth pays for smoothness is too high: he cheats himself, and cheats his readers of the truth.

Note

1. In *The New Republic*, June 15, 1959; *The Reporter*, May 28, 1959; and *Commentary*, May, 1959, respectively.

A Sentimental Education
Circa 1956

Irving Feldman*

Young men must grow up, must lose their illusions about themselves and their circumstances. Set on the anvil of reality, they will have to bear up under an indictment like that made by the father in Kafka's "The Judgment": "So now you know what else there was in the world besides yourself! An innocent child, yes, that you were, truly, but still more truly you have been a devilish human being!" And they will not leave the anvil until a death—that of a father or a child—has purchased their release. Such is the sentimental education through which Philip Roth conducts the two heroes of his long, uneven novel, *Letting Go*. They meet as graduate students, pursue their difficult friendship—one is married, grindingly poor, and dedicated to a life of stingy self-sacrifice, the other is at loose ends—and finally separate five years later as teachers.

"Devilish," however, is not quite the word for Gabe Wallach and Paul Herz, Roth's two unhappy young men, for their sins are, typically, those of omission, of failure. Rather, *Letting Go* seems to be patterned—not intentionally, so far as I know, but perhaps inevitably—on Flaubert's masterpiece of boredom, failure, and waste, *A Sentimental Education*. The comparison is, I think, worth pursuing. In both works the

*Reprinted from *Commentary*, September 1962, by permission; all rights reserved.

author wields the birch of bitter reality with harsh and depressing regularity on the backs of his heroes. In both, the twin heroes complement one another, though, characteristically, they are scaled down in the Roth novel. Gabe Wallach is a butterfly of sentiment, though without the strong romantic appetite of Frederic Moreau, his counterpart; he is, we are given to understand, always playing it safe, risking little in order to lose little; half-heartedly available, merely amenable, he has no clear idea of what he wants or of what others expect of him; his sentiments are, in fact, notably weak, he never gets behind on grading papers. Paul Herz, on the other hand, is a mole of duty where Flaubert's Deslauriers is a man of action, though of petty and blundering action. And there are a number of other resemblances, in the class backgrounds of these pairs, in the kinds of women who are available or not available to them, etc. What is more important is the similar disillusionment from which both novels spring. Flaubert wrote *Sentimental Education* in the 1860's looking back, under Louis Napoleon, on the betrayed hopes of the 1848 Revolution. And the broad subject of *Letting Go*, which begins at the end of the Korean War and concludes with the Recession of 1957, is the underlying hopelessness of the Eisenhower era.

This, I think, is at the heart of the reductions of *Letting Go*, it is what makes the man of feeling half-hearted and the man of duty torment and squander himself. Much of this is clearly calculated. The impoverished Paul Herz has, on first view, "the look about him of a dissatisfied civil servant, the product of some nineteenth-century Russian imagination." Yet he turns out to be not at all the Alienated Man of the 40's—he has gone "underground" not to subvert but to bear the world on his back. An industrious pursuer of scholarships, diligent at unhappiness, and something of a mama's boy. Like Gabe Wallach, he is a man of good will who succeeds only in acting in bad faith. Both, moreover, are arrayed against the background of their romantic elders: Gabe's father, Wallaceite, Reichian, yoga-ist, the romantic of health; Paul's Uncle Jerry, the romantic of (psychoanalytic) love; his Uncle Asher (who with his slangy, erudite, break-neck spieling is clearly meant to be Augie March at 50), the romantic of Bellovian (or Gidean) availability to experience; and, finally, Paul's father, the four-time failure, the romantic of business. Indeed, they are all failures—the health-maniac is terrified of his loneliness, the middle-aged lover is twice divorced, the bohemian Asher is a painter of buckeyes. Each of these paths is marked No Exit. And, generally, the past provides no issue for these young men; they are tethered to a sense of the limitations of their moral and biological inheritance, and even the children they must care for (or destroy) have been fathered by other men.

What, then, remains open to them? The future, except for the needle's eye of failure, is also closed. Unlike Flaubert's young men, they have no ambitions (except for a quite vague decency and happiness) and no careers. We are told that one is a writer and the other a scholar and that both are teachers, but, aside from some literary chitchat and some slight satire on academic types, we have no sense that they have any work. (Indeed, their work is so unimportant to Roth that he has implausibly made Herz the writer and Wallach the scholar, where the reverse would have been more plausible.) What, after all, are they doing in this world? And, amazingly, they have no contemporaries, no friends, no connection, that is, with the world at large; they have only their elders and their women and can measure themselves only against the demands made on them by their parents and their women. Let me give an example. The high point of Gabe Wallach's affair with the woman available to him comes at the onset of a brief illness. After two days of fever and sex he wakes up still ill but happy and convalescent. This is a characteristic moment—the passions have been exhausted and the world can be freely encountered. So, in *Sentimental Education*, Frederic Moreau finally gets a woman into bed. Unhappily, it is a courtesan who has come to the bed he had prepared for the woman he desires but can't have. Nevertheless, he is wakened at dawn by the sound of musketry and goes out into the streets of a Paris excited with its freedom. It is 1848! And Gabe? He listens to the old soap operas.

> Yes, there harassing the air waves were those same luckless couples who had struggled through my childhood . . . and who turned out to be struggling still. And recovering from a minor ailment, I discovered . . . reading in today's newspaper what the temperature had been the day before in all the major cities of the world, poring over the woman's page and racing results with little foothold in either world—it was all as cocoonish and heart-warming on the south side of Chicago as it had been fifteen years before on the west side of New York.

It is December 1956 and there are no more revolutions, not even in Hungary. There is no world, only yesterday's trivia and the balm of Pig Heaven. It is a sad sad fact, Roth's young men have only private lives.

And yet it seems to me that Roth is writing as much *out* of this wretched privacy as *about* it, for he seems to regard these exclusions of friendship and work, this public vacuum, as being serious, ultimate. Hence, the tedious earnestness with which he straps his young men to the problems of commitment to wife and family. Hence, for all the liveliness of much of the writing, the novel's cramped and fetid air. Everything takes place indoors, in apartments, in offices, in cars, in stores. The novel has only one public event, which is so cluttered with literary furniture that I wonder whether Roth himself clearly sees its significance. Paul Herz is returning to attend his dying father whom he has not seen since he had been turned out of the house for marrying a *shiksa*. He examines his life:

> It occurred to him now . . . that, no, he was not a man of feeling; it occurred to him that if he was anything at all it was a

man of duty. And that when his two selves had become confused—one self, one invention—when he had felt it his duty to
be feeling, that then his heart had been a stone, and his will,
instead of turning out toward action, had remained a presence
in his body, a concrete setting for the rock of his heart.

However, he resists seeing his father until, at the last moment, he rushes
alone to his funeral. There, in the cemetery, all the people from his past
are assembled:

No one moved, just himself, and what rushed to meet him: a
figure in black. And now at last he saw who that was too, yes,
and now he closed his eyes and opened his arms and what he
saw next was his life—he saw it for the sacrifice it was. Isaac
under the knife, Abraham wielding it. *Both!* While his mother
kissed his neck and moaned his name, he saw his place in the
world. Yes. And the world itself—without admiration,
without pity. Yes! Oh yes! What he saw filled him for a moment with strength. . . . He kissed nothing—only held out his
arms, open, and stood still at last, momentarily at rest in the
center of the storm through which he had been traveling all
these years. For his truth was revealed to him, his final premise
melted away. What he had taken for order was chaos. Justice
was an illusion. Abraham and Isaac were one.

The text is from Kierkegaard, Paul's gesture and vision from Camus, there
is perhaps a little Sartre, and, certainly, a lot of "Seize the Day." But the
Absurd here seems to me quite beside the point and helps make this
passage shrill and unconvincing. The healing, the joining of the man of
duty (Abraham) and of feeling (Isaac) can take place because the funeral
is a public event.

Roth's moral vocabulary is similarly contemporary: don't clutch,
don't push and pull, and let go—that is, fail, in order to seize the day.
And he is unremitting in dogging Herz and Wallach through their failures
to a final tentative generosity opposed to the self-consciousness implicit in
their difficulties of "feeling." But that one can win only by losing—perhaps this is the sentimentality of disillusionment. So, Gabe
Wallach succeeds in saving the Herzes' adopted child for them only when
he collapses before his intractable adversary. But it may be that the angel
presents himself for the wrestling match precisely to those who will
triumph over him. Why, in seeking to engage his characters, should Roth
put it that freedom comes from responsibility and not responsibility from
freedom? Maybe the answer is, 1956: Only careers in domesticity open to
talent. Similarly, *Letting Go* shows a healthy but constricting determination to avoid the other current sentimentalities—of individualism, of
love, of identity-finding, of availability. But, then, what excitement and
openness has life to offer in 1956? or in 1962? I recall that Flaubert, in the
midst of his dour and unrelenting realism, gives Frederic Moreau a
wonderfully magical love idyll at Fontainebleau. He is still with the

wrong woman, but such is the power of "love and Nature the eternal"! Gabe Wallach's convalescence from the flu also has some magical qualities. It's the fever. Anti-heroism is fine—when done on a large enough scale.

What seems to me the best thing in the novel comes where Roth exceeds this scale. It is an awkward thing but a pleasure to see in a writer who has won acclaim for being fresh, bright, sharpsighted, and winning, as Roth has. I am thinking of Paul Herz who, portrayed out of a venomous hatred, heavy and ugly at the beginning of the novel and comically predictable at its end, is often a memorable and powerfully drawn figure, though perhaps less a character than a portmanteau of insights. Gabe Wallach, on the other hand, is as absent and incredible a character as Neil Klugman of "Goodbye, Columbus." Since he is the narrator of about half the novel, this is a major misfortune. He is not a character, but a position: Central Park West, third-generation Jewish, Harvard, Henry James scholar, handsome, healthy, charming, cautious, gently guilty about his good fortune, wantless, sniffish, but not convincingly any of these. He is intended to be a sort of blank, the starved soul of the 50's, and a blank is all I get. He is outfitted, too, with a sodden, adenoidal prose (Harvard, I guess) that only quickens for some of Roth's satirical interludes (the one on the pure Brooklyn couple, Maur and Dor Horvitz, is particularly good). It is clear that Wallach's agreeableness is to be taken as a weakness, but when he is being agreeable he is just not interesting. I suppose it must be very difficult to put such a character at the center of a novel. I don't think Roth has brought it off. Given such a narrator and Roth's penchant for demonstrating everything and for showing off his fine ear for dialogue, of which there are a number of long, trivial, and distractingly colloquial tracts, it is no wonder that much of the last third of *Letting Go* should read like one of those heavy tomes with which women often carry on protracted affairs and which are called best sellers.

A Novelist of Great Promise

Stanley Edgar Hyman*

Television has destroyed boxing in our time, perhaps permanently, by killing the neighborhood clubs, at which young fighters learn their craft. As a result boys are brought up into the big time too soon, and acclaim and fortune are won by the semi-skilled, who then naturally continue to be semi-skilled. Consequently, we will probably never again see fighters with the artistry of Archie Moore or Ray Robinson.

In the literary arenas, the same thing is done by gushy reviewing. Philip Roth, whose first novel, *Letting Go*, has just been published (Ran-

*Reprinted from *The New Leader* (June 11, 1962), pp. 22–23, by permission of the journal.

dom House, 630 pp., $5.95), is a case in point. In 1959, at the age of 26, he published his first book, *Goodbye, Columbus*, consisting of the title novella and five short stories. It was greeted with a cascade of adulation, of which some remarks quoted on the back of the paperback reprint are a fair sample. "One catches lampoonings of our swollen and unreal American prosperity that are as observant and charming as Fitzgerald's," Alfred Kazin wrote in the *Reporter*. "At twenty-six he is skillful, witty, and energetic and performs like a virtuoso," Saul Bellow wrote in *Commentary*. "What many writers spend a lifetime searching for—a unique voice, a secure rhythm, a distinctive subject—seem to have come to Philip Roth totally and immediately," Irving Howe wrote in the *New Republic*.

The next year, *Goodbye, Columbus* won the National Book Award as "the most distinguished work of fiction published in 1959." Roth was promptly awarded a Guggenheim fellowship, as well as a grant from the National Institute of Arts and Letters with a citation saying in part: "*Goodbye, Columbus* marks the coming of age of a brilliant, penetrating, and undiscourageable young man of letters." Undiscourageable? Who had tried?

The merits of *Goodbye, Columbus* and its author are immediately evident. The novella shows a sardonic wit, and the sharp eye of a born writer. The Patimkin way of life, with its white hair "the color of Lincoln convertibles" and its 23 bottles of Jack Daniels, each with a little booklet tied around its neck, decorating the unused bar, has been rendered for all time. There are other sure touches: the cherry pits under Neil's bare feet in the TV room; the Ohio State sentimental record of the title. The long monologue by Patimkin's unsuccessful half-brother Leo at the wedding is a masterpiece: funny, moving, perfect.

But the faults of *Goodbye, Columbus* are as readily visible. The novella has no values to oppose to Patimkin values other than a small Negro boy who admires Gauguin's Tahiti, which seems a considerable overmatch. Some images are bad, like Brenda treading water "so easily she seemed to have turned the chlorine to marble beneath her"; the language is sometimes as inadequate as: "I failed to deflate the pout from my mouth." Most important, the novella shows Roth's architectonic weakness. Many of the incidents do not advance the action; the end is merely a running-down.

The stories show the same balance of strength and weakness. "Defender of the Faith" is the only one of them that seems wholly successful to me. "Eli, the Fanatic" reaches one high point of power and beauty, when Tzuref replies to all the smooth talk about the 20th century with: "For me the Fifty-eighth," but the rest of the story is rambling and diffuse. "The Conversion of the Jews," with its pat moral, "You should never hit anybody about God," is ultimately hokum, as "You Can't Tell a Man by the Song He Sings" is immediately hokum. "Epstein" is an inflated joke.

The minor result of the shower of praise and coin that Roth received was to make him arrogant. In a speech, "Writing American Fiction," at a 1960 symposium, he knocked off his elders and betters: Malamud displays "a spurning of our world," Salinger tells us "to be charming on the way to the loony bin," and so on. The major, and really unfortunate, result has been to convince Roth that he has nothing further to learn. Three years later, *Letting Go* appears with the same merits and the same faults as *Goodbye, Columbus*.

Let us get the faults out of the way first. Since the novel is six times as long as the novella, it shows Roth's architectural weakness six times as strongly. It never in fact becomes a novel, with a unified dramatic action, but falls apart into two narratives which have only a pat complementarity: the failure of Gabe Wallach in the world of personal relations, specifically with the divorcée Martha Reganhart, despite every advantage; and the limited success of Paul and Libby Herz in the same world, despite every handicap. For the rest, it is a series of comic set pieces and vignettes: dirty diapers and high thought among the instructors at Midwest universities; Swedish modern and espresso in Jewish apartments in Brooklyn; the Kodachrome European trips of Central Park West dentists.

The prose is still quite lame in spots. Characters experience "relief— though by no means total relief," and children eat, "manipulating their food like Muzak's violinists their instruments." There are letters that no one would ever have written, and long pedestrian explanations of past events by the author. In the style of college humor magazines, Roth will interrupt a scene to remark: "It's the little questions from women about tappets that finally push men over the edge." At the same time, there is a balancing pomposity; the book has no fewer than *three epigraphs*—by Simone Weil, Wallace Stevens, and Thomas Mann—any one of which would do for a dissertation on Covenant Theology.

A two-page history of the marital sex life of the Herzes has a clinical leadenness that would sink the most buoyant novel. Beyond that there is cocktail-party Freud. A pathetic event finally ends the liason between Gabe and Martha. Martha's older child, Cynthia, pushes her younger brother, Mark, off the top of a double-decker bunk, which results in Mark's death. Roth spends laborious pages showing us why—it was penis-envy! Finally, Gabe's weakness is Hegelian essence: "He is better, he believes, than anything he has done in life has shown him to be." Not being the sum of his actions, Gabe is not really anything in the book.

The virtues of *Letting Go*—of Roth, really—are equally impressive. He has the finest eye for the details of American life since Sinclair Lewis. When Margie Howells of Kenosha moves in with Gabe as an experiment in Bold Free Union, she comes with Breck shampoo, an Olivetti, an electric frying pan, a steam iron, and a copy of the *Oxford Book of Seventeenth-Century Verse*. The Spiglianos (he is the chairman of Gabe's department) have 11 budgetary tins in their kitchen, one labelled: "John: Tobacco, scholarly journals, foot powder."

Roth's ear is just as remarkable as his eye. When Blair Stott, a Negro on pot, talks hip, it is the best hip, and a delight. When Gabe and Martha quarrel over money, every word rings true, and the reader can feel a sick headache coming on. No manner of speech seems to be beyond Roth's powers. An elderly Midwest woman says to Gabe: "You talk to the top professors and you see if they're not Masons." Paul recalls necking with a girl in high school, sitting in her living room while her father called out from the bedroom: "Doris, is that you, dolly? Is somebody with you? Tell him thank you, dolly, and tell him it's the next day already, your father has to get up and go to work soon, tell him thank you and good night, dolly."

If Gabe is a thin Hegelian essence, Martha is a gorgeous rich *Existenz*. She *is* the total of what she does. "A woman at least realizes there are certain rotten things she's got to do in life and does them," Martha explains to Gabe. "Men want to be heroes." She is bawdy and vulgar, honest and decent, funny and heartbreaking. Gabe's effort, as he finally recognizes when he loses her, had been to turn her into a sniveling Libby. Martha's vitality dominates the book, and if Gabe's final "letting go" of the world is at all poignant, it is poignant chiefly in that he had a chance to keep Martha and failed.

The best of *Letting Go* comes from the marvelous quality of Roth's imagination. A fellow-dentist with whom Gabe's father goes ice-skating is characterized in a phrase; he only makes "little figure eights, and all the time, smiling." The failure of Paul's father in the frozen foods business is one magnificent sentence: "One day, creditors calling at every door, he got into the cab of a truckful of his frozen rhubarb and took a ride out to Long Island to think; the refrigeration failed just beyond Mineola, and by the time he got home his life was a zero, a ruined man." At her low point, Libby, who has converted from Roman Catholicism to Judaism on marrying Paul, tries to commit suicide; when that fails she decides to make potato pancakes, "to bring a little religion into her house."

Two episodes of almost indescribable complexity, at once awful and uproarious, are the clearest sign of Roth's great promise. One is Libby's abortion, which becomes entangled with the effort of an elderly neighbor, Levy, to steal a job-lot of jockey briefs from another elderly neighbor, Korngold; it culminates in a horrifying and splendid scene when they both invade the Herz bedroom just after Libby comes home from the operation. The other is Gabe's mad effort to persuade a scoundrel named Harry Bigoness to sign a legal document that will enable the Herzes to keep their adopted baby. Eventually Gabe steals the baby in the night and drives it to Gary, Indiana, to confront Bigoness.

Roth may be the Lewis of Suburbia, but he is potentially much more. His "Writing American Fiction" speech rejects all the easy affirmations of America, and concludes on Ralph Ellison's sombre final image of the Invisible Man waiting underground. Roth really does know how hard life is. *Letting Go* concludes with Gabe, who has tried to do good without attachment, as Lord Krishna recommends in the *Gita*, left with little good achieved and no attachments either. I think that after he has seasoned longer, after another book or two, if he is prepared to learn from his mistakes, Philip Roth will be a fine novelist. Providing, that is, that all the matchmakers and promoters leave him alone.

Marjorie Morningstar PhD

John Gross*

Half the novels ever written are about the anguish of growing up. Great expectations dwindle; illusions are lost; boys who run away must learn that they can't go home again. In the nineteenth century, when hopes run high, the raw young hero sets out with stirring ideals, Napoleonic aspirations. Today he is likely to be wary, circumspect, self-mocking from the very start. But no matter. You must still leap into the dangerous world, even if it turns out that the water is only two feet deep and you fall flat on your face. Each man must take the plunge for himself—it isn't enough to run vicarious risks arranging the lives of your friends. Life begins when you forget about your own uniqueness, stop quarrelling with your father, no longer try to cling to your dearest illusions—when you let go.

Such is the ambitious theme of Philip Roth's second novel. His first book, *Goodbye, Columbus*, which won him instant recognition and a string of literary prizes, made its points quickly: it consisted of a lively satirical fable about a poor boy and the daughter of a prosperous, boorish suburban family, and a handful of short stories. *Letting Go* runs to well over 600 pages, which is a couple of hundred too many. Still, it is better to be copious than tight-fisted, and Mr. Roth has the never-to-be-despised gift of readability: even when his story drags, or his characters are tiresome, the reader cruises along easily. It must be admitted that the men and women in *Letting Go* tend to go on and on. And on. But at least the dialogue is usually sharp and colloquial. Again, there is a great deal of superfluous description: every interior in the book is documented and furnished as thoroughly as if it were the Maison Vauquer. Old Dr. Wallach's scrolly Victorian sofa with its orange upholstery means more to his son that it does to the reader. But there it is: solid, plain to see, an indisputable fact.

We don't praise an architect, though, just because he uses bricks; Mr. Roth demands to be judged by his grand design. He has two heroes: Gabe Wallach, who tells his own story, and Paul Herz, who is exposed to a third-person narrative. Both are intellectuals, whose lives cross as

*Reprinted from *New Statesman*, 64 (November 30, 1962), 784, by permission of the journal.

graduate students in Iowa and later as university teachers in Chicago. Paul is 'in Creative Writing': shabby, obstinate, glum, and in a fretful way uncompromising. He marries a Catholic girl, and is promptly cut off by his family (and hers). The couple have a wretched time of it, what with an abortion, poverty, ill health, constant wrangling. When they try to adopt a child, unexpected obstacles trip them up at every turn. That they finally succeed, and escape from their misery, is due only to the intervention of Gabe Wallach, who drives himself to a break-down seeing the adoption through; the first decisive action of an indecisive man. Gabe is a poor little rich boy, a drifter, unwilling to commit himself. (His PhD dissertation, in case you haven't already guessed, was on Henry James.) He spends much of his energy resisting the advances of his father, a well-to-do, mildly cranky dentist who has been left a lonely widower in his Manhattan apartment. Women find Gabe attractive, and though he steers clear of permanent alliances he nearly meets his match in Martha, a tough, sensual divorcee. But in the end their affair dribbles away, and he is left straying around Europe, still puzzling out his own malaise.

Two full-length portraits, both of them blurred. Paul is vivid enough in the opening pages: harassed, long-suffering, a half-heroic half-absurd figure proclaiming *Beowulf* with a Brooklyn accent. He comes alive, too, in the squabbling and nag, nag, nag of his marriage. But great areas of his life are shrouded in mist. His main occupation is writing a novel. What is it about? Will he ever finish it? (As they say in Brooklyn, I should live so long.) Eventually it just gets lost along the way. Nor is the promising theme of his uneasy break with the past ever properly worked out. At first his family are shown as odious, mere caricatures. And on the religious gropings which follow his father's death, both Paul and his creator speak in riddles. Gabe is also the son of a weak father, but it's hard to sympathize with him in his sorrows. He's altogether too spruce, too well-fed. That's his problem, no doubt, but it still doesn't make it plausible that his struggle to save the Herz baby should be as epoch-making as he regards it. A man who has lived through a liaison with the redoubtable Martha is no longer a child. Long as the book is, the end of *Letting Go* is huddled up; Gabe comes across not as the 'mad crusader' he is intended to be, but as a busybody with time on his hands.

Mr. Roth is more successful with some of his minor characters. Sid Jaffe the stolid lawyer, Doris the ex-girlfriend, Fay Silberman the hard-drinking widow: these are well-observed, freshly drawn types. But they aren't enough to redeem the general cheapness of so much else in the book. Mr. Roth starts by quoting Thomas Mann and Simone Weil and Wallace Stevens, but his idea of what it means to be grown up is largely a mixture of aw-cut-the-crap bluster and an intolerable knowingness about lubricants and deodorants, menstruation and masturbation. Life in these pages is sour and soiled, full of small rancour. *Letting Go* is a book with a thousand wisecracks and scarcely a single joke.

This ugliness (and it's the ugliness of bad art, not of unsavoury subject-matter) is at its most grating in the specifically Jewish passages. Most of the men in the novel (though few of the women) are Jewish, and the more a character's Jewishness is stressed, the more likely he is to be presented as coarse-fibred, dirty-minded, *grob*. Paul's bohemian Uncle Asher is even more repulsive than Mr. Roth means him to be. A long, tedious digression involves old Levy's sordid scheme for swindling old Korngold out of his goods. (The item in question—it would be—is a consignment of underwear. Why not? But then again, why?) It's no compensation, but rather the reverse, that during this episode we're allowed to catch a glimpse of a sympathetic Jew with a concentration-camp number tattooed on his arm. Paul asks a rabbi to officiate at his wedding, only to be cursed and flung out. On the evidence shown here, it would be hard not to agree with Heine that Judaism isn't a religion, but a misfortune. Yet Mr. Roth isn't launching a wholesale attack: this is the faith to which Paul Herz tries to return, however ineffectually, after a hysterical reconciliation scene at his father's grave. It doesn't begin to fit together.

Perhaps it would have been as well for Philip Roth if he hadn't been cited again and again as a leading member of the new school of American-Jewish novelists. Without so portentous a label hung round his neck, he might never have been lured into writing such tawdry, incoherent stuff. Do American-Jewish writers form a school, anyway? It's easy to see why such an idea has won favour. We live in an age of anti-anti-Semitism; at the same time, it's agreeable to think of a generation of gifted critics, the Elders of the *Partisan Review*, as having made straight a path for their juniors, the young men 'in Creative Writing'. Yet traditional Jewish culture in America is dissolving, or being largely transformed into a minor variant on the standard American model. The immigrant novel, where a Jew was a Jew, has receded into history; and to search for intangible racial qualities among the assimilated is a dangerous game. Is Augie March twice or twenty times as Jewish as Holden Caulfield? Where is the Geiger counter which will give such readings?

There are novelists who write out of a wholly Jewish situation, and novelists who merely happen to be Jewish: it's tempting to leave it at that. But much of the best recent American-Jewish writing springs from an awareness that no such tidy distinction is possible. There's a splendid scene in Saul Bellow's *The Victim* where a group of men in a New York cafeteria are arguing about Disraeli, only half jokingly, in their own terms: 'And he was managing the firm?' said Goldstone. 'Bull and Company. The sun never sets on our stores. B. Disraeli, chief buyer? Here is a tradition both tenacious and fragmented, profound and artificial; one must tread with caution, but it's impossible not to see affinities, common nostalgias, old scars. Writers like Bellow and Malamud derive their blend of warmth and irony both from the intensity of the past, and from their ambiguous relationship with that past. From Jewish experience they abstract a metaphor for twentieth-century man: rueful, displaced, tragi-comic. Mr. Roth has borrowed a few externals from this tradition, but his high-gloss prose suggests another line of descent. He really belongs with a very different group of American-Jewish writers, the slick professionals like Irwin Shaw, Jerome Weidman or even Herman Wouk. He takes a big risk, in fact, when he lets one of his characters talk about *Marjorie Morningstar*.

But times change, and nowadays all the kids go to college. Viewed from one angle, *Letting Go* is simply another campus novel, complete with a phony head of the English Department supplied out of stock by Jarrell-McCarthy Inc. And both Gabe and Paul suffer from the usual trouble with intellectuals in fiction: they aren't intellectual enough. It isn't simply that they almost never talk about their work. They also seem to be indifferent to ideas, art, politics, untouched by the world beyond the nests which they are trying to build for themselves.

Paul retreats into domesticity as resolutely as any Victorian hero, even if he pins everything on one adopted child where once he might have fathered a swarming Victorian brood. And our last view of Gabe is as a lonely globe-trotter in an hotel lobby, still swathed in adolescent self-regard. This is the very reverse of letting go. Yet a long novel in which public themes are nowhere confronted is apt to induce the claustrophobia that comes from being trapped in somebody's else's private world. For all his virtuosity, Mr. Roth never persuades us that either of his sad young men is a hero (or anti-hero) of our time.

When He Is Bad

Robert Alter*

The kindest thing one can say about Philip Roth's new novel is that it is a brave mistake. It is easy enough to imagine how exasperated a writer of serious ambition must feel to find himself trapped, as Roth has been, by his own initial success, securely tucked away by the public into a special pigeonhole of genre writing. *When She Was Good* is Roth's strenuously willed effort to break out of the narrow precincts of Jewish urban and suburban life into the great open country of indigenous American fiction. Or rather, what used to be indigenous American fiction, since at a point in time when at least our literature has achieved something like a viable cultural pluralism, Roth must go back a generation and more to an age when one might still speak of a mainstream in the American novel. His models, therefore, are writers like Sherwood Anderson, Sinclair Lewis, Theodore Dreiser; correspondingly, his choice of

*Reprinted from *Commentary*, November 1967, by permission; all rights reserved.

materials seems peculiarly self-conscious and his treatment of them unhappily anachronistic.

All the action of *When She Was Good* takes place in and around a small town with the uncomfortably symbolic name of Liberty Center, somewhere north of Chicago "in the middle of America." The characters are all simple, inexorably average townfolk, white Protestants (with the exception of one disreputable Catholic family) of Nordic or Anglo-Saxon stock. Flaxen hair, blue eyes, and snub noses tend to cluster at the visual center of the novel against a sketchy background of school corridors, football fields, lovers' lanes, back porches, coke machines, old jalopies, and whatever else is generally included in everyone's inventory of Hometown, U.S.A. Roth clearly knows about all this, as almost anyone who has grown up in America would, but there is little evidence in the novel that he knows it firsthand, with an eye for the nuances of character and social gesture among such people, in such a setting.

Everything that happens in the novel occurs on a plane of flat generality and in consequence virtually nothing is altogether credible. Much of this is the result of Roth's unfortunate narrative technique, to which I shall return, but it is also related to his habit of building on ready-made formulas instead of actually imagining his subject. The principal action takes place in the years after World War II, and while Roth elsewhere has convincingly recreated the feel of this period in a New Jersey Jewish neighborhood, his midwestern Protestants float in a colorless temporal ambiance that could be as easily attached to 1890 or 1920 as to 1950. Unable to conjure up the period in the minds and life-style of his characters, Roth falls back on the formulaic device of merely reciting recollected cultural passwords of the era—Milton Berle on television, Dick Haymes singing "It Might As Well Be Spring," Harry Truman's loud sportshirts worn outside the trousers. Apart from this forced invocation of temporal setting, the use of mechanical formulas is less obtrusive, but more pervasive: it is, in fact, the armature around which plot and characterization are wound.

For in his attempt to create a bred-in-the-bone American heroine and a paradigmatic American marriage, Roth bases every major invention of character and event on the most familiar of formulas about the two sexes: American men, in their obsession with manliness, are supposed to be insecure about their masculinity, or not really men; and American women are supposed to be covertly domineering, subtly or brutally unmanning their men. Lucy Nelson, the protagonist of *When She Was Good*, has lived till the age of eighteen with a weak-willed, ne'er-do-well drunkard father whom she despises and a grandfather outwardly more successful but inwardly composed of the same pulpy stuff as his son-in-law. Predictably, Lucy becomes pregnant by a local boy who is every inch the weakling that her own father is, but she decides to have him make an honest woman out of her in the hope that through marriage she will be able to make a man out of him. The result, of course, is just the opposite of what she intends: husband Roy remains attached to his pathetic daydreams, his boyish snacks of Hydrox cookies, the distant tug of mama's apron-strings, while Lucy's attempts to confront him with his "responsibilities" make him aware only of the crack of the riding whip in her voice, the gleam of the castrating knife in her fierce eye. Such situations can only go from bad to hideous, and the animosity between Roy and Lucy finally bursts out in a forty-page domestic explosion, complete with obscenities hurled, blows struck across the face, and the meddling of obnoxious relatives. At the conclusion of all this, Lucy, half-insane with the sense of the injustices done her, flees into the night (as the saying goes), stopping finally at the lovers' lane where Roy first seduced her and where she now freezes to death in the snow, the perfect frigid American wife to the bitter, melodramatic end.

Many hypersensitive Jewish readers of *Goodbye, Columbus* accused Roth of Jewish self-hatred, though there is scarcely evidence for that in the stories themselves. What became clearer in *Letting Go* was that Roth suffered rather from a general deficiency in the sympathetic imagination of humanity. In his new novel, this deficiency of sympathy expresses itself in a kind of vendetta against human nature, at least in its characteristic American manifestations. Humanity is divided into those who are hateful and those who are merely contemptible, with most of the men falling into the latter category and a few rare creatures, like Roy's cigar-smoking, lecherous Uncle Julian, belonging to both groups at once. The title apparently refers elliptically to the end of the nursery rhyme: it is when Lucy is *good* that she is at her most horrid, and this could be applied almost equally well to every other character in the book. The novel reads, then, like *One Man's Family* written with the satirical moroseness of a Swift and none of Swift's genius.

This implacable attitude of Roth toward his personages may explain why he has written some remarkable short stories but has not yet proved that he can write a novel at all. In a short story, character can be exposed; in a novel it must be revealed. A novelist should be at least capable of seeing all around his characters, even to their attractive sides; to put this another way, he has to imagine at least the possibility of change and development in his personages. The characters of *When She Was Good*, on the other hand, are fixed in one anguished posture which we are made to see again and again—the men forever set in weak-kneed knavery around the central figure of the woman who, palpably victimized by them, unpityingly makes them her victims. Repeated for three hundred pages, this unvaried image of humanity is simply tedious.

The same word is inevitable in any description of the style and narrative technique. All the narration in the book adheres closely to the point of view of one character or another, with Lucy's naturally predominating. But since the consciousness of these characters, as Roth conceives them, is depressingly empty, containing little more than clichés and truisms, the whole novel is walled in with clichés without a chink of light from a world of intelligence and imaginative life that must exist somewhere on the outside. There is no analysis of motive, no realization of physical scene or atmosphere, not even the consolation of an occasional metaphor that strikes fire in the imagination. The entire book is made up of flat, unexpressive, unperceptive dialogue, summaries of the same, and summarizing accounts of action which paraphrase the language that would be used by the characters themselves to report it. *When She Was Good* is thus a textbook illustration of the imitative fallacy. One might forgive on the grounds of imitation an occasional sentence like, "Lucy herself had always thought of Joe as one big blah," but such sentences, in all their rhythmic deadness and all the stunted inadequacy of their adolescent vocabulary, comprise the whole texture of the novel's prose, from beginning to end. "No pity, no sympathy, no nothing," Roy is reported as saying to Lucy at one crucial juncture. "He was willing to let bygones be bygones, and to start in clean and fresh, and be a lot better off for the experience—if she was." Roth apparently does not give this to us in direct discourse because Roy's triteness in its original form would be just too embarrassing, but it is scarcely better in summary, and the prose throughout the novel never gets very much better than this.

A novelist, in one way or another, has to find a vocabulary to cope with the experience he presents, but Roth refuses to allow any adequacy of words either to his narrator or his characters. What Lucy wants is for people to be "innocent," "good," "just," "true," "strong," while those who threaten her are "wicked," "dirty," "cruel," "mean," "weak,"—and that is the full extent of the novel's moral vocabulary. The book wallows in authorially contrived misery with neither the language nor the imaginative vigor to make sense of that misery. Toward the end, Berta, Lucy's grandmother, confesses that "she was sick and tired of disorder and tragedy." In style and substance, this marks the exact level of the novel's response to the human condition. *When She Was Good* conveys not—as Roth may have intended—the vision of an American Tragedy but rather a nagging, frustrated, irredeemably banal sense of being sick and tired of disorder and tragedy, which, however, stubbornly and invariably prevail.

What Hath Roth Got

Jonathan Baumbach*

Philip Roth's new novel is a restrained horror story about the Puritan ethic, which owns part of us all, regardless of race, religion or creed. Dealing exclusively with white, anglo-saxon, midwestern America, a somewhat alien landscape for the author of *Goodbye, Columbus* and *Letting Go, When She Was Good* is a surprising tour de force, an accomplishment comparable, say, to Zero Mostel doing an extended imitation of Jimmy Stewart.

Roth's heroine, Lucy Nelson, takes on herself the burden of setting things right. The early part of the novel deals with the career of her grandfather (called—get it—"Daddy" Will), in whose house she grows up, her family supported and destroyed by Will's good intentions. Lucy's involvement with her father, which Roth handles with especially nice perception, is at the center of the novel. She is provoked—her mother too attached to her own father to be wife to her husband—to act in her mother's place, to become a kind of surrogate wife to her father. It is Lucy who calls the police when her father, in a drunken rage, hurts her mother. It is Lucy who, on another occasion, bolts the door against her father, locking him out of the house. The burden devolves on Lucy because the others refuse to act on their feelings. She acts *for* her mother, *for* her grandfather, confusing their desires with her own.

Lucy marries a man who is to some extent—perhaps more in the way she sees him than the way he is—like her father. She tries to do for her weak-willed husband, Roy Bassart, what she was unable to do for her father—make a good, hard-working man out of him, as if such a thing were in her power. She tries to be "good." Madness and tragedy result.

The novel, like the world it describes, is without texture. Roth is a marvelous mimic, which is perhaps his undoing here as a novelist. One can hear Daddy Will saying to Lucy, "You are just a schoolchild, and, maybe, just maybe, you know, you don't know the whole story of life yet. You may think you do but I happen to think different, and who I am is your grandfather whose house this is." Or Roy thinking: "She was small and had dark bangs and for a short girl she had a terrific figure (which you couldn't say was the case with Beverly Collison whom in his bitterness Roy had come to characterize, and not unjustly, as 'flat as a board.' "), Roth catches the rhythms of his characters' speech, the precise gestures that identify them for us. But not, I feel, what makes them human. The conception of the novel is much more compelling than the dull fact of its experience.

When She Was Good is a willful accomplishment, a good cause, a triumph of persistence and professional skill over imagination. It is the

*Reprinted from *Commonweal*, 86 (August 11, 1967), 498, by permission of the journal.

most successful technically and the least rich in texture of Roth's longer
fiction. The horror the novel delineates, which also, incidentally, informs
the paradox of our monstrous good intentions in Vietnam, is likely not to
be noticed, not to be experienced, by the very readers who will admire the
novel most, who will weep soap opera tears at poor Lucy's tragedy. Brave
in its ambitions, Roth's novel is too cautious and conventional in its form.
I kept wanting the novel to get away from its author, to violate at least for
a moment the logic imposed on it from without. I prefer the rich uneven-
ness of *Letting Go*, a book undervalued because it failed. *When She Was
Good* succeeds without life.

Brand Names and Others

J. Mitchell Morse*

Those who follow fashion—stepping along behind the drum majors
and majorettes of advertising—march with many different banners, but
all their parades move toward the marketplace. Fashion is salesmanship.
The desire to be fashionable is the desire to have what others have, do
what others do, be what others are. The sales media, offering themselves
to advertisers, announce with various degrees of delicacy that they cater
to this desire. *Cosmopolitan* says its readers buy what's in because they
have good taste, *Esquire* says its readers buy what's in because they are
sophisticated, *Seventeen* says its readers buy what's in because they are
impressionable, *Glamour* says its readers buy what's in because, having
grown up, they can now do what's in, those break-away girls, and the
MacFadden chain of confession magazines has boasted in at least one full-
page ad that its readers go for brand names and pay more than their
better-educated sisters, because, being mostly working-class wives, they
lack self-confidence. Race-relations note: the day after I wrote that last
sentence, *Ebony* announced that its readers, whose median family income
is $7,000, "are more impressed by quality brands than quick bargains"
because they know how to live.

All these motives, which are in essence one, are catered to almost as
naively by what in our quaint Briticism we call the book trade. The book
business. The business of producing, advertising and selling books. In that
it is a business it is to some extent like any other business; but in that it has
to do with books it is to some extent unlike any other business. I remember
when Macy's moved its book department from the first floor to the fifth;
when I asked why, I was told that it didn't bring in enough money per
cubic foot of space to pay its way on the first floor. A producer going into
business primarily to make money would do better in bottle caps or hair

*Reprinted from *Hudson Review*, 22 (1969), 320–29, by permission of the journal.

curlers. People who go into any aspect of the book business are almost all, however slightly, motivated by another motive as well: they like to be around books. Thus, confounding the two motives, they are ceaselessly tempted to believe that a good seller is a good book, to be impressed by a favorable review in *The New York Times*, and in the case of publishers to judge the quality of a manuscript at least partly by its estimated sales potential. They and the readers to whom they cater are roughy analogous to the horse lovers in Veblen's chapter on pecuniary canons of taste, "whose sense of beauty is held in abeyance by the moral constraint of the horse fancier's award." I know there are editors and even sales managers who will freely admit that this or that best seller on their list is a piece of trash, but such private judgments are not reflected in the professional judgments they back with the stockholders' money. And even so, even so, even so, the business office of a good publisher is sometimes affected by values that other businesses know nothing of, and a good book that nobody expects to have a large audience is backed with money because it is a good book. Not with a great deal of money, to be sure; but still, backed with money—printed, bound, advertised and distributed.

I say this out of respect for Louis Zukofsky and his new publishers, Grossman and Jonathan Cape.[1] We respect Zukofsky for his honesty more than for anything else. He isn't a very skillful writer or even a very careful one, but in everything he does we have the sense of a man trying in all simplicity to express the nuances of a subtle understanding. His technique is sufficient only to let the intention be perceived, not to fulfill it; he seems never to have realized that subtlety cannot be expressed without subtlety.

The new volume *Ferdinand* comprises in its ninety-four pages, along with a bibliography and a biographical note, two stories—"Ferdinand" and "It Was"—from the earlier volume *It Was* (Tokyo, 1961), which included in addition two other stories, "A Keystone Comedy" and "Thanks to the Dictionary." The two that are now reprinted are unmistakably better than the two that are not; they represent Zukofsky at his best as a writer of fiction; but they are distressingly flimsy in the details of construction, like summer houses personally hand-made by an architect who is a good architect but not a good carpenter. Here are a few weak joints spotted at random among many others. "Hard knocks in the past seemed responsible for many of his violent resentments and unexplained recurrent breaches short of sportsmanship." Why the "short"? Can Zukofsky have been unable to make up his mind between "breaches of sportsmanship" and "fallings short of sportsmanship"? Or was he playing one of his coy etymological games and expecting us to read "breaches" as "breakings"? Or didn't he know what he was saying? We can't dismiss this last possibility, for the very next sentence reads, "He was yawning excessively when he stepped into bed." "Got," yes; "sank," yes; "fell," possibly; "stepped," absolutely no. Ferdinand sees some Indians in Arizona who subsist by making "clay pots and baskets," meaning "baskets and clay pots." An Indian woman seems to him to exist like a hidden petal of a vine in the grass: "Though with respect to her, the sky, whose blue resembled the petals that are seen and glared over the empty road in the sun, might be hidden instead of her." Reading this sentence the way we naturally read English, we read "the petals that are seen and glared" and wonder what it means. Then we stop and reread and get "resembled the [visible] petals and glared." That's better, but the sentence still doesn't make sense: "Though, with respect to her, the sky might be hidden instead of her." God damn it, Zukofsky, what the hell are you trying to say? On almost every page we have to do the writer's work for him:

> Ferdinand's thought drifted back to the embassy. He wondered if the youngster who had replaced him there had made good, if anyone still could make good in a bankrupt country.
> All his family, father, uncles, distant cousins on both sides had been either farmers or gardeners, he heard the man say to his uncle.

After the "he" and the "him" in the first paragraph, we naturally assume that the "his" in the second refers to Ferdinand, and discover once again that Zukofsky has unintentionally misled us. And what bankrupt country?

But his rickety prose is worth repairing as we go along, which is more than can be said for most rickety prose—that is to say, for most of the prose now being written. "Ferdinand" is the story of a French foreign minister's son who, as a little boy whose parents had no time for him, had fallen deeply and permanently in love with the little daughter of a kindly Italian gardener who was like a father to him; since the gardener hoped to marry his daughter to an independent vineyardist, the boy dreamed of becoming one; of course he didn't, but went away to a lycee and the University of Paris and began to have casual mistresses and became an attache of the embassy in Washington; several years later, still unmarried, still romantically wishing he could be a vineyardist, etc., he resigned because France had been taken by the Nazis, started driving across the United States on a vacation with his exiled aunt and uncle, and deliberately smashed up the car and killed them all, re-enacting a childhood accident with a toy car. The End. Thus robbed of detail, the plot seems as corny as that of any nineteenth-century opera or twentieth-century movie. The car is an all too obvious symbol of his parents' way of life and the values they thought he shared; the aunt and uncle, who in fact had brought him up away from home, are all too obvious substitutes for his parents. And nevertheless the story is lyrical and true. It is a good story in spite of almost everything.

"It Was" is even more improbably true. It deals with a writer's long effort, conscious and unconscious, to write a perfect simple sentence that will put the only possible words in the only possible order; suddenly the sentence comes to him, and Zukofsky ends the story with it. Since the story is only four pages long, it should have been and doubtless was intended to be a little miracle of enclosure, a work of art whose subject is itself; but Zukofsky's prose, though better here than in "Ferdinand," is far from miraculous: his narrator's sentence, for example, in the absence of its imaginary context is not impressive. And even so, this story comes through, as most of Zukofsky's poetry comes through, largely on the strength of its good intentions. Our abjectly commercial writers, however skillful at their business, don't have good intentions. That was a difficulty Aristotle didn't have to consider when he said the invention was nothing and the performance all.

And speaking of commercial abjection, the congregation will please rise and sing All Hail the Power of Portnoy's Name.[2] As I write he is for the time being Lord of all, the hottest brand name in the market. By now everybody knows enough about him, and I don't find him worth discussing at length. Philip Roth belongs in the same abject bag as Leo Rosten, Harry Golden, Myron Cohen and Sam Levenson: like Leslie Fiedler's Montana ranch hand who on Saturdays gets all dressed up in a cowboy suit and walks the streets of Butte or Missoula as "the pimp of his particularity," a professional Jew-boy gets his kicks from catering to condescension.

In order to sell a particularity, we must simplify it, idealize it, and make it conform to popular preconceptions. This involves reducing it to a set of easy formulas that don't allow for any personal uniqueness. Though the conventions are different, *Portnoy's Complaint* is as conventional as the fiction in *Woman's Day*, where all adolescent daughters have braces on their teeth and all pre-adolescent sons have freckles. Portnoy is the ideal character towards whom a type of contemporary American novel has been working: The Neurotic Jewish Liberal Intellectual who is *nothing but* The Neurotic Jewish Liberal Intellectual. His mother is The Jewish Mother, Contemporary Comic Variety, whose life is limited to the kitchen and the bathroom. His father is The Jewish Lower-Middle-Class Father, Contemporary Comic Variety—constipation, flat feet and all. Alex Portnoy himself is nothing but a collection of contemporary cliches. He makes all A's in school. He is not athletic. He has all kinds of sexual difficulties because of his mother's smothering love. On his first try with a prostitute he is for aesthetic reasons impotent—just like Holden Caulfield. His mistresses are the standard goyische assortment: The Nice Middle-Western Corn-Fed Idealist, The Whorish Underwear Model, and The Liberal Connecticut Aristocrat. These people move in a swirl of contemporary cliches about Jews in general: Jews Have A Strong Family Life. Jewish Family Life Is Hell. Jews Are Either Extraordinarily Intelligent Or Extraordinarily Stupid And Gross. Some Intelligent Jews Are Also Gross. Some Stupid Jews Have An Innate Refinement—If Only They Could

Have Gone To College. Jews Are Not Athletic. Jews are Musical. Jews Are Sad. Jews Get Drafted Into The Army And Die In Battle Just Like Everybody Else. Jews Are Not All Communists. Jews Are Not All Rich. There Are Reactionary Jews. Jews Are Not Acquisitive. Jews Are Extraordinarily Generous. Jews Are Extraordinarily Kind. Jews Understand. Jews Are Nervous. Jews Are Neurotic. Jews Are Sensual. Jews Are Over-Sexed. Jews Are Over-Sensitive.

Since the defeat of the Nazis, the cliches of anti-Semitism among intellectuals have been largely replaced by these more benign ones. They are not equally harmful, but they are equally stupid, and they make me as a Jew almost as uncomfortable. Moreover, as is well known, group stereotypes tend to have a compulsive force: people tend to do what is expected of them, to play the role assigned to them; and if the role is undignified, the effort of rejecting it also conduces to a self-consciousness that would otherwise be unnecessary. Any attribution whatever of group characteristics, to any group whatever, threatens the individuality of members of the group, and to that extent is a form of hostility to them as individuals, however benign and friendly the attributors may feel. No man should have to keep fighting off cliches about himself. Or ignoring them either. As my son recently told an acquaintance, who was surprised that he wasn't interested in playing the stock market, "You've got your stereotypes confused. Jews steal watermelons and have natural rhythm." Philip Roth has the disease of masochistic conformity. He is a servile entertainer. *Portnoy's Complaint* is supinely acquiescent in every way: a series of burlesk skits. Many years ago I went to Boston to cover the trial of *Forever Amber*, and my background research took me to the Old Howard Burlesk Theater. There—five minutes from the courthouse—I heard a droopy-pants comedian singing "The Shithouse Blues" and saying aside to the audience between stanzas, "I'm Jewish." In my mind's eye now he seems to have the face of Philip Roth.

Writers like Isaac Bashevis Singer and Sholom Aleichem are another matter entirely. Human dignity doesn't preclude our laughing at ourselves—quite the contrary, it is precluded by the ways of life that never laugh or smile except at the expense of others. *The Adventures of Menahem-Mendl* is a very funny epistolary novel made up of letters between a schlemiel and his wife.[3] Who among us isn't a schlemiel now and then? Originally the letters appeared in various Yiddish newspapers and magazines over a period of eighteen years, beginning in 1892. In 1909 Sholom Aleichem selected, shortened, sharpened and arranged those he considered the best, and the resulting book has now been translated into English by his granddaughter, Tamara Kahana. Her witty command of English is equal to the piety. You don't have to be Jewish to enjoy Menahem-Mendl and his devoted Sheineh-Sheindl. All you have to be is human. Sholom Aleichem has often been compared to Mark Twain, but I think a better comparison would be to Sterne. I found *The Adventures of*

Menahem-Mendl as delightful as *Tristram Shandy*. (Observe students, how I avoided the cliche "He transcends his particularity." It wasn't easy.)

Jose Maria Gironella's *Peace After War* is not about Jews, but it does have a Jewish character whom I'd like to dispose of briefly before going on to more interesting books: Father Forteza, S.J.[4] In view of the extremely small number of Jewish Jesuits in the population (see Hannah Arendt's *The Origins of Totalitarianism*, p. 102), they seem to be disproportionately numerous in fiction. I think of Naphta in *The Magic Mountain*, whose name suggests a wrestler or a washing powder or one of the ingredients of Hell-fire, depending on one's cultural heritage and one's sensitivity to spelling; of Father Rothschild in *Vile Bodies*, whose name suggests money and George Arliss; and of Gabriel de Rennepont in *The Wandering Jew*, whose name suggests a good angel, a bad novel, and a bridge for reindeer. Bertie Stanhope in *Barchester Towers*—who was an Anglican first and last, but who in an aberrant interval became an acolyte of the Jesuits because he happened to be in Rome and then went with a group of them to Palestine to convert the Jews and was converted to Judaism—is doubtless a doubtful case, but he does illustrate a tendency of some writers to equate Jesuits morally with Jews. John Donne, in *Ignatius His Conclave*, calls Hell the chief synagogue, and the founder of the Society of Jesus its chief priest. John Jay Chapman in his xenophobic old age sums up all undesirable immigrants as "the Jesuit and the Jew." Even Joyce, who doesn't make the cheap equation, has characters who do. In *Ulysses* Buck Mulligan sneers at Stephen Dedalus: "O you inquisitional drunken jew jesuit!" And in *Finnegans Wake* the good Shaun lists among his bad brother Shem's indecencies the fact that he "went into the society of jewses." Father Forteza is not in this tradition; for, being a Jesuit in an authoritarian society that the author approves of, he is portrayed as a "good" Jew. At the same time, in case there are any Spaniards who distrust Jesuits . . . though of course not *all* Jesuits are Jews. Thus Gironella eats the insipid cake of servility and has it too. *Peace After War* is in the tradition of didactic novels whose characters make long dull speeches at each other by way of conversation, frequently in indirect discourse. It is set in Spain after the civil war, and its protagonists all welcome fascism, though with various degrees of warmth. Their differences are matters of nuance and timbre; all their heavy lame-brain discussions lead to the conclusion the clerico-fascist control is not only tolerable but desirable. Gironella is an official Great Writer in Spain, as Sholokhov is in Russia; the difference is that Sholokhov's novels, having more horses, make better material for the silver screen.

As I write, Spring is galloping like Isadora all over our suburban acre-and-a-quarter, and in her footsteps spring such flowers as sweet Elysium, Coryza, Epicanthus, Conundrum, Condominium, Vitalis, Lacuna, Hiatus, Cassandra, purple Persiflage, flowering Nexus, perennial

Petula, broad-leaved Platypus, climbing Parallax, trailing Nebula, creeping Abscissa, early-blooming Spinoza, Menander, Medusa and Lampedusa, and as I look out at these and at our little kitchen garden full of Colander, Spatula, Pyrex and Silex, how can I sneer at the suburban life? All this, and only 35 minutes from Wanamaker's and the Philadelphia Museum? We have the best of both worlds. Why should I sneer? What's eating all the writers who do, including those who admit that they like the suburban life?

Nothing is eating them, I gather, so much as a desire to sell more copies of their books; in the middle ages any writer could attack the ignorance and corruption of the lesser clergy with impunity and be widely appreciated, as long as he didn't question the dogmas; and in our time such harmless trap-shooting is something the customers expect and want to see. Meeting their expectations is a sure way to make them happy. One day last December the public address system in our suburban Woolworth's was out of order, and a clerk sadly told my wife, "It's hard, not havin' no music at Christmas time." She *wanted* to hear "Rudolf the Red-Nosed Reindeer," "I Saw Mommy Kissing Santa Claus" and "I'm Dreaming of a White Christmas" all day long. The book business caters to customers who have a similar habituation to certain accustomed features in the novels they read, and one of the most accustomed is an attitude that celebrates without endorsing, and mocks without threatening, the pleasant things that money can buy and the life that includes such things: in the absence of any need for pleasures of a purely literary kind, uncritical readers are impressed by books that confirm them again and yet again in their decent belief, of whose objective rightness they cannot be too often reassured, that money isn't everything. The Blintza Restaurant in Philadelphia, whose cabbage soup and friendly atmosphere we enjoy, has printed on the backs of its business cards the following incontrovertible truth: "MONEY CAN BUY A Bed but not Sleep, Books but not Brains, Food but not Appetite, Finery but not Beauty, a House but not a Home, Medicine but not Health, Luxuries but not Culture, Amusement but not Happiness, Boon Companions but not Friends, Flattery but not Respect." Novelists who have nothing less obvious to say may very well peddle such sure-fire wisdom; but serious novelists, who offer something more serious or at least funnier, should never put it in except for fun. The message of *Uncle Tom's Cabin* is that Slavery Is Wrong, and the message of *1984* is that Dictatorship Is Evil; but what is the message of *Hamlet*? That you shouldn't kill your uncle? That He Who Hesitates Is Lost? And what is the message of *Ulysses*? Say Yes To Life? The great works are not so easily summed up. I say this now because I have before me three good novels whose authors have succumbed to the temptation to be incontrovertible.[5] *Bullet Park, Expensive People* and *Mr. Bridge* are not about suburban life but about the inner lives of certain people who happen to live in the suburbs; nevertheless their authors go through the familiar routines of inferior novelists, as if they were no better.

"Well I suppose there's plenty to be sad about if you look around, but it makes me sore to have people always chopping at the suburbs. I've never understood why," says Eliot Nailles of *Bullet Park*; and then in the ensuing two paragraphs he unwittingly damns everything he consciously believes in. The giveaway here lies in the insensitivity of his first sentence, "Well I suppose there's plenty to be sad about if you look around"; earlier, trying to cope for the first time in his life with a seemingly senseless misfortune whose Oedipal cause he could not see, Nailles had thought, "Grief was for the others; sorrow and pain were for the others; some terrible mistake had been made." This is good writing about a serious subject, the changes that take place in the consciousness of a cheerful insensitive man under tests for which his thoughtless life has not prepared him; but Cheever himself as omniscient author mixes it up with a lot of quite ordinary chopping at the suburbs. Some of his sentences also are as rickety as some of Zukofsky's; he doesn't seem to know the uses of the suffix -ity: he speaks of "obsceneness," "obeseness" and "chasteness," for example; and his vocabulary is frequently inaccurate, as when he speaks of the "sameness" of the names of Hammer and Nailles. Cheever has always been an uneven writer, and he doesn't progress; in his hands, as in so many others, the English language shows signs of deterioration. Nevertheless, *Bullet Park* is worth reading for its serious intent and its frequent intervals of good execution. The best is the characterization of Paul Hammer, a homicidal maniac, entirely through his literary style.

Joyce Carol Oates does progress. *Expensive People* is the best of her books to date, and within it—shall I say like ontogeny recapitulating phylogeny?—she gets better as she proceeds. This is the story—cluttered up with parodies that don't work and a lot of easy inessential cliches and cliche set-pieces about the foolishness of suburban living and occasional explicit statements about how good it is anyhow—the story, I was saying, of an intelligent and sensitive boy's unrequited love for his cold beautiful mother, his conscious jealousy of and grudging sympathy for his crude father, and his growing distress at his mother's repeated adulteries and desertions, a distress that finally causes him to shoot her dead, and a good thing too, I say. Her name, Natashya, was originally Nancy. She addresses her son, whom she had seriously thought of aborting, as "you little fake." She belongs to the same great group as Paul Hammer's mother, Gloria, nee Gretchen. Natashya's son is the narrator: he writes a confessional memoir. The first part, which establishes the situation like the first act of a play, is full of elementary mistakes such as the use of "abandonment" for "abandon," "he's . . . did" for "he's . . . done," "climax" for "bottom," "invalid" for "valid" and "maturation" for "maturity," a sentence that inadvertently makes a typist raise her eyebrows with long-fingered grace, another that we have to read twice in order to be sure that it means that a lake was filled in, not created, another that is so clumsy it turns out not to be a sentence at all, etc., etc.; and we don't know whether to ascribe these to the highly intelligent boy or (things being as they are now with the English language) to Miss Oates. But in any case the quality suddenly begins to rise at the end of Part I and continues to rise throughout the rest of the novel, so that the last 48 pages sing and are brilliant. Miss Oates writes a very good brand of prose when she wants to and puts her mind to it. If she becomes a brand name—and it looks as if she may—she will be one of the better brands.

In 1896, after giving a series of Chautauqua lectures at Chautauqua itself, William James wrote, "Now for Utica and Lake Placid by rail, with East Hill in prospect for tomorrow. You bet I rejoice at the outlook—I long to escape from tepidity. Even an Armenian massacre, whether to be killer or killed, would seem an agreeable change from the blamelessness of Chautauqua as she lies soaking year after year in her lakeside sun and showers. . . . I have seen more women and less beauty, heard more voices and less sweetness, perceived more earnestness and less triumph than I ever supposed possible." (*Letters*, II, 43–4.) That is essentially the quality of the life lived by Mr. Bridge in the Crescent Heights suburb of Kansas City. Evan Connell's novel about him is a brilliant tour de force: a novel about tepidity that isn't tepid, quite the contrary, and a detailed portrait of a rather doughy *paskudnyak* with whom we sympathize even while we despise him. The fact that we find him not altogether unsympathetic is a large element in the deadliness of the portrait, some degree of sympathy being a necessary condition for credibility. Less blatant than Babbitt, less intelligent than Thomas Buddenbrook, he takes all the color and juice out of life. "I bleach," said Mother Sereda in *Jurgen*. Mr. Bridge bleaches. His children disavow his values, his wife unconsciously loses interest in him, his secretary tells him he has ruined her life by his impersonality, and he is bewildered. He hates Jews and Negroes; he loves listening to Nelson Eddy and Jeanette MacDonald; he thinks Roosevelt is wrecking the country; but he is not a churchgoer, he is not a pro-Nazi, he is not without spells of bewildered or self-satisfied reflection. He even has an element of kindness. His life is presented in a series of short episodes ranging in length from half a page to two or three pages, each complete in itself and structurally perfect: I suppose we could call them epiphanies. Novels come and go, but I think *Mr. Bridge* will be with us for quite a while. It can be read with pleasure again and again. That is the test.

Tony Nailles of *Bullet Park*, having been dropped from the high school football squad because of his low grades, started reading poetry, "as if he shared, with the poets, the mysterious and painful experience of being forced into the role of a bystander." That is of course the basic trouble of Paul Hammer, who lives on inherited money, and even of Tony's hard-working father, who makes a good living "pushing mouthwash" but can hardly force himself to go to work of such inconsequence every day. In Mike Nichols' *The Graduate* we have a society of hardworking bystanders who have no idea that anything ails them. The trouble with Frederick Exley's fictional character Frederick Exley is that—like Tony Nailles and the Graduate—he knows he is a bystander.[6] *A Fan's Notes*, which Exley calls a fictional memoir and a fantasy, is one of the best new novels I have read in a long time; Exley the character is worthy of comparison with Antoine Roquentin, Zeno Cosini, and Thomas Mann's Dilettante. This is Exley the novelist's first novel; I think we have here a new talent worth taking very seriously indeed. He does say "timidness" for "timidity," and now and then he does something equally clumsy, but on the whole he writes better than most established novelists. Don't miss *A Fan's Notes*.

Some established writers, like Hemingway and Faulkner, decline in their old age; some, like Hugh Walpole and E. M. Delafield, were never very good; for whatever reasons, it often happens that a book by an established or brand-name writer is of little or no value. I have before me an even half-dozen books of this kind.[7] In Kingsley Amis' *I Want It Now* the familiar Amis adult brat gets soft in the head at the end, a switch that isn't worth making because the character is of no human significance either before or after. Sybille Bedford's *A Compass Error* is a novel of blackmail and detection and the kind of actorish "sophistication" made popular by Somerset Maugham, Adolphe Menjou, David Niven and W. C. Fields. The Nobel Prize winner Knut Hamsun's early novel *Victoria* (1898), newly retranslated, is as full of theatrical sobbing and heart-clutching as all his other novels. When I ask college students what modern novels they consider "relevant," they usually mention the Nobel prize winner Hermann Hesse's *Journey to the East* and *Siddhartha*. They don't mention *Steppenwolf*; I'm afraid that in the future they may mention *Gertrude* (1910), now published here for the first time. Its only virtue is the negative one of not being mystical. It is a novel about love and musical creativity, full of pedestrian philosophizing and not in a class with *Jean-Christophe* or Thomas Mann's *Doctor Faustus*. Etienne Leroux's *The Third Eye* is a detective story written in a style that seems to be compounded of Ben Hecht, Rafael Sabatini, Anthony Hope, and the Burke who wrote *Limehouse Nights*, whose first name escapes me. *The New Yorker* publishes excellent stories from time to time, but most of its stories are rather bland and harmless. Jean Stafford's *Collected Stories* are of this kind: very smooth and well done, but hardly re-readable.

R. Prawer Jhabvala's *A Stronger Climate* is a collection of stories of a far higher order—of the very highest order.[8] Four of them, incidentally, also appeared in *The New Yorker*. All nine of them deal with the effects of India's heat, light and culture on Europeans who stay there more than briefly; the first six, grouped under the subtitle "The Seekers," deal with those who feel the voluptuous agony of surrender to a way of life that can only destroy them as it destroys most of those who were born to it; the last three, under the subtitle "The Sufferers," deal with those who realize that they have been destroyed. Mrs. Jhabvala, a Polish refugee from Nazi Germany, educated at London University and married to an Indian architect, must be listed among the very small number of Continental Europeans who have learned to write English better than most of us whose native language it is: Conrad, Nabokov, Isak Dinesen, Ludwig Bemelmans, and—if we overlook the accident of his birth in Wisconsin—Thorstein Veblen. That she belongs in such good company is evident on every page. I open the book at random (pp. 122–3):

> Georgia often returned to the subject of what they were doing for India. She had a lot of feeling for the country and wanted every young Indian to devote himself heart and soul to its uplift. She told Ranjit all the things he ought to be doing—building dams, teaching peasants to read and write, defending the frontier—all the things *she* would be doing if only she had had the good fortune to be born an Indian. In England nowadays, she said, one felt so frustrated—there wasn't anything to do, only things to protest against.

Have you ever seen a clearer characterization in so few lines?

Leonard Michael's *Going Places*[9] is a collection of stories less assured, less mature, and even, for all their use of newer techniques, less bold, the newer techniques having been tried and found true as long ago as—oh, say Biely's *Saint Petersburg* (1913), or Andreyev's "The Seven Who Were Hanged" (1908), and beyond him as far back as Sterne, and beyond him as far back as Rabelais, and beyond him . . . so that they are no longer as startling as they were when that old revivalist Joyce revived them in 1922. And even so, few people have the technical strength to use them without falling into formlessness, and Leonard Michaels uses them quite well. All honor and encouragement to him. This is his first book. It reminds me not so much of any other writer as of Chagall. But chiefly it is Leonard Michaels' own. He plays with language. Few writers of his generation can even work with it.

Finally, we have three works by old masters.[10] John Dos Passos' *One Man's Initiation: 1917*, first published in a bowdlerized edition in 1920, is now published unbowdlerized, with a long introduction by Dos Passos and a number of pleasing charcoal sketches from his Paris note-book. He wrote it in August, 1918, on the ship coming back from France after the expiration of his year's enlistment as a volunteer ambulance driver in France and northern Italy. Does that remind you of another American writer? The novel itself is full of spots that read somewhat like the early Hemingway:

> They tried to hide their agitation. The schoolmaster poured out more wine.
> "Yes," said Martin, "there are fine orchards on the hills round here."
> "You should be here when the plums are ripe," said the schoolmaster.

A tall bearded man, covered with dust to the eyelashes, in the uniform of a commandant, stepped into the garden.

"My dear friends!" He shook hands with the schoolmaster and the old woman and saluted the two Americans. "I could not pass without stopping a moment. We are going up to an attack. We have the honour to take the lead."

"You will have a glass of wine, won't you?"

"With great pleasure."

"Julie, fetch a bottle, you know which. . . . How is the morale?"

"Perfect."

"I thought they looked a little discontented."

"No. . . . It's always like that. . . . They were yelling at some gendarmes. If they strung up a couple it would serve them right, dirty beasts."

"You soldiers are all one against the gendarmes."

"Yes. We fight the enemy but we hate the gendarmes." The commandant rubbed his hands, drank his wine and laughed.

"Hah! There's the next convoy. I must go."

"Good luck."

The commandant shrugged his shoulders, clicked his heels together at the garden gate, saluted, smiling, and was gone.

It isn't Hemingway, it doesn't move with his speed, it doesn't have his concentrated force, but it is a product of the same situation and the same ways of sensibility that are reflected in Hemingway's good early prose, and it too reflects them. Dos Passos has not yet found what Henry James would have called his own note. This novel is of less interest in itself than as a document of literary history. Those who follow fashion don't like Dos Passos now, for reasons that need no recounting here; but I find the *U.S.A.* trilogy still valid and moving; I am absolutely certain that it will survive the current disfavor, and I find *One Man's Initiation* a welcome appendix to it.

Celine's *Castle to Castle* is a novel in which the old son of a bitch tells how tragically misunderstood he has always been, him a hero of the first world war and a uniquely righteous man in the second. Sartre once said that when the Nazis retreated from France they took Celine along with the rest of the baggage. This novel is a delirious account of his internment in Denmark along with Petain, Laval and other collaborators waiting for the end. It isn't in any way up to *Journey to the End of the Night* or *Death on the Installment Plan*; it is rather the obscene babbling of a gifted coward shaking with fear but still unable to resist dropping the names of the important people he knows and despises even as he despises himself and his publishers and his readers and his patients and his friends and his enemies and his benefactors and the court that convicted him and the court that exonerated him. The best parts of the book are three interviews that appeared originally in *The Paris Review* in 1960 and 1961. They are relatively sane.

Kawabata's two novels *Snow Country* and *Thousand Cranes* were discussed in the Spring issue of *The Hudson Review* by Edward Seidensticker, who translated them. Since I don't read Japanese and have not previously read anything of Kawabata's, I can do no better, by way of reviewing this joint edition, than say that Seidensticker writes beautiful English and that on the basis of his translation I agree with his high estimate of Kawabata. As Herbert Howarth has demonstrated, the Nobel Prize for literature has lost a great deal of the credit it should have by being awarded to writers whose merits had long since been discovered and who in many cases had very little merit anyhow, and also by incurring the suspicion that it was sometimes awarded on political grounds. But no such reproach is justified in the case of Kawabata, if the quality of the rest of his work is comparable to that of these two novels. The following paragraph, so unlike anything I know of in Western literature, introduces us, in fiction at least, to a new kind of beauty:

> The Milky Way. Shimamura too looked up, and he felt himself floating into the Milky Way. Its radiance was so near that it seemed to take him up into it. Was this the bright vastness the poet Basho saw when he wrote of the Milky Way arched over a stormy sea? The Milky Way came down just over there, to wrap the night earth in its naked embrace. There was a terrible voluptuousness about it. Shimamura fancied that his own small shadow was being cast up against it from the earth. Each individual star stood apart from the rest, and even the particles of silver dust in the luminous clouds could be picked out, so clear was the night. The limitless depth of the Milky Way pulled his gaze up into it.

Notes

1. Louis Zukofsky, *Ferdinand* (New York: Grossman Publishers, Cape Editions, 1968).

2. Philip Roth, *Portnoy's Complaint* (New York: Random House, 1969).

3. Sholom Aleichem, *The Adventures of Menahem-Mendl* (New York: Putnam, 1969).

4. Jose Maria Gironella, *Peace After War* (New York: Alfred A. Knopf, 1969).

5. John Cheever, *Bullet Park* (New York: Alfred A. Knopf, 1969); Joyce Carol Oates, *Expensive People* (New York: Vanguard Press, 1968); Evan S. Connell, Jr., *Mr. Bridge* (New York: Alfred A. Knopf, 1969).

6. Frederick Exley, *A Fan's Notes* (New York: Harper and Row, 1968).

7. Kingsley Amis, *I Want It Now* (New York: Harcourt, Brace and World, 1969); Sybille Bedford, *A Compass Error* (New York: Alfred A. Knopf, 1969); Knut Hamsun, *Victoria* (New York: Farrar, Straus and Giroux, 1969); Hermann Hesse, *Gertrude* (New York: Farrar, Straus and Giroux, 1969); Etienne Leroux, *The Third Eye* (New York: Houghton Mifflin, 1969); Jean Stafford, *The Collected Stories of Jean Stafford* (New York: Farrar, Straus and Giroux, 1969).

8. R. Prawer Jhabvala, *A Stronger Climate* (New York: W. W. Norton and Co., 1969).

9. Leonard Michaels, *Going Places* (New York: Farrar, Straus and Giroux, 1969).

10. John Dos Passos, *One Man's Initiation:* 1917 (Ithaca: Cornell University Press, 1969); Louis Ferdinand Celine, *Castle to Castle* (New York: Delacorte Press, 1968); Yasunari Kawabata, *Snow Country and A Thousand Cranes* (New York: Alfred A. Knopf, 1968).

Our Gang

Dwight MacDonald*

Philip Roth has become as hard to classify as Norman Mailer. His first book, "Goodbye, Columbus," a fitfully brilliant collection of short stories on Jewish-American themes, won the 1960 National Book Award. Was he the new Bellow? His next, "Letting Go" (1962), was a regression to conventional Jewish-American fiction, turgid with *angst* and alienation. The new Malamud? Five years later he published "When She Was Good," a psychological dissection of a sick (gentile) heroine in the context of a sick (gentile) society done with nineteenth-century amplitude. It didn't work. Is a new Flaubert or Eliot (George) possible?

Then, after a decade of false starts he found his true voice—like an actor who discovers his limitations and so his possibilities—with "Portnoy's Complaint" (1969), which didn't win the National Book Award. "Portnoy's Complaint" was the Jewish novel to end all Jewish novels (which it unfortunately hasn't), a ribald, frenetic Bronx cheer to the whole *schtick* all the more effectively disturbing because it was delivered with love and even a kind of nostalgic reverence. It was important to Roth personally—killing not the father but the momma. But its importance to him as a writer was greater: he discovered his congenial mode, satire, and his natural style, the vernacular, which he used with an unerring ear to get humorous effects that are most serious when they are funniest.

"Our Gang" is a political satire that I found far-fetched, unfair, tasteless, disturbing, logical, coarse and very funny—I laughed out loud sixteen times and giggled internally a statistically unverifiable amount. In short, a masterpiece. The most fantastic assumptions—fantasies we, alas, read daily in the papers and see nightly on TV—are worked out with the lunatic logic of Swift's "A Modest Proposal for Preventing the Children of Poor People in Ireland From Being a Burden to Their Parents and Country" (i.e., by fattening them for consumption as English breakfast bacon). How unfair can you get? "Our Gang" is a strong second. And as an inveterate American, I'm delighted by the way Roth's most extreme satirical

*Reprinted from *The New York Times*, November 7, 1971. Copyright © 1971 by the New York Times Company. Reprinted by permission.

flights—like those of Mark Twain, Ring Lardner and Nathaniel West—take off from a sound base of *volkische* knowledge; our lingo, and the national character it expresses, seems to alarm him as much as it did them and does me.

It all began with an appalling statement by our President last April, which I must admit I hadn't noticed—so much competition. Speaking *ex cathedra* from San Clemente, Mr. Nixon issued a bull that, with Mr. Roth's patient and tireless assistance, now appears more Irish than Papal. It is printed in caps at the beginning of "Our Gang":

> FROM PERSONAL AND RELIGIOUS BELIEFS I CONSIDER ABORTIONS AN UNACCEPTABLE FORM OF POPULATION CONTROL. FURTHERMORE, UNRESTRICTED ABORTION POLICIES, OR ABORTION ON DEMAND, I CANNOT SQUARE WITH MY PERSONAL BELIEF IN THE SANCTITY OF HUMAN LIFE—INCLUDING THE LIFE OF THE YET UNBORN. FOR, SURELY, THE UNBORN HAVE RIGHTS ALSO, RECOGNIZED IN LAW, RECOGNIZED EVEN IN PRINCIPLES EXPOUNDED BY THE UNITED NATIONS.

A mouse, surely, compared to the President's daily elephants; nothing worth squashing under a mountain of satire. Especially since President Nixon was meeting a clear and present danger; he had just discovered that "Under liberalized military procedures, the wives of servicemen were able to obtain abortions more easily than they would have under state regulations." He put a stop to *that* instantly—he's the Commander in Chief, after all—and if he only hadn't felt obliged to rig up a philosophical base for his ukase, "Our Gang" wouldn't have been written.

Eisenhower would never have been so gauche, nor his Republican predecessors in the twenties; but Nixon is more in the recent Presidentially articulate style, usually practiced by the Democrats. Also, as Roth's President complains to his Cabinet, when the Boy Scouts gather for a protest march on Washington with placards reading TRICK E. DIXON FAVORS SEXUAL INTERCOURSE, "*What did I say?*" Let's look at the record. I said *nothing!* Absolutely nothing! I came out for 'the rights of the unborn.' I mean if ever there was a line of hokum, that was it. Sheer humbug! And as if it wasn't clear enough what I was up to, I even tacked on 'as recognized in principles expounded by the United Nations.' "

One really feels for the President. The punishment seems excessive, considering his more serious crimes. But this was a crime against language, and Roth is a writer. I might add that the "sanctity of human life" (foetal division) bull shared the front page with the President's intervention to ease Lieutenant Calley's punishment after his fellow-officers had convicted him of killing Vietnamese civilians (adult division). And so there came that moment in a writer's life when the lemons and oranges and bells all click into place and the satirical jackpot is ready and Roth began to nurture from his little acorn an extravaganza of imposing dimensions and intricately branched consistency.

"Our Gang" begins with Tricky reassuring a citizen who is troubled lest Calley may have killed a pregnant woman, either inadvertently ("he assumed she was simply overweight," Tricky suggests) or advertently. On the latter option Tricky hypothesizes: "This woman presented herself to Lieutenant Calley for abortion with some kind of note, say, that somebody had written for her in English, and Lieutenant Calley, let's say, in the heat and pressure of the moment, performed the abortion, during the course of which the woman died." Such a case would be "abortion on demand," and Tricky admits he would be prejudiced: "I will disqualify myself as a judge and pass the entire matter on to the Vice President." "I think we can all sleep better at night knowing that," says the citizen.

The last chapter, "Tricky in Hell," takes place after his assassination (a baffling one because there are many groups with motives—the Boy Scouts, the Danes, for reasons too intricate, but logical, to go into here—and too many suspects, tens of thousands of them in fact, converging on Washington, each with his or her confession, claiming credit and insisting on being arrested by the overworked police force). Tricky is running against Satan for the Presidency of Hell: "My fellow fallen: Let me say at the outset that of course I agree with much of what Satan has said in his opening statement. I know that Satan feels as deeply as I do about what has to be done to make Wickedness all that it can be and should be in the creation. . . . And now let me say a word to those who point to my own record as President of the United States and contend that it is less than it could have been as regards suffering and anguish for all of the people, regardless of race, creed or color. Let me remind these critics that I happen to have held that high office for less than one term before I was assassinated. . . . Despite my brief tenure in the 'White' House . . . I think I can safely say that I was able to lay the groundwork for new oppressions and injustices and to sow the seeds of bitterness and hatred between the races, the generations and the social classes that hopefully will plague the American people for years to come. . . . I think I might point with particular pride to Southeast Asia."

His clincher is the Book of Job: "This document I am holding in my claw is the Holy Scripture. It doesn't lie. That is why it is nothing less than the Bible of our enemies." He quotes "the secret conversation between God and Satan" in Job, which does in fact show Satan as God's stoolie provacateur. "And did Satan spare Job's life, as God instructed him to? I am afraid the answer is yes, he did that too. We all remember, I am sure, that unhappy ending to that story. Job's faith was not broken. . . . And the Lord, as the record here states, 'gave Job twice as much as he had before.' "

In between these termini, Roth has constructed a complete mini-novel, coherent in its plot line and full of recognizable characters whose speech mannerisms are expertly parodied. As his epigraphs from Swift and Orwell suggest, his theme is the abuse of words; Erect Severehead, the Rev. Billy Cupcake and the members of Trick E. Dixon's Cabinet are especially memorable abusers. Each jigsaw piece is fitted with esthetic precision (or lunatic, if you prefer and do let's quarrel over words) into the ingenious and sustained narrative structure. I can't think of anything like it.

Of course it's all very exaggerated, one-sided, fantastic, etc. Common sense tells us that. But common sense is, as often, wrong. In the week I was writing this review, (a) Nixon's own nutrition expert, Dr. Jean Mayer of Harvard, called his proposal to cut a million and a half needy children from the Federally subsidized school lunch program "mean-spirited," and the House and Senate restored the cuts with no dissenting votes. (b) Will R. Wilson, the chief enforcer of Federal criminal laws, resigned, saying he sought to spare embarrassment to the Nixon Administration because of his association with a Texas stock manipulator. (c) Harold Goldstein, the economist at the Bureau of Labor Statistics who dealt with monthly unemployment figures, was relieved of this job because he had called last month's figures "mixed" while his boss had thought them "heartening." (d) Asked at a press conference whether he was planning to end "at least the American ground combat involvement" in Vietnam by the time he goes to Moscow in May 1972, the President replied, "The American presence in Vietnam, in terms of . . . ground combat forces and air power will be maintained to meet the objectives that I have often times spelled out, including . . . the return of our P.O.W.s and the ability of the South Vietnamese to take over the responsibility themselves." Next question.

"Swift's peculiarity," wrote Leslie Stephen, "is in the curious sobriety of fancy which leads him to keep in his most daring flights upon the confines of the possible." I think this might be said of Philip Roth's satire, also. Or, as his peer, Jules Feiffer, put it recently in a Playboy interview: "That's all satire is—creating a logical argument that, followed to its end, is absurd. . . . Satire concerns itself with logically extending a premise to its totally insane conclusion, thus forcing onto an audience certain unwelcome awarenesses."

Uplift

Frederick Crews*

We seem to be on familiar ground in the opening pages of *The Breast*. The hero, David Alan Kepesh, has Alex Portnoy's verbal gifts, his

*Reprinted from *New York Review of Books*, November 16, 1972, p. 18, by permission.

irony, his apparent public success, and his private hypochondria. If his life appears more stable than Portnoy's, so much the better, for Roth's specialty is pulling out the rug. We can be fairly sure that this Stony Brook professor of comparative literature, with his regular bowels and his tidy, if monotonous, *modus vivendi* with a nice young schoolteacher, is in for some awful surprise. When Kepesh gets an itch in the groin and becomes a kind of monogamous debauchee, grateful to be able to take the initiative with patient, neglected Claire, we know we won't get any Lawrentian smarm about the dark wisdom of the body. In Roth's work strong feelings, especially in the pelvic region, are always symptoms.

Kepesh deteriorates, all right, but not in a foreseeable way. In a few cataclysmic hours he suffers "a hermaphroditic explosion of chromosomes" and wakes up in Lenox Hill Hospital to find himself transformed into a 155-pound, dirigible-shaped female breast, with a five-inch nipple that's histologically reminiscent of his lamented penis. At the time of the soliloquy that constitutes the narrative, he has been living in a hammock for fifteen months, blind but not deaf, fed and drained by tubes, with his world constricted to doctors and nurses and a few visitors who do their best to treat this freak as the man he still is beneath his areola.

But the novelty of *The Breast* doesn't lie in its situation. Roth's work since *Portnoy* has been full of comic surrealism, and what happens to Kepesh is no more implausible than the fate of the talent scout Lippman, for example, in the brilliant story "On the Air." What is noteworthy is that Roth, having chosen a story line that looks ideally suited to his taste for outrageous sexual farce, has side-stepped the opportunity and instead written a work of high seriousness. *The Breast* has its laughs, but they seem like indulgences Roth has permitted himself along the way to an oblique, cryptic statement about human dignity and resourcefulness.

Kepesh's plight ceases to be funny as attention is diverted from his physical state to his agony of spirit. How can a man accommodate himself to the unthinkable? Why does the will refuse to surrender when the mind sees no escape? Kepesh's complaint, unlike Portnoy's, begins to subside as his dormant courage stirs. At the end Kepesh, now acquainted with his strength, dares to quote us Rilke's sonnet, "Archaic Torso of Apollo," with its bald concluding imperative: "You must change your life." Even hedged with sarcasm and ambiguity, the message is striking. It's as if Roth had wearied of the querulous, sardonic Portnoy and had decided to let Dr. Spielvogel have his say.

The shift of emphasis comes with notable suddenness after Roth's venture into political satire in *Our Gang*. The protagonist of that work, a president named Trick E. Dixon, is assassinated in the nude and stuffed into a water-filled baggie, to the approval of everyone but his widow, who "thinks that at the very least the President should have been slain in a shirt and a tie and a jacket, like John F. Charisma." Roth's humor in *Our Gang* is literally atrocious, his sense of being politically in the right licenses him to create a depersonalized, paranoid world in which sadistic fantasies are considered chic so long as they're directed against the right figures. To skim the book is to understand it. In describing *The Breast*, however, Roth speaks of his "distrust of 'positions,' including my own" (*NYR* interview, October 19); and the book itself moves fitfully toward transcendence, denying us one easy conclusion after another until we're finally prepared to grasp Kepesh's humanity without any overlay of ideas.

Reviewers who never cared for Roth's startling frankness and iconoclasm have already expressed pleasure with what they take to be his reformation. Even Trick E. Dixon, if he were a student of ideological currents in the arts, might be gratified to see our author moving from the aesthetic of Barbara Garson toward that of Henry James. To my mind, however, *Our Gang* and *The Breast* stand roughly equidistant from Roth's best mode, which is neither "political" nor "moral."

From the very beginning—from the moment when Neil Klugman, on the opening page of "Goodbye, Columbus," gets a glimpse of Brenda Patimkin's rear, Roth's forte has been the portrayal of compulsives whose human intelligence can't save them from their irrationality. The sharpness and energy of his work have to do with fidelity to the petty idiocies of the unconscious. In *Our Gang* he takes a holiday from characterization and simply lets fly at the Republicans; in *The Breast* he goes to the other extreme and, without detectable irony, subjects his hero to earnest lecturing from a psychoanalyst about "strength of character," "will to live," and even "Mr. Reality." What connects these seemingly opposite books is their common flight from the elements of Roth's finest art.

To be sure, those elements aren't absent from *The Breast*. Though Kepesh tells us that "reality has more style" than to punish wishes in a fairy-tale way, it's possible to infer that his fate is profoundly congruent with his disposition. Roth offers at least one obvious clue: once on Nantucket, with his mistress Claire's breast in his mouth, Kepesh wanted to leave it there instead of making orthodox love, and he confessed to an envy of her. Lesser indications of slippage in his male identity are scattered through the text. His ego has been bruised in a disastrous marriage; his arrangement with Claire (they have slept together but lived apart) looks like a phobic defense against what he calls the "dependence, or the grinding boredom, or the wild, unfocused yearning" of married couples; he has placed an unusual value on nonvaginal forms of intercourse, and he has almost entirely lost erotic interest in Claire before getting his premonitory itch. It's still quite a leap from these facts to becoming a female gland, but it also seems unlikely that Kepesh was selected at random by the prankster gods.

If we suppose that Kepesh's change is an exact condensation of his wishes and fears, the story does make detailed unconscious sense. Kepesh's fetishizing of Claire's breast has turned her into a fantasy-mother and himself into a nursing infant; now, it seems, he regresses further and merges himself with the breast as if there were no boundary between self and nurturing world. The breast is the womb and they are both Kepesh. To reach this apparent paradise, though, one must accept castration: the hero becomes blind, limbless and encased in female tissue like a eunuch. Yet paradoxically the mutilation permits a regrouping of masculine aims on a safer level: the Kepesh who had formerly submitted to Claire's advances "two, maybe three times a month" is now an imposing, permanently inflated organ, a quasi-penis, and he wants it serviced around the clock.

This isn't just intricate dream logic, it's also potentially rich irony. *The Breast* reads like a Midas story for an age whose mystagogues have seriously proposed that the Oedipal film be run backwards until we find ourselves polymorphous, guilt-free infants once again. Kepesh as breast is an object of constant mothering, with feeding and elimination looked after by others, with nonorgasmic pleasure in being rubbed and washed, and with a chance to "sleep the sleep of the sated" as he sways in his hammock. But what is it really like to have an infant's clamorous needs, and his powerlessness to get them satisfied on his own initiative, and his rage when he understands that a mother's patience is finite and her love divided?

Roth achieves real pathos in the moments when Kepesh, believing Claire to be too pure for inclusion in his new erotic script, fears he will lose her. Eventually he consents to a form of weaning, restricting himself to a fixed daily period of stimulation, having himself anesthetized before washing, and even accepting a male nurse, who can't arouse him because, in spite of everything, that would be "homosexual." Regression looks tempting, Roth seems to say, but—wait till you try it! Adult scruples aren't so easy to blot out, and stimulation of the skin "from a source unknown to me, seemingly immense and dedicated solely to me and my pleasure," is finally no substitute for freely exchanged love.

But has Kepesh actually regressed at all? Roth's irony is blunted by the tendency of his plot to deny any linkage between the hero's psyche and his outward state. Kepesh's heroism is measured by his increasing ability to forego explanations and simply acknowledge the technical fact that he is a breast in a hospital. His soliloquy thus has a curious, unintended effect of filibuster. Thanks to Roth's precise evocations, we as readers have never doubted since page 12 that Kepesh is a breast, and our minds move ahead to consider the poetic justice of this fate. But Roth scorns analysis and insists that his hero is a Job, not a Midas, and we eventually have to agree. Discerning a psychological feast, we're handed an "existential" crumb; isn't it grand to endure the absurd?

"You must change your life" but first, Mr. Reality might add, you must decide what's wrong with it. Nothing at all is wrong with Kepesh; as the victim of a colossal misfortune he need only keep a stiff upper nipple and exit to applause. By having even the psychoanalyst veto Kepesh's tentative efforts at self-awareness, by making his hero into a noble survivor, Roth loses control over the half-developed themes that would have saved his story from banality. It's as if Kafka were to bludgeon us into admitting that Gregor Samsa is the most stoical cockroach we've met, and a wonderful sport about the whole thing.

What makes an image telling, Roth accurately observed in his interview about *The Breast*, is not how much meaning we can associate to it, but the freedom it gives the writer to explore his obsessions. But has he explored his obsessions in this book, or simply referred to them obliquely before importing a *deus ex machina* to whisk them away? In a sense *The Breast* is a more discouraging work than the straightforwardly vicious *Our Gang*. Aspiring to make a noble moral statement, Roth quarantines his best insights into the way people are imprisoned by their impulses. What would Alex Portnoy have had to say about *that*?

The Great American Novel and *My Life as a Man*: An Assessment of Philip Roth's Achievement

David Monaghan*

Like their predecessors, *The Great American Novel* and *My Life as a Man* are flawed works, but contain enough of undoubted literary merit to reconfirm that Philip Roth is a writer who deserves our attention. However, critics continue to equivocate about the precise nature of Roth's achievement. There seem to be two main reasons for this equivocation. First of all, instead of dealing with his novels according to their merits, critics have allowed themselves to be distracted by side issues. For example, criticism of *Goodbye, Columbus*, *Letting Go*, and *Portnoy's Complaint* has tended to be over-preoccupied with Jewish cultural issues to the exclusion of discussion of the novels as literature. Mordecai H. Levine's "Philip Roth and American Judaism"[1] typifies this approach to Roth. For Levine, *Letting Go* succeeds because Gabe Wallach recovers his Jewishness, and *Portnoy's Complaint* fails because it creates negative feelings about the Jewish family and Judaism.

Roth's real achievements (and failures) have been similarly obscured by a group of critics who operate on the premise that, to achieve artistic success, a writer must be "committed." Stanley Cooperman's "Old Jacob's Eye? With a Squint"[2] is a rather subtle example of this type of criticism. Cooperman offers many perceptive insights into Roth's novels, but his

*Reprinted from *International Fiction Review*, 2 (1975), 113–120, by permission of the journal.

total argument is seriously weakened by his insistence that Roth fails as an artist simply because he finds the moral values of his society too empty to treat as anything but mannerism and because he regards the formal tradition as eccentric.

Roth criticism has also suffered from a tendency to force his novels into rigid categories. To approach *Goodbye, Columbus* as Jewish, *Letting Go*, and *When She Was Good* as naturalism, *Portnoy's Complaint* as pornography, *Our Gang* as political satire, *The Breast* as Kafkaesque allegory, *The Great American Novel* as sports fiction, and *My Life as a Man* as confession, serves only to fragment the canon of Roth's work and to obscure any unifying thematic and stylistic concerns it might possess. The task of Roth criticism must be to ascertain whether there are any logical principles behind his repeated experimentation and whether any consistent vision lies beneath his chameleon surface.

It would be impossible within the scope of this paper to carry out that task fully. However, if we are to grasp what Roth accomplishes in *The Great American Novel* and *My Life as a Man* we must make at least a preliminary survey of the territory. Varied as are the problems with which Roth's novels deal, there seems to be one main thread which runs through all of them, namely, the theme of failure of commitment. This basic conern is established through the characterizations of Neil Klugman in *Goodbye, Columbus* and Gabe Wallach in *Letting Go*, both of whom are essentially good men who suffer from an inability to attach themselves to anything of value. Neil skirts around the fringe of middle-class Jewish society, refusing either to embrace or to reject it, until that society finally reclaims Brenda, leaving him isolated. Similarly, Gabe fluctuates uneasily between his teaching job, his father, and a succession of women, until he, too, is left with nothing and no one. Probably the single decent person in a world of egotists, Gabe ends up the biggest failure because the others are all sufficiently self-interested to cling onto something: John Spligliano to academic success; Paul to Libby; Libby to her baby; Martha to respectable marriage; and Gabe's father to Cecilia Norton. Alexander Portnoy is cast in the same mold. As Assistant Commissioner of Human Opportunity he is involved in a professional world with others, but is uncommitted in personal relationships and continually falls back on his private world of masturbation.

Once we pay attention to this theme of lack of commitment, both *Our Gang* and *The Breast* which, at first sight, seem to represent breathing spaces between novels, can be accommodated into the mainstream of Roth's work. Roth presents Nixon, in the guise of Trick E. Dixon, as essentially a Roth hero, or more precisely, the mirror image of one. Whereas the others fail to commit themselves to good ends, Dixon is unable to commit himself to evil, and can only shuttle indecisively between his various advisors.[3] David Kepesh in *The Breast* is a grotesque exaggeration and simplification of Roth's earlier heroes. Like them he shies away from emotional involvement and feels happy only when he has a girl friend who is "even-tempered and predictable," and who offers "warmth and security," "without the accompanying burden of dependence."[4] However, whereas neither Neil, Gabe, nor Alex cherishes his isolation, Kepesh pursues aloneness single-mindedly, and it is appropriate that he eventually evolves into a gigantic Breast, the form most suited to his life style. As a Breast he can experience pleasure (he is intensely stimulated by manipulation of his nipple) but is almost completely cut off from others (he has no eyes or limbs and can barely speak).

This concern with lack of commitment is also central to *The Great American Novel* in which Roth presents a collective vision of the uncommitted hero in the shape of the Ruppert Mundy's baseball team. The archetypal Mundys are Ulysses S. Fairsmith and Luke Gofannon, both of whom are well-intentioned but emotionally stunted men. Fairsmith is distracted from the affairs of the real world by his determination to find divine providence at work behind all events, and Gofannon by his total involvement in baseball. Gofannon's human resources are so limited that he brings Angela Whittling Trust to despair by admitting that he loves a triple hit more than her (p. 253).

Once men such as these are called upon to deal with the crude reality of those who wish to exploit baseball for a profit, their failure is inevitable. Gofannon is soon traded away and Fairsmith allows himself to be used as a figurehead. When the Mundys are threatened with the loss of their stadium, Fairsmith agains fails to act, so convinced is he that the Lord has chosen his team to suffer trial and tribulation in preparation for a return to their former greatness.

Given that failure of commitment is responsible for its downfall, it is appropriate that the final Mundy team of 1942 and 1943 should be composed of men isolated from the world around them by their individual emotional and physical limitations and by the collective malaise of being the only homeless team in baseball. Typical Mundys are Nickname Damur, a fourteen year old boy who craves a nickname because he believes it will win him acceptance, and Hot Ptah, who is driven into embittered isolation by the loss of a leg.

As in Roth's earlier novels, so in *The Great American Novel* the failure of commitment seems to be irreversible. The Ruppert Mundys are eventually dissolved and all record of them obliterated, permitting the forces of free enterprise, which are turning American society into a place of injustice, prejudice, hypocrisy, and greed, to expand unchallenged.

The protagonist of *My Life as a Man*, Peter Tarnopol, and his fictional creation, Nathan Zuckerman, the major character in Tarnopol's "Useful Fictions," "Salad Days," and "Courting Disaster," seem at first sight to be very different from Roth's earlier heroes. Both quite deliberately become involved with women, Maureen and Susan in Tarnopol's case and Lydia in Zuckerman's, who "had suffered" and were "so brave"

(p. 70) and who thus seem likely to supply the *"moral content"* (p. 80) without which, as they have learnt from their study of literature, life is pointless. However, as each eventually realizes, even though the suffering which results from it is real enough, the commitment which they have sought is false because literary standards cannot be applied to real life. Whereas the world of literature is composed of lofty ideals and moral concerns, the real world is devoid of any serious purpose: "Of course what I also wanted was that my intractable existence should take place at an appropriately lofty moral altitude, an elevation somewhere, say, between *The Brothers Karamazov* and *The Wings of the Dove*. But then not even the golden can expect to have everything: instead of the intractability of serious fiction, I got the intractability of soap opera" (pp. 194–195). With this statement, Roth in many ways reaches the nadir of pessimism. Bleak as his earlier novels are, there is never any suggestion that the heroes' failure of commitment results finally from anything other than personal weakness. Now, Roth is asserting that there is nothing in the real world to which one can attach oneself. Oddly enough, however, *My Life as a Man* ends on a more assertive note than any of Roth's other novels. Having been made aware that reality is without value, and having been broken in the process of acquiring this knowledge, Peter Tarnopol proceeds to rebuild his life around literature, the one thing that retains its worth: "Literature got me into this and literature is gonna have to get me out. My writing is all I've got now" (p. 194). Although the novel concludes with Tarnopol still in retreat from the world, he is writing again and it seems likely that he will at last fulfill his ambition "to get to be what is described in the literature as *a man*" (p. 299).

Just as Roth's novels possess thematic unity, so a consistent principle underlies his technical experimentation. Essentially, Roth has been trying throughout his literary career to find an appropriate American mode. His early works draw on literary traditions, particularly the Jewish and the naturalistic, but more recently he has begun to seek for the authentic American voice in pulp fiction, newspapers, psychiatric jargon, and political speeches. *Portnoy's Complaint*, for example, owes much to the language of psychiatry and to pornography and *Our Gang* to political rhetoric. This tendency becomes particularly evident in *The Great American Novel* in which Roth embraces a broad range of popular American speech, drawn mainly from sports, politics, and television. The language of *My Life as a Man* is less pervasively pop than that of *The Great American Novel* since neither Tarnopol nor Zuckerman, the two central consciousnesses, possess a kitsch mentality like that of Word Smith, the narrator of the earlier novel. Nevertheless, in developing the thesis that reality is a soap opera, *My Life as a Man* repeatedly exposes us to the pop sensibility at work. This is most evident in "Salad Days," a brilliant exposé of *kitschmensch* as he manifests himself in the various members of the Zuckerman family.

The reasons for Roth's excursion into pop are made explicit in *The Great American Novel*: "Only *listen*, Nathaniel [Hawthorne], and Americans will write the Great American Novel for you" (p. 37). The fictionalized Hemingway's assertion that the Great American Novel will be written by "some dago barber sucking on Tums in the basement of the Palmer House" (p. 26), makes the same point.

To assess the achievement of Roth's two most recent novels, it is most profitable to approach them through their popular elements. *The Great American Novel* is the most ambitious of the two in this respect because it limits its frame of reference entirely to that of popular culture. The problems involved in making a successful statement through such limited resources are immense and there are few successful precedents in English (two which spring to mind are Lennon and McCartney's "When I'm 64," which employs irony and point of view to turn cliché into art, and Sylvia Plath's "Lady Lazarus," which limits its frame of reference to the nursery rhyme, the striptease show, and popular mythology about the Nazis, and draws much of its language from clichés). On the whole *The Great American Novel* does not manage to make art out of popular materials. However, it has many virtues and it might be as well to begin by pointing out areas in which it succeeds.

In *The Great American Novel*, Roth is not content to simply imitate the formal looseness of the popular work, but rather he tries to take full advantage of the freedom thus conferred upon him. In *Portnoy's Complaint*, *Our Gang*, and *The Breast*, Roth's bizarre and occasionally surrealistic humor is limited to a single, central subject—masturbation in *Portnoy's Complaint*, President Nixon in *Our Gang* and man as breast in *The Breast*. However, in *The Great American Novel*, Roth's imagination is allowed total liberty, and he introduces a multitude of bizarre and diverse incidents ranging from a visit to a brothel which specializes in treating its clients as babies to a baseball game featuring a clash between a forty inch tall batter and a thirty-seven inch tall pitcher. The results are often funny, if almost always on the edge of bad taste. Roth's account of the career of Base Baal, the great spitball pitcher, is typical. Throughout the incident, Roth comes close to disgusting rather than entertaining, particularly in his account of Baal's tendency to deposit mucus, or "stringy stuff" (p. 106) on the ball. However, Roth's scatological humor generally works well especially during the episode in which Baal makes his final gesture of revolt at the banning of the spit ball: "And so . . . the once great pitcher . . . did the unthinkable, the unpardonable, the inexpiable: he dropped the flannel trousers of his uniform to his knees, and proceeded to urinate on the ball" (p. 108).

Perhaps the single most imaginatively wild scene in the novel is the one involving the game between the Mundys and an asylum team. Roth's most obvious targets are the inmates who include a pitcher who refuses to throw because the umpire is staring at him. However, the real success of the episode derives from the behavior of the Mundys who, by taking the game seriously, prove themselves to be more insane than the lunatics. The prospect of a rare victory so distorts their perspective that when, for example, one-legged Hot Ptah is able to steal home from second, rather than admit that the fielder was simply too insane to return the ball, they convince themselves that he was "so darned stunned by it all, that finally by the time he figures out what hit him, we has got ourselves a gift of a run" (p. 183).

Roth's humor succeeds here because he not only invites us to laugh at the self-deceiving Mundys, but he also calls upon us to sympathize with their pathetic desire to win. This is particularly evident during the incident in which the coach and Deacon, the pitcher, confer about the latter's chances of maintaining a shutout in the face of a distracting base runner. We are amused by their appallingly sentimental baseball rhetoric and by their failure to realize that, rather than constituting a genuine threat, the runner is paralyzed by personal obsessions. At the same time, however, we are moved by their desire to relive past glories and by the genuine courage of the aging pitcher.

The formal looseness of *The Great American Novel* also allows Roth to fully exercise his parodic skills, which first emerged in *Our Gang*. It is, of course, with parody that Roth attempts to make art out of pop materials. By subtly exaggerating the absurdities and clichés of sports language, politics, and journalism, Roth at once stays within the bounds of pop and yet distances himself from it sufficiently to make a comment about the ability of the debased American language to effect a radical separation between situation and response. In the incident discussed above the Mundys are able to maintain the illusion that they are involved in a genuine contest only because they have the empty rhetoric of baseball to fall back upon. Cholly, for example, employs chiché to conceal reality by commenting, "Guess he wanted to stay in" (p. 172) as an uncooperative pitcher is removed in a strait jacket. A similar distortion of reality is achieved by Deacon's description of right fielder Parusha's feat of throwing out successive batters at first as "an exhibition such as I have not seen in all my years in organized ball" (p. 182). He is, of course, ignoring the fact that neither batter had attempted to leave the plate.

Political rhetoric comes to the fore as a justification for depriving the Mundys of their home park ("to help save the world for democracy," p. 49) and during the Red Scare which climaxes the novel. Although there is no solid evidence that Communists have infiltrated the Patriot League, nevertheless, a wholesale purge takes place simply because the American people suspend all judgment when faced with familiar rhetoric: "General, you talk to me of *stigmas*, but there is no stigma—there is only subversion! There is only conspiracy and sabotage!" (p. 323).

In that *The Great American Novel* is supposedly written by Word Smith, a journalist, Roth's satire on journalistic language necessarily pervades the whole novel. The first chapter, indeed, is devoted to an exegesis on Smith's style, which is built mainly around alliteration, antithesis, and lists. However, this part of Roth's satire is rather confusing because, although he is caught up almost entirely in the world of cliché, Smith is also the only character in the novel capable of understanding the truth about American life. No one else realizes that baseball operates according to the profit motive, that the Mundys were exiled for economic rather than Patriotic reasons, and that the Red Scare is a fake. Word Smith, then, would seem to contradict Roth's basic statement about the tendency of cliché to hide the truth. The contradiction seems unresolvable, and we can only presume that Roth failed to solve the problem of establishing a point of view that works through clichés yet transcends them.

The major faults of *The Great American Novel*, however, do not derive from its narrative technique, but from a general tendency towards superficiality and irrelevancy. These qualities, of course, must necessarily be present on the surface of any work written within pop conventions. Nevertheless, it is the job of the pop artist to somehow transcend the surface appearance. This, Roth, unfortunately, does not succeed in doing, or at least he does not succeed sufficiently to prevent us making unfavorable comparisons with his earlier realistic fiction. The strength of a novel like *Letting Go* lies in its presentation of character and environment, and these are replaced in *The Great American Novel* by a series of comic-strip types acting out their fates against a vividly-colored, but one-dimensional backdrop. Roth's intention is to overwhelm us with novelty and variety, and for a while this works. However, we finally begin to long for some level of complexity, for a character made up of more than a few eccentric gestures.

Roth's themes are similarly slight. The main theme, from which all the others stem, is that of innocence corrupted by materialism, and this is worked out at both the local and the archetypal levels. Roth's use of archetypes is often very witty because he is not so much seeking to ground American experience in something more universal as mocking the mythologizing tendencies of modern fiction. Thus, he introduces such crudely mythological figures as Gil Gamesh, the apparently invincible pitcher who is defeated by his mortality; Luke Gofannon, who dies by water; and John Baal, the evil force in the Mundys' team. Moreover, and this Roth would say is inevitable in any American novel, baseball is compared to the Garden of Eden. The local satire, however, lacks impact because it is often outmoded. For example, the admission of midgets into the league, a purely economic move wrapped up in rhetoric about the equality of man, is clearly intended as a comment on the admission of Negroes into baseball in the 1940's, and the Red Scare episode is directed against McCarthyism.

Besides being outmoded some of Roth's parallels are gratuitous. Thus, he constructs a series of pointless analogies between the assassination of Roland Agni and that of John Kennedy, under the general heading of "The Shot Heard Round the League" (p. 356). Similarly, in the midst of Bob Yamm's letter announcing his retirement from baseball, Roth introduces an amusing but irrelevant reference to Nixon's Checkers speech: "just about the only one I seem *not* to have failed is my chihuahua pup, Pinch-hit, who has sat in my lap all the while I have been composing this letter" (p. 204). Perhaps most irrelevant of all is Roth's account of General Fairsmith's attempt to convert African natives to baseball, which is organized around a series of references to Melville's *Omoo* and *Typee* and Conrad's *The Heart of Darkness* (pp. 304, 305).

The weakness of *The Great American Novel* perhaps taught Roth that it is impossible to construct a novel-length work entirely upon pop conventions, and in *My Life as a Man* he avoids such extremes of experimentation. By filtering his narrative through a non-pop mentality, Roth is able to record the workings of an essentially pop society, but he is also able to draw back from it. He can thus more easily achieve his aim of being both inside and outside of popular culture. This change of technique also means, of course, that *My Life as a Man* lacks some of the strengths of *The Great American Novel* in that its satire is neither so pervasive nor so freewheeling. However, this novel's faults do not derive from Roth's inability to handle pop materials, but from the overcomplexity of his point of view.

As with all of Roth's more recent fiction, the greatest strength of *My Life as a Man* derives from its satirical presentation of the stereotypes by which people live. The first story, "Salad Days," is an account of an existence conducted according to clichés. Mr. Zuckerman believes in life as a struggle and in Dale Carnegie; Mrs. Zuckerman is the all-suffering, all-loving, ever-cheerful mother. Their marriage is idyllic. Sherman, the elder son, follows a conventional path, beginning with an initiation into life and sex provided by the army, progressing through a brief period of nonconformity during which he becomes a jazz pianist, and concluding with marriage and a career in dentistry. His younger brother, Nathan, is led into revolt by, inevitably, Hemingway's *Of Time and the River*, and goes to a small college where he experiences a standard intellectual liberation. Nathan's sex life with Sharon Shatsky is based on pornographic clichés.

Roth's eye for physical detail and keen ear for speech patterns give flesh to his record of stereotyped life patterns. The dean of the college, who possesses a "briar pipe and football shoulders swathed in tweed" (p. 12), tells the freshman that "the ivy on the library walls . . . could be heard on certain moonlit nights to whisper the word 'tradition' " (p. 11). And Mrs. Zuckerman, who turns up at Nathan's school "dressed in the clothes she ordinarily wore only when she and her 'girl friends' went in to Philadelphia to see the matinee performance of a stage show" (p. 7), later asks her college-age son "why did Daddy ever buy the house, if not for you

to have a real boy's room, a room of your own for you and all your things?"
(p. 6).

While not as broad in its range as the satire in *The Great American
Novel*, the satire in *My Life as a Man* encompasses a greater social scope.
Whereas the earlier novel limits itself entirely to the culture of the masses,
the latter gives considerable attention to avant garde kitsch. Maureen
Tarnopol, with her pretensions to sensitivity ("I have my flute . . . I have
Group. I'm going to the New School," p. 275) is the main subject of this
aspect of Roth's satire. Roth is particularly successful in delineating
Maureen's therapy group which is presented to us through tantalizing,
fragmentary secondhand reports, most of which are accompanied by
Peter Tarnopol's caustic comments. Maureen's pseudointellectual friends
are debunked in similar indirect fashion (pp. 183–84).

Roth's satire in *My Life as a Man* finally has greater impact than that
in *The Great American Novel* because it supports a more subtle theme.
Whereas its predecessor contented itself with a rather superficial view of
the debasement of American ideals, *My Life as a Man* deals rather intricately with the differences between art and life. Roth's satire is not intended simply to mock American mores, but to reveal the tragicomic gap
between the life of moral seriousness and dignity presented by literature
and the crude farce of reality. The point of "Salad Days" is not that the
Zuckerman's are funny, but that, by living out stereotypes, they are
ultimately successful. Mr. Zuckerman's life of toil is rewarded at last with
"a brand new 'Mr. Z.' shoe store . . . at the two-million-dollar Country
Club Hills Shopping Mall" (p. 6). Sherman prospers as a dentist married
to "some skinny Jewish girl from Bala-Cynwyd" (p. 11), as does Sonia
with her "summer house in the Italian Catskills [which] had even more
pink 'harem' pillows in the living room that the one in Scotch Plains, and
an even grander pepper mill" (pp. 38–39). So long as he accepts clichés
Nathan also progresses successfully, academically and sexually. However,
once he tries to live by literary standards he inevitably fails.

Peter Tarnopol recognizes that it is precisely this gap between ideal
and reality which has reduced his life to a state of chaos. In deciding to
marry Maureen, he was making one of "those moral decisions that I had
heard so much about in college literature courses" (p. 193). The life which
results from this serious decision proves to be "a soap opera" (pp. 195,
304). Tarnopol equates his marriage with that of "Blondie and Dagwood,
or Maggie and Jiggs" (p. 270) and describes himself as "the Dagwood
Bumstead of fear and trembling" (p. 210). What he finally learns is that
"*You want subtlety, read* The Golden Bowl, *This is life, bozo, not high
art*" (p. 309).

My Life as a Man is flawed, not by any weakness in its use of popular
conventions, but because, in trying to suggest the complexity of "knowing" a person, Roth presents Tarnopol from so many perspectives that, in
the end, we find we know nothing at all about him. In addition to Tarnopol's exhaustive self-interpretation, we are offered a psychiatric

analysis (which is entirely at odds with Tarnopol's evaluation of himself), and two pieces of fiction, written by Tarnopol for therapeutic reasons, which are accompanied by three interpretations (two by characters we know little about, and one by Dr. Spielvogel, the psychiatrist). The reader is left wondering whether Tarnopol is a realiable narrator or, as he even suggests himself, whether he is too much in the grip of his obsessions to see things clearly. If we reject Tarnopol's point of view, should we then approach him through Dr. Spielvogel's analysis or through the "Useful Fictions"? If the latter, should we rely on one of the conflicting interpretations of them presented in the novel, or on our own interpretation? Ultimately, the novel gives us no fixed points of reference and we are left shuffling uneasily between shifting narrative perspectives.

Besides making the novel confusing, Roth's multiple points of view also serve to make it frequently static and boring. Tarnopol's attempts at understanding himself become tedious, and the long exchanges between patient and doctor, neither of whose judgments we can be certain about, finally reduce themselves to a tight circle of hypotheses about personality which give us little guidance or entertainment. The exchange between Spielvogel and Tarnopol about the ethics of Spielvogel using Tarnopol as an example in his article entitled "Creativity: The Narcissism of the Artist" is particularly dull. Well before the end of such episodes we begin to long to see the characters in action in order that we might judge them by what they do and by what they say in their everyday, less self-conscious conversations. *My Life as a Man* serves very much to underline the truth of Lionel Trilling's comment that "the great novelists knew that manners indicate the largest intentions of men's souls as well as the smallest."[5]

Roth's fiction can be viewed as a unified body and we should regard each novel as a serious attempt to express his vision of the failure of commitment. However, as an examination of *The Great American Novel* and *My Life as a Man* reveals, Roth has not yet been entirely successful in finding an appropriate form through which to filter this vision. Whether he will continue to experiment with popular conventions, or whether he will move in yet another direction, remains to be seen.

Notes

1. *College Language Association Journal*, 14 (December, 1970), 163–170.

2. *Twentieth Century Literature*, 19 (1973), 203–216.

3. Philip Roth, *Our Gang* (New York: Holt, Rinehart and Winston, 1971), particularly Chapter 3, "Tricky Has Another Crisis."

4. Philip Roth, *The Breast* (New York: Holt, Rinehart and Winston, 1972), p. 8. Subsequent references to Roth's novels will be cited in the text, and will be taken from the Holt, Rinehart and Winston editions of the novels. *The Great American Novel* was published in 1973 and *My Life as a Man* in 1974.

5. Lionel Trilling, "Manners, Morals and the Novel," in *The Liberal Imagination* (New York: Viking, 1950), pp. 211–212.

The Professor of Desire:
The Two Plums or
the Reawakening?

Daniel Walden*

In 1961, Philip Roth gave a talk at a B'nai B'rith ADL symposium in Chicago in which he attacked what he took to be the unreality and silliness of Jews who were being popularized around that time by Harry Golden and Leon Uris. Trying to come up with a story that would go to the heart of the particular Jewish ethos he had come out of, he vacillated between the Abel and Cain of his respectable middle class background, the Jewboy and the nice Jewish boy. What he had in mind was a Jewish family in which there was great warmth, dominated by the mother, in which the young Jewish boy envied the Gentile boy his parental indifference largely because of the opportunities afforded him for sexual adventure. The Jewish women in the stories were mothers and sisters, the sexual yearning was for The Other. From this talk, expanded into an essay, and from four abandoned projects, "The Jewboy," "The Nice Jewish Boy," "Portrait of an Artist," and "A Jewish Patient Begins His Analysis," Roth fashioned *Portnoy's Complaint*.[1]

Explaining *Portnoy's Complaint* to a class at the University of Pennsylvania, Roth once said, about Portnoy's predicament, "I don't think it's average. It's extreme. But the average is dramatized by this extreme case. The connection between [his] life imagined and [his] life lived furnished a lot of the tension and a lot of the comedy, such as it is." Commenting on the idea for *Portnoy's Complaint*, he remembered that "I didn't know how to use colloquial obscenity outside of dialogue. It's hard to figure how to do it. I needed an esthetic that would justify the language." The device of placing Portnoy on the psychiatrist's couch did the trick. "Finding the ploy of the analyst's couch—the condition of someone addressing the doctor, was the occasion for me. It freed me to organize."[2]

After *Portnoy's Complaint* was published, Alfred Kazin wrote that it was "the latest and most vivid example of the tendency among American Jews to reduce their experience to psychology."[3] Unfortunately, for Roth, what worked well for *Portnoy's Complaint*, which treated sex scandalously, as part of a shock technique, worked less well for those books that he has published since. Between *Goodbye, Columbus* and *Portnoy's Complaint* there was approximately a decade. Between *Portnoy's Complaint* and *The Professor of Desire* there was only seven years. It would have been natural to assume enormous differences in style, content and theme. But for Roth, the American Jew cannot claim exception from the special-

*This essay was written specifically for this volume and appears here for the first time by permission of the author.

ness of his forebears, nor can he rest comfortably being both Jewish and American. Where most writers in the Diaspora portrayed Jews sympathetically, Roth argued correctly that a writer's duty was to his own truth, his own vision. However, it seems to me that the quality of that vision can be examined. Roth should not be excoriated because he has written about Jews who are ugly and unpleasant, who are lechers or crooks. Neither should he be congratulated for it. But, when it appears that Roth's seriousness in preparing *Portnoy's Complaint* is worlds apart from the cavalier approach taken in the preparation of the *The Professor of Desire*, then a comment is needed. I have the strong feeling that most of *Desire* was written on the run, hastily, as an attempt to explain *The Breast* and as a result of a personal upturn in his life. I have a strong feeling that sociological considerations, in a religio-cultural context, can explain *The Professor of Desire*, its promise, its shortcomings. There is tension and comedy and obscenity in *Desire*, as in *Portnoy*. But the esthetic to justify the language and the book is in short supply.

In Philip Roth's *Portnoy's Complaint*, Alexander Portnoy's complaint is described as a struggle with his conscience about being identified with the Jewish community. "I don't want to escape," he says, but he also says, "yes I can—if I should want to."[4] Roth was making fun of Portnoy because he, Roth, couldn't get over his mother and father and being raised as "a little rabbi," like all good little Jewish boys. But he was also deadly serious. For he failed to realize that what kept him going, what Ibsen called the "Life-illusion," was the thought that he was not Jewish (in novel after novel, and short story after short story) when in reality his being Jewish, which gave him incentive for denying it, was the driving force of his life.[5] In the same way that millions have reinvented the wheel, so Roth discovered that the Jew is an archetype of the disjointed, dissociated modern man in America. The sense of rootlessness, of alienation and fragmentation, the search for personal identity and purpose, all constitute the dilemma of modern man and are a major source of the dysfunction of the modern American Jew. Add to that the more specific Jewish problems of homelessness and rejection, the conflict between tradition and assimilation, and the Jewish penchant for suffering, and you account for the search for a meaningful identity.[6] All of these Roth has used, knowingly or unknowingly, since he invented Neil Klugman, Ozzie, and Eli, in the late 1950s. And pushing Roth, it seems to me, was the need to force from the world that respect and admiration and love that he was never sure of as a Jew.

In my mind, this multi-layered explanation, with specific drive, accounts for almost every book and story Roth has written, including *The Breast*,[7] in which David Kepesh's life is first unfolded, and *The Professor of Desire*.[8] What Roth has done is to write a series of repetitious novels, initiation novels, in which the protagonist moves from the confines of the shtetl (or some variation thereof, as through a mother or father), an ordered and pervasive moral system, to the different but no less confining demands of Modern American society. True, Roth has given legitimacy to the traumas and shocks that resulted, to the seduction of the shiksas, to bizarre sex, which were denied most humans. Like Hemingway, or so many other authors, in Malcolm Cowley's words, he kept returning to the same themes, each time making them a little clearer to himself, as to others.[9] But just possibly, as D. H. Lawrence suggested, "all these naughty words . . . only reveal the state of mind of a man who has never had any sincere, vital experience in sex,"[10] at least until he met Claire in *The Professor of Desire*. In the past, Roth, or his persona, desired what was injurious to himself, even when it was stupid, simply, as Dostoievsky wrote, "to have the right to desire for himself even what is stupid and not to be bound by an obligation to desire only what is rational."[11] In *The Professor of Desire*, reawakening for the first time the brilliance and honesty of *Goodbye, Columbus* and "Eli the Fanatic," Roth appears to have gone beyond whiplashing himself, beyond repetition, beyond self-hate, toward understanding, toward what Bellow called some comprehensible pattern. But I said "appears" to have gone in that direction. Let's look at *The Professor of Desire*.

For the umteenth time Philip Roth has written about a Jewish boy who can't have fun without feeling guilty, who is surprised but delighted when he can say to himself, after having an affair with Elisabeth and Birgitta, "whichever I want I can have," and is then told by Helen, who at times is very discerning, "I wonder what it will be like when you can't have something you want (44)." But along the way there is much sex, especially triangular sex, as in *Portnoy's Complaint*, in which David and Birgitta and Elisabeth have sex, and then, after Elisabeth's departure, David and Birgitta and another. Then he marries Helen, whom he had known when he was eighteen and who returns at twenty-six, having run off to the Orient with an already married, mature man. But Helen's lover still claims her deepest feelings. At the end of a year of marriage, David is occupied sixteen hours a day with teaching classes, rewriting his thesis on romantic disillusionment in the stories of Chekhov, and taking full-time care of Helen who has become addicted to drink and dope. For once, David could not have what he wanted. When Helen's old friend Donald Garland visits, David sulks. After Helen leaves to join her lover in Kowloon he finds her in a Hong Kong jail; her ex-lover not only didn't want her back but, as a wealthy and powerful man, had arranged to plant cocaine on her and have her arrested.

With the divorce under his belt and a job at SUNY Long Island, David begins psychoanalysis with Dr. Klinger. Blaming his mother for his domestic habits, for not being able to forge ahead, he is told by Dr. Klinger that moral delinquency has its fascination for you. Meanwhile, when his parents come to visit, having sublet an apartment, he is harassed by one Wally who flirts with him over the phone. After his mother's death his father sells the Hungarian Royale, David has a misunderstanding with his department chairman's wife, and he finds out that he and Ralph Baumgardner, the department's poet, have much in common. But it is his relationship with Claire Ovington, aptly named, describing her clear-headedness and egg-like rounded character, that gives David loving kind-ness and a sane environment. At last, after dropping literary names throughout the book, Roth fixes on Chekhov's "Man in a Shell" to touch David and reveal to him the humiliations and failures "of those who seek a way out of the shell of restrictions and conventions, out of the pervasive boredom and stifling despair, out of the painful marital situations and the endemic social falsity, into what they take to be a vibrant and desirable life (107)." As a result, Chekhov and Flaubert being the influences, he writes forty thousand words of *Man in a Shell*. And all because Claire is a sturdy young woman, filled with common sense, devoted and trust-worthy. Still he is not completely happy. Occasionally he yearns for the bad, old, sex-driven days with Birgitta. During a trip with Claire to Europe he keeps imagining Birgitta with him. In Prague, driven to seek out the meaning of Kafka because of his sexual despair, he compares "the body's utter single-mindedness, its cold indifference and absolute con-tempt for the well-being of the spirit, to some unyielding, authoritarian regime (47)," and understands his lifelong problem. At last he knows the story of the professor's desire, his desire. He dreams of visiting Kafka's whore.

After a year together David and Claire no longer succumb to young desire. Kepesh will no longer quarrel or sulk or yearn or despair. Like Herzog presumably, he is willing to settle for what is. Suddenly, Helen Kepesh returns, married now to Les Lowry, wondering how Claire and Les have managed to be bright and pretty and good, while she and David are not, why David is a master repressive. David understands how he has always failed to be what people wanted or expected, and why he was never one or the other. During the visit of David's father, and his friend Mr. Barbatnik, it is learned that Claire visits a 93 year old woman each month from whom she learned to cook and garden. The implied question hanging over the scene is: what is David waiting for? Why doesn't he marry Claire? We now know that David and Claire have survived the mistakes of his twenties, the mistakes of her youth and adolescence. "And both of them knew that the most difficult and complicated part was only just beginning (179)." For David, the passion will be dead in a year, he believes, and he will be without desire. Robbed by himself of Claire. And yet, never will he forget Chekhov's overall philosophy of life, summarized by one of David's students: "We are born innocent, we suffer terrible disillusionment before we can gain knowledge, and then we fear death— and we are granted only fragmentary happiness to offset the pain (63)."

The Breast was an attempt to use Kafka to explain Philip Roth. *The Professor of Desire*, a more ambitious novel, appears to be an attempt to effect a reconciliation with life. The little boy who was Roth, the spoiled little brat who was twenty or thirty or forty and still a self-hater, was about to grow up and rejoin the human race unafraid at last of being a Jew, of being himself. Kepesh seemed to face the possibility of a fruitful union with a healthy woman, but not because she's a skiksa. Even the possibility of loving his mother and father, even though they are Jewish parents, was promised. But I wonder if Roth really had these in mind. Could he overcome the hold of his past? I wonder if Roth helped choose the picture on the dustcover of *Desire*, a painting of two plums. I can't help recalling the old joke and wondering how seriously we can take Roth. You know the one about the absent-minded professor, walking along with hands in pockets, fondling his jewels, suddenly saying, "Plums? Plums? Who bought plums?"

Just possibly, Roth, like Kepesh, has to learn from his mistakes of the past. He has to get his preoccupation with forbidden sex and being Jewish out of his system. Now that he seems to have accomplished that, and seems to have begun a reconciliation with his father and healthy womanhood, and his roots, he can use the extraordinary talents he has for the great books that are here promised but are yet to come.

Notes

1. See Philip Roth, "In Response to Those Correspondents, Students, and Interviewers Who Have asked Me: 'How did you come to write that book?' " *American Poetry Review*, 3 (August, 1974), 65–67.

2. In Walter Naedale's review of Roth talk, *Philadelphia Bulletin*, November 15, 1970.

3. Alfred Kazin, in the *New York Review of Books*, February 27, 1969, 3.

4. Philip Roth, *Portnoy's Complaint* (New York: Bantam, 1970), 254.

5. Henrik Ibsen, *The Wild Duck*, in Bennet Cerf, ed., *Sixteen Famous European Plays* (New York: Random House, 1943), 73.

6. See William Freedman, "American Jewish Fiction: So What's the Big Deal?" *Chicago Review*, 19 (1966), 90.

7. Philip Roth, *The Breast* (New York: Farrar, Straus and Giroux, 1972).

8. Philip Roth, *The Professor of Desire* (New York: Farrar, Straus and Giroux, 1977). Further references will appear in parentheses.

9. Malcolm Cowley, Introduction, in *The Portable Hemingway* (New York: Viking Press, 1944), vii–xxiv.

10. D. H. Lawrence, *The Letters of D. H. Lawrence*, ed. and with Introduction by Aldous Huxley, (New York: Viking Press, 1932), 563.

11. Fyodor Dostoievsky, *Notes from Underground*, tr. by Ralph Matlaw (New York: Dutton, 1960), 26.

Fathers and Ghosts

John Leonard*

In the 768 pages of Edmund Wilson's *Letters on Literature and Politics, 1912-1972*, there is a single mention of Philip Roth. Writing to the editors of this journal in 1964, Wilson complained about Roth's review of James Baldwin's play, *Blues for Mr. Charlie*: "Roth's article seems to me one of those scurrilous pieces of destructive analysis that the New York literati like to write in order to make themselves feel better when some other writer has become popular and is producing work of obvious value."

Yes. Now vee may perhaps to begin? No. When Roth gets his music right, as he does in *The Ghost Writer*, he is very good. And when he indulges his impulse to scandalize, as he also does in *The Ghost Writer*, he is very entertaining. "Of unknown duchesses lewd tales we tell," Alexander Pope pointed out. But Anne Frank?

The trouble with reviewing *The Ghost Writer* a few weeks late is that Roth has already explained it for us. He is ever explaining. Like David Susskind, he can't shut up. *The Ghost Writer*, he told readers of *The New York Times*, "is about the surprises that the vocation of writing brings," just as *My Life as a Man* "is about the surprises that manhood brings" and *The Professor of Desire* is "about the surprises that desire brings."

Elsewhere, in various essays and in reviews collected into *Reading Myself and Others*, he has advised us that *When She Was Good* was about "the problematical nature of moral authority and of social restraint and regulation," whereas *Portnoy's Complaint* "was concerned with the comic side of the struggle between a hectoring superego and an ambitious id. . . ." On the other hand, perhaps not: *Portnoy*, he says later on, "is about talking about yourself. . . . The method is the subject." Likewise, "The comedy in *The Great American Novel* exists for the sake of no higher value than comedy itself; the redeeming value is not social or cultural reform, or moral instruction, but comic *inventiveness*. Destructive, or lawless, playfulness—and for the fun of it" (Roth's italics).

This isn't Nabokov's ice-blue disdain for the academic ninnyhammers who went snorting after his truffles. Roth, instead, worries himself, as though a sick tooth needed tonguing. He is looking over his shoulder because somebody—probably Irving Howe—might be gaining on him: "This me who is me being me and no other!" as Tarnopol explained at the end of *My Life as a Man*.

Best, then, to try to ignore these verbal tags attached to the toes of the cadavers of bygone books. The art is elsewhere. If Roth was sincere

*Reprinted with permission from *The New York Review of Books* (September 2, 1979). Copyright © 1979 Nyrev, Inc.

with the readers of *The New York Times*—"When you publish a book, it's the world's book. The world edits it"—then he won't mind another gloss on the book at least one of us thinks he wrote this time.

Nothing much happens in *The Ghost Writer*. Forty-three-year-old Nathan Zuckerman—Tarnopol's alter ego in *My Life as a Man*—remembers back twenty years ago to a time when, as a very young writer of several published stories, he left an artists' colony in Vermont to seek the spiritual guidance of the reclusive E. I. Lonoff, a very much older writer, America's "first Russian writer," "the Jew who got away."

As the snow comes down, young Nathan and ironic Lonoff sit by the fire and talk literature. In the kitchen, Mrs. Lonoff, a New England Yankee, does whatever New England Yankee women married to eminent and gloomy Jewish writers do in kitchens. In the study, a beautiful young woman sorts Lonoff's papers, which are to go to Harvard. Nathan decides that the young woman is Lonoff's daughter; he also decides to fall in love with her. She is, in fact, Amy Bellette, an unspecified European, a displaced person, perhaps a survivor of the camps, brought by Lonoff to the United States after the war, and one of the best writing students he ever had at a nearby college that is probably Bennington.

Amy leaves. The Lonoffs and Nathan have dinner. Mrs. Lonoff has a tantrum, breaks a wine glass, suggests that Lonoff "chuck me out" and live, instead, with Amy: "I cannot bear having a loyal, dignified husband who has no illusions about himself *one second more*!" She goes to bed. Nathan and Lonoff return to the fire and talk some more literature: Kafka, of course, and Isaac Babel, and Felix Abravanel, another "Jewish-American" writer who, with his many wives and his hunger for publicity, is the very opposite of Lonoff. Lonoff has renounced life for art.

What sort of art? Stories

> in which the tantalized hero does not move to act at all—the tiniest impulse toward amplitude or self-surrender, let alone intrigue or adventure, preemptorily extinguished by the ruling triumvirate of Sanity, Responsibility, and Self-Respect, assisted handily by their devoted underlings: the timetable, the rainstorm, the headache, the busy signal, the traffic jam, and, most loyal of all, the last-minute doubt.

More snow falls. Nathan is prevailed on to spend the night in Lonoff's study, where he masturbates and reads Henry James and contemplates his problem. His problem is that his father, a Newark pharmacist who has always encouraged Nathan in his writing, disapproves of a new story that he feels will confirm "all our good Christian friends" in their anti-Semitism. His father has gone so far as to enlist a Jewish judge in Newark, who once helped Nathan get into college, to dissuade Nathan from his reckless course. The judge and his wife have sent Nathan a questionnaire. Sample question: "Can you honestly say that there is anything in your short story that would not warm the heart of a Julius Streicher or a Joseph Goebbels?" On the whole, Nathan would prefer another father, or, at the very least, the sanction of Lonoff to pursue his art.

Amy returns. Lonoff joins her in her bedroom. Nathan eavesdrops on them by standing on Lonoff's desk with the volume of Henry James as a footstool. Amy offers Lonoff her body, beginning with the breasts. Lonoff refuses. There is a Jimmy Durante routine that I don't believe for a minute because it's not Lonoff; it's the Philip Roth who professes affection for Henny Youngman and Tiny Tim.

And Nathan fantasizes that Amy is really Anne Frank; that Anne Frank somehow survived and came to the United States and found out she had written a best-selling book turned into a play and realized that if she revealed herself, even to *her* own father, her witness would be sullied. And he, Nathan, will marry her and introduce her to his relatives, and what will his relatives be able to say about his Jewishness when he is the boy who married Anne Frank?

The following morning. . . . The following morning is quite wonderful, and I don't want to give it away. Having begun *The Ghost Writer* in the manner of Chekhov, Roth finishes it off with a flourish of Tolstoy.

Is Lonoff a combination of Bernard Malamud and I. B. Singer, with the dust of Henry James? Is Abravanel—of whom Lonoff observes, "It's no picnic up there in the egosphere"—a combination of Saul Bellow and Norman Mailer? Is Nathan really the Philip of twenty years ago, misunderstood in New Jersey because of stories like "Epstein," "Defender of the Faith," and "Eli the Fanatic"? Is Quahsay Yaddo? For that matter, was Theodore Solotaroff a model for Paul Herz in *Letting Go*? Do Henry James and Kafka care?

These are not interesting questions. What matters more is the music. *The Ghost Writer* is an odd sonata, as if Mahler had tried his hand at a bit of Mozart and just couldn't resist bringing in one of his inevitable marching bands. Anne Frank, indeed. We will return to her.

But listen. Young Nathan on a winter Sunday walk with his father has been hearing what he doesn't want to hear. He is anxious to escape. His father tells him: "You are a good and kind and considerate young man. You are not somebody who writes this kind of story and then pretends it's the truth." And Nathan replies: "I *am* the kind of person who writes this kind of story!" His father pleads: "You're not." But

> I hopped onto the bus, and then behind me the pneumatic door, with its hard rubber edge, swung shut with what I took to be an overly appropriate thump, a symbol of the kind you leave out of fiction. . . . And what I saw, when I looked out to wave good-bye for the winter, was my smallish, smartly dressed father—turned out for my visit in a new "fingertip" car coat that matched the coffee-toned slacks and the checkered peaked cap, and wearing, of course, the same silver-rimmed spec-

tacles, the same trim little mustache that I had grabbed at from the crib; what I saw was my bewildered father, alone on the darkening street-corner by the park that used to be our paradise, thinking himself and all of Jewry gratuitously disgraced and jeopardized by my inexplicable betrayal.

That's painful music. So is Lonoff's wit. So is the wine glass smashed by Lonoff's despairing wife, whose name is Hope. The movements contrast; the coda is coming. One thinks of Roth at his high-strung typewriter, while the jackets of his books stare down from their frames on the living room wall in Connecticut. He is going great. He's in perfect control. The "I" for once is looking at other people and allowing them to make the interesting noises. This time, for sure, Irving Howe will have to say he's sorry.

But impulse sidewhelms him: Anne Frank. He has used her before, in *My Life as a Man*, as, over and over again, he has used Kafka and psychiatrists and Newark. Still, he hasn't used her as a sex object, as a wet dream, as a joke on his family. The *chutzpa* of it, appropriating the Ophelia of the death camps for his dark, libidinal purposes, his angry punch line. . . . He just can't help himself. "The delicate boy with the dirty mouth," as Wilfred Sheed described him somewhat admiringly, strikes again. In Roth's Franklin Library Memorial Swimming Pool, Irving Howe has the bends.

A certain courage is required. Take *that*, Hadassah!

Well. It seems to me that *The Ghost Writer* is less "about" the surprises that the vocation of writing brings than it is "about" fathers and ghosts. Except for Anne Frank, the ghosts and the fathers are pretty much the same. They include Kafka and Babel, Henry James and James Joyce, Tolstoy and Flaubert, not to mention Singer, Malamud, Mailer, Bellow, Howe, and Newark. In seeking sanction and a role model, Nathan will be disappointed and relieved: free.

Lonoff, as if Henry James could imagine being Jewish, represents "Purity. Serenity. Simplicity. Seclusion." He also represents, turning around his sentences instead of his life, repression, deferral, anality. He is a sponge dry of possibility. Abravanel,

> the writer who found irresistible all vital and dubious types, not excluding the swindlers of both sexes who trampled upon the large hearts of his optimistic, undone heroes; the writer who could locate the hypnotic core in the most devious American self-seeker and lead him to disclose, in spirited locutions all his own, the depths of his conniving soul; the writer whose absorption with "the grand human discord" made his every paragraph a little novel in itself, every page packed tight as Dickens or Dostoevsky with the latest news of manias, temptations, passions, and dreams, with mankind aflame with feeling—well . . .

according to Nathan, "in the flesh he gave me the impression of being out to lunch."

Nathan, whether or not he is Philip, is liberated to become whatever he desires: a breast, a penis, or a professor. If any professors are still listening, I would suggest that *The Ghost Writer* is "about" symbolic parricide.

This, of course, is a fantasy, like Anne Frank. Nevertheless, the method is the subject.

Literature obsesses Roth: the best pages of *Reading Myself and Others* are devoted to the others; and in his novels he will abandon his music, as Tolstoy abandoned his narrative, to lecture us on Mishima, Gombrowicz, and Genet, in addition to Kafka. So, I am convinced, do his critics obsess him, although he denies it in the pages of *The New York Times*: they insist that he be Lonoff or Abravanel or Harry Golden. They accuse him of being a Tiny Tim with unwarranted, and perverse, talent.

There's nothing wrong with an obsession with literature, even if it results in a sagging *The Breast*. It also results in such stories as " 'I Always Wanted You to Admire My Fasting'; or, Looking at Kafka." But there is something wrong with an obsession with critics: it brings out the David Susskind in Roth, and messes up the minds of some of his novels. Which was more important to Portnoy, "the settling of scores," or "the pursuit of dreams"?

Howe liked *Goodbye, Columbus*, with reservations: "a unique voice, a secure rhythm, a distinctive subject . . . ferociously exact," causing "a squirm of recognition," although he didn't like Roth's "mimetic revenge," his scoring of "points," his exploitation of subjects as "targets." Much later, of course, Howe would conclude that Roth lacked "literary tact" as well as good faith; that Roth was tendentious, narcissistic, and full of "free-floating contempt and animus," "unfocused hostility," and "unexamined depression."

Norman Podhoretz, back in 1962 when he was not quite as sanguine as he is these days about the perfection of America, complained that Roth endowed "the present condition . . . with the status of an inexorable fate against which there is very little point in struggling." According to this version of Podhoretz, "a particular form of economic organization and a particular set of political arrangements" can be, and maybe ought to be, changed.

Alfred Kazin complained of *Portnoy* that Roth wrote "without the aid of general ideas," which may be the same thing Howe meant by accusing him of a "thin personal culture," or Leslie Fiedler meant in saying he was a master of "the novel with minimum inwardness." Howe and Fiedler were closer to the crux when Howe noticed the way Roth was a bully in his stories and when Fiedler observed that "their terror and irony alike remain a little abstract—fading into illustrations of propositions out of Riesman. . . ."

One of the reasons that *The Ghost Writer* is so likable is that it is less a prisoner of ideas than any other fiction of Roth's since *Letting Go*. Form suggests substance; silence is allowed. One wants to hear more from Hope and Amy; one is obliged to imagine. Roth isn't *proving* anything; the multitude that he contains includes a trapdoor. The guillotine will be named later. But he hasn't gotten out of the library.

I say this with respect. One goes up and down on Roth. Accused of wallowing in the muck with *Letting Go*, he gives up some amplitude, a greed. Asked to acknowledge historical contexts beyond "the ambitious Id," he delivers the Soviet invasion of Czechoslovakia and the Holocaust. Convicted of assimilation on the evidence of his demonstrable enthusiasm for baseball and movies—see *The Great American Novel* and remember that he once reviewed films for *The New Republic*—he omits baseball and movies from subsequent fantasies. He is listening to the wrong people, which means he hasn't killed his father yet.

According to David Susskind, "The direction my work has taken since *Portnoy's Complaint* can in part be accounted for by my increased responsiveness to, and respect for, what is unsocialized in me." And, he explains, Gabe Wallach, Alexander Portnoy, and David Kepesh are "three stages of a single explosive projectile that is fired into the barrier that forms one boundary of the individual's experience: that barrier of personal inhibition, ethical conviction, and plain, old monumental fear beyond which lies the moral and psychological unknown."

Swell. But what we haven't heard about yet is what, beyond the barrier and the boundary, the Norman O. Brownies are doing with their unknowns. We watch, instead, Roth outbox his shadows, his fathers, the ghosts of the quarterlies and the seminar. Is Morris Dickstein right? Is Roth's "extremity" something "unearned"? I don't know, because I've been listening to the music. He should, however, abolish the shoulder he's looking over. The ghosts took Anne Frank to Studio 54. His father will forgive the conventional political intelligence that messed up *The Great American Novel* and excreted *Our Gang*.

Listen, fathers and ghosts, Roth cares too much about you, and he's only in his forties. He's a kid.

This ends another scurrilous, destructive analysis that the New York literati despise writing about lewd duchesses.

Dedalian Shades: Philip Roth's
The Ghost Writer

Joseph C. Voelker*

In *The Ghost Writer*, Nathan Zuckerman returns to Roth's fiction, this time as the budding young genius of a *Bildungsroman*. In an emblematic scene, Nathan climbs on the desk of Maestro E. I. Lonoff in order to eavesdrop on the sexual fall of a symbolic father, apparently taking place in the room upstairs. When the desk proves too low, Nathan slides a fat volume of Henry James's short stories onto it. Then, balanced precariously on book and desk, ear to the ceiling, he witnesses, not the seduction he expected, but the Master's heroic act of self-restraint. "Cover up, Amy," Lonoff tells his young would-be seductress. "Go to bed." Teetering atop the labor of his forebears, Nathan takes in the proud truth of artistic maturity. Lonoff, dubious wizard, knows his own power to enthrall perhaps a handful of readers. He also knows the cost of such power—a loss of illusion. Life holds little to tempt him; there are no second chances.

As autobiography, the emblem is sound. Philip Roth has done some daring and at times awkward balancing acts on the fictions of his literary fathers. His flamboyant performances have risked embarrassment and brought back surprising revelations. Roth has aspired to wizardry, and he has taken the measure of his own efforts against the legendary self-discipline of figures like Kafka, Flaubert, Joyce, Chekhov, and Henry James. He has chosen to become the disciple of those who risked betrayal of loved ones for the sake of "Art," and he has recorded, first, the shady deals with the self an artist will make in the name of "Truth," and second, the funny ways that the asceticism of art—unlike the asceticism of faith—permits certain necessary degradations. Roth's artist-protagonists—because Roth's masters allow it—are "unchaste monks." For the perfectly celibate, there are no stories.

If the autobiography that underlies *The Ghost Writer* is sound, it must needs be tentative, for Roth clearly expects to outlive even Tolstoy's 82 years. The pace of his development is slow, implying the long distance. Few other eras have confronted the writer with such an imposing set of proximate models or such an opportunity for an extended apprenticeship. Among his contemporaries, Roth has stood the longest on the desks of the great Moderns. He has spent twenty years learning to reflect the world after the manner of a James, a Flaubert, and, most recently, a Chekhov. Behind this labor there is both critical sophistication and imaginative power. "Reading Myself" is a title precisely chosen for such a procedure. It is Roth's means of hearing his own voice in his duets (trios, quartets)

*This essay was written specifically for this volume and appears here for the first time by permission of the author.

with the Moderns, of isolating that voice from the harmonies that support it. Short as it is, *The Ghost Writer* marks a new sense of tonal certainty. The novel begins and ends in a duet with Chekhov; its middle—the "madness of art"—is Roth on his own, and this time there are none of the lapses into discordant hysteria that marred *Portnoy's Complaint* or *Our Gang*.

In fact, *The Ghost Writer*'s music suggests that earlier apologetics, like those in "Looking at Kafka," were premature. In that piece, Roth confessed to a sense of impasse. Newark could not have sustained a Kafka—his art would have starved, not his protagonist. In other words, Roth's childhood could not provide great art's requisite suffering; the pain was insufficient to block out all voices but that of the victim. And too many voices add up to comedy. What Roth did not consider when he made those excuses, but what he seems to have discovered in *The Ghost Writer*, is longevity—the unromantic fact that not all significant experience occurs in childhood, that mature comedy is the product of imaginative pressure over considerable time, that Joyce, for instance, was a great Modern *and* a comedian.

The Ghost Writer displays one clear result of Roth's having gotten gracefully older: his novelistic budget can afford better furniture. In the opening moments of his visit with E. I. Lonoff at the older writer's New England farmhouse, Nathan finds himself voiceless. He can't tell the vivid story of his summers selling magazines in profane New Jersey, because he is unable to "utter even the mildest obscenity in front of Lonoff's early American mantelpiece." Such intimidations are commonplace for Roth's earlier protagonists: one thinks of Neil Klugman languishing in Short Hills, or Peter Tarnopol failing to come to terms with Susan McCall's East Side apartment. But Nathan, remarkably, sheds his discomfort. He begins to relish the conversational subtleties, the quieter forms of *angst*, even the well-bred little detonations of passion that a mantelpiece, a set of water colors, a study full of books make possible. Such refinements of emotion are unavailable on the Portnoy toilet. And when Nathan does masturbate—in Lonoff's study, in the very shrine of Lonoff's self-discipline—it evokes in him a mood of complex misery that generates the vision contained in the novel's third chapter, "Femme Fatale." The highly condensed imagining of Anne Frank's survival as Amy Bellette emerges from a condition in Nathan that begs for a most un-Rothian label: Nathan is *melancholy*. And, as Albrecht Dürer well knew, you can't have melancholy without furniture.

Joyce, as a first-generation Modernist, was more fortunate than Roth in two ways: he only had Ibsen and Flaubert as Oedipal obstructors, and he was born into a houseful of good furniture which was then sold out from under the family by a profligate father with bad luck in politics. One cannot imagine the Christmas dinner scene in Joyce's *Portrait* without the sideboard, the candelabra, the carpets, the family portraits.

The scene's moment of greatest sadness occurs in near silence—Stephen sees the enraged Dante's napkin ring fall from her lap, roll across the carpet, and come to a stop against the leg of an easychair. Anger has wrecked one opportunity for communal grace. The feast is broken. Later, after the furniture's repossession and the Dedaluses' move from elegant Blackrock to seedy Dublin, Stephen hears his father bellow, "Where's your bitch of a brother?" Casually, he picks a louse, corrects the error in gender, and saunters out the kitchen door. Furniture breeds restraint; it brings a necessary pressure to all encounters. But art thrives on downward mobility, and perhaps Roth's is the harder road. If he succeeds, we may in ten years time begin to take Henry James seriously again.

For all *The Ghost Writer*'s Chekhovian snow (and never was snow more Chekhovian), the book is a *Bildungsroman* with a Joycean theme. As Stephen denies his consubstantial father Simon for an "Old Artificer," so Nathan turns away from "Doc" Zuckerman to seek out some higher pedigree from the legendary E. I. Lonoff. But Roth's sense of his own belated Modernism underlies certain complications in Nathan's dilemma between loyalty to loved ones and loyalty to Art. Stephen's father is a man of brittle charm and small comprehension, who thinks to surmount his son's developing genius with his own ability to leap a five-barred gate or sing a tenor air. Doc Zuckerman's challenges are not so easily dismissable. A deeply caring man, he is also a sharp-eyed moral critic, who appears to have had at least one course with Lionel Trilling as an elective in podiatry school. The novel divides the Jews who take offense at Nathan's story, "Higher Education," into two types. The first is Judge Wapter, whose sly chauvinism and manipulative rhetoric characterize the attacks upon Roth that have been launched from Jewish Community Center lecture halls over the last twenty years. Wapter is simply the moral and intellectual equivalent of the Irish Joyce easily abandoned. The second type is Nathan's father; he is a kind of opponent Joyce either did not have to face or cared not to write about. Nobody Irish ever asked Joyce to write like Tolstoy, to achieve comprehensiveness of vision. Doc Zuckerman, on the other hand, says (and this is only part of it):

"The fact remains, son, that there is more of the family, much much more, than is in this story. Your great-aunt was as kind and loving and hard-working a woman as you could ever meet in this world. Your grandmother and all her sisters were, every last one of them. They were women who thought only of others."

"But the story is not about them."

"But they are *part* of the story. They are the *whole* story as far as I'm concerned. Without them there would be no story at all! Who the hell was Sidney? Does anybody in his right mind even think about him any longer?"

And if it is a sign of Modernism's lateness that consubstantial fathers are smart critics, the matter is doubly complicated for Roth by the flesh-and-blood reality of all available "old artificers." Not only are they un-mythic, there are too many of them. For Joyce, the imagination was a frontier; for Roth, it is a real-estate development, and the subdividing has reached an advanced state. Should Nathan get himself adopted by the flashy Felix Abravanel, who dwells on any edge he can identify, and still seems, to Nathan, "out to lunch?" Or should he choose E. I. Lonoff, the paunchy, unglamorous "Jew who got away?" If Joyce lurks behind Nathan's dilemma, pointing its complex belatedness, there is surely a specific Joycean text lurking behind that dilemma's solution. For Nathan chooses Lonoff—and then, on first arriving at his home, watches Lonoff build a fire. The older man's acceptance of routine, his regulated, uninspired service of art, his willingness *not to live* in order to write are caught in his fire-lighting technique:

> After directing me to one of a pair of easy chairs beside the fireplace, Lonoff removed the fire screen and peered in to be sure the draft was open. With a wooden match he lighted the kindling that apparently had been laid there in anticipation of our meeting. Then he placed the fire screen back into position as precisely as though it were being fitted into a groove in the hearth. Certain that the logs had caught—satisfied that he had successfully ignited a fire without endangering the two-hundred-year-old house or its inhabitants—he was ready at last to join me.

It is in a similar scene (in fact, the priest says, "A draft is said to help in these cases") that Stephen Dedalus confronts a counterfeit father, a self he will not become, in the Dean of Studies of University College, Father Butt. As their discussion of the fine arts and the useful arts makes its desultory way toward the subject of language ("tundishes," "funnels," and of course "detain") Stephen looks into the blank insipidness of the priest's routine, the failure of inspiration's light in the face before him, and knows he must turn his back on orthodox forms of priesthood.

Roth echoes the scene almost as a rebuke. Such momentous epiphanies prove hard to come by later in the century; even the hardest-earned certainties of youth erode under repeated inspection, in the light of longevity. Stephen's goodbyes are unequivocal (at least in intention); his hesitations are few and brief. His judgments may be wrong, but Joyce's narrative distance leaves it to the reader to decide. Far less distance separates the 45-year-old Roth from young Nathan Zuckerman. For Nathan, in *The Ghost Writer*, makes discoveries we usually associate with middle age. Lonoff is no Father Butt. Nathan, at 23, is prepared to learn that patience, discipline, an established routine get books written; he is willing to stay and witness the "madness" at their center.

It is interesting, then, that when Stephen Dedalus does hesitate, Joyce sounds a little like Roth. Every *Bildungsroman*, from *Wilhelm Meister* to *The World According to Garp*, contains a generic insight. Misunderstanding turns a young man into an artist. Then, absorbed in his craft, he forgets that his fictions conquer misunderstanding only in an interior arena. Publication brings an inevitable shock—now it is the art that is misunderstood, and violently. Stephen's "Villanelle of the Temptress" is suspect in its origins; we feel that no real poetry can emerge from such onanistic circumstances. But its reception, as Stephen sees, will be more shameful yet. There is the seed of Roth-like comedy in Stephen's vision of art's awkward presence at an Irish breakfast-table. A momentarily Jewish Stephen imagines the *goyim* at their feed:

> If he sent her the verses? They would be read out at breakfast amid the tapping of eggshells. Folly indeed! The brothers would laugh and try to wrest the page from each other with their strong hard fingers. The suave priest, her uncle, seated in his armchair, would hold the page at arm's length, read it smiling and approve of the literary form.

Admittedly, Stephen's grand manner ("Folly indeed!") restrains the scene's potential comedy, marks its bitterness. But the message of such a mortifying vision was clear to the young Joyce—he would have to leave Ireland for good. Perhaps the courage and the clearheadedness justify taking oneself a little too seriously.

In Roth, art misunderstood leads only to temporary abandonments—that is the theme of *The Ghost Writer*. Roth reduces Joyce's *non serviam* to a phone hung up in anger, a bus door that shuts with more melodrama than finality. Roth's gestures toward exile are arc-points on a circle from outrage to reconciliation and back again. Nathan doesn't have the phone disconnected; as he climbs into the bus, he promises to be back in a few months. He is older than Stephen because he knows he will put up with people. Joyce, to the contrary, sailed away from Ireland and landed on the planet "Art." For him, circles meant futility and writing was Faustian—memory's summoning of spirits to impersonate the dead. And like Luigi Galvani, Joyce knew how to make the frog's leg twitch to his tune. Oliver Gogarty and many another Dubliner deeply resented that ability. It robbed them of their ontological assurance, made them feel dead and buried before their decades were even up. Roth writes about the living as though they are alive, almost, it seems, in order to keep them alive.

Thus Nathan's counterpart to Stephen's Villanelle, the *Bildungsroman*'s obligatory work-of-art-within-the-work-of-art, is titled "Femme Fatale," concerns a temptress, and yet remains devoid of the Joycean necromancy. In fact, it is all about survival. Chapter Two of *The Ghost Writer*, "Nathan Dedalus," delineates Nathan's guilty predicament. He has written and intends to publish a story that his father believes will disgrace the Jews. Chapter Three, "Femme Fatale," responds to that guilt. It is a fantasy, partially induced by masturbation, in which Amy Bellette, Lonoff's young houseguest, turns out to be Anne Frank, who has miraculously survived the death camps. She is a *"femme fatale,"* first, in being a young woman of startling beauty, and second, in having to pretend to be dead. She knows that, were Anne Frank known to be alive, her book would have no meaning. For thousands of her readers, Anne Frank's death makes the holocaust real. The price is high. In order to be a great Jewish writer, she must be dead to her own father, "now sixty." Like Stephen's Villanelle, Nathan's fictional daydream invents a woman, but primarily as a means for brooding upon the self. Stephen's poem—after we acknowledge its technical brilliance, its perfect *fin de siecle* lyricism—proves to be poor stuff when measured as a conscious apprehension of either Emma Clery or its young creator. Mostly it linguefies Stephen's lust, providing thereby a chance for Joyce to make cold, ironic success out of Stephen's failure. "Femme Fatale" is considerably more complicated. It too displays immaturity. It is the verbal correlative of Nathan's deeply childish longing for parental forgiveness, and no more adult in its origins than Stephen's delicate pornography. Nathan's grandiose daydream of marrying Anne Frank and taking her home to the folks suggests that he is a long way from coming to grips with the dilemma of art and betrayal.

But "Femme Fatale" works in other ways. One of the more interesting is as a parable of time passed. The fiction that Amy Bellette is Anne Frank carries a more deeply pondered message to the world's Doc Zuckermans, to those judicious critics who yet insist that art operates on no alternate planet, that stories are about people. Had Anne Frank survived, she would embarrass us all by falling in love, or buying furniture, or wanting to interview movie stars. Stephen's "E.C." is an occasion for self-indulgence, but Nathan's Anne Frank is a fictional mirror for himself, one that rewards scrutiny. Outside the mirror "Anne Frank" stands Nathan, wondering if he must be dead to his own father to be free to write about Jews. Outside Nathan Zuckerman stands Philip Roth at 45, facing a dilemma that, if it is still unsolved, is at least masterfully articulated. We don't ask fiction to solve dilemmas, but to clarify them, calmly. Behind the guilty exposures of "Higher Education" and the elaborate apologies of "Femme Fatale" lies Roth's demand that his audience stop measuring art against martyrdom.

The Ghost Writer is a book full of the sense of belatedness—belatedness toward the Jews of Europe and toward the masters of fiction. With impressive economy, Roth has made an accounting toward both. The really sane thing—for both Roth and his readers—is to be thankful for the richness and the restraint of its comedy, "Joycean," "Chekhovian," or what have you.

ESSAYS

The Earthly City of the Jews

Alfred Kazin*

When John Updike brilliantly conceived Henry Bech, who was in everything he did, and especially in what he couldn't do, "the Jew as contemporary American novelist," Updike was having his fun with that once unlikely but now well-known American product, Bellow-Malamud-Roth. Bellow said that the constant linking of these names reminded him of Hart, Schaffner and Marx. But irritating as it might be to one proudly gifted and much-honored novelist to be linked with other *Jewish* names, Bellow more than any other American novelist of his ability used the modern Jewish experience in his work.

Most of Bellow's characters were Jews, his non-Jewish characters (rare enough) were, like Allbee in *The Victim*, obsessed with Jews or, like Henderson, clamorously produced wittily agonized definitions of human existence remarkably like those of the Jewish protagonists in Bellow's novels—Joseph in *Dangling Man*, Asa Leventhal in *The Victim*, Tommy Wilhelm in *Seize the Day*, Augie March, Herzog, Mr. Sammler. Over and again in Bellow's novels there were the parents who to tyrants in eastern Europe had been nothing but Jews, and in the slums of Montreal and Chicago saw nothing but their own experience reflected back from the neighborhood. There was a natural, enchanted repetition of the Jewish neighborhood, the Jewish family circle, the Jew as college intellectual, radical, dreamer, explorer of lowlife—the Jew discovering worlds new to him. "Look at me going everywhere!" Augie March cries out after pages devoted principally to the emancipation and enlightenment of Augie's senses—"Why, I am a sort of Columbus of those near-at-hand!" More than anyone else, Bellow connected one novel after another with a representative Jew in order to represent Jewish experience itself.

This emphasis on one people's collective idiosyncratic experience, an emphasis so intense that it seems to follow from some deep cut in Bellow's mind, is nevertheless intense in attention rather than partisan. Bellow is positively hypnotized by the part of human life he knows best, as a novelist should be, and he sees everything else in this focus. But without being detached and "impartial" about the long Jewish struggle for survival, he is fascinated and held by the texture of Jewish experience as it becomes, as it can become, the day-to-day life of people one has created. This is very different from writing about people one names as Jews but who, no matter how one feels about them, are just names on the page. Texture is life relived, *life* on the page, beyond praise or blame. In Bellow's first novel, *Dangling Man* (1944), the hero writes of himself: ". . . . To him judgment is second to wonder, to speculation on men, drugged and clear, jealous, ambitious, good, tempted, curious, each in his own time and with his customs and motives, and bearing the imprint of strangeness in the world." To Asa Leventhal in *The Victim*, crossing over to Staten Island,

> the towers on the shore rose up in huge blocks, scorched, smoky gray. . . . The notion brushed Leventhal's mind that the light over them and over the water was akin to the yellow revealed in the eye of a wild animal, say a lion, something in-human that didn't care about anything human and yet was im-planted in every human being too, one speck of it, and formed a part of him that responded to the heat and the glare . . . even to freezing, salty things, harsh things, all things difficult to stand.

In *Seize the Day*, where the West Side of New York is the most living, throbbing character, Tommy Wilhelm, trying to make a confident ap-pearance with a hat and a cigar, feels that the day is getting away from him: ". . . . the cigar was out and the hat did not defend him . . . the peculiar burden of his existence lay upon him like an accretion . . . his entire chest ached . . . as though tightly tied with ropes. He smelled the salt odor of tears in his eyes. . . ." In the sunshine of upper Broadway there was "a false air of gas visible at eye-level as it spurted from the bursting buses."

This air of having lived, of experiencing the big city in every pore, of being on the spot, is the great thing about Bellow's fiction. It is this living acrid style—in the suddenly chastened, too glibly precise, peculiarly assertive bitterness of postwar American writing, with its hallucinated clarity about details, its oversized sense of our existence, of too many ob-jects all around (what desolation amidst wonders!)—that made us realize Bellow as an original. He is a key to something that would emerge in all the American writing of this period about cities, the "mass," the common life. This was not the "minority" writing of the poignant, circumscribed novels of the 1930s. Even in the best of them, like Daniel Fuchs's *Low Company, Summer in Williamsburg, Homage to Blenholt*, one had been aware that "Jewish" equals ghetto. Bellow had come out of a ghetto in Montreal, the Napoleon Street that makes one of the deeper sections of *Herzog*. But what made him suddenly vivid, beginning with what was later to seem the put-on of *The Adventures of Augie March* (1953), was his command of a situation peculiarly American, founded on mass experience, that was as far from the metaphysical wit in Kafka as it was from the too conscious pathos of the Depression novels. With Bellow an American of any experience could feel that he was in the midst of the life he knew.

What was perhaps most "American" about it was the fact that despite all the crisis psychology in *The Victim, Seize the Day, Herzog* there was a burning belief in commanding one's own experience, in putting it right by thought. Each of these narratives was a kind of survival kit for a period in which survival became all too real a question for many Americans. The Jewish experience on that subject—and what else had the experience been?—seemed exemplary to Americans, especially when it came armed with jokes. Goodbye to Henry Roth and how many other gifted, stunted, devastated Jewish novelists of the Thirties. In book after book Bellow went about the business of ordering life, seeing it through, working it out. He was intimate with the heights-and-abyss experience of so many intellectual Jews, the alternating experience of humiliation and the paradise of intellectual illumination. And it was this depiction of life as incessant mental struggle, of heaven and hell in the same Jewish head,[1] that made Bellow's readers recognize a world the reverse of the provincial, a quality of thought somber, tonic, bracing, that was now actual to American experience yet lent itself to Bellow's fascinatedly personal sense of things.

In all of this Bellow became a style-setter for those many writers emerging in the Fifties who found in him a kind of paradigm for taking hold, for getting in there, for being on top of the desperate situation. And indeed no one was more impressed by this angle of life, this sense of command, this ability to be *imaginatively* in charge, than Bellow himself, whose books, one after another, were usually founded on a protagonist who was the nearest possible spokesman for himself. Just as the success story of American Jews "making it" was represented by a bewildering succession of changes in their lives, so Bellow's novels, each registering a different state of awareness but all coming together as successive chapters of the same personal epic, made the nearest and best literary expression of the disbelief behind a Jewish ascent that was also haunted by the Holocaust. Bellow expressed both the American facts and the disbelief.

Here was an American Jewish writer who had a powerful sense of his own experience as imaginative, yet could beat other Jewish intellectuals at putting the universe into a sentence. He was as clever as a businessman but racked by a sense of responsibility to his "soul." Bellow underwent all these phases in his fiction. But at the center of each narrative was always a hero, a single mind and conscience, adventurous but forever counting the cost of existence. Above all, the Bellow persona was an hallucinated observer of what Sartre called the "hell that is other people"—he brilliantly sized up the strength in other people's arms, lives, faces, seeing what they had to say to the predominating self's vision at the heart of each

Bellow novel. The man had been an anthropologist, a traveler, a musician, an editor of the University of Chicago's "great books"; he was a teacher, a lover, a liberated Jewish male and the most watchful of Jewish sons; he had found a way through the thickets of the big-city ghetto, the big-city university, the Depression, the merchant marine during the war; he had been a left radical, a welfare investigator; he was soon to become the sternest of Jewish moralists. And in all this Bellow influenced himself far more than others ever did, which is why book after book added up to what he had experienced and learned. The key belief was that right thinking is virtue and can leave you in charge of the life that is so outrageous to live.

The process of self-teaching thus becomes the heart of Bellow's novels, and the key to their instructiveness for others. One could compile from Bellow's novels a whole commonplace book of wisdom in the crisis era that has been Bellow's subject and opportunity. His novels are successively novels of instruction as well as existential adventure tales. The story as a whole tells, as the best Jewish stories always do, of the unreality of this world as opposed to God's. The hero struggles in a world not his own, a world run by strangers. The Jewish son has indeed lost the paradise that in childhood was within his grasp. In scripture this world is God's world; Jews must be grateful and obedient for being allowed to share it. In Jewish fiction this world is always someone else's world, though it is one in which Jews call themselves Jews and remain Jews. The so-called Jewish novel (there really is one, though only a few Jews have written it, and those who write it are not always Jews) takes place in a world that is unreal, never *our* world. The heart of the world is Jewish (said John Jay Chapman) but in Bellow's novels only one's mother and father have a heart. Bellow is in magnetized relation to the big-city environment, to the vertigo and clamor of New York, to the opulent yet sortable detail. But his is not a world in which a Jew feels at home. The Jew is always in some uneasy relation to "them"—he is a newcomer, parvenu, displaced person whose self-ordering becomes the issue in each book. In his humanist attack on anti-Semitism in France, *Jew and Anti-Semite*, Jean-Paul Sartre defined a Jew as someone whom others regard as a Jew. This understandably provoked Bellow by its lack of knowledge. When even "a prince of European philosophy" knows so little about them, Jews may wonder if this *is* their world. And so the Jew in Bellow's novels is a "stranger" because he really is one—not, like Camus's *"étranger,"* because he is free of other people's opinions to the point of total indifference. This representative Jew is involved in a catch-as-catch-can relationship to the world, that famous anchor of the old bourgeois novel, that keeps him lightly suspended just above the earth.[2]

But the vitality of Bellow's fiction comes from the importance of being a Jewish son, a figure of importance; this may be hidden from everyone but himself. The Bellow hero, though often distraught, has the powerful ego of Joseph relating his dreams to his jealous brothers. This hero is so all-dominating that other males tend to become distinct only if they are intellectuals who personify *wrong ideas.* Nonintellectuals, like the women in the later novels, tend to become "reality instructors," opaque emblems of the distrusted world. The central figure is the only pilgrim who makes any progress. From Joseph in *Dangling Man* to old Mr. Sammler, each of Bellow's heroes represents the same desperate struggle for life—by which he means a more refined consciousness. It is a concentrated example of the age-old Jewish belief that salvation is in thinking well—to go to the root of things, to become a kind of scientist of morals, to seek the ultimate forces that rule us.

Thinking is for Bellow the most accessible form of virtue. The "reality instructors" have become indistinguishable from the worldliness with which they are clotted. Bellow's recurrent hero, by contrast, is so concerned with thinking well that the imbalance between the hero and his fellows becomes an imbalance between the hero's thinking and the mere *activity* of others. Bellow is not a very dramatic novelist, and unexpected actions tend to be dragged into his novels—like Herzog's half-hearted attempt to kill his wife's lover—as a way of interrupting the hero's reflections. But evidently Bellow's personae attain their interest for *him* by their ability to express the right opinions. And not surprisingly, the protagonists of Bellow's novels are the voices of his intellectual evolution. A Bellow anthology would take the form of a breviary, an intellectual testament gathered from diaries, letters to public men and famous philosophers that were never mailed, arias to the reader à la Augie March, the thoughts of Artur Sammler that are neural events in the privacy of one's consciousness because they cannot be expressed to others—they are too severe, too disapproving.

Bellow has found fascinating narrative forms for the urgency of his many thoughts. He has been clever in finding a distinct *style* for so much silent thinking—from Joseph's diaries in *Dangling Man* to Herzog's equally incessant meditations and finally old Mr. Sammler's haughty soliloquies, where the style is one of the lightest, featheriest, mental penciling, an intellectual shorthand (here involving brusque images of the city) that answers to the traditional contractedness of Jewish thought. The favorite form for Jewish sages has always been the shortest, and Bellow's best fictions are his shortest. V. S. Pritchett, who admires Bellow for powerful descriptions of city life rare among "intellectual" novelists, thinks that in his long books Bellow "becomes too personal. There is a failure to cut the umbilical cord." Bellow's more lasting fictions will probably be those whose personae are not *exactly* as intelligent as he is—*The Victim* and *Seize the Day.*

In these books the weight of the world's irrationality, which is its injustice, falls heavily upon human beings who win us by their inability to understand all that is happening to them and why it is happening to *them*. Asa Leventhal at the end of *The Victim*, having been persecuted, exploited, terrified by a Gentile who accuses the Jew of having persecuted *him*, ends up innocently saying to his tormentor—"Wait a minute, what's your idea of who runs things?" Tommy Wilhelm in *Seize the Day*, who in one day realizes that he has lost wife, mistress, father, money, God, confronts the depths of his suffering only by identifying with a stranger into whose funeral he has stumbled by accident. These incomprehensions are truly evocative of the "existential situation" in contemporary fiction—that of individuals who are never up to their own suffering, who cannot fully take it in, who have learned only that their suffering has its reasons of which reason knows nothing.

Artur Sammler, on the other hand, is so openly Bellow's mind now, in its most minute qualifications, that one can admire the man's intellectual austerity and yet be amazed that Bellow's hero should be so intelligent about everything except his relation with other human beings. Sammler is an old man, a widower, with only one eye left to him by the Nazis; his wife was shot to death in the same Polish pit from which he managed to escape past so many dead bodies (the fable that haunts Jewish writers). Sammler is old, experienced, intelligent, cultivated. But none of these things accounts for the fact that Artur Sammler disapproves of everything he sees and everyone he knows except a vague kinsman, a doctor who got him to America and supports him. He dislikes all the women especially. The evident fact is that Mr. Sammler is the Jew who, after Hitler, cannot forgive the world, for he recognizes that its exterminations may be more pleasurable to it than its lusts. He has decided, not as the rabbis have decided but as Jewish novelists have decided in this first era of fiction by many Jews, that the "world" is a very bad place indeed. In God's absence human consciousness becomes the world; then the only thing for us, *Mr. Sammler's Planet* ends, is to know and to admit that we know.

The unsatisfactory thing about Mr. Sammler—a "collector" indeed, but of wisdom—is that he is always right while other people are usually wrong—sinfully so. More than most Jewish intellectuals, Artur Sammler is right and has to be right all the time. The Jewish passion for ideological moralism, for ratiocination as the only passion that doesn't wear out (and is supposed not to interfere with the other passions)—that passion has never been "done" in our fiction. There is no precedent for its peculiar self-assertiveness, so different from luxuriating in one's ego as a cultural tradition in the style of Stephen Dedalus. In Bellow's novel, insistently moralistic and world-weary, the hero is totally identified with his own thought. His total rejection of other people because of *their* thought sets up a lack of incident, an invitation to symbolic politics, like the now celebrated scene in which a Negro pickpocket follows old, delicate Mr. Sammler to his apartment house and exposes an intimidating penis, or the corollary scene in which Mr. Sammler's mad Israeli son-in-law—a sculptor carrying a bag of metal pieces—beats the same Negro almost to death near Lincoln Center.

Bellow's intellectual at-homeness with Sammler's thought is so assured that over and again one has the Blakean experience of reading thoughts expressed as sensations. But what is certainly not Blakean are the austere, dismissive jeremiads, the open contempt for the women in the book as crazy fantasists, improvident, gross careless sexpots, "birds of prey." There is a brilliantly immediate, unsparing knowledge of other people's appearance and limitations which in its moral haughtiness becomes as audible to the reader as sniffing, and is indeed that. There is so strong a sense of physical disgust with all one's distended, mad-eyed, pushing neighbors on the West Side that there seems nothing in the book to love but one's opinions.

So much self-assertion is a problem among contemporary American novelists, not least among Jewish writers who have been released into the novel under the comic guise of getting clinically close to their own minds. Jewishness as the novelist's material (which can be quite different from the individual material of Jews writing fiction) is constructed folklore. It is usually comic, or at least humorous; the characters are always ready to tell a joke on themselves. With their bizarre names, their accents, *their* language, they are jokes on themselves. And so they become "Jewish" material, which expresses not the predicament of the individual who knows himself to be an exception, but a piece of the folk, of "Jewishness" as a style of life and a point of view.

This sense of a whole folk to write about is indeed what Yiddish fiction began with late in the nineteenth century, and folklore remains a style, a manner, an attitude to life among many Jewish entertainers. But the appearance of this subject in the fiction of Bernard Malamud is so arch and clever a transposition into serious literature, a conscious piece of artifice, that one becomes aware of "Jewishness" in Malamud's language and style as the play within the play. The characters are all of a piece and of a tribe; they all speak with vigor the same depressed-sounding dialect, giving a Yiddish cadence to New York English that is pure Malamud and that makes his characters so aware of and dependent on each other that they have become a stock company ready to play any parts so long as they can keep their accents. In "Take Pity," a story that takes place in the next world (and is just as grubby), a recording angel or "census taker, Davidov, sour-faced, flipped through

> the closely scrawled pages of his notebook until he found a clean one. He attempted to scratch in a word with his fountain pen but it had run dry, so he fished a pencil stub out of his vest pocket and sharpened it with a cracked razor.

Rosen, a new arrival, tells the story of a refugee whose pitiful little grocery store is failing:

He was talking to me how bitter was his life, and he touched me on the sleeve to say something else, but the next minute his face got small and he fell down dead, the wife screaming, the little girls crying that it made in my heart pain. I am myself a sick man and when I saw him laying on the floor, I said to myself, "Rosen, say goodbye, this guy is finished!" So I said it.

The all-dominating poverty in the Malamud world and of any Malamud character reduces everything to the simplicity of a single tabletop, chair, carrot. No matter where the Malamud characters are—Brooklyn, Rome, or a collapsible hall bedroom in the next world—they are "luftmenschen," so poor that they live on air, in the air, and are certainly not rooted in the earth. In one of the "Fidelman" stories, a young art historian who finally makes his way to Rome encounters and is ultimately defeated by Susskind, a refugee from every country—in Israel he could not stand "the suspense." Poverty as a total human style is so all-dominating an esthetic medium in Malamud, coloring everything with its woebegone utensils, its stubborn immigrant English, its all-circulating despair, that one is not surprised that several of Malamud's characters seem to travel by levitation. They live not only on air but in it, one jump ahead of the B.M.T. All forms of travel and communication are foreshortened, contracted, made picturesque, as it were. Malamud has found a sweetly humorous dialect for the insularity of his characters. The outside world, which for Jews can be "another," does not even reach the consciousness of Malamud's Jews. They exist for each other, depend on each other, suffer each other and from each other with an unawareness of the "world" that *is* the definitive and humorously original element—and for which Malamud has found a narrative language whose tone derives from the characters' unawareness of any world but their own. Turning the tables on those who fear that the son of Yiddish-speaking immigrants might not be "proper" in his English, Malamud adopted a style essentially make-believe and fanciful, a style so patently invented by Malamud in tribute to the vitality of the real thing that the real humor of it is that someone made it up.

Malamud has always been an artificer. Even his first and only "non-Jewish" novel, *The Natural*, is a baseball novel with a deceiving drop in every curve. But from the time that Malamud left his native New York to teach in Oregon, and in what was distinctly a "new life" for him finessed his detachment and whimsicality into an operational set of characters and a terrain distinctly "Jewish," Malamud's own voice became that artfully dissonant irony that says in every turn: Reader, something out of your usual experience is trying to reach you.

Thus Malamud will describe in *The Assistant* Helen Bober reflecting on the life of the utterly spent man, the grocer who is her father: "He was Morris Bober and could be nobody more fortunate. With that name you had no sure sense of property, as if it were in your blood and history not to possess, or if by some miracle to own something, to do so on the verge of loss." The Bobers do not "live": they "eke out an existence." But though they address each other in the same toneless style, as if each word were their last,

> Why do I cry? I cry for the world. I cry for my life that it
> went away wasted. I cry for you—

the truth of this cadence, in its perfect fall of the voice, is so natural yet "made" that it takes us straight to Malamud's own wit behind the voice we hear. Of American Jewish writers, only Clifford Odets, in those plays whose original voice is now unrecognized (probably because it is assumed that all Jews talked this way during the Depression), took the same pleasure in creating this art-language from Yiddish roots. But Malamud is always wry, detached, a straightforward performer, who enjoys spinning some of this speech for the pleasure of seeing whether, with his odd freight, he can make it over to the other side. Gruber the outraged landlord in "The Mourners" says to the old tenant whom he cannot get rid of, "That's a helluva chuzpah. Gimme the keys. . . . Don't monkey with my blood pressure. If you're not out by the fifteenth, I will personally throw you out on your bony ass." Malamud is in fact so much of a "humorist" trying out situations and lines of dialogue for their immediate effect that Bellow once objected to the artifice of the last scene in "The Mourners," where the old tenant says Kaddish for the landlord who has been so cruel to him. "It struck him with a terrible force that the mourner was mourning him; it was he who was dead." Malamud's usual material, however, is so much about the violation of Jews, about actual physical deprivation and suffering, that obviously Malamud has returned the compliment to life, to the repeated violation of Jewish existence, by a kind of literary "violation," a studied contraction, in himself.

Certainly much of Malamud's humor as a writer lies in his conscious attitude of dissonance, his own wry "handling" of situations. What was oppressively pathetic in life becomes surreal, overcolored, picturesque, illustrative of a folk culture in the Chagall style rather than about Jews as fully grown individuals. His characters are all Malamud's children. Yet by the same logic of detachment, Malamud almost absently tends to turn his protagonists into emblems of "Jewish" goodness and sacrifice. In the best of Malamud's novels, *The Assistant*, which in the thoroughness of its workmanship, its fidelity to the lived facts of experience, its lack of smartness and facile allegorizing, is also the most satisfactory single Jewish novel of this period, even Morris Bober apostolically says what no Jew would ever say to a man taunting him, "What do you suffer for, Morris?" "I suffer for you." Morris Bober might live by this without thinking of it one way or the other. He would certainly be too absorbed in the struggle for existence to say grandly to an enemy, "I suffer for you." But *The Assistant* works all the time and all the way, it convinces, because of the tenacity with which Malamud has captured the texture of Morris Bober's grinding slavery to his store, his lack of energy, his lack of money, the terrible hours from six in the morning to late at night. It is the total poverty of the grocer that gives *The Assistant* the rigor of a great argument. (Malamud's stories sometimes tend to be picturesque and highly colored.) In *The Assistant* Malamud's strength is his total intuition of the folk idiosyncrasy involved. The sacrifice of Morris Bober is meaningful because he does not know to what he has been sacrificed.

Malamud's almost automatic identification of suffering with goodness, his old-fashioned affection for Jews as the people of poverty and virtue, is in any event a tribute to *his* past. It does not reflect the world Malamud has lived in since his own rise from the world in which Morris Bober rose in the dark every winter morning to sell the "Poilesheh" an onion roll for three cents. The hold of the past on Bellow and Malamud—of the immigrant parents, the slum childhood, the Hitler years that inevitably summed up the martyrdom of Jewish history—is in contrast with the experience of the "new" Jewish novelists, whose aggressively satiric star is Philip Roth.

Roth's natural subject is the self-conscious Jew, newly middle-class, the Jew whose "identity," though never in doubt, is a problem to himself, and so makes himself a setup for ridicule, especially to his son. The Jewish son now sees himself not as a favorite but as a buffer state. Far from identifying any of his characters with the legendary virtues and pieties of Jewish tradition, Roth dislikes them as a group for an unconscious submission that takes the form of hysteria. His first work, *Goodbye, Columbus*, builds up from dislikable outward attributes of the we-have-made-it Patimkin family out of Newark, the suburb to which they have escaped, the coarse sentimental father, the shrewish hostile mother, the dumb athletic brother, the brattish kid sister. Even Brenda Patimkin, girl friend to the sensitive narrator, Neil—an assistant in the Newark Public Library who is defined by his lack of status and his friendliness to a little Negro boy out of the slums who regularly visits the library to stare with ignorant wonder at a book of Gauguin reproductions—exists to betray him. Roth is so quick here to define people by their social place, and to reject them, that he does not always grant a personal trait to their intelligence. Brenda Patimkin seems more Sweet Briar than Radcliffe, just as the narrator Neil Klugman would not necessarily become a Newark Public Librarian just because *he* did not go to Harvard.

Yet what made Roth stand out—there was now a rut of "Jewish novelists"—was his "toughness," the power of decision and the ability to stand moral isolation that is the subject of his story "Defender of the Faith." There was the refusal of a merely sentimental Jewish solidarity. At a time when the wounds inflicted by Hitler made it almost too easy to express feelings one did not have to account for, but when Jews in America were becoming almost entirely middle-class, Roth emphasized all the bourgeois traits that he found. He cast a cold eye on Jews as a group; he insisted, by the conscious briskness of his style and his full inventory of the exaggerated, injurious, sordid, hysterical, that *he* was free. In story after story, in the contrasting voices of his long novels and his short, in his derisions, satires, lampoons, Roth called attention to the self-declared aloofness of his fictional intelligence by the way he worried surprising details and emphasized odd facts in people's behavior. Nathan Zuckerman, the narrator of the story "Courting Disaster," recounts his childhood habit, when given puzzles and arithmetic problems, of dwelling on points different from those he was expected to notice. This "seemingly irrelevant speculation of an imaginary nature" was to become in Roth's own work a stress on his thoughtfulness as an observer. But the marked overstress of oddities was Roth's way of focusing his real subject, social style. The *show* of any extreme, opened to the aroused fine eye of Roth as narrator,[3] became Roth's way of grasping people fictionally. Harriet in *Goodbye, Columbus*, about to marry into the Patimkin family, "impressed me as a young lady singularly unconscious of a motive in others or herself. All was surfaces, and seemed a perfect match for Ron, and too for the Patimkins. . . . She nodded her head insistently whenever anyone spoke. Sometimes she would even say the last few words of your sentence with you. . . ."

Roth wrote from sharpness as his center, his safety. Yet in a period when many young Jewish writers became almost too fond of "absurdity" as a style, and saw fiction as a series of throwaway lines, Roth—no Lenny Bruce even if he sometimes mimed like one—was notable for his moral lucidity and compactness. He had this ability to figure out a situation stylistically: the style of something was both its comedy and its allegory. Each of the stories in *Goodbye, Columbus* made a point; each defined a social situation without any waste and extended it to evident issues. Even when Roth, in his 1961 lecture "Writing American Fiction," found America "absurd," he insisted on defining the absurdity head-on, made it a problem to be solved, above all established its neatly laid-out *comic* reality. Two teen-age sisters in Chicago, Pattie and Babs Grimes, had disappeared, were rumored dead. It turned out that they had been living with two tramps in a flophouse. The mother gave interviews to the Chicago press and basked in her sudden fame. Roth found in this episode the kind of scandalousness, disorder all around, which he was always to take with the greatest possible seriousness, even when he mockingly imitated it:

> The American writer in the middle of the 20th century has his hands full in trying to describe, and then to make credible, much of the American reality. It stupefies, it sickens, it infuriates, and finally it is even a kind of embarrassment to one's own meager imagination. The actuality is continually outdoing our talents, and the culture tosses up figures almost daily that are the envy of any novelist. Who, for example, could

have invented Charles Van Doren? Roy Cohn and David Schine? Sherman Adams and Bernard Goldfine? Dwight David Eisenhower?

Roth seemed willing to meet the problem. But though the 1960s closed on more public disorder than Roth could have dreamed of, he did not become the novelist of this disorder, or even the journalist of it, as Mailer did. Roth significantly scored his first popular success with *Portnoy's Complaint*, which succeeded as a comic monologue with baleful overtones, very much in the style of a stand-up Jewish comic. The exactitude and fury of memory, the omnivorous detail going back to the most infantile rejections and resentments, captured perfectly a generation psyche which was more anchored on family, and more resentful of it, than any other. Now its novelists found the analyst's couch, the confession, the psychoanalytical recital, the litany of complaint, its most serviceable literary form.

In Portnoy the Jewish son had his revenge, as in Bellow's novels the Jewish son had his apotheosis. A whole middle class of sons and daughters, turning and turning within the gyre of the nuclear Jewish family—nucleus indeed of the Jewish experience and the first scenario of the psychoanalytic drama—found in Portnoy its own fascination with the details of childhood. It was this emphasis on the unmentionable, Roth's gift for zanily working out usually inaccessible details to the most improbable climax, like Portnoy masturbating into a piece of liver, that was the farce element so necessary to Roth's anger. There was the calculated profanation of mother, father, the most intimate offices of the body—a profanation by now altogether healthy to those therapeutized members of the professional middle class to whom everything about the body had become, like the possibility of universal destruction through the Bomb, small talk at the dinner table. Portnoy's howls of rage, love and anguish were so concentrated that this made them funny. Some of the incidents were so improbable that this alone made them necessary. Ronald Nimkin, the young pianist, hanged himself in the bathtub. Portnoy reminisces:

> My favorite detail from the Ronald Nimkin suicide: even as he is swinging from the shower head, there is a note pinned to the dead young pianist's short-sleeved shirt:—"Mrs. Blumenthal called. Please bring your mah-jongg rules to the game tonight. Ronald."

In any event, the Jewish mother had by now become such a piece of American folklore—I'll make fun of my ethnic if you'll make fun of yours—that *Portnoy's* success may be attributed to the fact that Roth was the first writer so obsessed with the Jewish family as to remove all the mystery from the Jewish experience. Roth secularized it all to the last micrometer of stained underwear, yet gave it his own "hard," fanatically enumerative quality. Whom do *you* suffer for, Alex Portnoy? I suffer for me. To be Jewish is to resent. What made Roth interesting in all this was that, with all his comic animosity, he was still glued to the Jewish family romance and depended on an "emancipated" Jewish audience as much as he depended on Jews for his best material. "Your book has so many readers!" I once heard an admirer say to Roth. "Why," she continued enthusiastically, "you must have at least six million readers!"

The "Jewish" identity of Norman Mailer lay precisely in the fact, as he said in *The Armies of the Night*, that to be a nice Jewish boy was the one role unacceptable to him. By this Mailer meant a rejection not of Jewishness—that would have been bourgeois and out of date—but of the sweetness, the conscious propriety that would have limited his social curiosity, social omnivorousness, his proven ability to play as many parts as possible in his books and through his books. More than any other novelist of this period (he was said to have "sacrificed" his career as a novelist to this) Mailer projected Mailer into the variousness of American life. He became not a famous novelist like Hemingway but, like another Mailer hero, Jack Kennedy, so much a personification of the ambitious American male that Mailer willingly offered himself up on the public stage as both a model and a hazard.

Mailer became recklessly and extravagantly a piece of American life because he was willing to prolong *his* individuality, *his* Jewish defiance, to the limit. He, for one, would find out in every nook and cranny of his psychic existence what it was like to be the most unassimilable Jew in American society. What was "Jewish" in this was his conscious exceeding of the group, and of other writers; he would be champ. As Disraeli said on becoming prime minister, "I have climbed to the top of the greasy pole." In a period when some Jews took pride in not being nice—"priests and Jews are civically timid," thought Kant—Mailer insisted on upsetting all expectations. He would play bad. But what was creative in this "role" was Mailer's belief in the validity of his most private thoughts. He made his fantasies interesting to many Americans. He would write as if, yes, he believed in the Devil. The Mailer who became such a laughable, publicizable part of the American consciousness was always there because he had somehow turned his most intimate wishes and fears into public symbols. Mailer accomplished what so few novelists were still able to do—he made his mind public. He was definitely not one of that minority group which will always feel excluded from the great American reality. He was inside this reality and on every side of it, willing to shift for a better view at a moment's notice. The voraciousness of American life, its power in human affairs, its fury of transformation, had found in Mailer a writer who would always find any and all of it "credible," who would never regard America as "a kind of embarrassment to one's own meager imagination."

Mailer began, in *The Naked and the Dead*, as a novelist traditional but forceful. Through the inevitable ups and downs of being a novelist—the second book, *Barbary Shore*, read like the deliberately off-beat book that will follow a best seller—Mailer wrote mysteriously about a Long Novel in the making that something equally important kept him from accomplishing to his satisfaction (his first sign of turning himself into a Cause). He wrote advertisements not for himself but for this Long Novel. There was as yet nothing he so much wanted to do as to beat Hemingway (his idol, personal and literary) at Hemingway's own game. The intense but speculative interest in politics again showed itself in *Barbary Shore*—a novel of conspiracy, a deliberate exercise in political paranoia about a radical in a Brooklyn Heights rooming house who is really a government agent. This plot, like many of Mailer's future intuitions about the amount of plot in American life, turned out to be an inspired guess. Many ex-radicals were now government agents and CIA money had been secretly channeled through cultural foundations to impress them with the importance of the right anticommunist line. But the depressed and windy monologue of the confessedly "sick" narrator, a war casualty, also signaled a moodiness of Mailer's, psychic, intellectual, political, that would never choose silence when it could box the universe with words. Mailer's many words would always depend on his psychic intuition into the staggeringly involved experience of our time. He was indeed an "existential" seeker of the truth the uncovering of which was the real value of any situation. Himself as the only oracle and prophet needed to grab the golden ring of truth as he spun round and round the carousel. "Truth" as the shifting existential fact. Prophecy as disclosure of the mysterious hidden will behind human behavior. The frantic joy of seizing the hidden "connections" of things. There was beauty, there was truth, with Mailer as the only discoverer you needed to know. These had obviously become more important to Mailer than the literary ideals that had prompted him to give out so many advance warnings, Joyce-like, of a great work in progress.

Mailer was not going to write his "long novel." This intended a tribute to an age that was already behind him—the age of the single masterpiece, the "perfect" work of art, to which a Joyce or Proust dedicated his life. But Mailer was going to turn his diagnostic skills, his personal verve, his instinct for all that could be taking place simultaneously in America, into a heady demonstration of personal insight. He would become a cultural force—that is, operating like a nineteenth-century man of letters—even as he insisted on himself as a threat to all those timid folk who would not follow him on his personal trek through the unconventional. Thanks partly to the influence of Wilhelm Reich's emphasis on sexual openness as the key to self-liberation in everything, Mailer now began *his* public confession and defiance. In *The Deer Park* he used ideological sex as a counterweapon to the Hollywood terrorized in the Fifties by the blacklist. As always with Mailer, "politics" as an arena of conflict was equal to sexuality, and had the same issue: never be a loser! Charles Eitel—I tell—the Hollywood director and ex-communist pushed out of the industry because he wouldn't tell—finally yields to pressure from the producers. He is down to his last resources in Desert D'Or, Palm Springs. But since Eitel finally gives in, what is he doing as a propagandist of sexuality as "knowledge"—and why does he fascinate us? Mailer's confidence in his ability to write a novel without caring any longer about The Novel was as striking in *The Deer Park* as his distraction. Eitel, supposedly the political refugee from both Stalinism and McCarthyism, and therefore a model American radical of our time, finally shows himself an alchemist. He is trying to change sex into pure spirit by way of his mistress, a wretchedly untalented nightclub performer who in fact excites him because in her own utter lack of confidence she is entirely at his mercy. Eitel the dominator (in bed) might or might not have had something to learn from the weakness of his mistress. But he had nothing to teach his alter ego, Norman Mailer, for whom sexual sensations communicated themselves as psychic events, Faustian claims to knowledge. Eitel and Elena settling into the routine of lovemaking:

> And Eitel felt changes in his body race beyond the changes in his mind, as though all those nerves and organs which he had tired almost to death were coming back to life, carrying his mind in their path, as if Elena were not only his woman but his balm. . . . They would explore a little further, he would come back with more.

Eitel in crisis "would gamble for knowledge . . . like a cave wanderer he would be able to wander into himself."

This claim to knowledge from within, romanticism as propaganda, based on the sacred intuitions of Mailer himself, was now to give Mailer's polemical imagination a fury of dissemination all over the American land that went beyond what anyone might have predicted of the dutiful naturalist behind *The Naked and the Dead* and the gloomy radical behind *Barbary Shore*. Even before he published *The Deer Park* Mailer had shown this ability to make his imagination public. One somehow knew not Mailer himself—that would always be too much for him and everyone else—but Mailer's fetishes, his drive, his necessary plunge into events, his ability to make connections between his psyche and American life. So insistent was this intuition, with Mailer's ability to spread every particle of as news to the outside world, that it imposed itself through *The Deer Park, An American Dream, Why Are We in Vietnam?*, not because these books communicated themselves as novels, but because they didn't.

Mailer's fantasies and ideas broke into the texture of every fiction he now wrote—and one remembered these books. Mailer succeeded in imposing his personal sense of things, as he did not his novels; his characteristic sense of imbalance, of different orders of reality to be *willed* together, did in fact reflect the imbalance between everyone's inner life and the constant world of public threat. This was the way the liberal imagination did in fact think of its problems. As a series of circles, not interlocking but fascinating each other; personality was a theater, politics another. Mailer's "new journalism" was to dramatize this split consciousness with radical gestures. The Marxist view of the world as a consistent piece of reality economic, social, cultural, could not have been less real at this time. Still, there was no escaping the violent eruptions created by the pressure on everything in sight of American power, wealth, the seeming unlimitedness of national and personal ambition. But whatever Mailer's fantasies of cultural authority in this situation, his several powerful insights were too scattered and spasmodic to make his *ideas* influential. As he said of *An American Dream*, "it might prove for some to be my most substantial attack on the problem of writing a novel of manners."[4] What made these novels, even the deliberately scatological farce *Why Are We in Vietnam?*, so effective as messages to the age (in between messages on the antiwar demonstration before the Pentagon, national political conventions, the heavyweight championship, the flight to the moon, women's lib) was the fact that in fiction, fortunately, Mailer could not incessantly be on top of all his material. He was traveling too fast, and despite every effort to show himself in control, looked more like the eye of the hurricane. He was always on the spot, a witness to his participation.

What was striking about Mailer's adventurist fiction was the sense of risk that for him pervaded everything in America. The American Faust was rushing to meet God or the Devil. Despite the bullying effect of his over-writing, Mailer's typical fantasy in *Why Are We in Vietnam?*, of a transistor planted in the body through the rectum that may "contact" the mind of God, did express the fright at the heart of contemporary consciousness. Since the Devil was assuredly loose again, man had desperately to reach the God whose hidden will was behind the force of things. This despair, Mailer's own frantic will despite his personal cockiness—this was to make the experience of reading him equal to a plunge into the age. We were at its mercy.

Bellow's Jewishness had increased over the years to the point where old Mr. Sammler's control, sobriety, wisdom had become the only protection against the age. Jewishness Mailer disliked because it limited and intellectualized. The world was too open, the disorder too flagrant, to permit oneself any identity but this possibility of total receptivity through oneself.

With his contempt for knowledge-as-control, his desire to leave all those centuries of Jewish tradition (and of Jewish losers) behind him, Mailer represents the unresting effort and overreaching of the individual Jewish writer who seeks to be nothing but an individual (and if possible, a hero). By contrast, Isaac Bashevis Singer represents the transformation of all Jewish history into fiction, fable, story. He accepts it for his own purposes. He is a skeptic who is hypnotized by the world he grew up in. No one else in modern Jewish writing stems so completely from the orthodox and even mystical East European tradition. No one else has turned "*the tradition*" into the freedom of fiction, the subtlety and mischievousness and truthfulness of storytelling. Singer, totally a fiction writer but summing up the East European Yiddish tradition in his detached, fatalistic, plainspoken way, represents a peculiar effortlessness in the writing of "Jewish fiction," when compared with the storminess of Bellow and Mailer. That is because Singer shares the orthodox point of view without its belief, and he meticulously describes, without sentimentalizing any Jew whatever, a way of life which was murdered with the millions who lived it. The demons and spirits so prominent in Singer's East European narratives have in his "American" ones become necessary to the survivors. "It is chilling," V. S. Pritchett noticed, "to know that he is describing ghosts who cannot even haunt because their habitat has been wiped out."

The occult presences in Singer's work represent that belief in another world which Singer grew up with, but which no longer necessarily represents "God's" world. There may very well be a God, since we are in the grip of forces so clearly beyond our power to understand and change them. But His, Its, inscrutability is the only attribute. Singer has transposed the terms without abandoning them.

There was a great religious tradition among Jews in eastern Europe. Orthodoxy was deeply habitual for millions, ritualized to the point where a pious existence was *interrupted* by one's outer existence. The inwardness of this "true" existence seems to have moved into Singer's work as a mental body, pages and pages. What is extraordinary in Singer's work is the conversion of the Jews—into storytelling. Singer was the son of an ultraorthodox Warsaw rabbi. He was brought up to follow the letter of the law that is all letter, punctilio, observance—the magnification in every possible instance of God's will, God's concern, God's observance of His creatures. There was a horror of the "unclean"—that is, the world itself. In his memoir, *In My Father's Court*, Singer describes his father firmly closing the windows of his study on the screams of a woman being raped in a Warsaw street. But his son the storyteller, though still in the orthodox costume of gabardine and wide-brimmed velvet hat, showed his independence by finally, one day, going out on the balcony to look at the life of Warsaw. He was to write about everything he knew in this unholy world, to sit apart from the tradition in order to describe the human experience of it. But some deep spirit of acceptance, still, not of God but of fact, enabled him to write and write with astounding ease—and without the tension so marked in his gifted brother Israel Joshua Singer (author of *Yoshe Kalb* and *The Brothers Ashkenazi*), who had a more painful struggle with tradition and family and was concerned with heresy and "immorality" as dramatic situations.

Isaac Bashevis Singer, who came to America in the 1930s and wrote for the Yiddish press, was after the war to become, through English versions of his work, the most widely accepted of all modern Yiddish writers. Living and writing in America, he somehow seemed the survivor and novelist of a whole tradition that had been destroyed by the Nazis and Communists, and that tormented its descendants in America because they had no access to it, perhaps had never had any—and so had no way of explaining why so many Jews had gone to their deaths.

Singer, who would not have presumed to offer an explanation, provided through his fiction the only one needed: the Jewish tradition. In English "translation" that was often adaptation, writing to Jews and non-Jews alike who could not read Yiddish, Singer became the fictional historian of the whole Jewish experience in eastern Europe because his extraordinary intelligence and detached point of view turned the heart of the tradition—acceptance of God's law, God's will, even God's slaughter of His own—into story, legend, fantasy. And Singer himself believed in acceptance: of human nature, the world's wickedness, God's total mysteriousness, the peculiarity of Jews themselves. The audience that read him week after week in the Yiddish newspaper was too close to view it as the last word, and many of these readers missed Singer's sophistication, artfulness and cunning use of the tradition in his work. Indeed, Singer was so cool in both senses of that American word that his gifts were not readily appreciated by other Yiddish writers. There is a brilliant and funny story by Cynthia Ozick, "Yiddish in America," about an unsuccessful Yiddish writer who cannot understand the fame of "Ostrover" and is convinced that it is all a matter of finding the right translator. But of course it was Singer's own lightness, ease and resourcefulness that convinced so many readers that, for all they knew, the tradition now lived only in the pages of Isaac Bashevis Singer. As Singer delightedly said, "I call myself a bilingual writer and say that English has become my 'second original!' "

Through this "second" language Singer reached American Jews often dominated unconsciously by the customs of their ancestors, but for whom the customs had disappeared with the ancestors. This gave Singer his unforeseen, ironic, much-enjoyed status as an American writer. He was the only American Jewish writer who knew the tradition so thoroughly that it was *in* him, and so he could simulate the credulity, the innocence, the timorousness, above all the unworldliness. Was it possible that in the twentieth century whole masses of people should have believed that *whatever* happened was God's will? Singer the storyteller had his own version of this: the wickedness of the world is never an "historical" accident, and what is happening has always happened. Things are as they are. The evidence of this world is to be accepted. Singer could thus make his characters real as Jews: they were the people of acceptance.

With such characters there would seem to be missing the decisive element in modern fiction—the indetermination of one's own existence to oneself, freedom as one's only heaven and hell. Unlike the many Jewish personae in modern American fiction, for whom a wholly willed, insistent claim on existence is the very theme of their striving and suffering, Singer's characters live in relation to God as the Power in and behind everything. They lived, the East European Jews were as a matter of fact the last generation to live, wholly in the eye of God—they lived to be responsive to God alone.

This mysterious fidelity, total obligation, meant that not individual characters but their way of life is the real matter of a Singer story. What the reader sees is never the individual's effort to determine his own life, but the fact that he is constantly being acted on—like the poor cuckold and unconscious saint in Singer's best story, "Gimpel The Fool"—by the whole force of his culture. There the dead wife appears to the husband she had cheated in every possible sense in order to keep Gimpel from blaspheming the tradition.

Of course Singer's characters include sinners like Yasha in *The Magician of Lublin* and those many demons, imps, sprites who move in and out of Singer's world as naturally as Jewish relatives—which they are. And in his bitter American novel, *Enemies: A Love Story*, he shows how irreparably the survivors of Hitler's and Stalin's camps had been crazed by the condemnation of Jews. But what Singer's many damaged and insatiable characters in America feel as the real force in their lives is still the Jewish tradition—because they cannot come to terms with it. The world is twice wicked because they cannot understand it. It has done everything to them, and still they do not live *in* it. They live in their imagination, as they did when they were believers.

Notes

1. "Up to their necks in dung," an old East European *rebbe* said of his seminarians, "they dream of ancient Assyria, Babylonia, Palestine."

2. An image in Kafka's parables.

3. Many of Roth's narratives are in the first person. This may be a necessity for him, since it enables him to change his voice without diminishing the sharp personal effect of "acting" someone like Portnoy. Monologue gives Roth a chance to act out traits, to "become" someone by a different patter.

In "On the Air," the hilarious but finally grotesque story of an intended journey to Princeton by one Lippman, a paranoiac talent scout who hopes to induce Einstein to become an "answer man" on the radio, Roth's delight in the man's spoken style *and* his mania, in the assorted freaks and horrors Lippman runs into at a Howard Johnson, finally makes the reader feel that while Roth will try out any situation, humanity is too mad and vicious to deserve this much attention.

4. *An American Dream* is in fact a novel of ambition, a snob document, which is why it is often unintentionally funny in its posturing. Barney Kelly on top of the Waldorf Towers describes himself as a "grand (not good) Catholic." "Once you're located where I am, there's nothing left but to agitate the web. At my worst, I'm a spider. Have strings in everywhere from the Muslims to the *New York Times*."

It is amusing to note how few Jews interrupt Mailer's recent communings with power. A noteworthy exception and a self-proving narrative is "The Time of Her Time," which was described in *Advertisements for Myself* as part of a "Long Novel." It puts the would-be-Irish hero, Sergius O'Shaugnessy, to grips with the ungiving Jewish girl, Denise Gondelman. IIe tries to conquer her in the contemporary style—to force her to satisfaction. But though he succeeds technically he has nothing else of her. And at the end she has a sexual insult for him.

A Denise Gondelman is indeed rare in Mailer's later fiction. He much prefers a devil figure like Deborah Caughlin Mangaravidi Kelly who is as socially important as she is wicked. Her husband says after he kills her, "She smelled like a bank."

Mailer's mythology of personal power works as episode in scene after scene of *An American Dream*. His fantasies are irrepressible, as in the descriptions of sex with Deborah's "Nazi" maid Ruta, on whom Rojack performs, mythically. As always in reading Mailer's descriptions of intercourse, one is impressed by how much of a war novelist he has remained.

In "The Time of Her Time" he is really inside the psychic "cave" the Mailer hero is always talking about. And the experience—the genuine internality described—is of a man's *sensations*, comparatively rare in other writers' unilluminating descriptions of sex as performance. And since sex as sex is comedy, not mythology, "The Time of Her Time" amuses the reader instead of instructing him.

Philip Roth

Mark Shechner*

"To each obstructed citizen his own Kafka."
"And to each angry one his own Melville."
"But then what are bookish people to do with all the great
prose they read—"
"—but sink their teeth into it. Exactly. Into the books, instead of into the hand that throttles them."

—Dialogue from Philip Roth's
The Professor of Desire.

The road of excess leads to the palace of wisdom.

—Blake

I knew something about Philip Roth before 1967. Since I had once
lived in Newark I had read *Goodbye, Columbus* and, the Jersey Jewish
world being a small one, had an aunt who claimed to know the real
Brenda Patimkin but wasn't about to tell. And I knew from the reviews
that Roth had published two novels subsequent to the *Columbus* stories
and that they were indifferently received. I knew that they were long and
not about Newark and I did not read them. I first looked into "Whacking
Off," a *Partisan Review* piece which some of my graduate student colleagues were passing about, just as some twenty years before their
grammar school counterparts had passed around *The Amboy Dukes*. That
was unique, for in our time and in that place, Berkeley, 1967, communities of knowledge did not as a rule form around fiction: we communed,
when we had to, over *Zap Comics*, zap politics, literary criticism, or
Country Joe and the Fish.

Our motives in recommending Roth to each other were clear enough:
spontaneous fraternities that form around texts are essentially confessional communities. If none of us bore all of Portnoy's anxieties or identified with each fear and every confidence, we all understood in our own
lives some portion of his complaint. Each of us had his oral or anal or
phallic secret that itched to be revealed. As outwardly sedate and

*Reprinted from *Partisan Review*, 41 (1974), 410–27, © 1974 by Partisan Review, by permission.

117

upwardly-mobile graduate students, we longed to be known to each other, behind our backs, as private sinners. And the serial publication of *Portnoy*, as it rolled on through "The Jewish Blues" and "Civilization and its Discontents" (in *New American Review*), assured us that Roth had secrets enough for all of us.

Since then, however, two things have complicated, without necessarily diminishing, my enthusiasm for Roth's writing. The first has been the discovery that my loyalty to *Portnoy* as a version of truth and my conviction that Roth has talent have not been widely shared, certainly not among Jews. The second source of complication is Roth's own work subsequent to *Portnoy*. While his voluminous writing of late has kept his talent on full, hilarious display, it has failed somehow to satisfy my own, somewhat unformed, expectations. The first matter, the opposition of *the* Jews, is of course no barrier to admiration. In the conflict between Roth and the numerous voices of Jewish disapproval, a conflict which goes back to 1959 and the publication of *Goodbye, Columbus*, Roth is right and his critics wrong. For their quarrel with him is not properly over literature or any aspects thereof but over culture, and institutional Jewry in America these days has a decidedly rigid, defensive notion of culture. That notion, I might add, may be a historical necessity and a condition of survival, but the Bar Lev lines of the heart do interfere with the reading of fiction. The second matter is that of Roth's talent and the uses to which he has put it which for me is a more serious matter. It too, though, points us away from literature and toward, in this instance, psychology. Everything about Roth's recent writing suggests the need for a psychological inquiry. *Portnoy's Complaint* itself calls to mind that little-known first book by Sigmund Freud: *Studies in Hysteria*. But these two faces of Roth-in-the-world, the Jew and the writer *cum* psychological man, are the two sides of his writer's identity. Roth the novelist and culture critic is also Roth the son. Observe the abundant filial torments of Alex Portnoy. Observe too Bruno Bettelheim's psychoanalysis of him in *Midstream*, with its peevish diagnosis of Alex's neurotic conflicts. Alex, after a mere six hours on the couch, is dismissed by his analyst, Spielvogel, aka Bettelheim, as a three-way loser. He is a bad patient, a bad Jew, and a bad boy. As therapy, Bettelheim's diagnostic putdown of Alex may look like a novelty but as criticism it is a cliche, just another sad complaint about what the critics mistakenly call Roth's "self-hatred."

That line of argument reached its fruition in Irving Howe's "Philip Roth Reconsidered" in the December 1972 *Commentary*. Howe complains there of Roth's personal and ideological assertiveness, of his stance of adolescent superiority to suburban Jewish life, of his nagging habit of "scoring points" instead of striving for imaginative plenitude, of his failure to render a "full and precise" portrait of his Jewish victims, and of his essential joylessness. This failure, Howe observes, is a failure of culture. Roth's stories and novels fall short of something like Tolstoyan amplitude because "they come out of a thin personal culture." Roth, we are told, has uprooted himself from "the mainstream of American culture, in its great sweep of democratic idealism and romanticism." Howe is not wholly wrong. Roth's anger is a crucial property of his art and his books bring laughter without bringing cheer. His failure of magnanimity is considerable and his ample wit sports a chilling, mechanical edge. A book like *The Great American Novel*, which draws its humor from an assemblage of freaks, cripples, dwarfs, stage Jews, and stagier *goyim*, adds little to his reputation for compassion. Nor will the book's loose collection of bits and routines earn him any points toward what Howe has called with Arnoldian sobriety, "compositional rigor and moral seriousness."

But for all that, Howe's lecture on Roth's cultural impoverishment is gratuitous. The trouble with it is that there is just enough truth in certain localized accusations to obscure the fact that Howe is entirely insensible of any of Roth's virtues and wholly unappreciative of skills that a critic of his stature and acumen might be expected to applaud. And to be insensitive to Roth's skillful deployment of language, to his overmastering wit, and to his gift for exact rendition of small psychological truths is no small failing in a critic. (As if we need reminders that the realm of *values* is not that of *taste*.) Clearly, it is not Roth's values as such that Howe is aggrieved by, but his character, and such is the animus of the essay that one might want to ask after hidden agendas, dim regions of mind whose force is everywhere apparent but whose reasons are everywhere veiled. In Howe's fatherly rush to deal out stern lessons in conduct, which has become his stock-in-trade ever since he became an elder statesman of letters, what the devilish son has actually been doing with his idle hands is hastily over-looked.

In all this delectable comedy of fathers and sons, Roth too has played his part, more consciously than Howe, for his image of himself as perennial Jewish son would seem to be at the very core of his identity. It surely has everything to do with his attachment to Kafka, another Jewish son with a painful and debilitating relationship to fatherhood (see " 'I Always Wanted You to Admire My Fasting'; or, Looking at Kafka," *American Review*). "Marrying is barred to me," confesses this Kafka to his father, "because it is your domain." But the sons we discover in Roth's fiction differ from Kafka's in this crucial respect: it is not the father's power that condemns them to impotence and bachelorhood; it is his weakness. The secret of the terror behind Roth's fiction is the realization that the father is impotent. In fact, Roth himself may be braced and encouraged by the opposition of the Rabbis, for the father's enmity is preferable to his adoration. "Others," he confesses in his Kafka essay, "are crushed by paternal criticism—I find myself oppressed by his high opinion of me!" There is no escape from the ineffectual father, for the son's oedipal guilt is renewed daily by the father's failures. "Make my father a father," cries Lucy

Nelson (*When She Was Good*), and she, a daughter, broadcasts this appeal on behalf of all the Roth sons, before and after.

Roth rewrites the opening sentence of *The Metamorphosis* this way: "As Franz Kafka awoke one morning from uneasy dreams he found himself transformed in his bed into a father, a writer, and a Jew." This Kafka is no gigantic insect with three pairs of legs quivering helplessly before his eyes but a man with three afflictions: Jewishness, talent, and fatherhood, the last, the greatest affliction of all. Imagine a Kafka, or a Roth, trying to love that brilliant issue of his loins known as a son. "Keep him away from me," screams a young, imaginary Roth in the Kafka piece. Jake Portnoy's bowels answer in frozen rage from the pages of an earlier book. Paternity is a legal fiction in Roth's books where sons and fathers turn out to be brothers under the skin, locked into generations by an unfortunate biological fate. What is Isaac to do when Abraham drops the knife and gets down on the chopping block with him? That is Roth's real dilemma. And that is why manhood in his books never gets farther than a dream of center field. The son's chief concern is not to escape his father's wrath but to short-circuit his sentimentality; the thing he doesn't want to do is make his father cry.

With fatherhood in doubt, all other relationships are in trouble. Relationships, in Roth's world, are painful experiments whose failures may be preferable to their shame-ridden successes. Men and women are natural enemies who do horrible things when they mistakenly get together, for marrying is surely as barred to Roth's sons as ever it was to Kafka's.[1] It is a good thing for Aunt Rhoda ("Looking at Kafka") that Dr. Kafka's problem is revealed to her *before* the marriage at that Atlantic City Hotel, for marriage is a fate worse than lifelong loneliness. Love is a front for aggression; sex is an occasion for failure; childhood is tragedy; adulthood farce. The family, according to Roth, doesn't pass on culture; it transmits symptoms. In such a world, to be a child is excruciating; to be a parent is unimaginable.

If Roth's books read like case histories, so does the profile of his entire career. It begins with an orderly and sedate fiction about straight-laced heroes who fail at some relationship or vital task and manifest their disappointment in "symptoms," spontaneous outbreaks of anger, unreason, or vertigo. Mrs. Portnoy calls them "conniption fits." The early books, the *Goodbye, Columbus* stories, *Letting Go*, and *When She Was Good*, with their repressed and driven characters, constitute a fiction of failed renunciation. Their heroes are all characters who repress desires which, as we might expect, refuse to go away and keep returning in the form of compulsive and irrational behavior. In *Letting Go*, the mutual renunciation of Gabe Wallach and Libby Herz (based on their mutual reading of *A Portrait of a Lady*) is prelude to six hundred pages of indecision (his), neurasthenia (hers), confusion, and sudden, irrational tantrums (theirs). In *When She Was Good*, the praise accorded to Willard Nelson in the very opening sentence tells us exactly what is wrong with him. "Not to be rich, not to be famous, not to be mighty, not even to be happy, but to be civilized—that was the dream of his life." A man who has given up that much might prosper in a novel of manners, but when Jamesian pretensions surface in a novel by Roth, things go haywire. When Roth hears the word *civilization*, he reaches for his discontents. And in fact, Lucy Nelson, who has learned from Grandpa Willard the virtues of small-town character armor, reaps its rewards when faced with the demands of pregnancy and abandonment. Her studied reaction-formations are revealed to be useless and she goes berserk with terror and righteousness.

Portnoy's Complaint advertises itself as Roth's psychic breakthrough, the book in which the Yid grapples with repression and lays claim to his Id. An oppressive childhood is dragged into the light; a wild sexual fantasy life makes its debut seemingly undistorted by style or euphemism; the Jewish mother in all her ambiguous effulgence replaces the father at stage center; her son's masturbation is magnificently confessed and celebrated; food is revealed to be an agent of both repression and liberation, and eating turns out to have something to do with love and sex. The book ends with nothing less than the primal scream, all ninety-six *a*'s and four *h*'s of it, after which Dr. Spielvogel delivers, and blows, the punch line. This book appears to deliver all the right confessions demanded of an analysis: confessions of undue bondage to the past, of secret humiliations and secret rages, of crimes against the family, of failures of the body and overcompensations of the will.

Post *Portnoy* we have been treated to the breakthrough books and stories: "On the Air" (*New American Review*), a savage and barely controlled saga of one day in the life of Milton Lippmann, talent scout; *Our Gang*, the book of pure malice: *The Breast*, an experiment in controlled regression with an old-fashioned stoical message; " 'I Always Wanted You to Admire My Fasting'; or "Looking at Kafka," a lecture turned fantasy of Franz Kafka's possible adventures in Newark; *The Great American Novel*, a four-hundred page free association around the theme of baseball, and *My Life as a Man*, a novel about marriage in the fifties. Up until the last book, which appears to return to older modes of writing, Roth's progress throughout this period seemed to bear an identifiable form: the early books, pre-*Portnoy*, were the documents of repression, the later writings, witnesses to the return of the repressed. Where Roth used to give us stoical characters who bore their misfortunes with the sullen nobility of the truly civilized until overtaken by sudden, irrational outbursts, he more recently has turned to showing us literary surfaces that look like primary process thought. Where repression was we now have rage; in lieu of symptoms we now get style.[2]

The accumulated work, the oeuvre, begins to come into view as a sustained exercise in self-analysis, on a scale otherwise unknown in American literature since Hawthorne, and Roth would appear to have the advantage of Hawthorne in both his imagination and his knowledge of neurosis, having read both Freud and Kafka. If we are taken aback by Roth's writing it is largely because we are not accustomed to all this digging and sifting of motives, this ceaseless pursuit of latent content through exhaustive self-inquisition and self-accusation. Upon its appearance, *Portnoy's Complaint* was the most spectacular attempt at Freudian fiction in recent American literature, not only because of the apparent boldness of its confessions, but because of Spielvogel's summary diagnosis, which challenged us with its crisp Germanic expertise. And despite the imposing clinical and theoretical apparatus of the latest book, *My Life as a Man*, the former, I think, is more successful as psychological fiction, perhaps because Alex manages to achieve with wit what Peter Tarnopol and Spielvogel (who is his analyst also) do with theory. Alex, to be sure, knows his theory also: he annotates his complaint with appropriate references to *The Standard Edition*, though he modestly claims to be reading only *The Collected Papers*. We know that he has read "The Most Prevalent Form of Degradation in Erotic Life," and that he practices it, and that he is familiar with *Civilization and Its Discontents*, as both text and dilemma. His furtive sexuality is supposed to mediate the demands of a clamorous, infantile id and a vigilant, righteous superego, and fails. Thus, according to Spielvogel: "Acts of exhibitionism, voyeurism, fethishism, autoeroticism and oral coitus are plentiful; as a consequence of the patient's 'morality,' however, neither fantasy nor act issues in genuine sexual gratification, but rather in overriding feelings of shame and the dread of retribution, particularly in the form of castration." That is a cogent and inclusive sentence and, in fact, the complaint (here meaning malady, not *geschrei*), stripped of its cultural paraphernalia and defensive wit, does make sense as a strategy for negotiating deep-psychic conflict. Moreover, believes Spielvogel, "many of the symptoms can be traced to the bonds obtaining in the mother-child relationship." The doctor has saved us some research here, though his categories, like most diagnostic labels, are textbookish and preemptive; they substitute the mannerisms of analysis for explanation, and if the analytic sections of *My Life as a Man* are any indication of what Spielvogel sounds like when he is under a full head of steam, we, and Alex Portnoy, should be more appreciative of his enigmatic silences in the earlier book. Still, he has the right idea: the fictional imitation of confession *is* confession and we as readers have some duty to make sense of what we are being so desperately told.

To set the stage for an analysis of our own we have to set the table, for *Portnoy's Complaint* is an exposé, no, a vaudeville, of the Jewish stomach. Food is to Jewish comedy and Jewish neurosis what drink is to Irish, though only Roth so far has taken the full anthropological plunge into the ethnology of the Jewish digestive tract. Roth's Jews are not a *people*, a *culture, nation, tradition*, or any other noun of rabbinical piety.

They are a *tribe*, which, after its own primitive fashion, observes arbitrary taboos and performs strange sundown rituals that look like obsessional symptoms. Roth's particular neurotic style of observing the world has this virtue: a lucid and unsentimental eye for styles of irrational behavior, his own included. As he sees it, the kosher laws are as primitive and irrational as any Australian fetish or Papuan cult of cargo, and the dietary antagonism of milk and meat in the Jewish diet is something, not out of Leviticus, but out of Róheim.

Portnoy's morality, not to mention his immorality, begins at the table. Here is *The Law* according to that Moses of Manhattan, the Assistant Commissioner of Human Opportunity for the City of New York. "Let the *goyim* sink *their* teeth into whatever lowly creature crawls and grunts across the face of the dirty earth, we will not contaminate our humanity thus." Thus spake Portnoy of the superego. Now let's hear a word from Portnoy of the id. "At least let me eat your pussy." It is in that spectrum of possibilities between phobic avoidance and insane lapping that the minute moral discriminations of Jewish life are made. For us, the word *moral* derives etymologically from the word *oral*.

When a sin is committed in the Portnoy home it is more likely to involve gluttony than lechery, though in the muddled dreamwork of a complicated and unreliable memory, primal crimes often become confused. "A terrible act has been committed, and it has been committed by either my father or me. The wrongdoer, in other words, is one of the two members of the family who owns a penis. Okay. So far so good. Now: did he fuck between those luscious legs the gentile cashier from the office, or have I eaten my sister's chocolate pudding?" This confusion never does get resolved. In the infantile moral system of this household, shared by parents and children alike, pudding and pussy may be equally taboo and proscribed with equal ferocity. Food, of course, is the first medium of love and authority for all of us, and where it retains its primal power, as it does for the Portnoys, young sinners may be heard to confess: "I'm eight years old and chocolate pudding happens to get me hot." It is understandable then that the table is the battlefield on which Alex's bid for manhood is fought and lost. The toilet and the bed are also put to military uses but they are later and secondary weapons and by the time Alex has understood their potential, the war is over. Rearguard actions still rage, however, and Alex's prime weapons are all the tricks in his stubborn oral trade: "having a mouth on him," refusing to eat, eating *chazerai* (or lobster or pussy), feeding his parents in turn, or, and herein shines forth his desperate genius, fucking his family's dinner. All strategies naturally fail since the field of battle has been chosen in advance and it favors whoever has got the ammunition.

Hunger striking fails as dismally for Portnoy as it does for Kafka's hunger artist. "I always wanted you to admire my fasting," confesses the dying hunger artist to a bored overseer. Portnoy, a tougher sort, would have survived such boredom, but in a household in which food is mistaken for love, hunger artistry is merely being a bad eater and earns not disinterest but a brandished breadknife and a perverse maternal appeal to a son's future manhood: which does he want to be, weak or strong, a man or a mouse?

The politics of food and guilt at the Jewish table have given rise to a unique taboo: *chazerai*. *Chazerai* is not necessarily unkosher food, unblessed or formally proscribed by the laws; neither the hot dog nor the cupcake is mentioned by name in Leviticus. But *chazerai*, while not unkosher de jure is certainly so de facto. It is cheap, processed, mass-produced snack food, gotten outside the home, behind one's mother's back. Its true purpose, as every Jewish mother knows, is to ruin her son's appetite for dinner—her dinner. Thus the eating of snacks after school is a betrayal, and the boy who stops for a burger and fries at fourteen will, at thirty, be stopping after work for a *shikse*, thus ruining his appetite.

For the son, naturally, *chazerai* symbolizes freedom, sexual freedom. For example, here is Alex's own dietary analysis of the difference between himself and Smolka, that same Smolka who gets blown by Bubbles Girardi after Alex, crestfallen, leaves her house having come in his own eye while bringing *himself* off. "He lives on Hostess cupcakes and his own wits. I get a hot lunch and all the inhibitions thereof." But for ultimate aphrodisiacal virtue there is the lobster, a terror beyond *chazerai*, an unambiguous threat to sanity and life. Sophie Portnoy's historic bout with lobster, paralysis, and an Irish insurance salesman is textbook hysteria. "See how I'm holding my fingers" she instructs her son, a neophyte in primitive religious phenomena, "I was throwing up so hard, they got stiff just like this, like I was paralyzed. . . ."

Sophie's symptoms are prophecies for her son. Within an hour of eating a lobster with brother-in-law Morty at Sheepshead Bay, Alex has his cock out on the 107 bus, "aimed at a *shikse*." It is to protect him from such madness that a mother must keep up her dietary vigilance. Naturally this education in taboo-by-diet falls to the mother, for she understands beter than anyone how food, love, power and possession are arranged.

Is it any wonder then that this same Sophie invites Jake's new cashier from the office for a nice, home-cooked Jewish meal? Hardly, for once Anne McCaffrey has dined with the Portnoys she's hooked, and not on Jake but on his wonderful *haimische* family. "This is your real Jewish chopped liver, Anne. Have you ever had real Jewish chopped liver before?" So much for that affair, for if lobster is the Spanish fly of the Jews, real chopped liver is their saltpeter, the all-inhibiting cold hors d'oeuvre of the constipated husband. Could Jake be slipping it to that new cashier on the side? Not after that meal. For this is a totem feast and that is *his liver* they're passing around.

So it is not just a happy conjunction of horniness and opportunity that sets Alex to banging that fresh liver behind the billboard *on his way*

to a bar mitzvah lesson. It is another symbol of Alex's private *Kulturkampf*, with the liver falling victim to his relentless, educated cock. What price such victory? To have your mother serve up the conquest two hours later, healthy as milk, dry as matzo, warm and safe as your own Jewish childhood. In other words, defeat. (In the "Salad Days" section of *My Life as a Man*, Roth tries to carry this oral logic over into the plant kingdom by having Sharon Shatsky entertain Nathan Zuckerman with a floor show in which she applies to herself a dildo that happens to be a zucchini. Though funny in its way, the scene lacks resonance; Judaism was never in turmoil over vegetables. Maybe that is why Peter Tarnopol's sister Joan, in reading the story, calls the scene "morally inconsequential.")
inconsequential.")

If Alex is telling the truth, and he must be unless this is the most opaque lie or deceptive screen memory known to psychoanalysis, his mother's purposes are plain and sinister. She wants nothing less than the annexation of her son, the full possession of and control over his manhood, and she'll have it by stalling his growth at a level of oral dependence. That is why mealtime is the likeliest occasion for Alex to make that libidinal leap to the toilet, for as long as he dines at home, his mouth belongs to mama. When his manhood droops, he seeks refuge in the sure successes of boyhood love, determined to win praise at least as a good eater. Similarly, in *My Life as a Man*, it is appropriate that Nathan Zuckerman tries to face down his "boyish" disgust and demonstrate to Lydia Ketterer and himself that he is a good man and a proper lover by eating her. The ability to eat anything is one of the many false definitions of manhood that Roth's heroes try on for size.

That food and love should be so consistently mistaken for each other is no mystery. The connection between them is built into our mammalian heritage, and the job of learning the difference is an ordinary childhood task that we all perform more or less badly. The terms of that task are named by Roth in two of his titles, *The Breast* and *Letting Go*, and they stand for the primal situations out of which his characters must negotiate a way of life. For these characters, letting go is a theme of desperate urgency, for entrapment, in the form either of captivity or self-repression, is their most abiding condition. Alex Portnoy's final scream is a gesture of letting go that is native to the Roth novel. At the moment of release, the bonds of repression are torn loose allowing anger to surge peremptorily to the surface. Thus the tantrum is serious business and sooner or later in these books one is bound to be thrown. In *My Life*, Peter Tarnopol's tantrum is a moment of sexual truth: it finds him donning his wife's panties and bra in order to show her, he later explains, that "I wear the panties in this family." In *Portnoy*, it constitutes Alex's final statement, the last desperate demand before Spielvogel interrupts to commence the analysis.

Holding on and letting go are terrors because they first were wishes and it is in the struggle between those wishes that Alex is paralyzed, not in that starchy tango of id and superego so scrupulously defined by the hopelessly Freudian Spielvogel. That conflict, nurtured by a Jewish family that does not know when to call parenthood quits, can ramify into the alimentary insanity of Alex Portnoy's love life. Every odd libidinal enterprise of his is an attempt to gratify those two needs and to be a man and a baby at the same time. Recall his fantasies of Thereal McCoy, the perfect prostitute, who calls him "Big Boy" (why not just "Big Mac?") and offers up a nipple the size and shape of a toll-house cookie. What more could the infantile rebel ask for than *milk and cookies on the same dish?* In the jungle of love, it is eat or be eaten.

Every character of Roth's seems to be stuck with this obligation, to satisfy deep-seated but contrary needs at once: to grow up *and* to regress; to let go *and* to hold on; to be autonomous *and* dependent. Totalists that they are, they are unable to find and occupy a human middle ground on which self-reliance need not be isolation or love entrapment. Thus Alex Portnoy steers clear of love by laying sexual traps for himself, insuring that his experiments in love will always end in defeat. His episodes of sexual boredom and his bouts with impotence are strategically timed. It is Peter Tarnopol who, seemingly on Alex's behalf, tries to break out of the circle of sexual isolation by getting married and manages, not unpredictably, to marry a woman he fears and despises. To be sure, Maureen Johnson is a fearsome woman, but that is why Peter wants her. He marries her *in order to destroy her*, and while any woman will do for that, it is a fine point of conscience that she should seem to deserve what she eventually gets.

This same dilemma underlies that curious little book, *The Breast*, which Roth wrote some time between *Portnoy* and *My Life* and which reads like a companion piece to both. In fact, if speculation about the book's origins is of any value, it is my guess that it is an addendum to *Portnoy's Complaint* and is perhaps one of those dreams that Alex must have produced in analysis but somehow failed to report to us. For its hero, David Alan Kepesh, reads like a primary process version of Alex, his repressed infant perhaps, his latent content. Kepesh appears to be the disguised fulfillment of Alex's most repressed wish which we may now guess is to undo his ill-fated sonhood altogether in favor of a generational merger, to become, not just an infant, but his own mother. To be more explicit, that is, more clinical, if this is a dream and if we know the dreamer, as I think we do, then we can say in our cold and diagnostic way that he has dreamed of becoming his own mother by way of a psychic retreat to that period of his own infancy when the sensory focus was too primitive and diffuse for him to know who was who. The advantages to such merger are obvious: it is a way of holding on and letting go at the same time, allowing you to *have* your mother without *having to deal* with her. (And the breast, for what this may be worth, confounds the kosher laws by being *both milchig and fleischig*.) In such a dream of primal merger, the dreamer is at last on his own, self-contained, androgynous, and pleasantly autoerotic, and can indulge himself forever at the sacred fount of life without two sets of dishes. But since this dream by Alex is also a story by Roth the fulfillment of this wish is bound to exact a price. It turns out that the dream of merger is also the dream of regression and the fairy tale of sexual self-sufficiency can turn into the nightmare of total helplessness. Thus Alex Portnoy's dream of independence and autonomy becomes David Kepesh's nightmare of isolation and entrapment.

Such a situation is not propitious for fiction; Kepesh's possibilities are too limited. He can only lie there and suffer and, in the end, grow tiresome. That is the condition of the infant after all; its demands are few, simple, boring, and endless, and since it can't act out its frustrated desires, it learns instead to moralize, to develop a superego and become wise. Kepesh's condition is in fact terrifying and yet the tone of *The Breast* seems askew because Kepesh refuses to be anything but sensible. Accordingly, while *Portnoy's Complaint* is protest fiction and a brief in behalf of letting go, *The Breast* is a conservative moral fable about the virtues of holding on. It hands us the dilemma of civilization and its discontents at the most primitive infantile level and comes out foursquare for repression. Alex, with his temper, is a tiger of wrath; Kepesh, with his Shakespeare and his Rilke, is a horse of instruction. But he may have no choice; all he can do is want, and want, and want, and learn how to behave when he doesn't get. Self-repression and parental control are stultifying annoyances for the likes of Alex Portnoy, but they are cruel necessities in the moral life of an infant, or a breast. That may be why *The Breast* is so unsettling a book, for to us, Kepesh's "mature" prescription of a daily anesthetic to reduce his polymorphous appetites reinforced by therapeutic doses of Shakespeare seems like a defeatist strategy for a meager endurance. We want a magical release from breasthood and Kepesh gives us, English majors all, the fake magic of poetry. We want the primal scream and he delivers lessons about Mr. Reality. Indeed, he is unique among the likes of Ozzie Freedman, Gabriel Wallach, Lucy Nelson, Alex Portnoy, and Peter Tarnopol; he never throws a tantrum. *The Breast* is the Rothian nightmare at its most radical and its most pedantic. Kepesh, having become his own mother or at least a part of her, thumps *her* bible; his text on renunciation and endurance may be wisdom but of a familiar Jewish kind. As breasts go he is an overachiever. Nipple and all, he is learning how to be a good boy, and an English professor. Which is to say, a professor of desire.

Or, if not exactly a professor, then a visiting lecturer and Jewish novelist like Peter Tarnopol of *My Life as a Man*. Tarnopol is a thirty-four-year-old writer—author of the celebrated novel, *A Jewish Father*—widower, neurotic narcissist, teacher, and outpatient who has squandered his talent and manhood in a marriage that has left him frantic, suspicious, over his head in debt and guilt, and only just able to turn the marriage into material for a book. That book is *My Life as a Man* itself, which consists of three parts: two stories or "useful fictions," as Tarnopol calls them—"Salad Days," and "Courting Disaster (or Serious in the Fifties)"—and an autobiographical novella, "My True Story," a true confession ingeniously done up in the style of a True Confession. It is an exposé of the desperate married life of a young writer. Due partly to the ironbound divorce laws of New York State and partly to the inexhaustible loyalty, or was it cunning, of Maureen Johnson Tarnopol, formerly Mezik, formerly Walker, the marriage had been dissolvable only by Maureen's death. It had been a trumped-up business from the start: founded upon a false pregnancy that was contrived with the aid of a urine sample Maureen had bought from a pregnant black woman for $2.25, and a phony abortion, for which a Jewish boyfriend had paid through the nose. Three years into this marriage, in the heat of the daily brawl, this one over Peter's brief affair with his undergraduate student, Karen Oakes, Maureen stages a mock suicide and threatens to expose her lascivious professor-husband to the university, and he reacts by firing off the last bullet in his emotional arsenal, a tantrum. He tears off his clothes and dons Maureen's underclothes. Confronted by her husband thus reduced, Maureen weakens and confesses her original sin and, as such things go in stalled marriages, turns her confession into an instrument of coercion: "If you forgive me for the urine, I'll forgive you for your mistress." Translation: if you'll forgive me for entrapping you, I'll forgive you for trying to get free. That is the *quid pro quo* of a true mugger. Now, 1967, four years after Peter's successful escape and a year after Maureen's death in a car crash that was possibly self-engineered, he is finally writing the novel, episode by bloody episode, in the monastic isolation of the Quahsay writer's retreat in Vermont.

Like David Kepesh, Peter Tarnopol is confounded by his predicament on two grounds: he has no idea how he got into it, and is impotent to discover a way out. Thus, like *The Breast*, *My Life* is largely a discourse on the ambiguities of entrapment, an inquiry into just how it is that a man can find himself so firmly beyond the pleasure principle just when he had so much pleasure to anticipate. As Roth conducts it, the inquiry is not so much philosophical as diagnostic. The two styles differ in the way, say, a Bellow novel differs from a Roth novel, for where Moses Herzog and Artur Sammler tend to make global inquiries like "What is this life?" and "What is the heart of man?" the likes of Portnoy, Kepesh, and Tarnopol pour their perplexity into more local and immediate questions: "How did I get *here* when I was just *there*?" and "Why is *she* doing *that* to *me*?" In the true Freudian spirit, they assume that predicaments point to faults and that answers should be formulated in terms of blame.

Tarnopol is quick to blame the culture. He was deceived into making that vain and calamitous gesture of a marriage, he believes, by the ethos or perhaps the superego of the fifties. For, in that decade,

Decency and Maturity, a young man's "seriousness," were at issue precisely because it was thought to be the other way around: in that the great world was so obviously a man's, it was only within marriage than an ordinary woman could hope to find equality and dignity. Indeed, we were led to believe by the defenders of womankind of our era that we were exploiting and degrading the women we *didn't* marry, rather than the ones we did.

And, as if the fifties weren't enough, there was the great tradition of literary high seriousness to contend with, a tradition epitomized for Tarnopol by an epigram from Thomas Mann that he had appended to *A Jewish Father* (and Roth had used for *Letting Go*): "All actuality is deadly earnest, and it is morality itself that, one with life, forbids us to be true to the guileless unrealism of our youth." Tarnopol is right here. The courtship of cultural superegos has always been the English major's game and Peter suffers the English major's fate—to have been done in by the tight-lipped moralism of the great Protestant tradition and by those ideas about honor, duty, and manly responsibility that can be gotten from a University of Chicago education. "To live well," saith the superego, especially one nurtured upon Dostoevsky, Conrad, Hawthorne, F. R. Leavis, and Mortimer Adler's *Syntopicon*, "is to suffer." The great dialogue of Western Man says a lot less than it should about the advantages of the pleasure principle.

The ubiquitous Dr. Spielvogel, who is Tarnopol's analyst too, sees things differently. What Tarnopol had taken for cultural coercion, he sees as the victim's collusion, as the "acting out" of his ambivalence, narcissism, and a libidinized aggression that was initially directed toward a "phallic mother" but subsequently displaced onto a wife. Indeed, so taken is Spielvogel with this diagnosis and the insight it gives him into the creative personality that he writes it up as a paper which he publishes while Tarnopol is still under his care. Speaking in his own voice he sounds like this: "It soon became clear that the poet's central problem here as elsewhere was his castration anxiety vis-à-vis a phallic mother figure. . . . In order to avoid a confrontation with his dependency needs toward his wife the poet acted out sexually with other women almost from the beginning of the marriage."

Castration anxiety, vis-à-vis, anxiety needs, *undsoweiter*. At first reading such prose is antiseptic and soul-deadening: here is interpretation by Freudian catchphrase, and Tarnopol is rightly outraged to find himself written up as just another humdrum instance of regression. Yet behind the diagnostic commonplaces is some ordinary sense about the origins of Tarnopol's emotional failures that makes his lament about the fifties and the moral liabilities of reading Conrad and Flaubert sound about as probing as a lecture by Werner Erhard.

What Spielvogel sees in this marriage is not a man victimized by an era that placed a premium on self-sacrifice and moral accountability but a tactical arrangement between two people who were out to enjoy some serious punishment. Behind his jargon is the suggestion that the marriage had its purposes for Tarnopol and that Maureen's duplicity not only posed a threat to him but opened up some opportunities as well. On Maureen's part, the signs of wanting something more than an Eddie Fisher-Debbie Reynolds version of "true love" are there from the start: she courts punishment with all the enthusiasm of a journeyman welterweight who is out to take a convincing dive. Even before the marriage, when she attacks Peter with her purse and he threatens, in his harmless way, "Clip me with that purse, Maureen, and I'll kill you," she responds, "Do it! Kill me! Some man's going to—why not a 'civilized' one like you!"

Of course it is not really possible to disentangle complicated motives at this level; it is only worth pointing out that Maureen's invitation to Peter to kill her is deeply felt on her part and Peter, in marrying her, picks up that strand in their relationship along with a good many others. Yes, guilt, submission, intimidation, sudden moral collapse, all those motives are obvious and correctly identified, and yet the fact remains that such marriages are only possible for a special class of men—those who don't like women. Maureen, to hear her tell it, had a talent for finding such men: Mezik, the alcoholic bartender in Rochester who made her blow his buddy while he watched, and Walker, the homosexual in Cambridge who promised to give up boys after the marriage and broke the promise. Tarnopol is more at home in such company than he imagines. What all three have in common is a dislike for women and a penchant for discovering in Maureen the right sort of woman—someone for whom their prearranged misogyny can seem like a just and natural hatred. Indeed, the circumstances of her death are ambiguous enough to suggest that it is Walker at last who kills her. He, at any rate, was driving, though, as so often is the case in mutual destruction pacts, he may have survived the sacrifice more or less accidentally.

The news of Maureen's death has hardly arrived when Peter finds himself contemplating his newest problem, girlfriend Susan McCall, who, until then, had merely been a pleasant burden: a helpless, mildly neurotic, leggy heiress who is incapable of an orgasm but cooks a marvelous *blanquette de veau* and expertly knows just how much kirsch to put on the fruit. In short, she is totally unsuited for life with an aspiring young hunger artist. Thus it is that *My Life* concludes with Peter, in tears from just having spoken to his father on the phone, turning to contemplate the newest threat to his freedom.

> I turned to Susan, still sitting there huddled up on her coat looking, to my abasement, as helpless as the day I had found her. Sitting there *waiting*. Oh, my God, I thought—now you. You being you! And *me!* This me who is me being me and none other!

No, this one is off to Quahsay and sexual quarantine, to a life of hard work, regular hours, calisthenics, a breakfast of hot cereal, and a simple boy's lunch. He is out to relive, if possible, the easy ascetic triumphs of those salad days when to finish your homework and clean your plate were the only evidence you needed that you were living the good life.

My Life as a Man is Roth's best sustained piece of writing since *Portnoy's Complaint* and perhaps, in all, his best book. Its prose is strong and mean and finely attuned to the gestures of real speech, especially the asperities of a lousy marriage and the aggressive banalities of the daily hustle. Roth listens to the language around him better than any writer in America today, and when he is listening well his prose is gratefully free from his characteristic mannerisms: those of precocious insight and those of high purpose. From the beginning he has had difficulty bringing his talent into working alignment with his material, a difficulty that comes in part from the conflicting claims of his two muses: Henry James and Henny Youngman. Books like *Letting Go* and *When She Was Good*, novels of high seriousness, were burdened by what now looks like an inauthentic sobriety of voice, while the exercises in pure Youngman: *Our Gang* and *The Great American Novel*, have tended to give in to their effects, to suffer from comic overkill. Such stylistic meandering reflects the instability of Roth's purposes. We see here a career based on splitting and isolation: a periodic identification with one of these fathers and a fierce struggle against contamination by the other. *My Life as a Man*'s flaws are characteristic: the periodic flat spots in which the writer seems to have lost interest, those hysterical dialogues that are a bit too frantic or a bit too long, and the open seams that show us how, and sometimes how awkwardly, the novel was assembled. And yet here, in a rare show of intrapsychic cooperation, Roth's comedy has bent itself to the expression of real pain, and his guilt and his irony have found common expression in the same medium. The resulting style sounds, as Peter Tarnopol observes, like a mixture of Dostoevsky and soap opera, but the novel has always been the sentimental genre, and *My Life* is, at worst, mainline domestic pathos with only some of the sex roles reversed. Roth has been successful here to the extent that the book's flaws feel like inevitable aspects of its texture. *My Life* is a hard story to tell: it *should* double back on itself a bit, feature a false start or two, or protest more than makes us comfortable—it should, for humility's sake, be told a bit clumsily.

Yet unlike *Our Gang* and *The Great American Novel*, whose awkwardness betrays the haste of their composition, the patchwork construction of this book feels like the result of hard work with intractable materials. My guess is that Roth has struggled long with this book and that its successes have not been easily achieved. In fact, it shows signs of having been in the works at least since 1967, which, computed in Roth time, is more than seven years ago. For not only did *Portnoy* begin to appear in 1967 but *When She Was Good* was also published in that year, a book that seems so ancient now that it might as well be a Sumerian tablet covered with some cuneiform scrawl. *My Life,* I think, makes some sense of that anomalous book at last, for an examination of the two books together strongly argues that both are attempts to manage and articulate the same situation, and that the first book's failure to contain this life in its fictions led Roth to reformulate his obsession in another, more direct, form. This choice has nothing to do with the preferability of "fact" to "fiction" since that is a meaningless distinction for any novelist. A writer soon discovers that he cannot really tell the truth, that is, be scrupulously faithful to actual events, and that he also cannot really lie: he can only choose a style of representation and trust it to be suitable to his psychological needs and capable of the right literary effects. While there is no measuring the psychic gains of Roth's representation of personal catastrophe as "true confession" in *My Life as a Man,* the literary gains are clearly substantial, for the book engages his talent fully, at its most frantic, its most ironic, and its most subtle.

Notes

1. This essay was written before the publication of Roth's *The Professor of Desire,* in which David Kepesh tries to set the record straight about the Roth hero's capacity for love. That book, in my estimation, is less convincing in its affirmations than are others in their flair for disaster. For brief notes on Roth's two novels since *My Life as a Man* see Mark Shechner, "Jewish Writers," in *The Harvard Guide to Contemporary American Writing,* edited by Daniel Hoffman (Cambridge: The Harvard University Press, 1979), p. 239, and Shechner, review of *The Ghost Writer* in *The Nation,* 229:7 (September 15, 1979), pp. 213–214.

2. In *The Professor of Desire* and *The Ghost Writer* Roth appears to have caught up with himself and effected a return to the controlled line of his earlier fiction. But with a difference: a keener awareness of the unruly forces that are poised just beyond the scrim of consciousness. The tension in these later books is the tension of suspended action, a brooding air of unnatural calm that promises disasters to come.

Philip Roth: A Personal View

Theodore Solotaroff*

One day in the fall of 1957, I was sitting in a course on Henry James at the University of Chicago. The semester had just begun, and there were a few new faces: one that I had been noticing belonged to a handsome, well-groomed young man who stood out in the lean and bedraggled midst of us veteran graduate students as though he had strayed into class from the business school. The text for the day was *Daisy Miller*, and toward the end of the hour, one of the other students began to run away with the discussion, expounding one of those symbolic religious interpretations of the story that were in fashion at the time everywhere but at Chicago. Eventually the instructor asked me what I thought of this reading, and in the rhetoric I had learned from my mentors among the Chicago critics, I said that it was idiotic. I was immediately seconded by the debonair young man, who, in a very precise and concrete way, began to point out how such a reading turned the purpose and technique of the story inside out. Like two strangers in a pickup basketball game who discover they can work together, we passed the argument back and forth for a minute or two, running up the score of common sense. It was one of those fine moments of communication that don't occur every day in graduate English courses, and after class we met, shook hands, and exchanged names. His was Philip Roth.

So began a relationship. Since we were leading complicated, busy, and quite different private lives, our paths didn't cross that much. But almost each time they did, a connection was made and the current flowed. Though I was five years older than Roth, we were rather alike in temperament—aggressive, aloof, moody, and, as graduate students go, worldly. We also had a number of things in common that turned us on to each other. We were from roughly the same background—the practical, coarse, emotionally extravagant life of the Jewish middle class—as well as from neighboring cities in northern New Jersey. So there was an easy, immediate intimacy of a more or less common upbringing—Hebrew schools and YMHA's, the boardinghouses and boardwalks of Belmar and Bradley Beach, the Empire Burlesque House in Newark; the days and ways of

*Reprinted from Theodore Solotaroff, *The Red Hot Vacuum* (New York: Atheneum, 1970), pp. 306–28, by permission.

possessive Jewish mothers and harassed Jewish fathers; the pantheons of
our adolescence where Hank Greenberg, John Garfield, Norman Corwin,
and Longy Zwillman, the outstanding racketeer in Essex County, were
enshrined; and so many other "Jewish" artifacts, experiences, nuances of
feeling and attitude, about which we found ourselves to be about equally
nostalgic and contemptuous, hilarious and burdened. At the same time,
we were both involved in the similar journey from the halfway house of
semi-acculturation, whose household deity was neither Sholom Aleichem
nor Lionel Trilling but someone like Jack Benny, into the realm of
literature and culture. In our revolt against the exotic but intransigent
materialism of our first-generation bourgeois parents, we were not in
school to learn how to earn a living but to become civilized. Hence our
shared interest in James. And, finally, we both thought of ourselves as
writers who were biding their time in the graduate seminars we took and
the freshman composition courses we gave. Hence our quick hostility
toward any fancy, academic use of James.

All of which meant that we were also somewhat wary of each other.
Since each of us served as an objectification of the other's sense of position
and purpose, we spent a lot of time secretly taking each other's measure,
comparing and contrasting. Also I had more or less stopped writing, except for term papers, while Roth was writing all the time and was getting
published. One of his stories had even been anthologized in a Martha
Foley collection; two others had just been bought by *Esquire*; and he was
also doing movie reviews for the *New Republic*. After a quarter or so Roth
dropped out of graduate school in order to concentrate on his fiction;
meanwhile I slowly forged on through the second year of the Ph.D. program. To our other roles came to be added those of the creative writer and
the critic, respectively.

During this year I read several of the stories in manuscript that were
to appear two years later in *Goodbye, Columbus*. Raised as I had been, so
to speak, on the short-story-as-a-work-of-art, the cool, terse epiphanies of
the Joyce of *Dubliners*, the Flaubert of *Un Coeur simple*, of Katherine
Mansfield and Hemingway, I didn't at first know how to respond to a
story in which the narrator says:

> Though I am very fond of desserts, especially fruit, I chose not
> to have any. I wanted, this hot night, to avoid the conversation
> that revolved around my choosing fresh fruit over canned
> fruit, or canned fruit over fresh fruit; whichever I preferred.
> Aunt Gladys always had an abundance of the other jamming
> her refrigerator like stolen diamonds. "He wants canned
> peaches. I have a refrigerator full of grapes I have to get rid
> of. . . ." Life was a throwing off for poor Aunt Gladys, her
> greatest joys were taking out the garbage, emptying her pan-
> try, and making threadbare bundles for what she still referred
> to as the Poor Jews in Palestine. I only hope she dies with an

empty refrigerator, otherwise she'll ruin eternity for everyone
else, what with her Velveeta turning green, and her navel
oranges growing fuzzy jackets down below.

But my resistance quickly toppled like tenpins. It was like sitting
down in a movie house and suddenly seeing there on the screen a film
about the block on which I had grown up: the details of place, character,
incident all intimately familiar and yet new, or at least never appreciated
before for their color and interest. This story of Neil Klugman and Brenda
Patimkin was so simple, direct, and evident that it couldn't be "art," and
yet I knew that art did advance in just this way: a sudden sweeping aside
of outmoded complexities for the sake of a fresh view of experience, often
so natural a view and so common an experience that one wondered why
writers hadn't been seeing and doing this all along. The informal tone of
the prose, as relaxed as conversation, yet terse and fleet and right on the
button; the homely images of "stolen diamonds," of the Velveeta, and the
oranges, that make the passage glow. Such writing rang bells that not
even the Jewish writers had touched; it wasn't Malamud, it wasn't even
Saul Bellow: the "literary" fuzz of, say, *Augie March* had been blown
away, and the actualities of the life behind it came forth in their natural
grain and color, heightened by the sense of discovery.

Such writing is much more familiar today than it was ten years ago:
indeed, it has become one of the staples of contemporary fiction. But at
the time the only other writer who seemed to be so effortlessly and accurately in touch with his material was Salinger. For a year or so after
reading *Catcher in the Rye*, I hadn't been able to walk through Central
Park without looking around for Holden and Phoebe Caulfield, and now
here was this young semblable of mine who dragged me off for a good
corned-beef sandwich or who gave me a push when my car wouldn't
start, and who, somehow, was doing for the much less promising poetry
of Newark, New Jersey, what the famous Salinger was doing for that of
Central Park West. Moreover, if Roth's fiction had something of
Salinger's wit and charm, the winning mixture of youthful idealism and
cynicism, the air of immediate reality, it was also made of tougher stuff,
both in the kind of life it described and in the intentions it embodied. Salinger's taste for experience, like that of his characters, was a very delicate
one; Roth's appetite was much heartier, his tone more aggressive, his
moral sense both broader and more decisive.

What fascinated me most about stories like "Goodbye, Columbus,"
"The Conversion of the Jews," and "Defender of the Faith" was the firm,
clear way they articulated the inner situation we sensed in each other but
either took for granted or indicated covertly—by a reference to Isabelle
Archer as a *shiksa*, or by a takeoff on the bulldozing glottals of our father's
speech, as we walked away from our literature or linguistics course. In
such ways we signaled our self-ironic implication in things Jewish, but

Roth's stories dealt directly with the much touchier material of one's efforts to extricate himself, to achieve a mobility that would do justice to his individuality. Social mobility was the least of it. This was the burden of "Goodbye, Columbus," where Neil Klugman's efforts early in the story to latch and hold on to the little wings of Brenda Patimkin's shoulderblades and let them carry him up "those lousy hundred and eight feet that make summer nights so much cooler in Short Hills than they are in Newark" soon take on the much more interesting, and representative, struggle to have her on his own terms, terms that lie well beyond money, comfort, security, status, and have to do with his sexual rights and ultimately his uncertain emotional and moral identity. At the end of the story, Neil stands in front of the Lamont Library and at first wants to hurl a rock through the glass front; but his rage at Brenda, at the things she had been given and has sacrificed him for, soon turns into his curiosity about the young man who stares back at him in the mirrored reflection and who "had turned pursuit and clutching into love, and then turned it inside out again . . . had turned winning into losing and losing—who knows—into winning. . . ."

Neil's prickly and problematic sense of himself, his resistance to the idea of being a bright Jewish boy with an eye for the main chance, for making sure, an idea that was no stranger to other desires—well, this was not simply fiction to me. Nor was the Patimkin package, where horse shows and Big Ten basketball and classy backhands still came wrapped in Jewish conformity and ethnocentricity. In story after story there was an individual trying to work free of the ties and claims of the community. There was Ozzie in "The Conversion of the Jews," who would not have God hedged in by the hostility of Judaism to Christianity; there was Sergeant Marx in "Defender of the Faith," who finally refused to hand over any more of his sense of fairness and responsibility to the seductive appeals of Jewish solidarity; or, on the other hand, there was Eli Peck, who refused to close the book of Jewish history to be more at ease with his landsmen in Suburbia. Or there was even poor Epstein, who managed to pry apart the iron repressions of Jewish family life to claim some final gratifications for himself. Or there was my special favorite, a very early story called "You Can't Tell a Man by the Song He Sings," in which a nice Jewish boy learns from two Italians—a juvenile delinquent and an ex-radical guidance teacher—that some dignities have to be won against the rules and regulations of upward mobility.

Such themes were as evocative to me as a visit from my mother, but I knew than I couldn't write the stories that embodied them in the way that Roth had. It was not just a matter of talent but of the intricate kind of acceptance that joins one's talent to his experience so that he can communicate directly. Though Roth clearly was no less critical of his background that I was, he had not tried to abandon it, and hence had not allowed it to become simply a deadness inside him: the residual feelings, mostly those of anxiety, still intact but without their living context. That is to say, he wrote fiction as he was, while I had come to write as a kind of fantasist of literature who regarded almost all of my actual experience in the world as unworthy of art. A common mistake, particularly in the overliterary age of the late Forties and Fifties, but a decisive one. So if I envied Roth his gifts, I envied even more his honesty, his lack of fastidiousness, his refusal to write stories that labored for a form so fine that almost any naturalness would violate it. The gross affluences and energies of the Patimkins, the crudities of Albie Pelagutti and Duke Scarpa, even the whining and wheedling of Sheldon Grossbart turned him on rather than put him off. Once, I remember, I balked. There is a scene in "Epstein" where his wife discovers his rash that they both believe is venereal, and an ugly and not very funny description follows of their fight in the nude. "Why all the *schmutz?*" I asked him. "The story is the *schmutz*," he snapped back.

Our relationship had its other ups and downs. After he dropped out of graduate school, Roth went on teaching in the college, an impressive post to me, if not to him (he was to give it up after a year and head for New York). And since he was publishing his work and looked to be making good use of his bachelor years, he seemed, at least on the surface (which was where my envy led me to look), to have the world by the tail. On the other hand, the world in those days seemed, at least on the surface, to have me by the tail. I was taking three courses at Chicago and teaching four at Indiana University Calumet Center, a glum building around which lay the oil refineries and steel mills to which most of my students returned from our discussions of Plato and Dante. On my salary of $3000 a year it was not easy to support my wife and two small boys. But, having wasted a number of years after college, I felt that I was getting somewhere. My students were challenging, to say the least, and some of the charm of scholarship had unexpectedly begun to descend upon me. Still the fact remained that Roth was visibly well off and I was visibly not, and it made certain differences. At one point I borrowed some money from him, which made us both uncomfortable until it was paid back. One evening he and his date, my wife and I, went to hear a lecture by Saul Bellow—our literary idol—and afterward went out for a beer. His girlfriend, though, ordered a scotch, and into the discussion of what Bellow had said and could have said there intruded an awkward moment at each round of drinks. Or there was a party he came to at my place to celebrate the arrival of bock beer (our version of the rites of spring). As I've suggested, Roth and I shared our past and our opinions much more than we shared our present lives. When we met, it was almost always at his place. My apartment, over in the Negro section, with its Salvation Army decor and its harassed domesticity, seemed both to touch him and make him nervous. I remember him sitting on the edge of a couch, over which I had just nailed on an old shag rug to cover the holes, waiting like a social worker while my wife got our oldest son through his nightly asthma. Then the other guests arrived, the beer flowed, and we turned on with our favorite stimulant—Jewish jokes and caustic family anecdotes—dispensed principally by Roth, whose fantastic mimicry and wit soon had us rolling in our chairs.

That evening came back to mind a few years later when I was reading Roth's first novel, *Letting Go*, which is set mainly in Hyde Park and which deals with the ethos of the graduate-student/young-instructor situation during the Fifties: the "Age of Compassion," as Gabe Wallach, the protagonist, aptly puts it. The story mainly follows Wallach's involvement with Paul and Libby Herz, a needy young couple (money is only the beginning of it), and with Martha Reagenhart, a voluptuous and tough-minded girl who has two children to support and who is looking for some support herself. Attracted both by Libby's frailty and by Martha's strength, and unable to make much contact with the surly Herz, Wallach, an attractive bachelor in comfortable circumstances, spends much of the novel sitting on the edge of his scruples, worrying whether too much or too little is being asked of him, a dilemma he shares with Herz, whose moral self-consciousness takes over whenever the point of view shifts to his side of the story. All of this reckoning of the wages of conscience is accompanied by cool, satirical observation, more successfully of the Jewish background of Gabe and Paul than of their professional life, which Roth used mostly to even a few scores. The best writing in the book came in the scenes in a Detroit boardinghouse when Herz's effort to push Libby through an abortion gets tangled up with the schemes of the retired shyster, Levy, to "help" the pathetic Korngold extract money from his son and to move the cases of underwear that Korngold hoards in his room, waiting for the market to improve.

Like a good many other citizens of Hyde Park, my wife and I furnished a trait here, an anecdote there, but the material was more thoroughly fictionalized in our case than in some others. What Roth was mainly drawing on, I felt, was a certain depressiveness that had been in the air: the result of those long Chicago winters, the longueurs of graduate school and composition courses, the financial strains, the disillusionment with the university (this was the period in which the Hutchins experiments were being dismantled and the administration was waging a reign of respectability in all areas), and the concomitant dullness of the society-at-large, which had reached the bottom of the Eisenhower era. But mostly this depressiveness was caused by the self-inflicted burdens of private life, which in this age of conformity often seemed to serve for politics, art, and the other avenues of youthful experience and experiment. One of the principal occupations in Hyde Park seemed to be difficult marriages: almost everyone I knew was locked into one. This penchant for early marriage and child-rearing, or for only slightly less strenuous affairs, tended to fill the vacuum of commitment for sophisticated but not especially stable young couples and fostered a rather pretentious moralism of duty, sacrifice, home therapy, experiment with domestic roles—often each other's—working things out, saving each other. It was a time when the deferred gratifications of graduate school and the climb to tenure and the problems of premature adjustment seemed the warranty of "seriousness" and "responsibility": those solemn passwords of a generation that practiced a Freudian/Jamesian concern about motives, pondered E. M. Forster's "only connect," and subscribed to Lionel Trilling's "moral realism" and "tragic sense of life." In contrast to today, everyone tried to act as though he were thirty.

Some of this Roth had caught and placed at the center of *Letting Go*. As the title suggests, the novel is a study of entangling attachments, beginning with Gabe's effort to release himself from his widowed father's possessiveness and ending with his frantic effort to complete, and thereby end, his intervention in the life of the Herzes, through helping them to adopt a child. In between, a host of characters push and pull, smother and neglect each other, usually under the guise of solicitude or obligation. At one point Wallach puts it for himself, Herz, and most of the others: "I knew it was not from my students or my colleagues or my publications, but from my private life, my secret life, that I would extract whatever joy—or whatever misery—would be mine." By "private life" he means relationships and their underlying *Realpolitik* of need, dependency, and control.

It was evident that *Letting Go* represented a major effor to move forward from *Goodbye, Columbus*. The theme of communal coerciveness and individual rights that dominates most of the stories had been opened out to deal with the more subtle perversions of loyalty and duty and creaturely feeling that flow through the ties of family, marriage, friendship. A very Jamesian theme: *The Portrait of a Lady* figures almost immediately in *Letting Go*, as a reference point for its interest in benevolent power plays. Also, in bringing his fiction more up to date with the circumstances and issues of his life, Roth had tried for a more chastened, Jamesian tone. The early chapters have some of the circumspect pace and restrained wit of the Master: well-mannered passages of nuance and implication, the main characters carefully observed, the theme tucked neatly away in the movement of action, thought, and dialogue. The book sails gracefully along for about 150 pages or so. Then it begins to turn as gray and bitter as the Chicago winter and, in time, as endless.

What went wrong? As I have indicated, the Hyde Park we had known had not been an especially chipper place, and there was plenty of reason to deal with it in terms of its grim domesticity. Still, Roth had laid it on and laid it on. If Gabe and Martha have the Herzes for dinner, the mutual strains will be as heavy as a bad Ph.D. oral, and afterward Gabe and Martha will fight about who paid for what. If Paul's passion for Libby revives at a party, it will cool before they can get around the cor-

ner. If some children are encountered at a playground with their grandmother, it is because their mother has just tried to flush herself down a
toilet bowl at Billings Hospital. In this morbid world, sibling rivalry leads
to homicide, intermarriage to being abandoned by both the Catholic and
Jewish families, adoption proceedings to a nervous breakdown. Not even
a stencil can get typed without fear and trembling.

All of which added up, I felt, not only to an exaggeration of the conditions but to an error of vision. I wondered if this *error* might have
something to do with the surface view we had of each other's lives: his apparent fortune, my apparent misfortunes: clearly the germ, at least, of the
Wallach-Herz relationship. As I was subsequently to realize, my view of
him that year was full of misapprehensions: behind the scenery of ease
and success he had been making his payments to adversity: a slipped disc,
for one thing; a tense and complicated affair, some aspects of which were
to figure in Gabe's relationship with Martha. On the other hand, behind
the scenery of adversity in a life like mine, there were positive purposes
and compensations that he had not taken into account, and that made the
struggle of those years tolerable and possibly significant. Though Wallach
is a scholar and Herz a novelist, they might as well be campus watchmen
for all the interest they have in their work, in ideas, even in their careers.
While this ministers to the central concerns of the novel, it deprives both
of them of force and resistance, for, stripped of any aggressive claim on
the world, they have little to do but hang around their women and guilti-
ly talk about "working it out"—the true title of the novel. The only
character who has any beans is Martha, which is partly owing to the fact
that, having two children to support and raise, her life intentions are to
some degree objective. Otherwise there are only the obsessive, devouring
relationships and the malaise they breed: Libby perpetually waiting to be
laid, Paul reminding her to put on her scarf, Gabe consumed by his sense
of his obligations and his distrust of it, Martha demanding that payment
be made for satisfactions given. From such characters, little natural
dynamic can develop, and Roth can only forge on and on in his relentlessly bleak way: now analytic, now satirical, now melodramatic—giving
Libby an adopted baby, Paul a religious turn, Martha a dull, dependable
husband, and Gabe a wild adventure in Gary with the extortion-minded
husband of the girl who bore the baby—none of it especially convincing,
none of it quite able to lift up and justify the burden of the pessimism.

In his essay on "Some of the Talent in the Room" Norman Mailer
wagered that the depressiveness of *Letting Go* had to do with Roth's
"working out an obsession." This seemed to me a shrewd observation,
though who in these days of obsessive fiction would 'scape hanging. In
Letting Go the obsession is with the power of women along with a male
queasiness about it that keeps both Herz and Wallach implicated, endlessly looking for moral means to cope with their emotional vulnerability. As
Wallach, for example, remarks at one point:

> There must be some weakness in men, I thought (in Paul and myself, I later thought) that Libby wormed her way into. Of course I had no business distrusting her because of *my* weakness—and yet women have a certain historical advantage (all those years of being downtrodden and innocent and sexually compromised) which at times can turn even the most faithful of us against them. I turned slightly at that moment myself, and was repelled by the sex toward which at bottom I have a considerable attachment.

This sort of observation hardly leads to insight or movement. It merely maintains an ambivalence by shunting the anger involved off on some courtly, literary track and letting the historical situation of women screen the personal guilt, the deep characterological misery that keeps men like Herz and Wallach in place and wide open. As the novel wears on, the anger if not guilt is more and more acknowledged in Wallach's case, as his priggishness is worn down by Martha and some of his true feelings begin to emerge. Still, the problem of coping with Libby and Martha, posited in moral terms that make it insoluble, nags away at the two men and their author. What they can't "let go" of is guilt, and it drags the book down with them.

When *Letting Go* came out, I was working at *Commentary*, a job that had come my way as the result of an essay that the *TLS* had asked me to write on Roth's recommendation. Since he hadn't liked the essay at first and since I was as touchy as Paul Herz proved to be about such matters as gratitude and pride, there had been a falling out. In New York, however, the relationship resumed, and with fewer of the disparities and diffidences that had made it tense and illusionary. As time went on, there were also reasons to level with each other: we were both separated, both in analysis, both in a state of flux. So we would get together, now and then, for dinner, and talk about problems and changes. One evening I dropped by his new place on East Tenth Street to borrow a book. It was bigger and much better furnished than mine, and he wanted me to know—screw the guilt—he intended to be comfortable here and to sink some new roots. But, for all that, the place looked as bare and provisional as mine: we might as well have both been living in tents, neither of us bachelors so much as husbands *manqué*. A portable typewriter was sitting on the dining-room table, and a lot of manuscript pages were spread around it.

"What's that?" I asked.

"It's a novel." He looked at it without much pleasure. "I've written it once, and now I'm writing it again."

It was strange to realize that he, too, got hung up. I had always assumed that he was like Chekhov, who said that he wrote "as easily as a bird sings."

Perhaps he noticed my silly smile. "You know something?" he said.

"There's not a single Jew in it." He went on about the strangeness of imagining, really imagining, a family that was not a Jewish family, that was
what it was by virtue of its own conditioning and conditions, just as the
Jews were, but which were not just those of "the others"—the Gentiles.
Something like that—though he put it, as always, more concretely—acting out, with that gift of mimicry that was always on tap, the speech and
the slant of some small-town citizen of middle America.

The novel, of course, turned out to be *When She Was Good*, two
years, and several more revisions later. It was easy to see why the book
had been a trial for Roth to write. Liberty Center is so far from his line of
territory that everything had to be played by ear, so to speak. The town
hardly exists as a place, as something seen in its physical actuality; it is
rather the spirit of the American Protestant ethic circa 1948, whose
people and mores, interests and values, emerge from the impersonation of
idiom and tone: Liberty Center as it might have been presented not by
Sinclair Lewis but by Ruth Draper. In order to bring this off, Roth had
had to put aside his wit, color, and élan, keep his satirical tendency tightly in check, and write the novel in a language of scrupulous banality. This
impersonality was far removed from the display of temperament that
animated "Goodbye, Columbus" as the life of the bitchy heroine, Lucy
Nelson, so meager and so arduous, is from that of the bitchy Brenda
Patimkin.

Yet, for all the improvisation and guesswork, the surface of *When
She Was Good* is solid and real, and though true to the dullness of Liberty
Center's days and ways, it is beautifully constructed to take on mo-
mentum and direction and to hit its target with shattering impact, like
some bland-looking object in the sky that turns out to be a guided missile.
As in *Letting Go*, the theme is the wages of possessiveness and self-righteousness, but as embodied by and embedded in Lucy Nelson's raging,
ball-breaking ego, it takes on a focus and power that had dissolved in the
miasmic male earnestness of the previous novel. There is no false gallantry
or temporizing about Lucy. Any ambivalence has been burned away, and
Roth presents her and her will to power dead-to-rights. Because of this
sureness of feeling, he can also present her in the round—terrible when
crossed but touching in her aspirations and inexperience, her baffled need
for a fathering trust, the victim as well as the avenger of her grandfather's
wishy-washy Good Samaritanism, of her parasitic father's disgrace and
her mother's passivity, of the family's stalled drive for respectability, and,
eventually, of her husband's arrested adolescence. But from the moments
early in the novel when Lucy turns in her drunken father to the police and
then bars his way back into the family, the blind force of her aggression,
screened by her faith in duty and responsibility and in her moral
superiority, begins to charge the novel and to shape her destiny. She is
unable to break off her romance with Roy Bassart until she has him safely
installed in photography school and thereby ends up pregnant. She refuses

the abortion she herself sought when it is offered by her father and when she learns that her mother had had one. She enters into a shotgun marriage with Roy, whom she has come to despise, with herself holding the gun. At each turn of her fate, skillfully paired with another and better alternative, it is Lucy's master emotion—her rage against her father—that directs her choice as surely as Nemesis. And some years later, when her father writes home from the jail he has landed in and thereby pulls her mother away from marriage to a man Lucy can finally respect, she turns it all against Roy in a climactic outburst of verbal castration, and then lets loose the furies of self-righteousness that drive her to madness and death. Like her grandfather's demented sister who had to be sent back to the state hospital because she followed Lucy to school and created a public nuisance, Lucy has been unable to understand "the most basic fact of human life, the fact that I am me and you are you."

In telling Lucy's story as circumspectly as he could, Roth has placed it within a context of cultural factors. Her grandfather had come to Liberty Center to escape from the brutality of the northern frontier, and the town stands in his mind, as it comes to stand in the reader's, as the image of his desire: "not to be rich, not to be famous, not to be mighty, not even to be happy, but to be civilized." Though Lucy rejects the tepid Protestantism on which Willard stands fast, she worships at the same shrine of propriety, which is the true religion of Liberty Center, and whose arbiters are the women. If men like her father and her husband founder in the complexities of society, it is the women who are supposed to straighten them out. They are the socializing agents, and the town's football stars and combat heroes, its reprobates and solid citizens, alike bow to their sway. When the high-school principal says to Roy and Lucy, "So this is the young lady I hear is keeping our old alum in line these days," he is referring to the community norm which Lucy will carry to an extreme.

Still, the cult of Momism in Liberty Center hardly added up to a pressing contemporary note, and the novel tended to be dismissed by most of the influential reviewers as slight, inauthentic, retrograde, or otherwise unworthy of Roth's talents. Coupled with the mixed reception of *Letting Go*, his reputation was slipping. Moreover, as much as I liked *When She Was Good*, it was further evidence that he was locked into this preoccupation with female power which was carrying his fiction into strange and relatively arid terrain. I knew that he had been writing plays in the last few years and had spent a lot of time watching the improvisations of the Second City Group—another part of our Chicago days that had accompanied us to New York—and I wondered if his own theatricality would lead him in that direction. But we seldom saw each other during this time. I was editing *Book Week* during the long newspaper strike, hadn't written anything for a year, and was going through a crisis or two of my own, and if we met at a party or something, we exchanged a word or two and looked around for more cheerful company. I remember thinking that we had both come a long way since Chicago—much of it out to sea.

A few months after *When She Was Good*, Roth published a sketch in *Esquire*. It was a memoir of a Jewish boyhood, this time told to an analyst, and written with some of his former verve and forthrightness. Even so, it ventured little beyond a vein that had been pretty well worked by now: the beleaguered provider who can't even hold a bat right; the shatteringly attentive mother; the neglected, unhappy sister; the narrator, who is the star of every grade and the messiah of the household. In short, the typical second-generation Jewish family; and after all the writers who had been wrestling with it in the past decade or two—Herbert Gold, Wallace Markfield, Bruce Jay Friedman, Arnold Wesker, Mordecai Richler, Irwin Faust, Roth himself, to name only a few—Roth's latest revelations were hardly news. Nor did a psychoanalytic setting seem necessary to elicit the facts of Jack Portnoy's constipation or Sophie's use of a breadknife to make little Alex eat. After five years of reading manuscripts at *Commentary*, such stuff was coming out of my ears. Perhaps Roth was only taking a small writer's vacation from the labor that had gone into his last novel or returning to the scene of his early success for a quick score. I hoped so.

But soon after came "Whacking Off" in *Partisan Review*: hysterical, raw, full of what Jews call self-hatred; excessive in all respects; and so funny that I had three laughing fits before I had gone five pages. All of a sudden, from out of the blue and the past, the comedian of those Chicago sessions of nostalgia, revenge, and general purgation had landed right in the middle of his own fiction, as Alex Portnoy, the thirteen-year-old sex maniac.

> Jumping up from the dinner table, I tragically clutch my belly—diarrhea! I cry, I have been stricken with diarrhea!—and once behind the locked bathroom door, slip over my head a pair of underpants that I have stolen from my sister's dresser and carry rolled in a handkerchief in my pocket. So galvanic is the effect of cotton panties against my mouth—so galvanic is the *word* "panties"—that the trajectory of my ejaculation reaches startling new heights: leaving my joint like a rocket it makes right for the light bulb overhead, where to my wonderment and horror, it hits and hangs. Wildly in the first moment I cover my head, expecting an explosion of glass, a burst of flames—disaster, you see, is never far from my mind. Then quietly as I can I climb the radiator and remove the sizzling gob with a wad of toilet paper. I begin a scrupulous search of the shower curtain, the tub, the tile floor, the four toothbrushes—God forbid!—and just as I am about to unlock the door, imagining I have covered my tracks, my heart lurches at the sight of what is hanging like snot to the toe of my shoe. I am the Raskolnikov of jerking off—the sticky evidence

is everywhere! Is it on my cuffs too? In my *hair?* my *ear?* All
this I wonder even as I come back to the kitchen table, scowl-
ing and cranky, to grumble self-righteously at my father when
he opens his mouth full of red jello and says, "I don't understand what you have to lock the door about. That to me is
beyond comprehension. What is this, a home or a Grand
Central station?" ". . . privacy . . . a human being . . .
around here *never*," I reply, then push aside my dessert to
scream "I don't feel well—*will everybody leave me alone?*"

And so on. A few minutes later Alex is back in his kingdom, doubled over
his flying fist, his sister's bra stretched before him, while his parents stand
outside:

> "Alex, I want an answer from you. Did you eat French fries
> after school? Is that why you're sick like this?
> "Nuhhh, nuhhh."
> "Alex, are you in pain? Do you want me to call the doctor?
> Are you in pain, or aren't you? I want to know exactly where it
> hurts. *Answer me.*"
> "Yuhh, yuhhh—"
> "Alex, I don't want you to flush the toilet," says my mother
> sternly. "I want to see what you've done in there. I don't like
> the sound of this at all."
> "And me," says my father, touched as he always was by my
> accomplishments—as much awe as envy—"I haven't moved
> my bowels in a week." . . .

This was new, all right, at least in American fiction—and, like the
discovery of fresh material in *Goodbye, Columbus*, right in front of
everyone's eyes. Particularly, I suppose, guess, of the "Jewish" writers'
with all that heavily funded Oedipal energy and curiosity to be worked
off in adolescence—and beyond. And having used his comic sense to carry
him past the shame that surrounds the subject of masturbation, and to
enter it more fully than I can suggest here, Roth appeared to gain great
dividends of emotional candor and wit in dealing with the other matters
in "Whacking Off." The first sketch maintained a distance of wry description between Portnoy and his parents, but here his feelings—rage,
tenderness, contempt, despair, and so on—bring everthing up close and
fully alive. And aided by the hard-working comedy team of Jack and
Sophie Portnoy, the familiar counters of Jewish anxiety (eating hamburgers and french fries outside the home leads directly to a colostomy;
polio is never more than a sore throat away; study an instrument, you
never know; take shorthand in school, look what it did for Billy Rose;
don't oppose your father, he may be suffering from a brain tumor)
become almost as hilarious as Alex's solo flights of passion. Against the
enveloping cloud of their fear and possessiveness, his guilt, and their
mutual hysteria, still unremitting twenty years later, Alex has only his sar-

casm and, expressive phrase, private parts. He summons the memories of his love as well as of his hate for them, but this only opens up his sense of his vulnerability and, from that, of his maddening typicality:

> Doctor Spielvogel, this is my life, my only life, and I'm living it in the middle of a Jewish joke! I am the son in the Jewish joke—*only it ain't no joke!* Please, who crippled us like this? Who made us so morbid and hysterical and weak? . . . Is this the Jewish suffering I used to hear so much about? Is this what has come down to me from the pogroms and the persecutions? Oh my secrets, my shame, my palpitations, my flushes, my sweats! . . . Bless me with manhood! Make me brave, make me strong! Make me *whole!* Enough being a nice Jewish boy, publicly pleasing my parents while privately pulling my putz! Enough!

But Portnoy had only begun to come clean. Once having fully entered his "Modern Museum of Gripes and Grievances," there was no stopping him. Or Roth. Having discovered that Portnoy's sexual feelings and his "Jewish" feelings were just around the corner from each other and that both were so rich in loot, he pressed on like a man who has found a stream full of gold—and running right into it, another one. Moreover, the psychoanalytic setting had given him now the freedom and energy of language to sluice out the material: the natural internal monologue of comedy and pain in which the id speaks to the ego and vice versa, while the superego goes on with its kibitzing. At the same time, Portnoy could be punched out of the analytic framework like a figure enclosed in cardboard and perform in his true role and vocation, which is that of a great stand-up comic. Further, those nagging concerns with close relationships, with male guilt and female maneuvering, from his two novels could now be grasped by the roots of Portnoy's experience of them and could be presented, not as standard realistic fare, but in a mode that was right up-to-date. If the background of *Portnoy's Complaint* is a classical Freudian one, the foreground is the contemporary, winging art and humor of improvisation and release, perhaps most notably that of Lenny Bruce.

In short, lots of things had come together and they had turned Roth loose. The rest of *Portnoy* was written in the same way—as series of "takes"—the next two of which were published in *New American Review*, the periodical which I was now editing. It may be no more than editorial bias speaking here, but I think these are the two richest sections of the book. "The Jewish Blues" is a sort of "coming of age in Newark, New Jersey," beginning with the erotic phenomena of the Portnoy household and carrying through the dual issue of Alex's adolescence: maleness and rebellion. On the one hand, there are those early years of attentively following Sophie Portnoy through her guided tour of her activities and attitudes, climaxed by a memory of one afternoon when, the housework all done "with his cute little assistance," Alex, "punchy with delight" watches his shapely mother draw on her stockings, while she croons to him "Who does Mommy love more than anything in the whole wide world?" (a passage that deserves to live forever in the annals of the Oedipal Complex). On the other hand—"Thank God," breathes Portnoy—there are the visits with his father to the local bathhouse, the world of Jewish male animal nature, "a place without *goyim* and women [where] I lose touch instantaneously with that ass-licking little boy who runs home after school with his A's in his hand. . . ." On the one hand, there is the synagogue, another version of the dismal constraints and clutchiness of home; on the other, there is center field, where anything that comes your way is yours and where Alex, in his masterful imitation of Duke Snider, knows exactly how to conduct himself, standing out there "as loose and as easy, as happy as I will ever be. . . ." This is beautiful material: so exact in its details, so right in its feeling. And, finally, there is the story of his cousin Heshie, the muscular track star, who was mad about Alice Dembrowsky, the leggy drum majorette of Weequahic High, and whose disgraceful romance with this daughter of a Polish janitor finally has to be ended by his father, who informs Alice that Heshie has an incurable blood disease that prevents him from marrying and that must be kept secret from him. After his Samson-like rage is spent, Heshie submits to his father, and subsequently goes into the Army and is killed in action. But Alex adds his cause to his other manifold grounds of revolt, rises to heights of denunciation in the anti-Bar Mitzvah speech he delivers to Spielvogel ("instead of wailing for he-who has turned his back on the saga of *his people*, weep for your pathetic selves, why don't you, sucking and sucking on that sour grape of a religion"); but then is reminded by his sister of "the six million" and ends pretty much where he began.

Still circling back upon other scenes from his throbbing youth, as though the next burst of anger or grief or hysterical joking will allow him finally to touch bottom, Portnoy forges on into his past and his psyche, turning increasingly to his relations with the mysterious creatures called "shiksas" as his life moves on and the present hang-ups emerge. His occupation is that of Assistant Commissioner of Human Opportunity in the Lindsay Administration, but his preoccupations are always with that one thing his mother didn't give him back when he was four years old, and all of his sweet young Wasps, for all of their sociological interest, turn out to be only an extension of the fantasies of curiosity and self-excitement and shame that drove Alex on in the bathroom. Even "the Monkey," the glamorous fashion model and fellow sex maniac, the walking version of his adolescent dream of "Thereal McCoy," provides mostly more grist for the relentless mill of his narcissism and masochism. All of which Portnoy is perfectly aware of, he is the hippest analysand since Freud himself; but it still doesn't help him to give up the maddeningly seductive voice inside his head that goes on calling "Big Boy." And so, laughing and anguishing and analyzing away, he goes down the road to his breakdown, which sets in when he comes to Israel and finds that he is impotent.

I could go on writing about *Portnoy*, but it would be mostly amplification of the points I've made. It's a marvelously entertaining book and one that mines a narrow but central vein more deeply than it has ever been done before. You don't have to be Jewish to be vastly amused and touched and instructed by *Portnoy's Complaint*, though it helps. Also you don't have to know Philip Roth to appreciate the personal triumph that it represents, though that helps too.

The Jew's Complaint in Recent American Fiction: Beyond Exodus And Still in the Wilderness

Alan Warren Friedman*

On the appearance of that recent cultural phenomenon known as *Portnoy's Complaint*, Philip Roth said that right now this work "is an event. In two years it will be a book." It is an event that happens at a time when more than the usual number of American myths and idols lie under attack or already shattered, not in embassies abroad but in the streets of America herself, those streets that hordes of eager immigrants once knew were paved with gold, and which are now peopled by a radical and convulsive skepticism that finds the past not a history play but a tragedy—or worse, a farce. In *Waiting for the End*, Leslie Fiedler writes of a simpler time, the relative innocence of the late 1950s, when the enemy was still without, and when "the Jew who thinks he is an American, yet feels in his deepest heart an immitigable difference from the Gentile American who thinks he is a Jew, need only go abroad to realize that, in the eyes of non-Americans, the difference does not exist at all"[1]—because both are equally hated, equally berated, by angry crowds shouting in front of our embassies, "Americans go home!" Increasingly during the 1960s and now the 1970s, Americans who put each other on trial in Chicago and elsewhere for what they think as they cross state lines are reduced to shouting such slogans at themselves—and then having to confront the fact that they *are* home.

"Land of equal opportunity," "land of the free and home of the brave," "manifest destiny"—like those of us who grew up in the fifties, and then had to do so again in the sixties, all the grand and noble truisms by which we were taught American history in high school have lost their innocence and, like Roth's Portnoy, we spend our time trying to define what has replaced it. The latest truism to go is "the melting pot"—that overheated, cracking vessel filled with its congealing, lumpy mass incapable of becoming a chemical combination through any process known to man—when ethnic is in, who values a melting pot?

*Reprinted from *Southern Review*, 8 (Fall 1972), 41–59, by permission of the journal.

Jews, and Roth's are only among the most recent exemplars, know all about the ambiguous consequences of attempted assimilation. Like other people, only more so, the Jew remains a cultural schizophrenic, a concatenation of past and future haunted by a sense of his own uniqueness, and simultaneously blessed and burdened by his heritage and his vision. The heritage teaches him that he is something special, a creature umbilically linked to a historical grandeur and sense of destiny that, however, best manifests itself through the suffering of its exemplars and which defines them whether or not they seek to escape it. His vision is that of his Promised Land, the land of milk and honey that seems always to lie just beyond his reach.

Bernard Malamud's *The Fixer*, Yakov Bok, who defines history as "the world's bad memory" and being a Jew as "an everlasting curse," says, "We're all in history, that's sure, but some are more than others, Jews more than some" (pp. 314–5). The Jews enter history, of course, in Egypt, when Moses promises them freedom and salvation, and they go with him, reluctantly, against their better judgment, out of their centuries-old comfortable slavery in the stranger's land that gave them roots, out into the wilderness and history. The Biblical account of Exodus (as opposed to Leon Uris' pop-heroic version) reads like the saga of an unhappy marriage or of the generation gap, for it tells of a God, in a manner foreshadowing Roth's Portnoy and his problems, constantly trying to prove to a doubting people that he exists, that he knows his own identity, that he has relevance—first with his flat Cartesian assertion to Moses: "I am that I am," and then his increasingly tangible but still somehow unconvincing magical tricks. He turns rods into snakes, makes plagues descend, holds back and unleashes waters, slakes the thirst of the multitude demanding, "What shall we drink?" He rains manna on them when they cry out for food—"Would to God we had died by the hand of the Lord in Egypt . . . for ye have brought us forth into this wilderness, to kill this whole assembly with hunger"—but like the stereotyped Jew lusting for food, they then insist on meat instead of manna: "and the children of Israel . . . wept again, and said, Who shall give us flesh to eat? We remember the fish, which we did eat in Egypt freely; the cucumbers, and the melons, and the leeks, and the onions, and the garlic: But now our soul is dried away: there is nothing at all besides this manna, before our eyes." And they get a response they did not anticipate, though they certainly should have. God tells Moses: "Say unto the people, Sanctify yourselves against tomorrow, and ye shall eat flesh: for ye have wept in the ears of the Lord . . . : therefore the Lord will give you flesh, and ye shall eat. Ye shall not eat one day, nor two days, nor five days, neither ten days, nor twenty days; But even a whole month, until it comes out at your nostrils, and it be loathsome unto you: because that ye have despised the Lord which is among you . . . and while the flesh was yet between their teeth, ere it was chewed, the wrath of the Lord was kindled against the people, and the Lord smote the people with a very great plague."

God's refrain throughout the exodus is, I shall do this or that or the other thing, "and ye shall know that I am the Lord your God." But except when directly confronted by overwhelming power, no one seems to take Him very seriously. This chosen people, reluctantly bearing the burden of that dubious distinction, continues its unending series of complaints and demands, which stimulates God, alternately, to indulgence and un-governable fury. One can't help wondering about *His* inner needs that he complusively keeps seeking to satisfy them through this agnostic, earthy people who have little ultimate use for Him. No wonder he keeps punishing them—for like a good Jewish mother, he is frustrated at having devoted himself, squandered himself, even sacrificed himself, to keep them fed, to give them opportunity to better themselves, to see that they have a decent life and don't consort with *goyish* idols—and they have the effrontery to be less than fully grateful.

The continuing problems of the Yahweh-Israeli relationship explain the long period of exile; for, even on foot, it really doesn't take forty years to get from Egypt to Jericho. But arriving at Canaan and realizing they are expected to fight for it, predictably, "all the children of Israel mur-mured against Moses and against Aaron: and the whole congregation said unto them Would God that we had died in the land of Egypt! or would God we had died in this wilderness! And wherefore hath the Lord brought us unto this land, to fall by the sword, that our wives and our children should be a prey? were it not better for us to return into Egypt? . . . And the Lord said unto Moses, How long will this people provoke me? and how long will it be ere they believe me, for all the signs which I have showed among them?" Only Moses' plea saves the Jews from extinction, but they are doomed to the forty years of exile, until such time as a new generation shall have grown up among a presumably chastened people. But, as God knows best of all, they are incorrigible, "stiffnecked": "And the Lord said unto Moses . . . this people will rise up, and go whoring after the Gods of the strangers of the land . . . and will forsake me, and break my convenant which I have made with them. . . . For when I shall have brought them into the land which I sware unto their fathers, that floweth with milk and honey; and they shall have eaten and filled themselves, and waxen fat; then will they turn unto other gods, and serve them, and provoke me, and break my covenant."

There is, then, a kind of foreordination to the fact that the modern Jew, the Jew beyond Exodus, remains in the wilderness. He too doesn't really expect eternality *and* absolution *and* milk and honey *and*—well, peace and joy and youth and beauty; but to hunger for verities and en-counter only reality, who needed to journey across a lifetime of wilderness and arrive at journey's end only to discover more wilderness and more lifetime? The Promised Land for the Jew, then, is a place in which to die as well as live, and although it has been given to him he must work to earn it, to produce the milk and honey that exist only insofar as he creates them (and usually having to do so without cows or bees); and though it may be called a place of respite, of cessation of wandering, it is still a wasteland—and one puts down roots there at his own risk, tentatively, circumspectly, for the indifferent arid sand will starve, burn out, bury whatever encroaches and attempts to grow there. And so the Jew, trembling and chosen, trembling *because* chosen, simultaneously enacts and unintentionally parodies the world's success story—the alienation and feebleness, the dream, the struggle, the achievement—and then the wondering if it is all worth it, especially since he achieves nothing permanent and stable, but only more struggle and uncertainty.

It should be no surprise, especially to Jews, who have been there before, that, beyond Sinai, lies more of the same, a Negev Desert of the mind offering an unceasing challenge for man's questing spirit—necessarily questing because rootless. Exodus defines man's condition as process, a constant becoming. The Jew knows, though he often forgets and needs life to remind him, that the Promised Land too is a process and not a goal, a place where one goes to eat forbidden fruit (as Portnoy takes great delight in graphically demonstrating) because such an act at least proves you're alive and in a position to make things happen—even if only for the worse. In general, the Christian view, looking towards Judgment Day and eternality beyond, says that being of the Elect means you've got it made, if not immediately then ultimately. The Jew's already been to his Promised Land, and he finds that it's not so great, in fact seems a little steep at the price; and he would like to know if maybe there isn't something just a little fancier in stock, perhaps something a little more like what the *goyim* are getting over in their neck of Paradise.

All of this is not to say that the Jew does not acknowledge the existence of his God and the possibility of a divine superstructure; he does acknowledge these—at least if pressed hard enough. But he's not only not obsessed by them, he also doesn't spend much of his time looking in that direction. The Jew lives in and of this world, for of all Western religions Judaism is the most secular and agnostic, the least concerned with considering this world as a stage in some larger process and pointed towards some otherwordly ultimate. The Jew knows that God is not a man and that he must try to be one, and so he looks within and builds what he can with the inadequate raw material he discerns there. His agnosticism and secularity lead him to humanism, to an intense concern that the day to day events of the here and now be lived in compassion and consideration, in love and peace—all the tender and lost virtues rarely actualized in a world basically indifferent to the human moment. The Rabbi's eulogy over Morris Bober, the finally-worn-out grocer in Malamud's *The Assistant*, makes the same point in more concrete terms.

The rabbi gazed down at his prayer book, then looked up.

"When a Jew dies, who asks if he is a Jew? He is a Jew, we don't ask. There are many ways to be a Jew. So if somebody comes to me and says, 'Rabbi, shall we call such a man Jewish who lived and worked among the gentiles and sold them pig meat, trayfe, that we don't eat it, and not once in twenty years comes inside a synagogue, is such a man a Jew, Rabbi?' To him I will say, 'Yes. Morris Bober was to me a true Jew because he lived in the Jewish experience, which he remembered, and with the Jewish heart.' Maybe not to our formal tradition . . . but he was true to the spirit of our life—to want for others that which he wants also for himself. He followed the Law which God gave to Moses on Sinai and told him to bring to the people. He suffered, he endu-red, but with hope. . . . He asked for himself little—nothing, but he wanted for his beloved child a better existence than he had. For such reasons he was a Jew. What more does our sweet God ask his poor people?" (p. 180)

The Jew come to America feels doubly estranged—a continuing anomaly, an outsider in the wilderness which is the gentiles' Promised Land. "It is not surprising that he becomes, in Isaac Rosenfeld's phrase 'a specialist in alienation.' "[2] In *Making It*, Norman Podhoretz writes of his father:

A skeptical, reticent, highly private man, he never got caught up, as so many of his contemporaries did on their journey from East European orthodoxy to Western-style modernity, either in socialism or in any one of the organized varieties of ideological Jewish nationalism. He was sympathetic to socialism but not a socialist; he was a Zionist, but not a passionate one; Yiddish remained his first language, but he was not a Yiddishist. He was, in short, a Jewish survivalist, unclassifiable and eclectic, tolerant of any modality of Jewish existence so long as it remained identifiably and self-consciously Jewish, and outraged by any species of Jewish assimilationism, whether overt or concealed. (pp. 29–30)

The attitude here is ambiguous, for the father is surely to be admired for his insulation from the "ism" of the moment, for his immunity from the follies of his fellow Jews. Yet the detachment also implies a lack of commitment, a continuing sense of outsidedness. Leslie Fiedler has written that

All flights, the Jewish experience teaches, are from one exile to another; and this Americans have always known, though they have sometimes attempted to deny it. Fleeing exclusion in the Old World, the immigrant discovers loneliness in the New World; fleeing communal loneliness of seaboard settlements, he discovers the ultimate isolation of the frontier. It is the dream of exile as freedom which has made America; but it is the experience of exile as terror that has forged the self-consciousness of Americans. (*End*, p. 84)

Paradoxically, then, the Jew is also right at home in America, for alienation is a deeply American theme. He is divided between adhering to the old ways and fully adopting the new—as in the true and typical story of the immigrant who had been a rabbi in the old country; in America, unable to speak English, he naturally finds no job as a rabbi—so he becomes a rich furniture salesman. And the polarizing pressures function all the more traumatically because they are inherent, inherited rather than acquired, products of dual stereotypes: the Jew as Shylock the evil money-grubber or the *nouveau riche* at their crudest and most flagrantly ostentatious; and the obsessive scholar, ashen pale, totally oblivious to material concerns and mere physical functionings—the product of "the Einstein syndrome," which proclaims (as any Jewish mother will tell you) that all Jewish boys are born brilliant.

In another sense, the Jew in America is no longer the anomaly he once was—that of one more written about than writing. Back in the 1920s and 1930s there were not only no major Jewish writers, there were (with a scattering of exceptions like Lionel Trilling and Ben Hecht and Mike Gold) few who were significant at all. With specific reference to the thirties, Fiedler—an archetypically brilliant Jew with the usual problems and then some—has written:

> Even in the creation of the Jew, a job the Jewish writer in the United States has long been struggling to take out of the hands of the Gentiles, there is no Jewish writer who can compare in effectiveness to Thomas Wolfe. Just as Sherwood Anderson and Hemingway and Fitzgerald succeeded in making their hostile images of Jews imaginative currencies in the twenties, Wolfe succeeded in imposing on his period a series of portraits derived from his experiences at New York University; enamelled Jewesses with melon breasts; crude young male students pushing him off the sidewalk; hawk-beaked Jewish elders, presumably manipulating the world of wealth and power from behind the scenes.[3]

Clearly a major change has transpired between those earlier decades and the fifties and sixties; Jews today, though they may not be more certain of their own identity than anyone else, have nonetheless asserted their right to the dubious privilege of writing about themselves—and, in fact, of telling the *goyim* who *they* are.

Several recent commentators have suggested that, to the extent that such processes have locatable origins, the place to begin is with Hemingway's *The Sun Also Rises*, with its stereotyped Jewish antagonist named Robert Cohn:

> Less than a decade after the war that signified the end of Protestant supremacy in American culture, white Protestant

Hemingway was able to control the destiny of his Jew with complete confidence, outfitting him with all the Jew's cliché characteristics (doesn't drink, doesn't know when he isn't wanted, is a wet blanket, is too intellectual and unspontaneous, and so on), using him to set off the Protestant types who are the code followers. Hemingway thoroughly humiliates Cohn through his Jewish pugnaciousness, and then dismisses him.[4]

Jewish writers of the fifties and sixties, Fiedler suggests—writers like Bellow, Malamud, and Roth—though under Hemingway's influence for a time, are not descendants of him and his at least literarily anti-Semitic contemporaries, "but are rather anti-Hemingways, avengers of the despised Robert Cohen [sic], Jewish butt of *The Sun Also Rises*" (*End*, p. 64). They claim Hemingway's caricature as a legitimate character, embrace him as their own, and place him at the center of their still geocentric universe. He has been transformed into the modern equivalent of the hero, someone whose existence somehow matters because he radiates intensity and because, like it or not, he bears the seeds of his culture.

The book that permits the exorcism of Hemingway's ghost for the Jewish writer is Bellow's *Henderson, The Rain King*. Bellow had already made the attempt once. On the first page of his novel, *Dangling Man*, his protagonist denounces the Hemingwayesque "code of the athlete, of the tough boy. . . . If you have difficulties, grapple with them silently, goes one of their commandments. To hell with that! I intend to talk about mine, and if I had as many mouths as Siva has arms and kept them going all the time, 1 still could not do myself justice." The exorcism, however, was not to be so easily accomplished, and it was not until 13 years later that Bellow made the more extended and successful effort in *Henderson, The Rain King*. Though its protagonist is not Jewish, it is the parody of Hemingway that all right-thinking American-Jewish writers had unconscioulsy been awaiting. The title character, who shares Hemingway's initials, is a middle-aged American millionaire who fails to find happiness or peace by trying to raise pigs or cope with his family. He flees to Africa, rejects the safari approach to seek out the natives, becomes a kind of local deity through no talent of his own except brute strength and sheer stupidity, discovers that one is akin to the kind of animal one identifies with, has his vision, and then flies safely out of Africa and back, presumably, to connubial bliss and domestic tranquility—an ending whose very hopefulness, especially cast in such a form, mocks those achieved by Hemingway's protagonists, and of course by Hemingway himself.

Concerning being Jewish and an American and young and an intellectual in the 1930s, Lionel Trilling writes that it had nothing to do with religion or Zionism—for he and others like him had rejected the religion and were generally either indifferent to or actually opposed to the founding of what is now Israel (in the mid 1940s Alfred Kazin called Zionists "dreary middle-class chauvinists")—"our concern with Jewishness was about what is now called authenticity . . . that the individual Jewish person recognizes naturally and easily that he *is* a Jew and 'accepts himself' as such." Writing from the vantage point of 1966, Trilling is able to say that

> Nowadays one of the most salient facts about American culture is the prominent place in it that is occupied by Jews. This state of affairs has become a staple subject of both journalism and academic study—for some years now the *Times Literary Supplement* has found it impossible to survey the American literary scene without goggling rather solemnly over the number of Jews that make it what it is; foreign students have withdrawn their attention from the New Criticism to turn it upon The Jew in American Culture.[5]

To make the same point in a slightly different way, Fiedler quotes Gore Vidal—an *au courant* writer but, alas, not Jewish—as writing "in mock horror (but with an undertone of real bitterness, too) . . . : 'Every year there is a short list of the O.K. writers. Today's list consists of two Jews, two Negroes and a safe floating *goy* of the old American Establishment . . .' " (*End*, p. 88).

This is not to say that Jewish writers (any more than their co-religionists in other fields) have completely taken over the scene—though sometimes it does seem as if such is the case—or that we even know what we mean when we speak of Jewish writers today. In the thirties, Trilling says, "we undertook to normalize [the Jewish present] by suggesting that it was not only as respectable as the present of any other group but also as foolish, vulgar, complicated, impossible, and promising."[6] Trilling was, of course, ahead of his time; for it is only after the apocalyptic events of the thirties and forties, only in the context of the fifties and sixties, the context of, on the one hand, the civil rights movement spearheaded to a large extent by young Jews and, on the other, that of the scandals associated with non-Jews like Billie Sol Estes, Bobby Baker, and others, that the necessary merging of stereotypes can occur so as to produce an Abe Fortas—a classically brilliant Jew driven by greed—and result in a hue and cry throughout the land that is not a ritualistic witch hunt, does not even hint at a condemnation on the grounds of Fortas' being a Jew. And on a slightly different level a Norman Podhoretz (himself a living variation on the Portnoy theme of outsidedness as "in-ness") can come along and make a fortune by writing opening about "making it" in this country. He writes that "the immigrant Jewish milieu from which I derive is by now fixed for all time in the American imagination as having been driven by an uninhibited hunger for success. This reputation is by no means as justified as we have been led to believe, but certainly on the surface the 'gospel of success' did reign supreme in the world of my childhood." Yet today it is far more significant, he adds, that American culture itself both embodies materialistic values and seeks to deny them, instilling in us curiously contradictory feelings

> toward the ambition for success. . . . On the one hand, we are commanded to become successful—that is, to acquire more . . . worldly goods than we began with, and to do so by our own exertions; on the other hand, it is impressed upon us by means both direct and devious that if we obey the commandment, we shall find ourselves falling victim to the radical corruption of spirit which . . . the pursuit of success requires and which its attainment always bespeaks. . . . On the one hand, our culture teaches us to shape our lives in accordance with the hunger for worldly things; on the other other hand, it spitefully contrives to make us ashamed of the presence of those hungers in ourselves and to deprive us as far as possible of any pleasure in their satisfaction. (*Making it,* pp. xii–xiv)

What has happened is that America herself has become a Jewish mother surrogate, supreme creator of schizophrenia in all her sons.

Thus, Trilling's implicit notion, that "beyond alienation"—to borrow the title of a recent book by an American-Jewish critic named Marcus Klein—lies assimilation for the Jew who wants it, seems a truism. For the contents of the broken melting pot have escaped and covered the land; and who shall be an outsider, an alien, when everyone is? The individual Jewish writer, then, like the Pole and the Italian and the Irishman before him, but unlike the black who follows him, is at last free to seek his own orientation and direction, to write Christian allegories like Nathanael West or obsessive moral fables like Bernard Malamud or middle-class suburban exposés cast in the form of a Jewish joke like Philip Roth. Contemporary Jewish writers, then, are neither monolithic nor univocal; they speak with many voices though they share the same tongue and the same questioning attitude towards the equivocal world their variety of protagonists try gamely to survive in.

Salinger's half-Jewish protagonists, for instance, are kids of all ages, adolescents (like Holden Caulfield) and brittle post-adolescents like the aptly named members of the Glass family; like miniature Hemingway heroes, they are at once tough and wide-eyed, sophisticated and sentimental, persistently expectant and disappointed—which is appealing and moving when the characters are young, but which becomes cloying when they remain unchanged through puberty, marriage, parenthood, religion, insanity, menopause, suicide, and so on. And yet they have their visions of fulfillment, as when Zooey Glass offers his sister the inescapable Fat Lady of the typical radio or television audience ("the eternal vulgarian," Ihab Hassan calls her[7]) as Jesus Christ himself. Malamud offers us the opposite: narrow, suffering Jews, unwilling victims of a heritage they thought to reject. In the short story "The German Refugee," for example, the title character flees to America from Nazi Germany and his non-Jewish wife, and then commits suicide after learning that she embraced Judaism and was executed in the gas chambers. Malamud's characters are old, even the young ones—old and tired and bitter and complaining about a world set against them by definition and which asks them to endure more of the same and keep on shrugging benignly. And, surprisingly, mostly they do, and achieve in the process a crummy but miraculous dignity which allows life to go on going on and meaning to remain a potential.

Bellow's early protagonists are young seekers somewhat akin to Salinger's. (Augie March, for instance, says, "I have always tried to become what I am. But it's a frightening thing. Because what if what I am by nature isn't good enough?") His later and more interesting ones are middle-aged ex-athletes rebelling against a kind of male menopause that seems to threaten them with an eternity of their present condition unless they break immediately and violently out of their inertia through the conquest of untamed jungle (as in *Henderson, the Rain King*), or of women (in *Herzog*), or of self (in *The Last Analysis*). At the beginning of their works it appears that they have already been wherever it is they are going to get, are too blind to know this, and so in a frenzied, picaresque manner strive to attain or recapture a world and a way irrevocably gone. Yet they end, oddly enough, like Malamud's characters and like *Portnoy's Complaint*, at a beginning, or at least a stasis, a still point in the turning world where, if anywhere, beginnings are still possible.

Though the level of formal education varies greatly, the typical protagonist for all these writers—and Roth's Portnoy may be the paradigmatic personification—is highly intellectual and articulate. Unlike Robert Cohn who is mocked because he talks too much, the protagonist of the modern American-Jewish novel takes pride in being an obsessive self-confessor whose verbal diarrhea is, he thinks, preventive medicine against the constipation he will surely inherit from his father. But unlike their fathers, such characters know too much to remain passive, stoical, and silent, and too little to discover ultimate consoling responses to the unending questions they feel constrained to ask about the inadequacies of their world and its strange inhabitants—themselves most especially. Tragic heroes they're not; they don't suffer grandly, they just sort of have aches and pains all over. Tragic heroes are psychotic, possessed of a monomaniacal sense of grandeur; but the Jewish hero like Portnoy is neurotic—and he whines about it (and why not? it hurts just as much whether he's made to suffer by others or himself), but his whining itself is often a thing of glory, so brilliant that it impresses him, dazzles him—and he revels in it, drinks (non-alcoholically) to it, indulges himself in it, plays it for all its worth before whatever audience he can capture by mesmerization or money, whether it be Portnoy's analyst, Zooey Glass's Fat Lady, the group of psychiatrists gathered to watch the closed-circuit performance in Bellow's *The Last Analysis*, or the myriad recipients, living and dead, of Herzog's endless letters.

And on top of everything else, to add to his joy and his woes, the Jew has a mother. As a rule tragic heroes do not have mothers. One who does, Shakespeare's Coriolanus, a huge-statured military commander, causes major problems for the critics because of his dominating mother (appropriately named Volumnia) and his uncomfortable relationship with her; they don't know whether he is superman or, as Aufidius the rival general calls him, a boy of tears. Now any Jew with a mother will recognize immediately that Coriolanus' duality is the quite normal consequence of his trying to please his mother who wants, inevitably, lovingly, two impossibly contradictory things of him: that he be hailed by the world for his unique achievements and that he fulfill himself according to *her* vision of human greatness; that is, that he be totally independent—"As if a man were author of himself" (*Coriolanus*, Act V, scene iii, line 36)—and simultaneously totally dependent upon the self-sacrificing mother who has given him the best years of her life, worked her fingers to the bone for him, scrimped and went without, and asks for nothing in return—except that he be exactly what she needs him to be. If we see Coriolanus, then, as a precurser of Portnoy, a kind of "my son, the Roman tyrant," it all makes perfect sense. Volumnia will do literally anything to have her son achieve her definition of his role, but God help him if he attempts to strike out on his own. The moral, I suppose, is that if you're going to have a mother you'd better be Jewish—at least then you'll know where your troubles are likely to originate.

Oedipus and Hamlet also had mothers, and, at least in the case of Oedipus, in both senses of that phrase. But Jocasta and Gertrude are not only embodiments of political power, they are also good-looking, sexy females, worth murdering kings to possess. The Jewish mother is, on the other hand, the tender and dumpy seat of domestic authority, by definition harrassed, middle-aged, long suffering, and simultaneously so emasculating towards any handy husbands or sons and of such delicate sensibilities that even the vaguely risqué, the barest hint at anything having to do with that dirty of dirties, the ultimate four-letter word if it only had the money to buy one more—S-E-X—that one can't help but wonder where all the Jewish kids keep coming from—certainly not from such mothers as these.

Like Malamud's characters, Roth's are Jewish all the way, only their humor has turned to feverishly pitched self-deprecation rather than bitter resignation. Here is Portnoy, who has just been warned by his mother, yet again, about eating French-fried potatoes out because "*tateleh*, it begins with diarrhea, but do you know how it ends? With a sensitive stomach like yours, do you know how it finally ends? *Wearing a plastic bag to do your business in!*" (p. 32). Portnoy's response is typical of his theatrical exasperation:

Where was the gusto, where was the boldness and courage?
Who filled these parents of mine with such a fearful sense of

life? . . . These two are the outstanding producers and packagers of guilt in our time! . . . Please, who crippled us like this? Who made us so morbid and hysterical and weak? . . . Is this the Jewish suffering I used to hear so much about? Is this what has come down to me from the pogroms and the persecution? from the mockery and abuse bestowed by the *goyim* over these two thousand lovely years? (pp. 35–7).

What Roth has written is a nervous Jewish *bildungsroman*, its protagonist stretched on the analyst's couch during the entire novel, circling in and around his rites of passage from innocence to neurosis, trying to define his experience as an assimilated, heritage-rejecting American Jew who still feels himself as one apart, unique, doomed to be different from the fellow Americans he longs to embrace as his own. "Look, I'm not asking for the world," he says,

I just don't see why I should get any less out of life than some schmuck like Oogie Pringle or Henry Aldrich. I want Jane Powell too, God damn it! And Corliss and Veronica. I too want to be the boyfriend of Debbie Reynolds—it's the Eddie Fisher in me coming out, that's all, the longing in all us swarthy Jewboys for those bland blond exotics called *shikses*. . . . Only what I don't know yet in these feverish years is that for every Eddie yearning for a Debbie, there is a Debbie yearning for an Eddie—a Marilyn Monroe yearning for her Arthur Miller—even an Alice Faye yearning for Phil Harris. . . . Who knew, you see, who knew back when we were watching *National Velvet*, that this stupendous purple-eyed girl who had the supreme *goyische* gift of all, the courage and know-how to get up and ride around on a horse (as opposed to having one pull your wagon, like the rag-seller for whom I am named)—who would have believed that this girl on the horse with the riding breeches and the perfect enunciation was lusting for our kind no less than we for hers? Because you know what Mike Todd was—a cheap facsimile of my Uncle Hymie upstairs! And who in his right mind would ever have believed that Elizabeth Taylor had the hots for Uncle Hymie? (pp. 151–2).

Both Alexander Portnoy and his mother (the only Mrs. Portnoy he ever knows), are firm believers in "the Einstein syndrome"—especially as personified by Alexander Portnoy. As in *Making It*, perhaps the central theme in *Portnoy's Complaint* (and one virtually ignored by the reviews) concerns the use and abuse of the intellect and, more specifically, the ambiguous role of the intellect in Jewish culture. Traditionally, the Jews view intellect as an end in itself, a dubious but supreme sign of specialness because it bestows more responsibility than freedom; if a means to anything, then to unworldly success: the disputatious role of Talmudic scholar. But the young Jew's assertation of his *own* intellect often takes the form of a total rejection of his Jewishness—the culture, the religion, the people—as when Portnoy, age fourteen, refuses with atheistic integrity to get dressed up on Rosh Hashanah. Looking back on the scene, which hurts rather than amuses, Portnoy mocks the self-righteous younger version of himself—yet it is typical not only of a certain stage in the life of the recently bar-mitzvahed, third generation American Jew, but also of Portnoy throughout his life. For while he intends his intellect as a moral force, an instrument for improving the lot of at least those who fall within the province of the Assistant Commissioner of Human Opportunity for the City of New York if not of the entire world, it becomes a pious means for making money, fame, and females. The thirty-three-year-old Portnoy knows that the self-assertion of the fourteen-year-old Portnoy is essentially a sham: a gut-level attack on his parents cast in the form of an intellectual statement; but though Portnoy's confessional, like Podhoretz's, reveals a great deal of self-consciousness, both are still able to maintain the natural arrogance that supposedly accrues to those of superior intellect and, simultaneously, to perfect that intellect in the service of worldly success. The dichotomy leads invariably to obsessive self-deception, guilt, and a despairing need to escape what pursues from within. Portnoy's neurosis results primarily from rebelling against what he hates (and yet also loves) in his mother and finding it in himself—the prejudice against *goyim*, for example, which he compensates for by taking to bed every blond, blue-eyed, button-nosed, seemingly unobtainable *shikse* he can get his hands on, seduce, do acrobatic tricks with, abandon, and then feel guilty about—all the time striving to put "the id back in Yid . . . , and the *oy* back in *goy*" (p. 209). Podhoretz quotes Freud (himself of course a Jew) on the mother-son origins of such paradoxical role-playing: "A man who has been the indisputable favorite of his mother [Portnoy on his father: 'Among his other misfortunes, I was his wife's favorite.'] keeps for life the feeling of a conqueror, that confidence of success which frequently induces real success" (*Making It*, p. 57). "Let's face it, Ma," says Portnoy, "I am the smartest and neatest little boy in the history of my school! Teachers . . . go home happy to their husbands because of me" (p. 14). And yet, "When I am bad I am locked out of the apartment," and from his bed at night he can "hear her babbling about her problems to the women around the mah-jongg game: *My Alex is suddenly such a bad eater I have to stand over him with a knife*" (pp. 13, 43). Who but a Jewish mother, of whom Portnoy's is but an epitome, would sacrifice everything—even, or perhaps the word is especially, her husband—in order that her son may succeed, and then winds up revelling in her sacrifice and mocking the success? What other kind of mother makes her sacrifices with such complete and utter commitment that she can threaten the object of all her sacrificing, the pride and joy of her whole life, with immediate and total extinction if he should fail by one iota to achieve in direct proportion to the extent of her sacrificing?—an achievement which is impossible since her sacrifice knows no bounds, is always greater than one can imagine, measure, or equal. And so Portnoy, now an adult, successful and famous, is still making the same complaint:

> Whenever my name now appears in a new story in the *Times*, they bombard every living relative with a copy of the clipping. Half my father's retirement pay goes down the drain in postage, and my mother is on the phone for days at a stretch and has be be fed intravenously, her mouth is going at such a rate about her Alex. In fact, it's exactly as it always has been: they can't get over what a success and a genius I am, . . . but still, if you know what I mean, still somehow not entirely perfect. . . . All they have sacrificed for me and done for me and how they boast about me and are the best public relations firm (they tell me) any child could have, and it turns out that I still won't be perfect. Did you ever hear of such a thing in your life? I just refuse to be perfect. (pp. 107–8)

The anguish Portnoy expresses comically here is real and intense—for he, too, would like to have achieved the all he intended when he started out, the all that lies always beyond the actual. What Portnoy will not, cannot, say is that the intensity of their involvement in his life is not only cloying but also beautiful, and valuable beyond anything he has attained by repudiating them. As Portnoy knows all too well, and has been at pains to demonstrate throughout the session that is his book, his life is immeasurably less perfect than they will ever know. And the resulting guilt—the sense of having achieved nothing of substance (though thriving as the world measures these things) and the need to maintain the façade of success—leads, naturally enough, to his taking the offensive, to his evading introspection by accusing his parents of unforgiveable acts.

For some undefined sin, Moses was barred from bringing his people into the Promised Land towards which he had led them for forty years. Where Moses failed to go there Portnoy has gone, and what he learns, among other things, is that Moses was better off—at least he could still maintain his vision uncontaminated by reality. After all the gentile girls he's had in order to prove how much he belongs *here*, Portnoy (in a section Roth ironically calls "In Exile") goes to Israel to discover that, for once, the Jews are the WASPS, and he finds that the discovery renders him impotent—first, with a small, voluptuous Israeli lieutenant and then with a beautiful idealist who reminds him of, of all people, his mother. As Portnoy puts it: "Doctor: *I couldn't get it up in the State of Israel!* How's *that* for symbolism, *bubi*? Let's see somebody beat that, for acting-out! Could not maintain an erection in The Promised Land! At least not when I needed it, not when I wanted it, not when there was something more desirable than my own hand to stick it into . . ." (pp. 257–8). The girl from the kibbutz, who calls him "nothing but a self-hating Jew, . . . a shlemiel," towers six feet over the prostrate, defeated Portnoy who starts to sing,

"Im-po-tent in Is-rael, da da daaah," to the tune of "Lullaby in Birdland."

"Another joke?" she asked.

"And another. And another. Why disclaim my life?"

Then she said a kind thing. She could afford to, of course, way up there. "You should go home."

"Sure, that's what I need, back into the exile."

(pp. 265–9)

And so it's back to America, the diaspora, the Promised Land for Gentiles, back to the alienation which defines him there as it defined the Jews during the forty years in the desert and throughout their history—back because a successful Jewish nation makes neither historical nor sexual sense, and because Portnoy has conceived of Israel not as process, something alive and changing—as Exodus teaches us it is—but rather as something fixed and determined. Besides, only in America can he spite his mother by seducing *shikses*, the only form of love apparently granted Portnoy's perverse penis—at least until the end and the hopeful hint of a beginning with which Roth concludes both the book and what is, after all, only Portnoy's first session of self-analysis and self-definition. The book ends with a cry for help and the possibility of a beginning, a return to process and promise. Eliot's anti-Semitic Gerontion asks, "After such knowledge, what forgiveness?" But self-willed ignorance is not the Jew's way; for Portnoy, now fully conscious heir of Jewish tradition (like Malamud's Yakov Bok), only after such confrontation and self-revelation as that which comprise his book may forgiveness, and therefore viable self-definition, possibly follow. Such endings would seem to be the only kind possible in American-Jewish novels. Perhaps they are the only kind possible in a world that remains defined by mortality and flux. Perhaps, and I suggest this with great temerity, they are (if we but knew it) the only kind we need.

Notes

1. *Waiting for the End: The Crisis in American Culture and a Portrait of Twentieth Century American Literature* (New York, 1964), p. 102. Subsequent references to this work are cited in the text as *End*.

2. Irving Malin, *Jews and Americans* (Carbondale, 1965), p. 14.

3. "The Breakthrough: The American Jewish Novelist and the Fictional Image of the Jew," *Midstream*, 4 (Winter 1958), p. 17.

4. Michael J. Hoffman, "From Cohn to Herzog," *The Yale Review* (Spring 1969), p. 342.

5. "Afterword," *The Unpossessed* by Tess Slesinger (New York, 1966), pp. 319–21.

6. *Ibid*, p. 320.

7. *Radical Innocence* (New York, 1961), p. 283.

The Sadness of Philip Roth:
an Interim Report

Joseph C. Landis*

In its January 1962 issue, *Esquire* presents a small portion of Philip Roth's forthcoming novel (to appear late this spring), with the announcement: "This is a section from his first novel, a much-awaited literary event." There is no exaggeration in this statement. The same anticipation awaited the appearance of *Goodbye, Columbus*—Roth's first and thus far only book, a collection of five short stories and a novella. The publication of that collection in 1959 confirmed the already widespread impression left earlier by his stories in the *New Yorker* and *Commentary* that a young writer of great vigor and promise had appeared on the scene. Among his reviewers were Saul Bellow, Leslie Fiedler, Irving Howe, and Alfred Kazin. His honors included a National Book Award in 1960 as well as the Daroff Memorial Award of the Jewish Book Council of America, also in 1960, for the best "work of Jewish interest" in fiction. And he and Bernard Malamud have since been frequently coupled as artists of large talents who write about Jews.

For this very subject matter Roth became the center of a controversy that has only recently subsided. In Yiddish as well as in English he has been severely attacked for distortion in his portraits of Jews.[1] With equal warmth he had been defended for his honesty. Leslie Fiedler congratulated him on having "already received the young Jewish writer's initial accolade: the accusation of anti-Semitism. . . ." And Saul Bellow encouraged him: "My advice to Mr. Roth is to ignore all objections and to continue on his present course."

Now that the dust of controversy has settled, it is possible to see Philip Roth in a clearer perspective and in the light of two recent contributions to *Commentary*. His talents are large enough to warrant an interim report.

Despite their sharp dispute, Roth's friends and foes found themselves in curious consort: they agreed on the acerbity of his portraits and they saw in that acerbity Roth's essential quality. Like Neil Klugman in the story "Goodbye, Columbus," Roth is indeed fiercely satirical, at times

*Reprinted from *The Massachusetts Review*, 3 (Winter, 1962), 259–68. Copyright © 1962. The Massachusetts Review, Inc., by permission.

even cruel. Klugman, as Irving Howe emphasizes, means "cleverfellow" in Yiddish, and Roth's tone and style are those of a clever fellow, sometimes even of a wise-guy. But if the *u* in Neil's name is pronounced short instead of long, Klugman in Yiddish comes to "sadfellow," "mourner." If Roth is a clever fellow in his portraits, he is perhaps even more a mourner, a man made deeply sad by the spectacle of what he sees. In the controversy, this sad undertone seems to have escaped the notice it deserves. If Roth is indignant at the values of a prosperous world, he is also saddened by the sheer pathetic emptiness, the comfortable meaninglessness, the petty superficiality of the lives he sees. Under the ferocity of his satire is a terrible sadness that is ultimately the more important quality of his vision, a sadness that life has become merely a comfort station for easing tensions. The world of Roth's fiction is not one damnably dedicated to making money; it is a world dedicated to nothing, desiring nothing except "normalcy." What oppresses Roth above everything is the insignificance of those normal, humdrum, comfort-seeking lives, the pathetic waste of time.

The lives he pictures are wholly unrelated lives—unrelated to any real group or community or indeed to any other human being. Utterly lonely lives, they have not even Carlyle's "cash nexus" as a bond between man and man. They make no real contact with one another. In pursuit of their own ends, they merely brush against one another. Despite all the zipping and unzipping, they are really loveless lives. Those of his characters, like Epstein, that yearn for love, do not find it. Lives are empty and cold, full of food only, like the Patimkin refrigerators. When lives are ruffled, Freud becomes a tranquilizer to soothe them back to insignificance. Even those that dream and hope, like Neil Klugman and the little Negro boy, find that someone else has taken their books out of the library.

What grieves Roth most is the awareness that normalcy has, like a Procrustes' bed, truncated the range of life, excluding on the one hand the embrace of aspiration, the exhilaration of wonder, and on the other the acceptance of suffering. From this sadness grows Roth's ferocity, directed mainly against those who deny life, against the cowards who fear it, against all who would reduce it to safe insignificance, against all who flee from self and suffering. It is beneath the dignity of man not to sacrifice and suffer—to seek repose is a travesty of the realities of life and the potential of man. Roth is committed to his unheroic heroes who yearn and aspire, who want to climb out of the morass "up the long marble stairs that led to Tahiti." Such a hero is "the little colored kid who liked Gauguin" (in "Goodbye, Columbus"), who dreams of island paradises, and who taunts the library lions and growls at them though they are but stone: "Then he would straighten up, and, shaking his head, he would say to the lion, 'Man, you's a coward. . . .' Then, once again, he'd growl." Here we perceive the essence of Roth, the source of his sadness and his ferocity: "Man, you's a coward." And he shakes his head sadly. Then, once again, he growls.

In "Goodbye, Columbus," Brenda Patimkin's sin is not so much that she has affronted Neil and his dignity as a human being. Her greater sin is her cowardice, her dream-destroying fear. Hers is not merely a betrayal of Neil or betrayal of love; it is a betrayal of herself, and of life. Neil's return to his work in the library on the day of the Jewish New Year is not the act of desecration that it seems. It is meant to be an act of dedication to dreams and meanings and values symbolized by the library. The return to work is Neil's own goodbye, Columbus, a goodbye to the sad values and empty lives that are normal in America—a land sometimes referred to in the Yiddish as "Columbus's *medineh* [country]." That his renewal of himself should take place on the New Year is symbolically appropriate.

Neil is relatively fortunate. He is free to hope again. But not Epstein. It is given to Goldie Epstein, his wife, to pronounce the most terrible sentence in Roth's book: "You hear the doctor, Lou. All you got to do is live a normal life." Underlying the farce and the ferocity of "Epstein" is the grief of Epstein's outcry to his nephew: "You're a boy, you don't understand. When they start taking things away from you, you reach out, you *grab*—maybe like a pig even, but you grab." And after the outcry there is the sad defeat that seals Epstein's fate. His rash and his yearning are merely an "irritation," which the doctor promises to clear up "So it'll never come back." And underneath the sadness of Epstein's defeat is the sadness of Roth's own sense of man's defeat. The rash in man is only an irritation which the world will all too soon and irrevocably clear up so it'll never come back.

This same awareness is what gives other stories of rash men, like "The Conversion of the Jews" and "Eli the Fanatic," a dimension that some of Roth's critics have missed. One of our most perceptive critics thought "Conversion" little more than a lesson in tolerance: "The point—'You shouldn't hit me about God, Mamma. You should never hit anybody about God'—is altogether too clear; there really isn't a story apart from it." But "Conversion" is far more than (perhaps even far from) a plea for tolerance or "a beautiful treatment of a young boy coping with comparative religion," as another reviewer put it. In "Conversion," as in all Roth's stories, is implicit a plea for dreams, for life's wonders, for aspiration to the meaningful and the miraculous and the bold. It is a plea for the conversion of the Jews—but to Judaism. And now. For like the lover in Andrew Marvell's "Coy Mistress," from which the story's title seems to be taken, we have not "world enough and time," and any coyness *is* a crime.

In "Conversion," Ozzie Freedman is approaching thirteen, the symbolic age of adulthood in Judaism, the age at which full moral responsibility is assumed. And Ozzie Freedman discovers God.

> His mother was a round, tired, gray-haired penguin of a
> woman whose gray skin had begun to feel the tug of gravity
> and the weight of her own history. Even when she dressed up
> she didn't look like a chosen person. But when she lit candles
> she looked like something better; like a woman who knew
> momentarily that God could do anything.

Ozzie tries unsuccessfully to reconcile his sense of miraculous Divinity and miraculous life with the domesticated, naturalized, and reasonable local Deity of Rabbi Binder. The contest is reflected in the names. The efforts of the youth aspiring to freedom outrage the Rabbi who binds and is earthbound. Ozzie is unable to understand why a God who could "make all that in six days . . . why couldn't he let a woman have a baby without intercourse." When Ozzie finally blurts out his pent-up protest, "You don't know anything about God!" and Rabbi Binder unintentionally bloodies his nose, Ozzie seeks refuge on the roof of the synagogue. As he looks down at the crowd in the street below, at the Rabbi, "normal" in his faithless faith, at Blotnik the Caretaker, who had "memorized the prayers and forgotten all about God," Ozzie's mother cries up to him with splendidly unconscious irony, "Don't be a martyr, my baby." But to Roth the history of Judaism is the history of a faith so deeply held that it embraced martyrdom and gloried in the miraculous potential of life. Jews have always been martyrs, and it is, ironically, their martyrdom that has kept them alive, that has made their history significant and transformed them as Ozzie's mother was transformed in the glow of the Sabbath candles. To be a Jew is to be a martyr. And Ozzie, not "my baby," but preparing to be a man, is the only one who senses that meaning—Ozzie and to a lesser degree his friends who urge him to "be a Martin" in counterpoint to his mother's pleas for his safety. "He's doing it for them," Rabbi Binder explains, not really aware of the truth that Ozzie's dilemma involves all the young, all who aspire to be men. Neither side quite aware of the implications of their words, they stage a debate whose real meaning concerns the nature of life. In the background of the debate is the bored appeal of the firemen, who were called to catch Ozzie in their net: "Look, Oscar, if you're gonna jump, jump—and if you're not gonna jump, don't jump. But don't waste our time, willya?" Oblivious to meaning, they are eager to return to normalcy.

The debate is resolved by a leap that provides a subtle and complex affirmation of the theme of conversion. As a sexual symbol, Ozzie's ejaculation of himself from on high into the firemen's net below affirms the creative wonders of life. And as an act of martyrdom his leap into the "net that glowed . . . like an overgrown halo" becomes paradoxically a moral symbol of his conversion to Judaism and to life. As a moral symbol this act of "madness" is a jolting reminder that to assert one's faith in a world overwhelmed by everyday, petty reasonableness requires an act of martyrdom and fanaticism.

To think of Roth as a social realist (as some of his critics seem to do) is to miss the outcry of such a story and to find in the mad act of its ending a dissipation of its vision. But Roth is more than a realist. His heroes are, in varying degrees, mad—or seem so to a normal world. It takes an act of "madness" to crack the smooth glaze of its tiled life, an act of "fanaticism" like Eli's in "Eli the Fanatic." Eli asserts his identity and like Ozzie assumes the responsibility of martyrdom. His education begins when, as attorney for the Jews of suburban Woodenton, who wish only to "protect what they value, their property, their well-being, their happiness," he tries to reach an accommodation within a newly-established yeshiva of refugees: let the activities of the yeshiva be restricted to its own grounds, and above all let its strangely clad teacher give up his caftan and wide-brimmed hat and adopt American dress in town. The request is reasonable enough in a world striving for normalcy. But the headmaster informs Eli that "The suit the gentleman wears is all he's got," a remark whose meaning Eli slowly comes to realize: the Nazis have taken everything from him except his identity in a tradition of martyrdom for faith. When he is finally forced to wear the tweeds that Eli provides for him, he leaves his own clothes at Eli's door. The "greenie's" unspoken message becomes clear. Eli must himself take up the identity which the normality-seeking Jews of Woodenton have forced the greenie to shed; Eli and the Jews of Woodenton must accept the heritage of faith and martyrdom that is symbolized by the suit. Eli's earlier words acquire an added dimension: "In a life of sacrifice what is one more? But in a life of no sacrifices even one is impossible." There is no doubt as to which of these is life and which is death.

Having donned the greenie's clothes, including the ritual undergarment worn by every orthodox Jew, Eli goes to the greenie as though to seek forgiveness and direction. The greenie points his finger skyward, and Eli has a "revelation." Like Ozzie he is converted. Wearing the strange attire he shows himself in all the streets of Woodenton as the greenie had done wearing Eli's tweeds. And now Eli is ready to show himself to his new-born son in the maternity ward, to pass on to his child the ancient heritage. When his wife begs him, "Please, can't you leave well enough alone? Can't we just have a family?" the answer is obvious. "No." But the penalty for "No" is martyrdom. He is seized on either side by solicitous interns. "But he rose suddenly . . . and flailing his arms, screamed: '*I'm the father!*'" before undergoing the martyrdom of modern man—sedation. Not the son this time. The Father himself. *El li*. My God.

In contrast to the wooden life of Woodenton is the life of the yeshiva with its eighteen students, a number symbolic of life in Jewish tradition. It is perhaps pressing a point to see in the headmaster's name, Tzuref (not a common name, if, indeed, a name at all), an amalgam of the Yiddish and Hebrew words *tzureh* (trouble) and *refueh* (remedy). It is perhaps also pushing too far to read in the name of Eckman, the tranquilizing, normalizing analyst of the story, the pun in Yiddish signifying both man's tail and man's end. But whether or not the names were thus chosen, the men themselves represent these conflicting forces in Roth's world. Eckman wins. Normalcy is the opiate of the people.

Even a story like "Defender of the Faith" grows out of the same vision as "Eli" and the others, the same hatred of normalcy and cowardice, the same insistence on the acceptance of suffering which life requires of man. Grossbart, the Jewish rookie who uses his Jewishness in every weasel way to avoid the unpleasantness of army life and, finally, to get himself removed from a shipment to Pacific combat, Grossbart, like Henry VIII, first bearer of the title, is a betrayer, not a defender of the faith. But in the complex ironies that are typical of a Roth ending, he begins the process of conversion, of becoming a defender, by accepting man's fate of suffering. And Sergeant Marx, the Jewish combat veteran who has Grossbart put back on the Pacific shipment, accepts the knowledge and the guilt of his own vindictiveness and the suffering that is the penalty of that knowledge. He discovers another dimension of martyrdom. In fact, from the final paragraphs of the story there begins to emerge a complex sense of crime and punishment, guilt and innocence, a sense of man's moral capacities. But from the final paragraphs only. The story, which has been praised for its construction, is, apart from these paragraphs, nothing but construction. The complex humanity implicit in the final vision, the compassionate sadness that is as characteristic of Roth as his satiric ferocity, is apparent nowhere else in the story. Only a venomous portrait emerges. Of all Roth's stories that require serious consideration, "Defender" is the least successful because less than any other it translates its meanings into human terms; because more than any other it is untrue to the intention and the vision enunciated in its closing lines and characteristic of its author. And also, perhaps more than any other, it reveals the limitations of that vision.

The debate around Roth has unfailingly pointed out that he is a Jewish writer. The designation needs some explanation. Mark Harris implies that Roth is too narrowly Jewish when he charges Roth with writing about "the small memory," not "the national adventure." It is true that danger lurks for the regional writer, whether his regionalism is geographic or ethnic—the danger of provincialism or parochialism. Yet Roth is not guilty of such weakness. The middle class Jews he writes about are distinguished by their Americanism rather than their Jewishness; the problems he discerns, the voids and the failures, are not distinctively Jewish at all. Roth's concern *is* with the large national misadventure in normalcy. Irving Howe, on the other hand, observes that Roth does not draw upon Jewish tradition at all, that he fails to use the positive values in Jewish life. The remark is especially interesting in the light of Roth's own charge against Bernard Malamud that as a writer he "has not shown specific interest in the anxieties and dilemmas and corruptions of the modern American Jew. . . ." Change "specific interest in" to "much knowledge of" and one gets the charge of the Yiddish critics against Roth. And there is much justice to this accusation. He does not write about the problems that American Jewish life is deeply concerned with: its struggles to maintain or transmit or define its moral values, its cultural creativeness, its scholarship, its relation to Jewish life in other lands. Nor does he write about the problems of self-definition that face multitudes of Jews or the dilemmas that arise from the impact of two moral heritages. Roth does not really deal with the complexities of the Jewish experience in America.

And yet it is overstating a point to deny his relation to Jewish tradition. Not only does he make skillful symbolic use of tradition, custom, and language; ultimately, all of Roth's stories are about the conversion of the Jews. But to what? Roth's weakness lies in the vagueness with which he formulates that tradition and in the resulting softness of his outlook. Although faith and martyrdom, affirmation of life and acceptance of suffering are in the Jewish tradition, that tradition embraces far more than these concepts and defines them within a specific moral context. Since Roth uses these concepts symbolically, since his stories convey no real sense that he takes them literally, definition becomes doubly imperative for him. Faith in what? Martyrdom for what? In his assertion of these values he is strangely reminiscent of Sholem Asch, who was also intrigued by faith and martyrdom. But Asch thought he was talking literally about Judaism when he romanticized these aspects of the Jewish past. Roth's stories give every indication that he does not wish to be taken literally. His recent explicit statement confirms these impressions: "For myself, I cannot find a true and honest place in the history of believers that begins with Abraham, Isaac, and Jacob. . . ."[2] The result is an element of vagueness and generality in his fiction where there should be hard clarity. What kind of island paradises to dream about? What kind of life to live now, shaped by the dream? The "madness" and martyrdom of an Ozzie Freedman or an Eli Peck are not in themselves values. And "since madness is undesirable and sainthood, for most of us, out of the question, the problem of how to live *in* this world is by no means answered; unless the answer is that one cannot." These words are Roth's criticism of Salinger. They are equally applicable to Roth. "The only advice we seem to get from Salinger is to be charming on the way to the loony bin."[3] What advice do we get from Roth? We need to know his values, to see his vision of how to live in the world and how to die in it. It is this soft center in Roth, this lack of a hard moral position that, throwing the emphasis of his stories onto the satire, leaves an aftertaste of pessimism and prevents the compassion from fulfilling itself. Neil Sadfellow's longings are never clearly articulated, so that Neil Cleverfellow's satiric tone remains uppermost in our recollections. Roth's weakness is not, as several of his critics have charged, that his stories are too thematic. His real weakness is that ultimately they lack a theme, a vision and a visionary sense of life, a hard center. Steps—even marble ones—must lead somewhere.

And now there is the prospect of Roth's first novel. Does *Letting Go*, as the work is tentatively titled, have the weighted core that will prevent the false impression of merely raucous satire or evasive parable? The *Esquire* selection is too brief to offer any positive answers, but there are enough departures from both the manner and the matter of the first stories to suggest that the appearance of *Letting Go* many indeed be a literary event of large magnitude.

Notes

1. So great was the outcry that the Jewish Book Council announced, in February of 1961, its decision to consider in the future only fiction characterized by "an affirmative expression of Jewish values" as well as by literary merit.

2. Roth's untitled contribution to "Jewishness and the Younger Intellectuals—A Symposium," *Commentary*, XXXI (April 1961), 351.

3. "Writing American Fiction," *Commentary*, XXXI (March 1961), 228.

Philip Roth and the Rabbis

Allen Guttmann*

It is no surprise that the most famous of the stories of conversion is by Philip Roth. Of Jewish writers a generation younger than Saul Bellow and Norman Mailer, he is the most talented, the most controversial, and the most sensitive to the complexities of assimilation and the question of identity. Roth's first collection of a novella and five stories, *Goodbye, Columbus* (1960), received the National Book Award, the praises of those writers generally associated with *Partisan Review* and *Commentary*, and considerable abuse from men institutionally involved in the Jewish community.[1] Two stories were the focus of resentment: "The Conversion of the Jews" and "The Defender of the Faith."

Ozzie Freedman, the inquisitive hero of "The Conversion of the Jews," asks the questions that any intelligent boy wants to ask, questions like those young Mary Antin put to her teachers. How can Jews be the Chosen People if the Declaration of Independence affirms that all men are created equal? How can an omnipotent God who made the heavens and the earth be *unable* to "let a woman have a baby without having intercourse"?[2] (p. 141) Rabbi Marvin Binder cannot handle questions of this sort. He sends for Mrs. Freedman. When Rabbi Binder attempts to explain to Ozzie why it is that "some of his relations" consider airplane crashes tragic in proportion to the number of Jews killed in them, Ozzie shouts "that he wished all fifty-eight were Jews." (p. 142) Mrs. Freedman is summoned again.

Ozzie is punished and becomes prudent, but Rabbi Binder feels an unacknowledged urge to force another confrontation with his recalcitrant pupil. Forced by Binder's nagging demands, Ozzie drops his reticence and re-asks his question: "Why can't He make anything He wants to make!" While Rabbi Binder prepares his answer, another child causes a disturbance and Ozzie takes advantage of the commotion:

> "You don't know! You don't know anything about God!"
> The rabbi spun back towards Ozzie. "What?"
> "You don't know—you don't—"
> "Apologize, Oscar, apologize!" It was a threat.

*From *The Jewish Writer in America: Assimilation and the Crisis of Identity*, by Allen Guttmann. Copyright © 1971 by Oxford University Press, Inc. Reprinted by permission.

"You don't—"

Rabbi Binder's hand flicked out at Ozzie's cheek. Perhaps it had only been meant to clamp the boy's mouth shut, but Ozzie ducked and the palm caught him squarely on the nose. (p. 146).

Ozzie flees from the room and climbs to the building's roof and locks the door. The crowd gathers, the rabbi begs him from the street not to be a martyr, and his schoolmates—eager for sensation—urge him, "Be a Martin, be a Martin!" (p. 155) His mother comes and the child becomes the teacher. Ozzie catechizes from the rooftop:

"Do you believe God can do Anything?" Ozzie leaned his head out into the darkness. "Anything?"

"Oscar, I think—"

"Tell me you believe God can do Anything."

There was a second's hesitation. Then: "God can do Anything."

"Tell me you believe God can make a child without intercourse."

"He can."

"Tell me!"

"God," Rabbi Binder admitted, "can make a child without intercourse." (p. 157)

Mrs. Freedman agrees and Ozzie leaps into a safety net. Although one critic has assured us that Ozzie's leap "becomes paradoxically a moral symbol of his conversion to Judaism and to life,"[3] the form of the catechism and the imagery are unmistakably Christian: ". . . right into the center of the yellow net that glowed in the evening's edge like an overgrown halo." (p. 158) It is a doubly parabolic descent. The economy of characterization and the simplicity of the fable make the allegorical implications unavoidable. Was it not written that a child shall teach them?

In Roth's collection, Ozzie's story was followed by "The Defender of the Faith," in which the protagonists are Sergeant Nathan Marx, a veteran of World War II, and Sheldon Grossbart, a trainee under Sergeant Marx's care. Sheldon Grossbart, ironically named "Big Beard," begs cravenly for special treatment on the basis of the ethnic bond between him and the sergeant. Although military tradition sanctifies Friday nights to "G.I. parties" (i.e. everyone scrubs the barracks and prepares for Saturday morning inspection), Sheldon points out that Jews must attend religious services. Sergeant Marx allows the request and goes, another night, to attend the services he hasn't gone to for years. Then he thinks he hears Sheldon cackle, "Let the goyim clean the floors!" (p. 172) The sergeant begins to worry. When the captain in charge of the company informs him that Sheldon's congressman has called the general to complain about the Army's non-kosher foods, Sergeant Marx's ambivalence increases. The captain's outrage is deftly captured:

> Look, Grossbart, Marx here is a good man, a goddam *hero*.
> When you were sitting on your sweet ass in high school,
> Sergeant Marx was killing Germans. Who does more for the
> Jews, you by throwing up over a lousy piece of sausage, a piece
> of firstcut meat—or Marx by killing those Nazi bastards? If I
> was a Jew, Grossbart, I'd kiss this man's feet. He's a goddam
> hero, you know that? And *he* eats what we give him. (pp.
> 180–81)

It turns out that Sheldon himself, not his father, wrote the letter to the
congressman, that Sheldon will use his Jewishness to draw advantage for
himself from the persecutions of others, that Sheldon does not even have
the excuse of sincerely held faith. Given a chance to go to town for
Passover, he heads for a Chinese restaurant. The penultimate turn of the
screw comes when Sheldon arranges, with a Jewish acquaintance at head-
quarters, to be removed from orders that send him to the Pacific, where
the war has not yet ended. At this moment, Sergeant Marx decides to defend the faith; he has the orders changed so that Sheldon Grossbart goes
with the rest. Sheldon shrieks, "There's no limit to your anti-Semitism, is
there!" (p. 199) Sergeant Marx calls himself vindictive, but he may also be
seen as the defender of a democratic theory by which the accidents of
birth give no exemption from our common fate. He acts from a sense of
justice that is, finally, humanistic in its universality.

Given only those two stories, an unsympathetic reader might suspect
that Roth holds a wholly negative view of Jewishness and of Judaism, but
the first and final stories of *Goodbye, Columbus* and Roth's first novel,
Letting Go (1962), are longer and more complex. The long title story
plays with names. Although the story is certainly about the country
discovered by the Genoese explorer, the words are from a phonograph
record dedicated to memories of Ohio State University, located at Columbus, Ohio. The record is owned and utilized as a devotional aid by Ronald
Patimkin, an athletic young man who is about to enter his father's
business, where he will "start at two hundred a week and then work
himself up." (p. 61) Through sales of kitchen sinks, phenomenally good
during the war years, the Patimkins have risen to suburban wealth. Is not
cleanliness more profitable than godliness?

The Patimkin family has whatever goods the world calls good. Their
refrigerators burst with fruit; their trees are hung with sporting goods.
Beefy Ronald Patimkin is a type unrelated to the pale scholar of the *shtetl*
and the exploited needle-trades worker of the ghetto. Harvey Swados has
noted this with characteristic acuteness:

> We might measure the distance that has been traveled by con-
> trasting Hemingway's Jewish athlete of the Twenties, Robert
> Cohn, the boxer, forever attempting with fists or flattery to
> join the club, the expatriate Americans who exclude him, to
> Philip Roth's Jewish athlete of the Fifties, Ronald Patimkin,

who hangs his jockstrap from the shower faucet while he sings the latest pop tunes, and is so completely the self-satisfied muscle-bound numskull that notions of Jewish alienation are entirely "foreign" to him.[4]

Brenda Patimkin, the family's older daughter, is a paragon of Olympic virtues; she plays tennis, she runs, she rides, she swims. In the pool, she is a far cry from the *Yiddishe Momma* of yesteryear. "I went," says her boy friend,

> to pull her towards me just as she started fluttering up; my hand hooked on the front of her suit and the cloth pulled away from her. Her breasts swam towards me like two pink-nosed fish and she let me hold them. Then, in a moment, it was the sun who kissed us both, and we were out of the water, too pleased with each other to smile. (p. 17)

And, as Leonard Baskin lamented in a recent symposium, "For every poor and huddled *mikvah* [ritual bath], there is a tenhundred of swimming pools."[5] In this suburban world, the past seems passé indeed.

Brenda Patimkin stands on the magic casement of a world sharply contrasted to that of Neil Klugman's Aunt Gladys, a woman of the immigrant generation. Immediately after the first poolside scene, Roth shows us the milieu from which Neil Klugman (i.e. "wise man") wants to rise:

> That night, before dinner, I called her.
> "Who are you calling?" my Aunt Gladys asked
> "Some girl I met today."
> "Doris introduced you?"
> "Doris wouldn't introduce me to the guy who drains the pool, Aunt Gladys."
> "Don't criticize all the time. A cousin's a cousin. How did you meet her?"
> "I didn't really meet her. I saw her."
> "Who is she?"
> "Her last name is Patimkin."
> "Patimkin, I don't know," Aunt Gladys said . . . (pp. 3–4)

Aunt Gladys does know that a growing boy should eat. But Neil is not about to be satisfied with the food she makes the center of her life.

Neil has his chance. He dates Brenda, watches her at tennis, runs around a track (that may or may not symbolize the final futility of his efforts), basks in the hard sunshine of her father's wealth. He is accepted as her fiancé, as a future worker in the porcelain vineyard of Patimkin sinks.

The marvels of money, and simple physical beauty, are counterpointed by the vision of Gauguin's Tahiti. In the downtown library where Neil works, a little Negro boy comes daily to stare at a book of reproductions of Gauguin. His moan of pleasure is poignant: "Man, that's the fuckin life. . . . *Look, look*, look here at this one. Ain't that the fuckin *life*?" (p. 37) But the breadfruit-and-wild-flower life is unobtainable for the little Negro boy, except in fantasy; Neil's dream of classless, creedless hedonism turns out to be equally unobtainable. He bullies Brenda until she purchases a contraceptive diaphragm, but when he goes up to Boston to spend the Jewish holidays in unholy union with her, he learns that she has left the diaphragm behind, where her mother discovers it. The affair is over. Neil is convinced that the discovery was intentional, Brenda's way out. He goes off and stares into the glass that walls Harvard's Lamont Library and asks himself questions that Roth leaves to the reader's imagination. Then he takes "a train that got me into Newark just as the sun was rising on the first day of the Jewish New Year. I was back in plenty of time for work." (p. 136) The days he meant to spend in carnival he spends at work. He cannot join the Patimkins, cannot use Brenda to rise up "those lousy hundred and eighty feet that make summer nights so much cooler in Short Hills than they are in Newark," (p. 14) but he cannot remain in the world of Aunt Gladys either.

The suburbs that Neil Klugman aspires to are the ones that Eli Peck, inhabitant of Woodenton, lives in. The last story of *Goodbye, Columbus*, "Eli, the Fanatic," is the most complex and difficult to interpret. (It has certainly drawn the most contradictory interpretations.) The contrasts in this story are extreme, for the highly assimilated "successful" Jews of Woodenton are suddenly confronted by a group of Jews more strange and Orthodox than Neil's Aunt Gladys. The newcomers are from Eastern Europe, refugees from unnamed but clearly suggested persecutions; they open a *yeshiva* in pastoral Woodenton, whose names indicates both its forested environment and its hardness of heart.

Eli is the tragic go-between. Standard critical opinion holds that the "demarcation [in the story] between good and evil is absolutely clear,"[6] but this is simplification. In truth, both sides in the suburban dispute are equally rigid. With a comedy painfully true to life, Roth demonstrates how far the nominal Jews of Woodenton are from their ancestral faith. One of Eli's friends argues with him on the telephone:

> Sunday mornings I have to drive my kid all the way to Scarsdale to learn Bible stories? And you know what she comes up with, Eli—that this Abraham in the Bible was going to kill his own kid for a *sacrifice*! You call that religion, Eli? I call it sick. Today a guy like that they'd lock him up. (pp. 276–77)

From this position, an Orthodox *yeshiva* is simply incomprehensible. But the caftan-clad Jews of the *yeshiva* are equally unable to understand the Americans or to realize why Eli and his neighbors are upset. Eli's desperation is intensified by his pregnant wife's devotion to the dogma of the followers of Sigmund Freud. Eli pats his wife's belly and says, "You know what your mother brought to this marriage— . . . a sling chair, three months to go on a *New Yorker* subscription, and *An Introduction to Psychoanalysis.*" His wife answers, "Eli, must you be aggressive?" (p. 259) There is no comfort for him.

When *Weltanschauungen* collide, it is Orthodoxy that yields. Although Eli prevails on Mr. Tzuref (i.e. troubles) to dress his assistant in one of Eli's greenish tweed suits, Eli cannot stand the sight of the "greenie" dressed in his clothing, like a vision of another self. Tormented, guilty, unable to withstand the pressures from every side, torn apart by conflicts of identity, Eli breaks down, dons the black clothing deposited by the Orthodox at his door, and wanders through the town like the Last of the Just. He goes to the hospital to see his newborn son and tells him,

> . . . I'll keep the suit at home, and I'll wear it again. I promise. Every year on the nineteenth of May, I'll wear it. I promise. All day. I won't work, I won't talk, I won't do anything but walk around with this black suit. And when you're old enough, I'll get you one, and you'll walk with me. . . . (pp. 297–98)

Eli is interrupted by the men in white with needles in their hands.

It has been argued that Eli's transformation is a "conversion into the essential Jew," whose essence is to suffer for the truth;[7] it has also been argued that Eli has been touched by "the strange power of an authentic religion."[8] A third view is that

> Eli's grotesque attempt at atonement is doomed to failure: it cannot be understood or accepted by his neighbors, for it is private and also dishonest in the sense that Eli can no more own the experiences that make orthodox dress a truthful expression of the Greenie's identity, than he can disown that part of himself which belongs to Woodenton.[9]

The third version seems closer to the truth, but Eli's fanatical act is pathetic rather than dishonest. There is only one path across the psychic abyss that separates Woodenton from the *yeshiva*—madness. Eli's fate is truly a tragedy and not an expiatory aberration. He has been driven to insanity, at least for the moment, by the hardness of the zealots who have treated him as a fanatic.

Support for this interpretation can be found in an extraordinary response made by Roth to a symposium conducted by *Commentary*: asked about his sense of identity, he answered with a statement and a question serious almost to solemnity:

> I cannot find a true and honest place in the history of believers that begins with Abraham, Isaac, and Jacob on the basis of the heroism of these believers, or of their humiliations and anguish. I can only connect with them . . . as I apprehend their God. And until such time as I do apprehend him, there will continue to exist between myself and those others who seek

> his presence, a question . . . which for all the pain and long-
> ing it may engender, for all the disappointment and bewilder-
> ment it may produce, cannot be swept away by nostalgia or
> sentimentality or even by blind and valiant effort of the will:
> how are you connected to me as another man is not?[10]

To put the matter more abstractly, martyrdom proves the martyr's commitment to his beliefs but cannot validate them. It seems improbable that
Roth intended Eli Peck to affirm an apprehension that he himself was
unable to achieve.

Like Neil Klugman and Eli Peck, like Ozzie Freedman and Sergeant
Marx, the hero of Roth's first (and best) novel is caught in the middle, but
the dilemmas confronted by Gabe Wallach are less specifically Jewish and
more easily universalized. *Letting Go* (1962) is a series of episodes in
which Gabe Wallach becomes increasingly involved with people to whom
he is not emotionally committed.

While doing graduate work at the University of Iowa, Gabe receives
the impetuous embraces of Marjorie Howells, a *shikse* from Kenosha,
Wisconsin, who revolts "against Kenosha as though Caligula himself were
city manager."[11] (p. 27) In her eyes he is the exotic outsider; to please her,
he proclaims himself her Trotsky, her Einstein, her Moses Maimonides,
but he knows that he's none of these and was not meant to be. In Chicago,
where he takes a job in the university, he becomes involved with Martha
Regenhart, a divorcée with two children, but the affair has an air of im-
permanence, and Gabe's admiration for his departmental chairman is, to
speak mildly, limited:

> Spigliano is a member of that great horde of young anagram-
> ists and manure-spreaders who, finding a good deal more am-
> biguity in letters than in their own ambiguous lives, each year
> walk through classroom doors and lay siege to the minds of the
> young, revealing to them Zoroaster in Sam Clemens and the
> hidden phallus in the lines of our most timid lady poets. (p. 63)

And Christ in the work of every Jewish writer?

Gabe's rootlessness has tragic consequences for others. In a grotesque
and horrible disaster, one of Martha Regenhart's children kills the other.
The moment is followed by the climax of a crazy situation in which Gabe
acts as go-between for a couple who attempt illegally to adopt the baby of
a girl whom Martha had encountered at work. The girl turns out to be
married to a brutal and stupid man appropriately named Harry Bigoness.
Gabe rushes back and forth until, at last, he decisively seizes the baby and
brings it to his childless friends.

In contrast to Gabe, Roth sets forth a circle of characters committed
to adjustment. Claire Herz, once known as "hot Claire Herz," has become
"an outstanding mother." (p. 96) Dora and Maury Horvitz lead lives dic-
tated by the *New Yorker*. Of him she says, "Maury is a very Jewish fella."

(p. 186) The one possible affirmative contrast to Gabe and Martha is the intermarried couple, Paul and Libby Herz.

The Herzes are almost as important within the structure of the novel as narrator-hero Gabe Wallach. They had married against the will of their parents: Libby's conversion to Judaism, she explains to Gabe, was "switching loyalties": it

> somehow proved to them [the Herz family] I didn't have any to begin with. I read six thick books on the plights and flights of the Jews, I met with this cerebral rabbi in Ann Arbor once a week and finally there was a laying on of hands. I was a daughter of Ruth, the rabbi told me. In Brooklyn . . . no one was much moved by the news. Paul called and they hung up. I might be Ruth's daughter—that didn't make me theirs. . . . And my father wrote us a little note to say that he had obligations to a daughter in school, but none to Jewish housewives in Detroit. (pp. 21–22)

Nonetheless, their marriage, economic difficulties, quarrels and reconciliations, suggest a way of life that is neither aimless nor complacent. It is for them that Gabe secures the illegitimate baby—for the intermarried couple, an adopted girl.

From this book, Roth went on to write a novel without Jews, almost without urban scenes, a novel that rivals and perhaps surpasses *Main Street* and *Winesburg, Ohio* as portraits of small-town America, but *When She Was Good* (1967) falls outside the bounds of this study—except insofar as it proves what everyone should have known: Philip Roth is a thoroughly assimilated American writer. Roth's next book was quite another matter.

Alexander Portnoy, the desperately comic narrator of *Portnoy's Complaint* (1969), is derived from the same sociological sources as Neil Klugman and Eli Peck and Gabe Wallach, but the literary mode in which he grotesquely lives and suffers is the novelized joke, the night-club gagster's ethnic line drawn out to nearly three hundred pages. In the hot pursuit of the blonde *shikse* by the Jewish libertine, Leslie Fiedler has seen the myth of Samson and Delilah, which allegedly underlies American Jewish fiction to the end of the 1920s.[12] Whether or not the argument holds for Abraham Cahan and Ludwig Lewisohn, none can doubt that Alexander Portnoy's sexual adventure is freighted with social significance:

> I don't seem to stick my dick up these girls, as much as I stick it up their backgrounds. . . . Columbus, Captain Smith, Governor Winthrop, General Washington—now Portnoy. As though my manifest destiny is to seduce a girl from each of the forty-eight states. As for Alaskan and Hawaiian women, I really have no feeling either way, no scores to settle, no coupons to cash in, no dreams to put to rest. . . .[13] (p. 235)

His conquests are a series of *shikses* (preceded by a series of *shikses* whom he failed to conquer). Kay Campbell of Iowa, "The Pumpkin," is a ludicrous version of Gabe Wallach's Marjorie Howells. With her family, among the "real" Americans who live on farms and never raise their voices in argument, Portnoy celebrates Thanksgiving. Finally, *he* rejects *her*, looks higher in the social system: "Another gentile heart broken by me belonged to The Pilgrim, Sarah Abbott Maulsby—New Canaan, Fox-croft, and Vassar . . ." (p. 232) And lower in the system too. His most serious affair is with an illiterate from West Virginia, Mary Jane Reed, nicknamed "The Monkey," for whom he represents the exotically Hebraic, just as Gabe Wallach did for Marjorie. Miss Reed is outrageously vulgar; en route to a party given by Mayor John Lindsay, Portnoy appeals to her, "Don't make a grab for Big John's *shlong* until we've been there at least half an hour, okay?" (p. 211) Portnoy abandons her in Athens, after sexually intricate escapades in New England and in Rome. In Israel, however, he is impotent. Exhilarated by a world in which everyone, even the longshoremen, is a Jew, Portnoy picks up a female lieutenant and is sexually helpless. He listens to her idealistic lectures on the superiority of Israeli socialism to American capitalism and then attempts to rape her. She is strong but he is stronger—and impotent. She tells him in a fine exchange of insults ("Tomboy," "Shlemiel") that he is a victim of the Diaspora, another Jew who hates himself.

There is no doubt that he does. There is no doubt that his childhood is an Oedipal joke: "She was so deeply imbedded in my consciousness that for the first year of school I seem to have believed that each of my teachers was my mother in disguise." (p. 3) Her overprotective, overabundant love and her vindictive demands for love in return combine to drown him in guilt. Portnoy's father is, of course, a failure, Freud's anal type write large, writ grotesquely, a consumer of All-Bran and Ex-Lax and prune juice, a salesman of insurance to Negroes in the slums of Newark. His rage is related to the Boston-based insurance company that gives him stationery with his name printed beneath a picture of the *Mayflower* but makes it clear that he is forever on his way to America and can never arrive. Portnoy's own secret rebellion is a denial of Judaism; he claims to be an atheist and not a Jew.

Now, at the age of thirty-three, he is Assistant Commissioner on Mayor Lindsay's Commission on Human Opportunity, but still an undutiful child in the eyes of his ever-watchful parents. He can turn upon them and imitate their transparent nag into one of the classic parodies of the excesses of assimilation: he mimics Mother on Seymour Schmuck:

> I met his mother on the street today, and she told me that Seymour is now the biggest brain surgeon in the entire Western Hemisphere. He owns six different split-level ranch-type houses . . . and belongs to the boards of eleven synagogues, all brand-new and designed by Marc Kugel, and last year with his

wife and his two little daughters, who are so beautiful that
they are already under contract to Metro, and so brilliant that
they should be in college—he took them all to Europe for an
eighty-million-dollar tour of seven thousand countries, some of
them you never even heard of, that they made them just to
honor Seymour, and . . . in every single city . . . he was asked
by the mayor himself to stop and do an impossible operation on
a brain in hospitals that they also built for him right on the
spot. . . . (pp. 99–100)

Et cetera, et cetera. But what of poor Portnoy? He lies on Dr. Spielvogel's
couch while the doctor, presumably, takes notes for the essay that is cited
in the epigraph-in-the-form-of-an-encyclopedia-entry. He, Portnoy, is
the "Puzzled Penis."

What are we to make of his puzzlement? Is the book a Jewish joke or
is it a joke about Jewish jokes? If the latter, which seems more probable,
then it is—like Black Humor—a kind of terminus, a suggestion that the
satirist of assimilation has grown tired of the harvest he himself desired. A
good place for a satirist to stop.

Notes

1. The exception among the *Partisan Review* critics is Jeremy Larner, who wrote that
"Roth . . . seeks only to cheapen the people he writes about" ("The Conversion of the Jews,"
Partisan Review, XXVII [Fall 1960], 761).

2. Philip Roth, *Goodbye, Columbus* (Boston: Houghton Mifflin, 1959).

3. Joseph C. Landis, "The Sadness of Philip Roth. An Interim Report," *Massachusetts
Review*, III (Winter 1962), 264.

4. Harvey Swados, *A Radical's America* (Boston: Little Brown, 1962), p. 174.

5. Leonard Baskin, ed. "My Jewish Affirmation—A Symposium," *Judaism*, X, No. 1
(Fall 1961), 291–352.

6. Dan Isaac, "In Defense of Philip Roth," Chicago Review, XVII (Nos. 2 & 3,
1964), 92.

7. Theodore Solotaroff, "Philip Roth and the Jewish Moralists," *Chicago Review*, XIII
(Winter, 1959), 92.

8. Isaac, "In Defense of Philip Roth," p. 94.

9. Irving and Harriet Deer, "Philip Roth and the Crisis in American Fiction," *Min-
nesota Review*, VI (No. 4, 1966), 359.

10. Philip Roth, "Jewishness and the Younger Intellectuals," *Commentary*, XXXI (April
1961), 351.

11. Philip Roth, *Letting Go* (New York: Random House, 1962).

12. Leslie A. Fiedler, "Genesis: The American-Jewish Novel through the Twenties,"
Midstream, IV (Summer 1958), 28.

13. Philip Roth, *Portnoy's Complaint* (New York: Random House, 1969).

In Defense of Philip Roth

Dan Isaac

And still the rabbis rage.

Philip Roth continues to be the unfortunate recipient of irrational and inappropriate criticism—perhaps even the more for his forthright statement of artistic purpose in the December, 1963 issue of *Commentary*. In this article he formulated a brilliant credo of aesthetics, founded on the proposition that the artist is concerned with ". . . all that is beyond simple moral categorizing." The essay also contained a collection of excerpts from hate letters and rabbinic sermons indicating just how much hostility Roth's stories had engendered in the Jewish community. One of them likened Roth to Hitler; another asserted that the Medieval Jew would have known what to do with him. And a rabbi, in a personal letter to Roth, wrote: "You have earned the gratitude of all who sustain their anti-Semitism on such conceptions of Jews as ultimately led to the murder of six million in our time." This published catalogue of abuse should have shamed his detractors into silence and produced, if not an ascending dialectic, at least an intelligible dialogue of disagreement. But it only served to encourage certain rabbis to continue the attack.

In the summer edition of *To Our Colleagues*, a little journal circulated among Reform rabbis supplying them with usable quotes for sermons, these statements appeared:

> Philip Roth, of "Goodbye Columbus" fame, constantly depicts the Jewish characters in his short stories and novels as depraved and lecherous creatures.[1]
> The only logical conclusion any intelligent reader could draw from [Roth's] stories or books, is that this country—nay that the world—would be a much better and happier place without "Jews."[2]

I quote these statements not for the purpose of refuting them (any undergraduate of average intelligence could do that), but because they point up the need for a reasoned analysis of Philip Roth's writings. What is the peculiar power of his stories that renders rabbis irrational?

*"In Defense of Philip Roth" by Dan Isaac first appeared in *Chicago Review*, 17, nos. 2 and 3, Fall/Winter 1964. Copyright © 1980 by *Chicago Review*. Reprinted by permission.

Such a delicate investigation should be preceded by a few basic statements concerning the underlying assumptions and prejudices of the critic. First, I am a rabbi and, secondly, I am rather ashamed of the tawdry rhetoric and third rate thinking employed by my colleagues in their attack upon Philip Roth. Not only do I absolutely reject the naive formula of, "Is it good for the Jews," as a proper yardstick for the judging of literature, but I maintain that a writer has the freedom and right to choose his characters and make of them whatever he wants so long as it suits his purpose. I admit to having enjoyed most of Roth's writing. And finally I would argue and hope to demonstrate that when Roth is properly understood he is not only a good writer but that he can also be in fact "*good* for the Jews."

Philip Roth is generally concerned with society and its values—the new society that second generation Jews are emerging into and recreating. "Goodbye, Columbus," the novella that lends its title to a collection of stories, suggests the complex and irrational position of the rich, semi-assimilated Jew in suburban society. The sporting goods tree, the old refrigerator filled with fruit, the active Jewish club lady who has never heard of Martin Buber, are part of a series of signs and indices telling us exactly what has happened to Jewish life. When an extra place is set at the Patimkin table for Mickey Mantle every time the Yankees win a doubleheader, we have not only a sign of the corruption of Jewish tradition but an indication of where modern Jews look for their messiah. Mr. Patimkin, who has made his money manufacturing sinks, is the last member of a dying tribe. Proud of the hard bump in his nose, representing the last vestige of visible Jewishness, he is equally proud that he has the money to have his daughter Brenda's nose fixed.

The whole story is suffused with a sense of reduction. It is a satiric demonstration of how the house of modern Judaism rests on a base of vulgar and mindless materialism. Ron Patimkin's wedding gives us an entire gallery of the *nouveaux riches*.

> There was Mrs. Patimkin's side of the family: her sister Molly, a tiny buxom hen whose ankles swelled and ringed her shoes, and who would remember Ron's wedding if for no other reason than she'd martyred her feet in three-inch heels, and Molly's husband, the butter and egg man, Harry Grossbart, who had earned his fortune with barley and corn in the days of Prohibition. Now he was active in the Temple and whenever he saw Brenda he swatted her on the can; it was a kind of physical bootlegging that passed, I guess, for familial affection. Then there was Mrs. Patimkin's brother, Marty Kreiger, the Kosher Hot-Dog King, an immense man, as many stomachs as he had chins, and already, at fifty-five, with as many heart attacks as chins and stomachs combined. He had just come back from a health cure in the Catskills, where he said he'd eaten nothing but All-Bran and had won $1500 at gin rummy. When the

photographer came by to take pictures, Marty put his hand on
his wife's pancake breasts and said, "Hey, how about a picture
of this!" His wife Sylvia, was a frail, spindly woman with
bones like a bird's. She had cried throughout the ceremony,
and sobbed openly, in fact, when the rabbi had pronounced
Ron and Harriet "man and wife in the eyes of God and the
state of New Jersey."[3]

The long, sad monologue of Leo Patimkin, whose territory is "from
here to everywhere," tells of how his wife made "oral love" with him after
seders because she got drunk from the wine. Jewish holidays, rather than
representing a heightened sense of reverence for Jewish values, turn into
opportunities for licentiousness. Rosh Ha-Shonah is merely a chance for
Neil to get off work and go up to Boston to continue his sexual romance
with Brenda. When he leaves her and returns to work on the Jewish New
Year, a skillful irony has been woven into the story. Neil participates in
serious self-searching and undergoes a personal rebirth not because he
believes in the religious efficacy of Rosh Ha-Shonah, but simply because
the holiday has provided him with an opportunity to see his girl.

It is not just Jewish life that suffers bitter satiric and ironic reduction.
New Jersey, just the other side of the Hudson, is seen as ". . . the swampy
meadows that spread for miles and miles, watery, blotchy, smelly, like an
oversight of God." We get this again in a longer passage, revealing a
superb sense of social awareness and poetic perception.

> The park, bordered by Washington Street on the west and
> Broad on the east, was empty and shady and smelled of trees,
> night, and dog leavings; and there was a faint damp smell too,
> indicating that the huge rhino of a water cleaner had passed by
> already, soaking and whisking the downtown streets. Down
> Washington Street, behind me, was the Newark Museum—I
> could see it without even looking: two oriental vases in front
> like spitoons for a rahjah, and next to it the little annex to
> which we had traveled on special buses as schoolchildren. The
> annex was a brick building, old and vine-covered, and always
> reminded me of New Jersey's link with the beginning of the
> country, with George Washington, who had trained his scrappy
> army—a little bronze tablet informed us children—in the very
> park where I now sat. At the far end of the park, beyond the
> Museum, was the bank building where I had gone to college. It
> had been converted some years before into an extension of
> Rutgers University; in fact, in what had once been the bank
> president's waiting room I had taken a course called Contem-
> porary Moral Issues.[4]

This long lyrical passage, this hymn to Newark, New Jersey that sees not
only the modern irony that allows a bank to be so easily converted into a
school, but can with a sense of pride look back into time and connect

George Washington with whatever modern meaning the place might have—all of this immediately brings to mind the writing of Fitzgerald in *The Great Gatsby* with its intermingling of romantic innocence and materialistic corruption. And all of it associated with the ethos of a particular period and the personality of a nation. In short, Philip Roth treats Jews as *people*, and people—ancient and modern—are corruptable.

"Goodbye, Columbus" could easily be thought of as F. Scott Fitzgerald looking for Zelda, thirty years later in Jewish New Jersey. I have even seen it suggested that this story represents the Gatsby-meets-Daisy-in-Louisville incident in *The Great Gatsby*.[5] Roth has not only a heightened sensitivity to the sweep of the past, but can read the future in the matrix of the present.

> Patimkin Kitchen and Bathroom Sinks was in the heart of the Negro section of Newark. Years ago, at the time of the great immigration, it had been the Jewish section, and still one could see the little fish stores, the kosher delicatessens, the Turkish baths, where my grandparents had shopped and bathed at the beginning of the century. Even the smells had lingered: whitefish, corned beef, sour tomatoes—but now, on top of these, was the grander greasier smell of auto wrecking shops, the sour stink of a brewery, the burning odor from a leather factory; and on the streets, instead of Yiddish, one heard the shouts of Negro children playing at Willie Mays with a broom handle and half a rubber ball. The neighborhood had changed: the old Jews like my grandparents had struggled and prospered, and moved further and further west, towards the edge of Newark, then out of it, and up the slope of the Orange Mountains, until they had reached the crest and started down the other side, pouring into Gentile territory as the Scotch-Irish had poured through the Cumberland Gap. Now, in fact, the Negroes were making the same migration, following the steps of the Jews, and those who remained in the Third Ward lived the most squalid of lives and dreamed in their fetid mattresses of the piny smell of Georgia nights.[6]

Roth does what Fitzgerald was never able to do until late in his life—display a sense of sympathy for a social or racial class one rung below, standing just where the narrator might have stood a generation earlier.

This juxtaposition of Negroes to Jews is not accidental, indeed is integral to the movement and meaning of "Goodbye, Columbus." The most touching incident in the story relates Neil's feeling for the little colored boy who wants to look at "the Go-again pictures" in the "heart" section. The boy is Neil's secret sharer. Both crave an immediate experience of the sensual. And Neil discovers the boy to be an important companion in his dream where both are leaving the island of Polynesian maidens, who are saying to them as they sail away, "Goodbye Columbus, goodbye."

The title has multiple meanings. For Ron, Brenda's basketball playing brother, it is a final farewell to the time and place where he was important and a star. The one thing Ron can do beautifully has no permanent value in the money-making world, and even now—but a short time after graduation—he looks back with nostalgia and a sense of loss to his years at Columbus, Ohio. John Updike built a whole novel around such a character, but Philip Roth puts him on display as just another sad victim sacrificed to the new cult of adjustment and security. Updike's character is sympathetic because he fights back, but Ron Patimkin submits and salves his wounds with the manufactured sentimentality of a recorded document describing his senior year at Ohio State. Narrated by a solemn Edward R. Murrow voice, it stoically intones at the conclusion, "Goodbye Columbus, Goodbye." Neil, who at first only hears this last line, and not the whole record until later in the story, has a dream that is partially provoked by his own associations to the tag line. He, too, suffers a sense of loss, but it is an anticipatory loss of the freely given sensuality that both he and his secret sharer, the Negro boy in the library, are enjoying in different ways. When Neil first saw Brenda at the beginning of the story, he thought of her as a Polynesian maiden; and the dream correctly suggests that he is a Columbus of the sensual, discovering for the first time the fresh virginity of her young and inviting body. The dream also foreshadows the outcome of the story—the renunciation and loss of what looked like love.

That the dream should include the young Negro boy, when seen alongside the observations of how Negroes are moving into Jewish neighborhoods, provides the story with a perceptive and prophetic social vision. Just as the middle class Mid-westerner and the powerful head of a mob of bootleggers were able to enter the sophisticated society of the East in the Twenties, the Jew is doing it now—and the Negro will be next!

Unlike Gatsby, Neil refuses to pay the price. He will not sacrifice his moral integrity for a comfortable position in the Patimkin household, even if it means losing Brenda. Indeed, the final dimensions of the story more readily suggest Nick Carroway's decision to give up the girl who cheats at golf, the slightly immoral sportswoman Jordan Baker, than Gatsby's fatal quest.

Neil is at least half aware of some of the less savory emotions that make up his complex desire for Brenda. At the beginning it clearly partakes of aggressive social climbing, not unmixed with some envy of what he does not have. After making love to Brenda for the first time, it feels just like beating her spoiled younger sister in a game of ping-pong. Twice he tells himself and the reader that he is on the verge of proposing marriage. But each time he substitutes a provocative act for what would have been a very reassuring one. The first time he thinks of marriage, he instead suggests to Brenda that she acquire a diaphragm. The idea completely unnerves her, as it robs the relationship of its romantic spontaneity. In spite of Brenda's reluctance Neil pushes the matter, never giving her the word of assurance she seeks, arguing only his personal pleasure. The second time he considers suggesting marriage occurs at the conclusion of the story when he goes to Boston to visit her. She is upset because her mother has discovered the diaphragm in her drawer. Neil, instead of acting as a source of sympathy, aggressively and accusingly attacks her for, what is at worst, an unconscious slip. When Brenda indicates she will spend her Thanksgiving vacation with her parents rather than with him, Neil leaves her. Had Neil been a little more comforting and loving to a girl who had just registered them in a Boston hotel as man and wife, perhaps her choice would have been different.

Neil knows of the frightened insecurity beneath the beautiful, proud, self-assured facade. He has seen her angry rivalry with her mother, and made love to her in the attic at her command when she could not find the hundred dollar bills her father had hidden for her inside the old sofa. If sex partakes of an aggressive acquisitiveness for Neil, Brenda uses it to console herself for what she imagines to be an unsuccessful struggle with her mother. The discovery of the diaphragm not only hurts her mother, but forces her to pay attention to Brenda and open her arms wide to her. It is not only a struggle with the mother, but for the mother.

A careful reading of this story suggests that neither Neil nor Brenda is in love with the other. Each practices a half-unconscious act of self-deception so that each can more freely enjoy both the psychological and sensual gratifications that their sexual relationship provides.

There is something of love there, too; or at least a good potentiality for it. But any final judgment about how well it might have worked, changing this or postulating that, is impossible. The reason: Neil is an unreliable narrator, and he not only does not give us enough real information, but his own judgment is too clouded by his involvement with the entire Patimkin family. Neil is too worried about himself become a kitchen sink man under Mr. Patimkin's tutelage, or the horse that wins the race under Brenda's. This self-concern prevents him from ever exploring the depths of Brenda's soul, and leaves the impression with the reader that she has none. With his rich imagination, Salinger-like sensitivity, and intelligent tone, Neil is certainly a sympathetic center of reflection; but his judgment is flawed by an intense reaction to the pleasures and dangers of the only real antagonist of the story—the vulgar materialism of middle class Jewish life.

This is not to say the story is irreparably flawed. The antagonist, modern Jewish suburban life, is real and accurately described. Neil's rejection of Brenda is meant to represent a rejection and condemnation of this way of life. Since this is the obvious and successful purpose of the writer, it might be too much of a scruple to suggest that Brenda, with Neil's help and love, could become something else. Indeed, it would have turned the story into a sentimental romance and shoved the social criticism to the rear, burying it under the triumphant emotion of emerging love.

Whatever the faults, "Goodbye, Columbus" is a rich and deeply moving story, provocative in many directions. It marks the successful working of a significant theme: the rejection of Jewish life, not because it is too Jewish, but because it is not Jewish enough, because it is so dominated by and infused with the American ethos that it partakes of the same corruption, offering no significant alternative.

II

The bulk of Jewish writing in the past fifty years comprises a very limited genre. Two stock types become so dominant that they reduce the literature to the level of soap opera. One found either gentle faded photographs of traditional Jews pathetically out of joint, or the action shots of so many anxiously driven Sammy Glicks assimilating with a vengeance, on the make and out for the whole world. The rabbi who had read nothing more sophisticated than a genre writing that trades in stereotypes was bound to be disturbed by the writing of Philip Roth.

The characters created by Philip Roth are men in the middle, lacking a sure sense of values. They are continually concerned with complex alternatives. Placed in problematic situations, they are forced to think their position through and come out with a new formulation. Two value systems clash and a sympathetic character makes a significant choice.

"Defender of the Faith" is a clear demonstration of this technique. Sgt. Marx, a war hero returned to the states to conduct basic training, has no special sense of his Jewish identity. But when a young soldier in his company begins to manipulate his sympathies on the basis of their common Jewish background, this sense is tugged and wakened. The effect of Sheldon Grossbart and his shrewd maneuvers is exactly opposite to what he intends. Repelled by the young boy who seeks special favors, Marx is even more disgusted by his commanding officer who manifests a crude streak of casual prejudice: "Marx, I'd fight side by side with a nigger if the fellow proved to me he was a man." When this officer falsely quotes Marx to the brass hats in Washington as saying that certain Jews tend to be pushy, Marx finds himself pushed against his will into Grossbart's corner. Trapped between two antipathies, two grotesque distortions of attitudes toward Jewishness, Marx is forced to redefine his identity.

Ironically, Marx's sense of Jewishness is so completely aroused that he becomes hostile to the obnoxious and selfish Grossbart when the screw of manipulation is turned one notch too tight. On discovering that Grossbart has succeeded in having his orders changed so that he will be sent to Ft. Monmouth instead of the Pacific, Marx uses all his influence to change them back again. This action partakes of the vindictive, as Marx himself admits. But he has done it, he tells the angry and hurt Grossbart, "for all of us." Sgt. Marx has taken an action that appears callous and even "anti-Semitic," unless understood as arising out of an honest conflict that profoundly wrestles with the problem of how best to serve Jewish interests. The solution is one that sacrifices the interests of one not very likeable member of the tribe to an abstract principle of absolute justice. The concerns of Judaism are consequently translated from simply self-preservation, to a prophetic vision of universal justice. Sgt. Marx's small action recapitulates the most significant transformation of social thought during the biblical period.

All this makes the story sound more rhetorical than it truly is. There is yet one element to be mentioned that permits multiple interpretations of the total plot. The reader is allowed to see the psychological workings of the central character's mind, and is therefore able to second guess some of his avowed motives for acting. The reader is even prompted in this direction by Marx's admission of vindictiveness. Whether or not the action that sends a boy off to combat and possible death is based on lofty principle is left for us to determine. At the end of the story the reader and critic is the man in the middle.

"Eli the Fanatic" is an even more interesting variation of this approach to plot. Here the central character has a history of nervous breakdowns; hence the significance of anything he does can be easily disqualified on psychological grounds. Eli Peck, chosen to be spokesman for the Jewish community because of his legal background, has the unpleasant assignment of asking a group of refugees to move. They have established a Yeshivah and are violating zoning laws that make no allowance for a school in the area. But the legal concerns are merely a ruse and rationalization. The Jewish community, located in a suburb of New York City, is worried what their Christian neighbors will think when they see these Orthodox Jews with their black clothes, beards, and *peos*.

By making both the rabbis and their homeless charges former inmates of German concentration camps, Philip Roth has set up sign posts for sympathy so that no one could possibly be pulling for the wrong side. The demarcation between good and evil is absolutely clear. Not only does Eli have to contend with the anxiety of representing a bad cause, but his wife is about to give birth for the first time. If this weren't enough, Eli learns that one of the rabbis was castrated by the Nazis. All of these vectors of anxiety impinge upon Eli, forcing this man in the middle to seek a compromise that will permit the Yeshivah to remain, and simultaneously to put to rest the fears of his Jewish neighbors. He convinces the castrated rabbi to take off his black gabardine and dress in a green tweed suit of Eli's. But then the extraordinary and unexpected happens. Eli dons the clothes he has persuaded the rabbi to give up, and walks through the center of town to pay his first visit to his new born son.

The large question of Eli's mental stability causes the validity and courage of the act to come into question. It can be interpreted in two diametrically opposed ways. It is either a manifestation of an intense neurosis that drives a man to parade his deviation from expected norms, or an act of immense courage that overcomes the pressures toward conformity in order to demonstrate one's true identity. Is Eli a saint or a nut? A prophet or a fool? The story is carefully structured so that you can almost read it either way.

Almost, but not quite. The signs are subtle, but they suggest an answer. It is the sharp and biting depiction of Eli's wife that points the way. Herself in therapy, she is constantly trying to "understand" Eli when he is upset. Playing the therapist with him, she always assumes in a condescending way that whatever Eli is excited about is only a cover for deeper and more chronic turmoil. This becomes an ongoing *ad hominem* attack that is never willing to face the rightness or wrongness of his opinions. Acts and attitudes are reduced to a psychological necessity, and as such are dismissed. This is a perfect caricature of the psychologically oriented literary critic whose interpretation of this story would end after pointing up the evidence for viewing Eli as a guilt-ridden compulsive. The ridicule Roth heaps on Eli's wife indicates what he thinks of her, and he accomplishes it by just letting her talk. In one instance she claims to be having a kind of Oedipal relationship with her unborn child. A pretty good example of *a priori* reasoning.

Eli is to be taken very seriously, because within him two competing cultures are struggling for dominance. American's homemade moral system of rational pragmatism does battle with a weaker but more ancient and durable adversary, traditional Judaism. Certianly Judaism has its obtuse absurdities, its tale of a divine request for child sacrifice. But is it any more absurd than Main Street, Suburbia, USA, as we get it from Roth:

> The Mayor's wife pushed a grocery cart full of dog food from Stop N' Shop to her station wagon. The President of the Lions Club, a napkin around his neck, was jamming pennies into the meter in front of the Bit-in-Teeth Restaurant. Ted Heller caught the sun as it glazed off the new Byzantine mosaic entrance to his shoe shop. In pinkened jeans, Mrs. Knudson was leaving Halloway's Hardware, a paint bucket in each hand. Roger's Beauty Shoppe had its doors open—women's heads in silver bullets far as the eye could see. Over by the barbershop the pole spun, and Artie Berg's youngest sat on a red horse, having his hair cut.

And on it goes, documenting the nightmarish quality of the American quotidian.

In the final scene Roth underlines the myth and ritual of modern medicine. Eli stands talking to his baby, telling him how he will always commemorate this day by walking around once a year in a black suit, when the doctors descend upon him to give him a shot. Roth very carefully contrasts the white of the doctors—white shoes, white gowns, white skull caps—with Eli's black. And we see in the last paragraph of the story that these colors are meant to communicate a complicated metaphoric meaning:

> And in a moment they tore off his jacket. The cloth gave in one yank. Then a needle slid under his skin. The drug calmed his soul, but did not touch it where the blackness had reached.

What we have here is medical science, metaphoric for all of modern thought, winning a false and superficial victory over ancient Judaism. A false victory because the black, with its associations of things sour, stale, and old, also represents the strange power of an authentic religion that touches an area of the soul inaccessible to tranquilizing drugs.

Can there be any doubt that Philip Roth means to condemn a society that turns zoning laws into subtle instruments of persecution? If Eli is a fanatic, he is a prophet as well. But the society he seeks to instruct with a dramatic act is too corrupt, too insulated, too hard of heart even to try to understand the meaning of Eli's suffering. Eli is trying to redeem the viciousness, masking itself in a sophisticated modern rationalism, of the American Jew. But none of his neighbors are sensitive enough to see, to feel, to understand. Once again modern society is the real villain; and the American Jew, to the extent to which he has steeped himself in America's peculiar mythos, is a visible sign of this villainy.

No wonder, then, that the rabbis rage at the writing of Philip Roth. He has exposed and ridiculed the very system that has nourished American Judaism to an unparalleled position of wealth and power. "Goodbye, Columbus" continually implies what "Eli the Fanatic" boldly states: American Judaism has become the willing servant of an immoral society, corrupted by the very force it should oppose.

Unfortunately, but perhaps significantly, none of the many rabbinical attacks on Roth faced Roth's challenge in a responsible way. Their immediate reaction was a bad mannered defensiveness. Rabbi David Seligson, as reported in the New York *Times*, could only wonder about gifted writers "Jewish by birth, who can see so little in the tremendous saga of Jewish history."[7] Unwilling to admit that Philip Roth's writing was either entertaining literature or a significant indictment of American-Jewish values, these rabbis retreated to the position of public relations men interested only in preserving a popular image of the modern Jew.

The story "Epstein," included in the *Goodbye, Columbus* collection, has been a particular target of rabbinic discontent. It prompted Rabbi Seligman's attack on Roth's character gallery, including "a Jewish adulterer . . . and a host of other lopsided schizophrenic characters."[8] Once again the rabbinic criticism backed away from a real and fruitful confrontation. "Epstein" is an extremely disturbing narrative, but not because it merely suggests that a modern Jew can be an adulterer. This is the substance of the rabbinic apologetic protest—the portraying of a Jew who is an immoral man. In truth, the story is explosive because it makes such a convincing case for a feeling of sex-loathing in a middle-aged man who looks at his wrinkled wife beside him in their bed. What really rankles with the rabbis is an adulterer who is a sympathetic character in a story containing many comic elements. But have they forgotten that one can condemn the act and yet forgive the man? Epstein, seen with full knowledge and imaged with compassion, is a pathetic figure. He is the victim of his own frightening, and simultaneously comic, fantasies—the fears and hopes of a man who stands on the brink of advancing age.

A Jewish adulterer improbable and unrealistic? One need only turn to the latest murder trial in the Chicago papers. Irwinna Weinstein, accused of being an accomplice to her husband's murder which took place on the evening after Yom Kippur Day, claimed that her husband instead of attending afternoon services had himself been having an affair with a neighbor who happened to be the chief witness. The court then called the rabbi to the stand to determine whether or not the murdered man had indeed been in the synagogue on Yom Kippur afternoon, or might have been, as his wife suggested, also involved in adultery. The man with whom Irwinna Weinstein had been having an affair had already confessed to the killing. The whole situation was ugly and shameful, and the Yom Kippur setting sounded like the plotting of an eager writing who had too ready an eye for irony.

But this really happened. If it were fiction it would accomplish a kind of viciousness that is never present in the writing of Philip Roth. For he has achieved the rare gift, perhaps most prominent in the prophecies of Jeremiah, of a clear and critical social vision accompanied by an overflowing sense of compassion for his suffering central characters.

At every turn the published rabbinical responses to Philip Roth misfire and fail to face the real issue: To what extent can a civilization compromise its values in order to survive, and still retain its distinct and original integrity? Roth's fiction suggests that in some quarters the struggle is already over. Judaism has gone through the quiet metamorphosis demanded by American society and emerged as a co-operative, acquisitive member of the new frontier. That American rabbis resent this indictment is understandable; but to attack the critic rather than to face the criticism is unforgiveable.

Any man who has served as a rabbi in America can come up with ten true tales about Jews that are more evil and absurd than anything Roth has written of. Instead of attacking Philip Roth for what they all privately know to be true, these rabbis would do well to use his stories as sermon texts, and thereby attempt to alter through illustration and argument the faulty fabric of American-Jewish life.

Notes

1. Rabbi Saul I. Teplitz, "From Rabbi to Rabbi." *To Our Colleagues*, vol. 4, no. 8 (New York, 1964), p. 9.

2. Rabbi Theodore Lewis, quoted by Rabbi Teplitz, p. 9.

3. Philip Roth, *Goodbye, Columbus* (New York: Houghton Mifflin Company, 1959), pp. 105–6.

4. Roth, p. 30.

5. James Friend, "Nakedness and Night Again: The Influence of *The Great Gatsby* on Philip Roth's *Goodbye, Columbus*." An unpublished essay that considers *Goodbye, Columbus* a modern interpretation of *The Great Gatsby*, and makes an incident by incident comparison of the two.

6. Roth, p. 90.

7. Cited by Philip Roth in "Writing About Jews," *Commentary*, December 1963, p. 447.

8. *Ibid.*

Laughter in the Dark: Notes on American-Jewish Humor

Stephen J. Whitfield*

No one has been able to generalize successfully about what is funny, or what makes it funny, or what makes some funny things last. Saul Steinberg once said that "trying to define humor is one of the definitions of humor." Everyone knows how deadly it is to attempt to explain a joke; for to analyze humor is to vivisect, to kill a living thing in the very act of examining it. It is tempting simply to assert that the essence of comedy may be ultimately unfathomable, and leave it at that.

But someone still has to try to straighten out the place after the hysterics have had their hour on the couch and the anarchists their night at the opera; and the method of my approach to madness differs from the primarily literary analysis of American-Jewish humor represented by Ruth Wisse, Robert Alter and Allen Guttmann. In its focus on the social implications of the subject, this article is more attentive to what makes Sammy run than to what makes Saul Bellow. For humor—both expressed and appreciated—is central to the subculture of American Jewry, the kind of badge Jews pride themselves on wearing, an acknowledged sign that certifies membership in a community. At the moment humor is a way, in a relatively tolerant society, of keeping up the resistance level to what many Jews fear, which is less the loss of faith than the loss of identity. Many can live more easily with disbelief than with utter assimilation; and since we moderns play for lower stakes than salvation, humor makes more sense than in the past. It is one of the dominant threads of memory and group consciousness, a style that disarmingly proclaims that "we" are still different from "them."

For humor is *cosa nostra, unser shtick*, our thing. It percolates through the associations of Jews, helping to sustain not only individual energies but collective resources as well and to define one group's place in the amorphous and anxious society that is America. Russell Baker once observed that, unlike himself, Art Buchwald *looks* like a humorist. Baker did not mention that Buchwald also happens to look Jewish, and the distinction between those two attributes has by now become blurred. The companion of Scott Fitzgerald in his last years has recalled how the novel-

*Reprinted from *Midstream* (February 1978), pp. 48–58, by permission of the journal.

ist enjoyed going to "a Jewish delicatessen, and he would ask the names of things. I think 'knish' just floored him. He would ask again and again for it just to hear it pronounced." Phyllis Diller has acknowledged that just to hear Jackie Mason "talk makes me laugh. He wouldn't have to say anything funny—that very thick Russian-Jewish accent just makes me fall down." When salted with Yiddish, wisecracks seem to have the added preservative of folk wisdom; and like so many stereotypes, the Gentile impression of Jews as jesters has more than a tincture of truth.

For even among non-professionals within the Jewish community, the comedian's impulse to work the room can be irresistible. For example, Alfred Kazin has recalled his first meeting with the most subtle and mordant of recent American historians, Richard Hofstadter: ". . . Of course he was telling jokes, doing the impersonations that would regularly send his friends to the floor . . . Then and afterward, for 34 years, he could reduce me to more helpless laughter than any professional jokesmith in American life." Bellow remembers the critic Isaac Rosenfeld as a "marvellous clown" who "loved hoaxes, mimicry, parody . . . With Isaac, the gravest, the most characteristic, the most perfect strokes took a comic slant." The daughter of the philosopher Morris Raphael Cohen recalls his capacity to "swap Yiddish jokes for hours on end." *Newsweek* reported that an emeritus Grossinger's *tummeler*, Mel Brooks, is enough of a friend of a CUNY literature professor named Joseph Heller for the latter to assure us that the private rather than public Brooks is the more funny and intelligent. Philip Roth, self-styled disciple of Henny Youngman as well as a National Book Award winner for fiction, admired Lenny Bruce's work but considered himself funnier than Bruce, who was after all a professional nightclub comedian.

Never mind that Roth was, in my opinion, right; consider the implications. Think of the likelihood of friendship between, say, Thomas Wolfe and W. C. Fields, or between James Baldwin and Richard Pryor. Nor is it likely that William Styron has ever felt himself in competition with Johnny Carson, or Truman Capote with Red Skelton, or that they ever felt they just might be better than pros who had emerged from the crucible of the Catskills. Therefore, it seems appropriate that the first major American novelist who was also a Jew, Nathanael West, had for a brother-in-law a Marx Brothers scenarist. It seems appropriate that the only play written by today's most respected American novelist (and he's also a Jew) has for a protagonist a Jewish professional comic.

Saul Bellow's play, *The Last Analysis* (1964), prefigured the rise of the Jewish comic as a less peripheral figure within American popular culture. *Lenny* for a while was inescapable, with both the Broadway play and the Hollywood movie implying that because Bruce was rough he must have been a diamond. (Mordecai Richler's disclaimer that Bruce "didn't die for *my* sins" is a useful hint that, however malicious the prosecutions may have been, he was the sort of person who would have self-destructed

in Sodom and Gomorrah. Nevertheless, Bruce's influence on other comedians has been important, the interest in his career enormous.) Several
other works of fiction and drama have made a Jewish comic the central
character, such as Wallace Markfield's *You Could Live If They Let You*,
in which a put-down artist named Jules Farber is trapped inside his own
hysterically unpleasant identity. Irvin Faust's *A Star in the Family*
chronicles the career of Bart Goldwine, who never made it to the
Palladium. The French novelist Romain Gary's *Dance of Genghis Cohn*
deals with the dybbuk of a nightclub comedian killed in a Nazi extermina-
tion camp who haunts his German tormenter—a mixture of "slapstick"
and horror that has become something of a specialty of the house of Israel.
Of Neil Simon's major plays, the least funny is *The Sunshine Boys*, the odd
couple redivivus as two aged comedians. "You're a funny man, Al,"
Willie tells his ex-partner, who replies: "You know what your trouble
was, Willie? You always took the jokes too seriously. They were just jokes.
We did comedy on the stage for forty-three years, I don't think you enjoyed it once." "If I was there to enjoy it," Willie responds, "I would buy
a ticket."

It is Willie who is closer to Judaic tradition, in which the question of
the enjoyment of life is hardly a pressing one. Genesis 21:6 reports that in
her old age Sarah gave birth, an idea she found so amusing that her son
was named Isaac ("he shall laugh"). But laughter is an uncommon
response both in and to the Bible, and the Old Testament figures are not
memorable for their levity. The Greeks at least made Thalia, the muse of
comedy, one of the three Graces; and Homer permitted his gods to laugh.
Even the Purim spiel, the farcical recycling of the Book of Esther in which
the town wag—the "Purim rabbi"—did parodistic send-ups of sermons
and rabbinic responsa, dates from the Middle Ages. And it was the *shtetl*
that institutionalized the *badkhen*, the emcee at weddings, the remote
ancestor of the so-called Toastmaster General of the United States,
George Jessel, and of the roastmasters of the Friars Club. The jesting of
the *badkhen*, according to Zborowski and Herzog's *Life is With People*,
could be "simple or folksy" or dependent on "a wide range of learning—
satirizing and parodying the flights of *pilpul* and drily deflating scholarship with free use of puns, homonyms, and innuendo."

But Jewish humor as we recognize it today is more immediate in its
origins. It can barely be traced much earlier than the 18th century. It was
sparked by the friction of emancipation, by the fateful encounter with
Christian neighbors of the Jews emerging from the ghettos of the West
and the *shtetlach* of the East. Since telling a joke is an oral art, historical
records yield few gems that can be dated with certainty. But in written
form Jewish wit can be found little earlier than Heinrich Heine, who,
along with Ludwig Boerne, is credited with the invention of the German
feuilleton, the casual humorous monologue in which a few Jews have ex-
celled, from the Viennese cafe wits to S. J. Perelman and Woody Allen.

Heine helped transmit to Jews who came after him the pertinence of irony, the prism of double and multiple meanings simultaneously held and accepted. It is the natural response of a people poised between two worlds: one, the matrix of ghetto and *shtetl*—to which they can no longer return; the other, the civil society of the West—in which they could not be fully at ease.

In the United States, at least since the third wave of immigration beginning in the late 19th century, that note of irony could be heard, with all the ambivalence and ambiguity, all the tension and estrangement, all the posturing and self-consciousness, all the desire to go native and the fear of letting go, all the sense of inferiority and sense of the ridiculous that marginality in American life implies. (I do not know whether Georg Simmel or Thorstein Veblen should be credited with refining the concept of marginality, but whoever it was deserved the rest of the afternoon off.) Though Jews have been sufficiently within American culture to accept its ideals as if by osmosis, their own social acceptability has rarely been complete. To the banker Otto Kahn has been attributed the definition of a kike as "a Jewish gentleman who has just left the room." Though anti-Semitism in America has been relatively mild, its Jews have had reason to deem their fate poignant and odd and thus requiring the palliative of laughter. To be a Jew, Philip Roth has written, is "a complicated, interesting, morally demanding, and very singular experience, and I like that."

However singular that experience may be, the precise ways in which "we" are still different from "them" are hard to pin down. In Walter Bernstein's script for *The Front*, Woody Allen's Gentile girl friend remembers that in her family the worst sin was to raise one's voice; Allen confesses his own family's worst sin was to buy retail. Lenny Bruce may have committed the fallacy of misplaced concreteness in one of his most famous routines:

"I'm Jewish. Count Basie's Jewish. Ray Charles is Jewish. Eddie Cantor's goyish. B'nai B'rith is goyish; Hadassah, Jewish. Marine Corps—heavy goyim, dangerous. Koolaid is goyish. . . . Evaporated milk is goyish even if the Jews invented it. Spam is goyish and rye bread is Jewish. . . . As you know, white bread is very goyish. Fruit salad is Jewish. Lime jello is goyish. Lime soda is *very* goyish." However sly the redistribution of ethnic categories, what is also very Jewish is the marginal man's fascination with difference, with mapping out the boundaries of Jew and Gentile on their common ground in America. Onto that ground came kids who had practiced one-liners and whole monologues the way other kids in other ghettos had practiced hook shots and lay-ups, with comedy providing a form of handling the need for the security of an ancient and consoling identity as well as the hunger for acculturation and normality.

Humor thus served as an opiate of the Jewish masses, a painkiller for the incongruities of an exilic past so terrible at its worst that it was daring to hope for a messiah competent enough to redeem it, a past so strained with the extreme compensations of messianism and idealism that on *Succot* the pious Jews of Europe prayed for rain for the crops of Palestine even though neither the crops nor the Jewish settlements of Palestine existed. Against such exorbitant demands placed upon common sense, a humor could develop that might deflate the absolutism of the purely interior life, a humor that might engage the paradox of both the absurdity of such dreams and their necessity for Jewish survival. The distinctiveness of Jewish humor, Robert Alter has argued, is this need to set the limits of the ordinary and the mundane upon the pretensions of the mythic and the apocalyptic, the need to reduce the extravagance of idealism to the proportions of the familiar. A proverb like "If you want to forget all your troubles, put on a shoe that's too tight" not only softens the central fact of Jewish history, which is suffering, but has its reverberations in the New World as well. Much of the hilarity of Mel Brook's 2000 Year Old Man is due to the effect of an endearingly accented *zeyda* who domesticates historical romance and punctures the transcendance of legend. (Shakespeare is denigrated for his sloppy penmanship, Napoleon is vaguely remembered as "short, right?") The most predictable structure of a Woody Allen witticism is the juxtaposition of the lofty and the immediate, getting at least a smile out of the wish that even the Almighty might be housebroken: his parents's values were "God and carpeting." I once noticed an inadvertent example in the form of a reminder note a rabbi taped on his refrigerator: "Write open letter to Rabin. Call repairman."

The savoring of juxtapositions and paradoxes comes naturally to a people that is both vilified and Chosen, a people whose place in society is so bizarre, so problematic, so defined by others as well as themselves. There may be little point in being Jewish without this awareness of ambiguity, this sense of how bittersweet life is, this recognition of how apt is the symbolism of the Hillel sandwich that mixes *haroset* and *moror* on Passover the way the *badkhen* mixed and manipulated the emotions at weddings. The psychic imperative to "swallow pain with a smile," as Langston Hughes said of black Americans, may explain the high saline content of Jewish humor, that un-anatomical proximity of funny bones to tear ducts. Judaic law does not prohibit graven images among our comics. When *Esquire* put Woody Allen on its cover, it boasted: "We did it! We finally did it! We got Woody Allen to laugh!" Picture others as disparate as Myron Cohen and George S. Kaufman and Shelley Berman and Bert Lahr: they are so melancholy, so unlike the expectations we might have of jolly clowns. They don't even bother to laugh on the *outside*; and though we are assured of the value of laughing when it hurts, many Jewish comics are almost unsettling in their own apparent failure to achieve catharsis through comedy.

The bleakness may be due to an especially troubled encounter with the limitations of the human condition itself. At its most acute, it is a *comédie noire* based on the desperate knowledge that we will each soon be led away, one by one, into the darkness. Laughter is thus the response to a cosmic punch line, to the paradox of love and death, to the odd necessity of having to live together and having to die alone. (Pardon the shorthand.) Comedy suggests a certain dignity in being able to exit laughing, and it is the imprisonment of mortality that especially perturbs some of these humorists. John Yossarian, an Assyrian-American in the novel *Catch-22* (but a Jew in Heller's earlier manuscript version), wants to "live forever or die in the attempt." Brooks, the creator of the rapidly aging 2013 Year Old Man, has proclaimed his desire for "immortality in my lifetime." "Why are our days numbered," Woody Allen asks, "instead of, say, lettered?" And in *Love and Death*, the Allen character realizes that "everyone has to go sometime. I have to go at 6 a.m. It was supposed to be 5 a.m., but I have a good lawyer." Dorothy Parker's fear of dying was best expressed in her poem "Résumé": "Razors pain you;/Rivers are damp;/Acids stain you;/And drugs cause cramp./Guns aren't lawful;/Nooses give;/Gas smells awful;/You might as well live."

The protagonist of *Death of a Salesman* made the awful decision not to live, and yet Arthur Miller has noted his own great hilarity in writing his play. Oddly enough this desperate laughter binds Miller to Kafka, who laughed till the tears came to his eyes as he read his tales aloud to his friends. In describing Kafka's attitude toward the universe, one critic was reminded of the joke of the man seen fishing in a bathtub. "Anything biting?" a friend asks. "Of course not, dummy"—goes the reply—"can't you see this is a bathtub?" Inhospitable though the universe is, unsatisfying though life is, most of us cannot play long enough, knowing that the only game in town is fixed. And humor is the impulse, before we are taken away by the *malekh-hamoves*, the Angel of Death, to fling a custard pie in the face of ultimate defeat.

But there is a special animus to Jewish humor, for some of the descendants of those who had to wear yellow badges on their sleeves grew up even in America with chips on their shoulders. Humor, or more precisely wit, has been not only a shield against the outside world but also a weapon against the *goyim*, a way of getting even. It, too, is one of the needle trades. Perelman once told an interviewer that he sprinkles Yiddish words in his feuilletons "for their invective content. There are nineteen words in Yiddish that convey gradations of disparagement from a mild, fluttery helplessness to a state of downright, irreconcilable brutishness." Wallace Markfield has observed that for some comedians Yiddish "is like a wet towel in the hands of a locker-room bully; it cuts, slices . . . shames, undermines, puts down"; and I can only add that the incorporation of its vocabulary has helped give our American prose a whiplash sting. The stand-up comic's greatest boast, after his or her act is done, is to offer backstage post-mortems like "I killed them out there" and "I knocked them dead." Comic license means that its practitioners are licensed to kill. "I don't want to make just another movie," Brooks has insisted. "I want to make trouble. I want to say in comic terms, 'J'accuse.' " And even though he himself need not be taken too seriously on this point, gall is indivisible from the style of the likes of Don Rickles and David Levine. Even in the world of "entertainment," some Jewish comics are merchants of menace who sometimes seem ready to unlatch the door in the back of the brain and let some of the scorpions out. It is significant that Freud's *Wit and Its Relation to the Unconscious* defines wit so heavily in terms of hostility and aggressiveness and that so many of his examples are Jewish jokes.

Cruelty is rarely far below the surface in comedy; the ridicule of foibles is rarely far from the contempt for flaws. Laughter is an acceptable way to disguise the derision we may privately feel for the hapless victim toward whom we are supposed to display compassion. In offering us a compromise between the pity that conscience requires and the smug relief of having avoided the fate of the luckless, American-Jewish humor also skirts the edge of nastiness. In *The Day of the Locust*, West wrote that "it is hard to laugh at the need for beauty and romance. . . . But it is easy to sigh." Yet his two major novels, populated with grotesques, are usually considered early veins of black humor, toward which it is not easy to sigh. The characters in Roth's *The Great American Novel* include a baseball squad from an insane asylum, a couple of midgets (one of whom is hailed as "a credit to his size") and a one-armed outfielder whose handicap enables a batter to score an inside-the-mouth home run. *Love and Death* shows a convention of village idiots. Brooks is especially pleased with the scene in *Young Frankenstein* in which a blind monk clumsily plays host to the monster. And although Brooks reacted vehemently to the charge that in *Blazing Saddles* Mongo's name is an abbreviation for mongoloid, it strains credulity that the director would have ignored the association that audiences might make. A wall has thus been breached which, according to the psychiatrist Theodore Reik, had been erected around Jewish humor in Europe: "Mockery at a crippled condition, physical affliction and ugliness as well as old age, with its many complaints, is amazingly rare as a subject of Jewish witticisms." The dangers of the coarsening of sensibility, especially in our century, cannot be dismissed; there was a need for walls against sadism and ugliness.

But even if Dr. Reik's claim cannot be fully substantiated for American brands of Jewish humor, the relative absence of cruelty toward the helpless and the handicapped may be credited not only to the recalcitrance of humane values but to the substitution of targets, to displacement. Hostility takes the form, as Dr. Reik and many others have noticed, of masochism, of the self-deprecation that—as an Israeli amazon informs Alexander Portnoy—may be the essence of Diaspora humor. Again it is Heine, the first of those Enlightenment Jews to recognize that life is—or at least should be—a tale told by an ironist, who gets there first:

"I cannot relate my own griefs without the thing becoming comic." It is not so much that Jews see themselves as victims but that the victimization is rendered ludicrous and thus bearable in the very act of shrill insistence. Playing sorrows fortissimo may drown out the silence of God.

Neil Simon once distinguished between "writing Gentile" (for example, *Barefoot in the Park*) and "writing Jewish" (for example, *The Odd Couple*), by which he meant more than inflections and phrasing: Jewish is more than black cherry soda and rye bread; it is "martyrdom, and self-pity, and 'everything terrible happens to me.' " For Portnoy, whose confession ends with a primal scream, for the Peter Tarnopol of *My Life as a Man*, for Gene Wilder's Leo Bloom in *The Producers* and his Dr. Frankenstein, for the Alan Arkin characters in *Little Murders* and *Hearts of the West*, for Joe Ancis (the ur-Lenny Bruce and reputedly the funniest man in Brooklyn), the title of Freud's first major book is applicable: studies in hysteria. The eponymous hero of *Herzog* wonders if he is "out of his mind"; his creator claims that the novel "makes comic use of complaint." One conclusion to be drawn is that the stoic ideal is goyish, having a tantrum is Jewish.

A good example is Simon's own Mel Edison, the frantic middle-aged prisoner of Second Avenue, the wisecracking victim of civilization and its peculiarly urban discontents. He hears everything. The heat is oppressive, tropical. The toilet doesn't stop flushing. He gets indigestion from a health-food restaurant ("I haven't had a real piece of bread in thirty years. . . . If I knew what was going to happen, I would have saved some rolls when I was a kid"). The garbage outside is piled up so high that Edison predicts their fourteenth-floor apartment will soon be on the second floor. After six years of therapy, his psychiatrist has died; and when his wife Edna suggests treatment with another, he replies: "And start all over from the beginning? . . . It'll cost me another $23,000 just to fill *this* doctor in with information I already gave the dead one." When his wife demands not to be spoken to "like I'm insane," he replies: "I'm halfway there, you might as well catch up."

From Jack Benny, who was (according to Fred Allen) "the first comedian in radio to realize that you could get big laughs by ridiculing yourself instead of your stooges," to Rodney Dangerfield, whose insignia is the plaintive "I don't get no respect," the Jewish comic has bent the self-definition of martyrdom to his own purposes. There are undoubtedly biographical explanations here, in that several comedians seem to have found their vocation already as children too puny to use their fists against bullies and chose to live by their wits instead. Such traumas were then transmuted, as in Perelman's shuddering recollection of a grammar school "fiend incarnate, a hulking evil-faced youth related on both sides of his family to Torquemada and dedicated to making my life insupportable. . . . Too wispy to stand up to my oppressor, I took refuge in a subdued blubbering, which soon abraded the teacher's nerves and earned me the reputation of being refractory. . . ." As a child Woody Allen once won two weeks at an inter-faith camp, "where I was sadistically beaten by boys of every race, creed, and color." (In *Sleeper*, the line is altered: the Allen character was once even beaten up by Quakers.) Even in the scene in which Portnoy acknowledges the self-deprecatory quality of Jewish humor, he is both sexually frustrated and physically overpowered by the six-foot kibbutznik, Naomi.

But Jewish jokes go well beyond this emphasis on helplessness. So completely are faults, vices, embarrassments, shames lingered over that it is not easy to decide whether such humor was created by Jews or by anti-Semitic Gentiles. Jewish humor accepts some of the very accusations of anti-Semites, then turns those crimes inside out, and thus blunts the impact and absorbs the shock of bigotry. Marginal men and women thus nervously discharge their own anxieties by giggling at them and thereby escape their spell. You think that's bad? the Jew tells the anti-Semite. Can you top this? . . . Markfield's Jules Farber wags his finger at south Florida matrons and spits out: "Remember, never be ashamed that you're Jewish; it's enough that *I'm* ashamed that you're Jewish." Jews not only kid their own ostensible group characteristics but also, paradoxically, attack some brethren for not being Jewish *enough*—hence the in-group popularity of jokes about Reform Jews. With the patent decline of anti-Semitism since the end of the Second World War, Jews have become comfortable enough to realize—as the success of musicals like *Funny Girl* and its star attests—that a nose with deviations *isn't* such a crime against the nation. The humorist can be less effectively stigmatized as an informer to the *goyim*, who can now hear in-jokes on talk shows and read them in *Portnoy's Complaint* and other best-sellers, which is after all where the gripes of Roth are stored.

The animus remains, for American Jewish humor is fueled with vitriol and concocted to wash away protocol. One of the ways to puncture the pretensions of the Gentiles is to make them marranos, secret Jews, as in all the jokes whose punch lines reveal that certified *goyim* like Santa Claus, Richard Nixon, Billy Graham and the Pope break out into Yiddish. There are Jewish-accented Indians in *Cat Ballou* and *Blazing Saddles*, Jewish-accented robots in *Sleeper*, a Jewish-accented black cabbie in *Bye Bye Braverman*. Sherlock Holmes has become Shlock Holmes, and James Bond has become Israel Bond, agent oi-oi seven.

Jews have also been relatively free to explore the area beyond the rim of good taste, free to press their noses—their less-than-classic profiles—against the glass of form. Freud himself cited several jokes about the indifference to propriety by which Jews recognized their own differentiation from Gentiles. Among Einstein's favorite nonscientific reading during his final years at Princeton was Emily Post's manual of etiquette, passages of which caused him to cackle with delight. (The fact that the rules governing the conduct of ladies and gentlemen must have seemed to Einstein about as exotic as the winter ceremonial of the Kwakiutl is another bewildering proof of the difficulty of classifying humor.) Groucho Marx once wrote to the sleazy gutter rag *Confidential* as follows: "If you continue to publish slanderous pieces about me, I shall feel compelled to cancel my subscription." Even S. J. Perelman, whose literary persona is at least shabby genteel, repatriated himself from England several years ago because he had found "too much couth" there. Another Marx Brothers associate, Herman Mankiewicz, once attended an elegant dinner party, drank too much during dinner, and then vomited on the table. Mankiewicz himself broke the hushed silence by assuring the host: "It's all right— .... The white wine came up with the fish."

Given this sort of heightened self-consciousness about propriety, it should not be surprising that the first movie not so much *in* bad taste as *about* bad taste, *The Producers* (with its play-within-a-film of a Nazi musical on Broadway), should be by that Flatbush fabulist, Mel Brooks. Jewish humor has more than its share of crudeness and lewdness as well, for they are human equalizers when social barriers are raised and tradesmen and peddlers are forced to enter from the rear. If genteel society condemns the "dirty Jews," then the accused will sometimes perversely admit to the charge, indeed affirm a certain kind of faith—I stink, therefore I am—as a way of asserting the commonness of the dust from which all of us have sprung and to which even the genteel will return. William James, hearing Freud deliver his 1909 lectures at Clark University, considered him "a dirty fellow"; and what movie critics call "lusty" in foreign films, Billy Wilder once complained, they call "dirty" in his films. No wonder then that in recent years so many of those associated with blue language—Roth, Norman Mailer, Allen Ginsberg, "Dirty Lenny"—have been Jews, as have been their attorneys, as is Gershon Legman, who is the leading scholar of pornography, the Linnaeus of the limerick, the author of a veritable Syntopicon of *shmutz*. When Woody Allen's psychiatrist asked him if he considered sex dirty, he replied, "Yes. If you do it right." Insistence upon a shared humanity with the Gentiles helps explain why these figures illustrate the warning issued by Rabbi Akiba that "jesting and levity lead a person to lewdness."

Had Lenny Bruce been better educated, had he read for instance Denis de Rougement's *Love in the Western World* (a study of how, between the eleventh and twelfth centuries, the French invented love—that is, the romantic version, the idealization of passion), he might have added to his list that love is goyish, sex is Jewish. From Alex Portnoy (who wanted to "put the id back in Yid") to the compulsive, aging adolescents in *Carnal Knowledge*; from the leering and aggressive opportunist that was Groucho's screen personality to the characters Woody Allen has played—all are essentially prisoners of sex with a remarkably high recidivism rate. In much of American Jewish humor, love is folly and an illusion. Except for some artificial sweeteners added to the endings, Billy

Wilder's best comedies have all the romantic sentimentality of a police blotter. They are as far removed from the romantic ideal as the domestic pieties of a Sam Levenson are from Sophie Portnoy, whose parental love is perceived as disguised aggression, a will to power that threatens autonomous manhood with infantile dependency. Even when other Jews—in Hollywood, on Broadway, in the radio and television studios—have sold dreams of redemptive love, much of the aim of American Jewish humor has been to illumine the disparity between fantasy and actuality, to cross the chasm between ideal and real by walking upon a banana peel.

Yet such humor is dependent on those public dreams and official pieties for its own ironic effects. Take, as only one minor example, the post-World War II consoling myth of the "good German." The notion was briefly mocked in *One, Two, Three* by director-scriptwriter Billy Wilder (whose mother perished at Auschwitz), and more directly and savagely in Mordecai Richler's novel *Cocksure*, in which a British gentleman after the War "had collected case histories and compiled a book, elegantly produced if necessarily slender, about all the charitable little acts done by Germans to Jews during the Nazi era. Here a simple but good-hearted sergeant offering spoonfuls of marmalade to Jewish children before they were led off to the gas chamber, somewhere else a fabled general refusing to drink with Eichmann or a professor quoting Heine right to a Nazi's face." But generally a direct encounter with the Holocaust has been avoided; even Brooks did not mention the almost-unmentionable in *The Producers*, as though even bad taste has its limits—at least so far. Perhaps because one "good German" was not associated with the war against the Jews, Werner Von Braun has been a favorite target. He was satirized in the Tom Lehrer ditty about the "widows and cripples in old London town/Who owe their large pensions to Werner Von Braun," the "big hero" who "learned to count backward to zero." He was also lampooned as Dr. Strangelove (admittedly with elements of Herman Kahn and Henry Kissinger thrown in as well). And when Hollywood produced a film about the cosmetic aspects of the rocket engineer's career entitled *I Aim for the Stars*, Mort Sahl offered a subtitle: But I Hit London.

So much for one myth anyway. Philip Roth has argued that American social reality, refracted through the prisms of publicity and celebrity, has become too rich for novelists to keep up with, that the facts of national life are too wildly improbable and irrational to sustain the standard methods of verisimilitude. Indeed, we now know that almost anything can happen on television, including murder and the confession of murder; and we are braced to expect almost any affront to dignity, any insult to the intelligence, any banality, any assault on privacy. We should not be astonished if Indira Gandhi shows up as a special guest on The Merv Griffin Show, seated next to a crooner, a starlet and a guru, or if Jean-Paul Sartre and Simone de Beauvoir go for the big prize on The

Dating Game. The media may have become *the* great American subject, and humorists have tried so hard to keep up that parody is almost synonymous with American Jewish humor itself.

For example, *Mad* magazine mimics comics, movies, advertisements. Much of *Your Show of Shows* consisted of TV take-offs on movies, while *The Groove Tube* is a movie send-up of television. Like Allen, Perelman specializes in parody for the *New Yorker*; and even Perelman's autobiographical pieces are often accounts of silly movies ("Cloud-land Revisited"). All of Brooks's films except one have been parodies (the show biz success story in *The Producers*, the Western in *Blazing Saddles*, the horror pic in *Young Frankenstein* and now the films of Hitchcock in *High Anxiety*). Until *Annie Hall*, all of Allen's films except one were parodies (the prison escape film in *Take the Money and Run*, the political film in *Bananas*, the science fiction film in *Sleeper*, the Russian novel in *Love and Death* and parts of *Everything You Ever Wanted to Know about Sex*). Bernard Malamud's *The Natural* is not only a satire on baseball but a parody of "The Waste Land." Among Portnoy's zaniest impulses is the magnification of his shame into newspaper headlines, to see how his crimes would look when validated in the media.

It may be an important limitation that, in darting so naturally from the unconscious to commerce and from the id to the ad, some comics have so little to draw upon except their own sometimes recondite knowledge and memory of movies, comic books, sports, radio shows and other forms of popular culture. Many humorists are too heavily dependent not upon the direct observation of social incongruities and human folly but upon the ways in which they have already been treated, however inadvertently, in the media; and that world is simply not thick enough to be consistently explored by truly adult minds. The risks of vacuity, tediousness and preciousness should not be minimized, and it is dreary to contemplate the endless recycling of the effluvia of the popular arts.

But what salvages the best of American Jewish humor is often the continuation of Heine's achievement in shaping language itself for comic purposes. The Jews are not the only people to claim to have talked to God but are, I think, the only people to have talked *back* to God, to have attempted to bargain and negotiate. Soon after Freud devised the method that the Viennese nicknamed "the talking cure," the Catholic intellectual Charles Péguy succinctly presented the case for Jewish verbal resourcefulness: the Catholic has been reading for two generations, the Protestant for three centuries; the Jew has always read. One might add that the Jew has long been talking about, arguing about what he has read, in contrast to the depiction of the saint in Christian mythology as mute or possessing a speech defect. The sufferer in modern Jewish lore undergoes, like Bellow's Philip Bummidge, Roth's Portnoy and Tarnopol, Erica Jong's Isadora Wing, the talking cure. The polar opposite of the Christian saint who is struck dumb is the Jew who *shpritzes*, the perpetuator of an oral tradition

(Scheherazade should have been Jewish). "Interior monologue, free association, stream of consciousness—these are the fancy words for the *shpritz*," Albert Goldman writes. "Out . . . in the Bensonhurst-Borough Park Delta of Jewish humor, the Basin Street of Jewish jazz . . . Lenny (Bruce) first learned to be funny . . . funny being equivalent to vital, strong, honest, and soulful. Funny guys were the guys who told the truth. Guys with an original point of view, a private language, a sound. The Jewish equivalent of the black jazzman. A hero." What dazzled Dick Gregory about Bruce was that "here's a man [who] can do three hours on any subject."

The first talking picture was also one of the first to deal explicitly with a Jew, the cantor's son who became *The Jazz Singer*. In the pantheon of immortal silent film comedians are no Jews, who have historically been more comfortable within the world of sound than gesture, of idea rather than image. There are exceptions: the drawings of Saul Steinberg and the caricatures of David Levine (although, to strengthen the generalization, the cartoons of Herblock and Jules Feiffer depend upon the cleverness of captions and dialogues), the pregnant silences in the skits of Jack Benny, the sublime grace of Harpo Marx and the silly mugging of Jerry Lewis. And yet even the most physical of the Jewish clowns of the 1950s, Sid Caesar, was a master of mimicry of fake foreign languages. Even he required scripts from what ought to be considered the Groton of gag-writers—for Brooks, Simon and Allen all rendered unto Caesar the things that were Caesar's before they established careers of their own.

At its most authentic, Jewish humor demonstrates a sensitivity to language as the vehicle of truth, has helped verbalize anxieties, has contributed its desperanto to the articulation of the modern mood. Jews have dominated comedy record albums if not silent films ("hear O Israel" to Nichols and May, to Sahl, to Shelley Berman, to David Frye) and have altered the form of professional joking, as Wallace Markfield has remarked, from "the old-style Bob Hope-type monologue, with its heavy reliance upon a swift sputter of gags plucked from card indices, then updated and localized. It is involuted, curvilinear, ironic, more parable than patter. A Jackie Mason, for example, will start from a basic absurdity . . . [and] work around, over, and along it like a good Talmudist."

The pious Jew who explicates the mysteries of the word is not too distant a relative of the comedian who encounters life through the exercise of intelligence, even when it is intelligence itself that is being kidded. Consider the following joke supposedly explaining the "secret of telegraphy," of which Immanuel Olsvanger found three versions. The Arabic version asks us to "imagine a huge dog having its head in Beirut and its tail in Damascus. Pull the dog's tail in Damascus and the bark will be heard in Beirut." Here is the Russian version: First Russian: "Imagine a horse, its head in Moscow and its tail in Tula. Pinch the horse's nose in Moscow and it will wag its tail in Tula. And so it is with telegraphy." Second Russian: "Yes, but how do they telegraph from Tula to Moscow?" (Something may be getting lost in translation.) And now the Jewish version: First Jew: "Imagine, instead of the wire, a dog, whose head is in Kovno and whose tail is in Vilna. Pull the tail in Vilna and the bark will be heard in Kovno." Second Jew: "But how does wireless telegraphy work?" First Jew: The very same way, but without a dog."

Though the Jewish version renders the explanation of telegraphy as futile as ignorance of it, the very mockery of the circularity of reasoning pays a certain tribute to the need to make the universe a little less perplexing. Perhaps that is why Philip Roth felt himself in competition with Lenny Bruce, or why Joseph Heller feels at home with Mel Brooks, or why Woody Allen is the thinking man's comedian despite his own limited formal education (he was expelled from one college for "cheating—it was a rather delicate situation because it was with the Dean's wife"). Much of Allen's humor is based on an exaggeration of the word, an excess of ratiocination. He is too clever for his own good; he's the kind who would have been a stowaway on the *Titanic*. He thinks too much: he couldn't marry one woman because she was an atheist, and he's an agnostic, and they could not agree "what religion *not* to raise the children up in." Woody Allen is a survivor of the mythical village of Chelm, where the responses to life are theoretically plausible and practically ridiculous—intellectuality gone berserk, as the unexamined promise moves inexorably if unpredictably toward its bizarrely inappropriate conclusion. Kidnapped as a child, Allen was freed when FBI agents surrounded the house and, since they had failed to bring along tear gas cannisters, instead "put on the death scene from *Camille*. Tear-stricken my abductors gave themselves up." Several years later Allen was briefly hired by an advertising agency to prove that it would employ minority groups. Placed at the front desk, Allen "tried desperately to look Jewish," even reading his "memos from right to left. But I was eventually fired for taking off too many Jewish holidays." In such routines the spaciousness of the interior life of the Jew is simply further inflated with laughing gas; it is not perforated from outside but exploded from within. But from late 19th century Russia comes a story (my immediate source is the American Constitutional historian Leonard Levy) which best shows the imperative to make sense, the compatibility of the comic spirit with the ideal of rationality:

When Jews could not travel outside the Pale of Settlement without official permission, an aged scholar from Odessa was finally able, after months of negotiation, to be allowed to travel to Moscow. After one train stop, a young man got on and sat down opposite him. The old scholar looked at him, and the following interior monologue took place: "He doesn't look like a peasant, and if he isn't a peasant, he probably comes from this district. If he comes from this district, he must be Jewish because this is a Jewish district. But if he is Jewish, so where could he be going? I'm the only one in the district who has permission to travel to Moscow. To what village would he not need permission to travel? Oh, just outside Moscow there's a little village of Mozhaisk, and to Mozhaisk you don't need permission. But whom could he be visiting in Mozhaisk? There are only two Jewish families in the whole of Mozhaisk, the Linskys and the Greenbaums. I know the Linskys are a terrible family, so he must be visiting the Greenbaums. But who would undertake a trip at this time of the year unless he were a close personal relative? The Greenbaums have only daughters, so perhaps he's a son-in-law. But if he's a son-in-law, which daughter did he marry? Esther married that nice young lawyer from Budapest. What was his name? Alexander Cohen. Whom did Sarah marry? Sarah married that no-goodnik, that salesman from Zhadomir. It must be Esther. So if he married Esther, his name is Alexander Cohen and he comes from Budapest. Oh, the terrible anti-Semitism they have there now. He probably changed his name from Cohen. So what's the Hungarian equivalent of Cohen? Kovacs. But if he's a man who changed his name from Cohen to Kovacs, he's a man who shows a basic insecurity in life. However, to change his name because of anti-Semitism, a man would need status. So what kind of status could he have? A doctor's degree from the university." At this point the old scholar got up, tapped the young man on the shoulder and asked, "Dr. Alexander Kovacs?" "Why yes," the young man replied, "but how did you know?" "Oh," said the old scholar, "it stands to reason."

Philip Roth's Would-be Patriarchs and their *Shikses* and Shrews

Sarah Blacher Cohen[*]

In Genesis Abraham cherished both his Hebrew wife, Sarah, and his Egyptian concubine, Hagar. Though Sarah could not provide him with a male heir until he was a hundred, Abraham dwelled harmoniously with her and shared all the fruits of his God-given prosperity with her. Yet Sarah is depicted as more than the complacent sharer of her husband's good fortune; she is elevated to the position of Abraham's most sagacious mortal advisor. She is concerned that Abraham's line be perpetuated and selflessly bids Abraham leave her tent to impregnate her more fertile handmaiden, Hagar. Also Sarah, after miraculously giving birth at ninety to her own son, Isaac, prudently instructs Abraham to banish Hagar and her son, Ishmael, for fear he will usurp Isaac's rightful inheritance. All of Sarah's counsel Abraham willingly heeds, never doubting that she has his and his descendants' best interests at heart. His compliance to her wishes in no way detracts from his tribal leadership or interferes with his personal sovereignty. Nor, for that matter, does it diminish his regard for Hagar. Knowing Hagar in the biblical sense and begetting Ishmael are not guilt-ridden activities for Abraham. On the contrary, bedding a bedouin, especially if it leads to the siring of a male offspring and the multiplying of the species, is in Abraham's time considered a most noteworthy achievement. Nor does Abraham callously terminate his fourteen-year relationship with Hagar or harbor any ill feelings toward her when she threatens the welfare of his household. Only when he has God's assurance that Hagar will not be abandoned and a new nation will emerge from her son does Abraham send her into the wilderness.

But those were patriarchal times when the Abrahams did not feel their authority undermined by women or need to win their approval. Secure in their leadership, they were free to enjoy the pleasures of female society and family solidarity. However, in twentieth century America, in Jewish-American households among others, the fathers have had to abdicate their power in the domestic sphere to scramble after power in the

[*]Reprinted from *Studies in American-Jewish Literature*, 1 (Spring 1975), 16–23, by permission of the journal.

world at large. Their clans they have reluctantly left in control of the mothers. While these mothers have not always ruled wisely and merited being extolled as "women of valor," except in funeral eulogies, they are not the emasculators they are made out to be on the analysts' couches or the vipers they are depicted as being by the Philip Wylie novelists. Yet there are men today who aspire to be venerable patriarchs, but whom the systems, the external socio-economic one or their own psychological one, force to be vengeful little boys who blame their powerlessness on their *Yiddishe mommes* and other women who faintly resemble them. Such petulant *puers* are found bellyaching through Philip Roth's novels.

In *Goodbye, Columbus* the bellyaching takes the form of wry anti-feminine mockery, so subtle that Neil Klugman, the *klug* or clever hero who expresses it, is not always aware of its misogynistic import. Since Neil's mother is in Arizona curing her asthma, he unwittingly directs his maternal hostility at Aunt Gladys, the first generation relative with whom he stays. Overlooking her generosity and assiduous efforts to please, he exaggerates only her flaws: her forced-feeding tactics, her hysterical concern for the starving Jews of Israel, her strict avoidance of pleasure and her contempt for wealthy, less observant co-religionists. Uncle Max, who lives in the same apartment and obviously shares some of the same values as Aunt Gladys, is never the object of Neil's reproach. He somehow is miraculously free of all pettiness.

The same kind of gender bias colors Neil's view of the Patimkins, the *nouveau riche* suburban Jewish family whose daughter, Brenda, he's courting. He amusingly notes the arrested locker-room development of son Ron, who becomes awash with sentimentality listening to the record of his Ohio State football triumph. He unsparingly describes the coarse behavior of father Patimkin, the hard-driving parvenu of kitchen and bathroom sinks. However Neil mentions their redeeming features as well. Ron may be the uncultivated "super-jock," but he has an endearing canine loyalty and exuberance. Mr. Patimkin may be the scorner of idealism in the business world, but he is a paragon of love and devotion in his home. Not so the mother of the house. She has, according to Neil, no compensatory good graces. As the Jewish-American princess who has become queen of the split-level palace, she impresses him as an unenlightened and mean-spirited monarch. He finds her ignorant of the teaching of Judaism, inconsistent in her religious practices, too permissive in the rearing of her children and inhospitable to strangers.

Neil is quick to discover Mrs. Patimkin's obnoxious traits, but it takes him longer to discover Brenda's, perhaps because he has convinced himself she is so very unlike a Jewish girl. Compared to the other Jewish ladies at the country club pool with their "Cuban heels and boned-up breasts," the barefooted Brenda in her simple "black tank suit" reminds him of "a sailor's dream of a Polynesian maiden" (14). Unlike his seden-tary cousin, Doris, who in search of suitors reads *War and Peace* at the poolside, Brenda is an athlete par excellence. She expertly dives, grace-fully swims, plays a champion's game of tennis and energetically runs the mile. A female equivalent of the Hemingway sports hero, she effortlessly wins Neil's adoration. So enchanted with her is he that, like the Hem-ingway heroine, he begins to lose his own identity and assume Brenda's. Wearing identical sneakers, sweat socks and khaki bermudas, and forsak-ing his contemplative life for her active one, he even begins to look like her. However, the more intimately he comes to know her, the more he realizes that beneath her free-spirited gentile "phys.ed." exterior, lies an uptight, demanding Jewish girl. That she bobs her nose to avoid looking Jewish does not prevent her from absorbing the values of her narrow-minded Jewish mother. Just as acquisitive and over-indulged as her mother, Brenda views Neil as a compliant junior version of her father whom she can manipulate at will. Believing she is entitled to anything she wants, she initally has sex with Neil in her home as a pleasurable in-tramural sport, and not because she has any strong feelings for him. But once she grows accustomed to having Neil about, she assumes he will want to marry her and give up his unprestigious librarian's job to become a promoter of Patimkin sinks. When Neil does not propose marriage to her and proposes instead that she buy a diaphragm, Brenda is angry she can-not have her way. And when she does finally purchase a diaphragm, she carelessly leaves it at home for her Hadassah mother to discover. Her cen-sure Brenda can bear, but her father's disappointment in her and his veiled threat that he will stop buying her clothes if she continues her affair with Neil she finds too difficult to accept. Compelled to choose between her prosperous father and his impoverished younger surrogate, Brenda, in true Jewish Electra fashion, chooses her Daddy.

But this is Neil's interpretation of the affair and his analysis of Brenda. Why, if he were so fond of Brenda and thought her so singular did he not inform her of his dissatisfaction with her offensive ways? That is to say, why in his own enlightened way did he not try to tame the shrew? Why, if he were seriously interested in her did he not make some long-range commitment to her? Why did he make getting a diaphragm a primary condition for their staying together? The answer to these ques-tions is obvious: He wanted to terminate his affair with Brenda because he was incapable of maintaining any permanent relationship with a flesh and blood woman, particularly a Jewish one. As he himself describes his feelings for her early in the relationship, "I did not want to voice a word that would lift the cover and reveal that hideous emotion I always felt for her, and is the underside of love. It will not always stay the underside . . ." (27) That "hideous emotion" drives him from her and causes him to return to the library where he can once again see the only person with whom he feels a kinship: the little Negro boy who comes to look at Gauguin's pictures of Tahiti. Like the little boy who takes esthetic delight in the paintings of island beauties, Neil takes esthetic delight in his

Polynesian dream maiden, Brenda. Moreover, like the boy who prefers not to check the Gauguin book out of the library and take it home, Neil prefers not to take his dream maiden home and live with her. Thus what he and his little friend choose to settle for are fleeting visions of the Ideal and continual partings with it.

Alexander Portnoy also cannot remain too long with those women who figure in his fantasies and those who exist in real life. But unlike Neil Klugman, who never fully explains the psychological reasons for his female antipathies, Portnoy over-explains the causes for his grievances. The entire novel is in fact an endless litany of little lord Portnoy's grievances primarily against the unholy Madonna, Sophie Portnoy. His conception of her determines his attitude and behavior toward the subsequent women in his life. As a child Portnoy marvels at her many accomplishments: her magican's feat of making jello with peaches suspended in it, her humanitarianism of giving the black cleaning lady cans of high-grade tuna for lunch. But he also remembers his mother in more disconcerting roles. She is a seductress who, as she puts on her nylons and girdle before him, calls him her "little lover" and praises him for his docility and good marks in school. She is an insidious food-pusher who, if he will not become addicted to three wholesome meals a day, threatens to castrate him with the bread knife. During his adolescent years he finds her even more pernicious. Unlike the matriarch Sarah, happy to wean Isaac so he would not be dependent on her, Mrs. Portnoy refuses to abdicate control over his teenage eating and excretory habits. So dictatorial is she when he asserts his autonomy that he believes there's been "a mix-up of sexes" in the house, with his mother acting the way his father should act.

Since his father is not a powerful figure of masculinity whom he can emulate, Portnoy struggles to avoid identifying himself with his omnipotent mother. He is not only plagued with homosexual fears, but he is panic-stricken he may turn into a girl and even have babies. But when he accompanies his father to the Turkish bath, his panic is dispelled. Proud of his father's privates, Portnoy is temporarily assured of his own manhood and is capable of uttering the same prayer which the Orthodox Jew recites each morning: "Thank God, I was not created a woman."

The other way Portnoy proves to himself he is not a woman is to engage in excessive masturbation and heterosexual activity. If his sexual apparatus is in good working order and taxed to the limit, he can never be accused of being a non-functioning male. However, Portnoy is limited to the kinds of women with whom he can function. According to his sophomoric classification of things, there are two kinds of females: *shikses* and shrews, or more specifically, prurient gentile lasses and prudish Hebrew harridans. And like other mother-bound heroes who seek out the alien woman to gratify their latent Oedipal desires, Portnoy chooses the *shikses* to satisfy his lust. But the *shikses* he consorts with are not all alike, as he naively supposed. They are all sexually compliant, but some are more compliant than others.

The sluttiest one is Thereal (the real) McCoy, the creature of his puberty fantasies. He imagines her carrying out his most perverse erotic wishes and being extremely grateful for the opportunity to do so. Her real-life counterpart is Mary Jane Reed, an uneducated ex-fashion model whom he nicknames the Monkey for her lascivious dexterity. In their relationship she takes the sexual initiative, devising ingenious voluptuary games to entertain him. Deeming it an honor to sleep with a Jewish intellectual, she subordinates her needs to give him pleasure. Hoping that he will someday marry her, she strives to conform to his image of the ideal woman. But her efforts are doomed to failure. No matter how respectable or literate she becomes, in Portnoy's parochial eyes she will always be a *shikse*, the unkosher, forbidden woman.

Unlike the self-assured patriarch Abraham, who could treat Hagar magnanimously, the insecure thirty-three year old *puer* Portnoy must degrade his gentile mistress. Certain that his mother would condemn his actions, he projects the punishment he expects to receive for his transgressions onto Mary Jane. He also makes her the object of the rage which he originally intended to direct at his mother but was too inhibited to do so. Moreover, to stifle any incestual feelings he might have, he must dehumanize Mary Jane, treating her like a copulating machine rather than a sensitive individual, so she will not bear the slightest resemblance to his mother. Thus he lectures her on her inadequacies, forces her to have sex with an Italian whore, drives her to suicidal desperation and deserts her in a foreign city. And all of this cruelty is through the courtesy of the virtuous Portnoy, the New York City Assistant Commissioner of Human Opportunity.

Portnoy reacts differently to the more high-toned Christian women. Just as Dick Diver saw in Nicole Warren "the essence of a continent," Portnoy finds the more genteel gentile ladies to be symbolic of America. Differentiating his conception of America from that of previous generations, he rhapsodically exclaims:

> O America! America! it may have been gold in the streets to my grandparents, it may have been a chicken in every pot to my father and mother, but to me, a child whose earliest movie memories are of Ann Rutherford and Alice Fay, America is a *shikse* nestling under your arm whispering love love love love love! (164–165)

Not only do full-grown Hollywood sirens embody America for Portnoy, but young blonde maidens represent the new world to him. Humbert Humbert's childhood love affair with an idyllic nymphet caused him to remain exclusively enamoured of nine to fourteen-year-olds; so Portnoy's pubertal adoration of a little Christian skater causes him to be hopelessly infatuated with "bland blond exotics" (171) in later life. In Portnoy's youth this fair-haired descendant of Sir Walter Scott's Rowena is not only a symbol of grace and purity, but with her red, white and blue outfit, she is "Miss America, on blades" (170). He yearns to possess her as well as the charmed life he imagines her to lead with her dignified parents and one-family house. He fantasies his own imperfections will miraculously vanish when this perfect creature kisses him. Like the self-hating Jew who thinks he will lose his tell-tale Jewish characteristics by marrying a non-Jew, Portnoy imagines that his nose and name will not matter when he is lost in the arms of little Miss America. He also hopes that through prolonged association with the ideal *shikse* he will somehow become like her even more desirable older brothers, the *shkotzim*, those "engaging, good-natured, confident, clean, swift, and powerful" (163) college football stars. Then Portnoy believes he will have all the treats which radio and the movies promise to every other "all American *goy*" (164): a date with Judy and "chestnuts roasting on the open fire."

When Portnoy does attend college in predominately Christian mid-western America and meets the ideal Christian coed, the "artless, sweet-tempered" Kay Campbell, he can't allow himself to appreciate his good fortune. Spending Thanksgiving with her parents, he feels he is an in-terloper who will be ostracised as soon as his Jewish identity is discovered. Since Portnoy is one of those Jews who want to change their noses not their Moses, the only way he can conceive of being the Campbell's son-in-law is by having Kay convert to his faith. When she sees no need to renounce Christianity for Judaism, he uses her refusal as an excuse to ter-minate his relationship with her. Pitying himself for being the rejected Jewish male, he is the one who has rejected the gentile female, not because of her unwillingness to become a Jewess, but because she has come frightening close to conquering his chosen prison.

When Portnoy graduates from college and law school, he also graduates from mating with a middle-class *shikse* to coupling with an upper class one. Just as he attempted to depersonalize Kay Campbell by calling her "The Pumpkin" because of her pigmentation and the size of her buttocks, he calls Sarah Abbott Maulsby "The Pilgrim" because of her distinguished New England origins and her finishing school propriety. Whereas Portnoy genuinely likes "The Pumpkin," he dislikes many of "The Pilgrim's" personality traits, yet he has an affair with her. Like the black man, who, by raping white women, thinks he is getting his piece of America, Portnoy believes that by fornicating with a WASP debutante, he is making inroads into the monied WASP establishment. As he tells his doctor: "I don't seem to stick my dick up these girls, as much as I stick it up their backgrounds—as though through fucking I will discover America. Conquer America—maybe that's more like it" (265). But Port-noy, like the black man, also wants to wreak vengeance on America for exploiting his ancestors. He therefore forces "The Pilgrim" to engage in degrading sexual acts to compensate for the degradation his father suffered at the hands of his gentile New England employers. Since Portnoy is consumed with making "The Pilgrim" the scapegoat for his WASP hostility, there is no opportunity for love to develop between them. Thus he abandons her to remain with her own people in New Canaan, Connecticut, and sets out to find his own people in old Canaan, Israel.

But Israel is not the land of milk and honeys who are eager to be sweet to Portnoy. The Jewish women he meets there are not promiscuous and are very discriminating about whom they choose as lovers. The one Sabra who captures his fancy initially reminds him of "The Pumpkin" in that she is innocent, idealistic and earnest. But when he impetuously proposes marriage to her, he notices that she takes on the characteristics of his mother. Acting as if she were the Holy Land's most righteous priestess, she castigates him for his moral laxity and self-deprecation. With scant patience for his weakness, she orders him to go home and mend his errant ways. Portnoy, however is determined to sexually defile this priestess, but finds himself impotent to do so. Thus, yearning to discover a nice Israeli girl and live as a patriarch of old in the Promised Land, Portnoy meets an eligible candidate, but reacts to her as if she were a Jewish Jocasta. And so guilt-ridden, he goes back into the wilderness where as a little boy he continues his psychoanalytic games with Dr. *Spielvogel.*

In *The Breast*, the *novella* Roth published right after *Portnoy's Complaint*, he explores the consequences of one of the worst fears which Portnoy has: "What if breasts began to grow on me . . . ? What if my penis went dry and brittle and one day, while I was urinating, snapped off in my hand" (43)? For David Alan Kepesh, the hero of *The Breast*, such a fear turns out to be his secret desire and ultimate destiny. From the soliloquy that forms the *novella* we learn that Kepesh is the scarred veteran of a mutually destructive six-year marriage and more recently the enervated participant of an uninspired two-year love affair. The women with whom he "had worked out a way of living together—which in part involved living separately" (8) is a non-distinctive, predictable school teacher with the gynecological name of Claire Ovington. But what draws Kepesh to Claire are not her ovaries but her breasts. Not only does he want to become a suckling baby again, but filled with *udder* envy, he would like to have breasts of his own. With his own massive protuberances he need no longer feel like an inferior flat-chested male, but can identify himself with those superior hyper-mammaferous mothers. But Kepesh's fate is not to be a hermaphrodite. Through "a massive hormonal influx," "and endocrinopathic catastrophe" he is converted "into a mammary gland disconnected from any human form" (12). While such a metamorphosis is a cruel blow of fortune, being a breast is not as vile as being a cockroach. Indeed for the regressive Roth hero such a transformation has decided advantages. He does not have to be the aggressive male, straining to be successful in the competitive world. He can be a "big brainless bag of tissue, desirable, dumb, passive, immobile, acted upon instead of acting, hanging, *there*, as a breast hangs and is *there*" (61). He also does not have to worry about losing his sexual prowess and gratifying demanding women. In the past he had barely managed to respond to Claire's advances "two, maybe three times a month"; now he is, as one male critic noted, "an imposing, permanently inflated organ, a quasi-penis and he wants it serviced around the clock" (Frederick Crews, Review of *The Breast* by Philip Roth, *New York Review of Books*, November 16, 1972, p. 18). Perhaps most pleasurable of all, in his infant-like state he can have all his needs instantaneously satisfied with nurses as mother figures, feeding, cleaning, massaging and lavishing him with affection. Even Daddies have not deserted him for the office. His own father and his surrogate one, the psychoanalyst, Dr. Klinger, are constantly at the hospital, offering him support to accept his lot. And, except for an occasional "tempest in a D-cup" (Bruce Allen, Review of *The Breast* by Philip Roth, *Library Journal*, October 1, 1972, p. 3182), Kepesh learns to "keep a stiff upper nipple" (Crews, p. 19) and resigns himself to being a breast.

Thus it would seem that Roth's Jewish-American heroes are more immature than the first Hebrew, Abraham. He could respect his women and appreciate their contributions, while Neil Klugman and Alexander Portnoy can only denigrate women and engage in juvenile retaliations against them. Unlike Abraham from whose bosom the nation could derive strength, David Alan Kepesh can only be a bosom who lives off the strength of others. From patriarch to *puer* to bust, the Roth hero has appreciably diminished in stature.

The Great American Novel

Walter Blair and Hamlin Hill*

The comedy in *The Great American Novel* exists for the sake of no "higher" value than comedy itself; the "redeeming" value is not social or cultural reform, or moral instruction, but for *comic inventiveness.* Destructive, or lawless, playfulness—and for the fun of it. . . . It was . . . a matter . . . of discovering in baseball the means to dramatize *the struggle* between the benign national myth of itself that a great power prefers to perpetuate, and the relentlessly insidious, very nearly demonic reality. . . .

Now the discovery of thematic reverberations, of depth, of overtone, finally of meaning, . . . would seem to contradict what I have said about wanting fundamentally to be unserious; and it does.

—Philip Roth, 1973

Comic skirmishes between the genteel and the learned, on the one hand, and the unpolished and untutored, on the other, in this country have lasted for at least two and a half centuries. We have seen them turning up again and again. Teen-age Ben Franklin had his earliest alter ego, Silence Dogood, speak sharply against collegians and professors. Pedants collided with Dutch burghers, Yankees and settlement roughs in Irving's pages. Parson Wilbur's erudite epistles set off Hosea Biglow's Yankee lingo poems. Educated reporters wrote polished frameworks that were incongruous because they were cheek by jowl with Southwestern vernacular tall tales. Scientists, pontificating lecturers, and local colorists contrasted amusingly with Far Western humorists, Phunny Phellows, and rustics of various regions. Urban wits showed up quirks of clod hoppers and square ladies in Dubuque.

Beginning in 1939, thanks to an arresting article by Philip Rahv, a new statement about the old opposition received widespread discussion. Writing not about American humor but about American literature, Rahv in "Paleface and Redskin" noticed that a great many of our writers might usefully be classified as one or the other: "The paleface [such as T. S. Eliot and Henry James] continually hankers after religious norms, tending

*Reprinted from *America's Humor: From Poor Richard to Doonesbury*, by Walter Blair and Hamlin Hill, copyright © 1978 by Oxford University Press, Inc., by permission.

toward a refined estrangement from reality. . . . at his highest level the paleface moves in an exquisite moral atmosphere, at his lowest he is genteel, snobbish, and pedantic." As for redskins, such as Whitman, Twain, Anderson and Wolfe: "Their reactions are primarily emotional, spontaneous, and lacking personal culture. . . . In giving expression to the vitality and to the aspirations of the people, the redskin is at his best; but at his worst he is a vulgar anti-intellectual, combining aggression with conformity, reverting to the crudest forms of frontier psychology."

Philip Roth found it useful, some years later, to quote Rahv's classification when explaining the nature of some very funny books that he had written. Roth made a stir as a fiction writer and critic when he was twenty-three, and by the time he was twenty-six, in 1959, his articles and fictions about what he called "a cockeyed world" had won him recognition as one of the country's leading writers. In 1973, in "Reading Myself," a self-conducted interview which enabled him, conveniently, to both ask and answer questions, Roth, now forty, surveyed his career. He started, he believed, pretty much in the paleface camp. He wrote his stories and novels in the tradition of James, Tolstoy, Flaubert and Mann, "whose appeal was as much in their heroic literary integrity as in their works."

Roth was somewhat uneasy, though, about what he had written, because (as some delightful low humor that had intruded into his fiction showed) he had affinities with the redskins—"the aggressive, the crude, and the obscene." As a kid, he had loved the schlemieldom of a vaudeville and nightclub standup comic, Henny Youngman. Later he had gone for "Jake the Snake H., a middle-aged master of invective and insult, and repository of lascivious neighborhood gossip," and "Arnold G., an unconstrained Jewish living-room clown whose indecent stories of failure and confusion in sex did a little to demythologize the world of the sensual for me in early adolescence." He decided that "it was to the low-minded and their vulgarity that I owed no less allegiance than I did to the high-minded with whom I truly did associate my intentions." But though he owed them no *less* allegiance, he also owed them no *more*. He was "fundamentally ill at ease in, and odds with, both worlds." He found himself in the position of a "redface"—"sympathizing equally with both parties in their disdain for the other, and as it were recapitulating the argument within the body of his own work." In *Portnoy's Complaint* (1969), *Our Gang* (1971), and *The Great American Novel* (1972), though both parties were active, there was much more of the Roth who had alliances with redskins than there had been in his earlier works. (We omit consideration of two largely humorous books written after *The Great American Novel—The Breast* and *My Life as a Man.*)

Like his part-time idol, Henry James, Roth has always been more articulate than most fiction writers about his aims and methods. So he watched and described himself moving toward "the comic 'recklessness' that I've identified with my old mentor, Jake the Snake." *The Great*

American Novel in some ways was a climax. Jake's subversive influence, Roth guessed, "could not develop to its utmost, until the *subject* of restraints and taboos had been dramatized in *a series of increasingly pointed fictions* that revealed the possible consequence of banging your head against your own wall" [our italics].

The move from paleface territory to *Portnoy's Complaint* took several steps. "On the Air" told about "a series of grotesque adventures . . . as extreme in their comedy" as anything that would go into the novel; but it stopped when it was "only a story." A two-hundred-page manuscript used "jokey dialogue and comedy that had the air of vaudeville turns"—something Roth "liked and hated to lose"; but since he wasn't satisfied with it, he didn't publish it. A play with funny moments and laughable dialogue that he relished "lacked precisely the kind of inventive flair" that he wanted. More steps eventually carried the author to the actual start of the writing. He defined his final step as that of "discovering Portnoy's voice—or more accurately his mouth—and discovering along with it, the listening ear: the silent Dr. Spielvogel." In other words, what at last made composition possible was Roth's invention of a framework which, barring the final sentence, was implied but not dramatically represented. Except for that sentence, the book was a mock oral tale.

Reading this dramatic monologue, antiquarians who garner old jokes will recognize a slew of familiar friends. *Portnoy* is stuffed with Jewish-mother-and-son jokes, such as the tall talk of one momma about Her Son the Doctor: "he's so important . . . that in every single city in Europe that [he and his family] visited he was asked by the mayor himself to stop and do an impossible operation on a brain in hospitals that they had built for him right on the spot." Portnoy, for the most part, is a traditional schlemiel; but even when he isn't one, he comically pretends to be. Naomi's description of his "ghetto humor," as she calls it, summarizes not simply a Jewish but also an American comic dynasty: "Everything you say is somehow always twisted, some way, or another, to come out 'funny'. . . . In some little way or other, everything is ironical, or self-depreciating." Naomi, "the Heroine, that hardy, red-headed, freckled, ideological hunk of girl," gives Alex a chance to be an updated *alazon* when he tries to rape her. Having with great difficulty forced her body down beneath him, the bluffing braggart loftily tells her she must submit: "Down, down with those patriotic khaki shorts . . . unlock your fortressy thighs! Make ready, Naomi!" Then, since he is impotent—"But of course I couldn't." Though the 1969 version plays up not fighting strength but virility, the boast is about physical prowess, just as it had been a hundred and fifty years earlier.

As with *Portnoy*, both written and oral humor helped Roth write his ferocious *Our Gang*. This time, he converted his "indignation and disgust," as he put it, "from raw, useless emotion to comic art." This savaging pre-Watergate satire against Richard Nixon, his attitudes and his associates, credited literary antecedents in two epigraphs, one from Jonathan Swift's masterpiece, *Gulliver's Travels*, and the other from George Orwell's "Politics and the English Language." In interviews, Roth spoke of James Russell Lowell's *Biglow Papers* and the Nasby letters as native forerunners. He also mentioned as models for his "broadly comic" book the antics of Charlie Chaplin, Laurel and Hardy, Olson and Johnson, Abbott and Costello, and the Three Stooges. Finally, a book containing speeches and monologues by "Trick E. Dixon," using as it does many of its model's favorite locutions, almost had to be shaped by impressionists, notably the vicious David Frye, who had been using them lavishly in television shows and night club acts.

A number of readers found this book hilarious, and as *The White House Transcripts* show, it was prophetic. But its ferocity, like that of Northern and Southern Civil War satirists, made it amusing only to those who shared the author's hatreds; and five years after it came out, its topicality makes reading it tough going. It was useful, though, as a cathartic, and its surrealistic fantasies—particularly those of its last two chapters—exercised inventive powers that would be used to the utmost in *The Great American Novel*.

Literary and oral influences, this highly self-conscious artist makes clear, affected this novel. Roth mentions three "gifted writers" who had "gotten quite a yield" from baseball as material for fiction—Ring Lardner, Mark Harris, and Bernard Malamud. He may not have encountered—or he possibly forgot—a fantastic short story that Thurber first published in 1942, "You Could Look It Up," worth mentioning because, like Roth, Thurber had a midget play on a struggling baseball team. Possibly he didn't see the hit musical *Damn Yankees* (1955), or the novel it dramatized, which melded the Faust legend with a pennant race. He shows no awareness of Robert Coover's *The Universal Baseball Association, Inc.* (1969), about a lunatic farther gone than Roth's, who dreamed up a wonderful baseball team and details concerning its fantastic games. Again, he could have missed Claude Brion Davis's prior use—almost—of Roth's title when he wrote "*The Great American Novel*" (in quotes), in which, like Roth, Davis had a journalist try to create the elusive masterpiece. (Even if Roth knew none of these, it is worth noticing that other writers used quite similar gambits.) But Roth did mention in his "Acknowledgements" *The Fireside Book of Baseball* and *Percentage Baseball* as books from which he borrowed incidents. And since burlesques and parodies dot the pages, one can easily spot writings running back to the Middle Ages and down to the present as acknowledged and unacknowledged forebears.

In his "Acknowledgements," Roth also credits an oral "source": "The tape-recorded recollections of professional baseball players that are deposited at the Library of the Hall of Fame in Cooperstown . . . have been a source of inspiration to me while writing this book, and some of the most appealing locutions of these old-time players have been absorbed into the dialogue." Although Portnoy poor-mouths them, he proves by commenting on them that his creator was familiar with standup comedians Sam Levenson, Myron Cohen, Henny Youngman, and Milton Berle. George Plimpton in a 1969 interview asked Roth whether he might have echoed Lenny Bruce's comic routines. The novelist said that he thought well of Bruce as a mimic and social commentator, but guessed that a literary work—Kafka's *Metamorphosis*—had influenced *Portnoy* more. Bruce's biographer, Albert Goldman, however, described Roth's performances in private gatherings that were quite Bruce-like:

> Philip Roth . . . was a fantastically funny man years before *Portnoy's Complaint* was published. He broke up his friends at parties, flew off in conversation into marvelous fantasies, did all sorts of voices and dialects, rehearsed old radio shows, exhibited exactly the same sense of timing, meter and delivery as any professional comedian.

This sounds like Alex Portnoy on the couch or the author quoted at length in *The Great American Novel*, Word Smith.

A forty-five page "Prologue"—proportionately one of the lengthiest "frames" for a boxed narrative in the history of our humor—introduces Smitty, an eighty-seven-year-old ex-sports-writer. His three-hundred-and-thirty-five page novel and six-page "Epilogue" follow.

Smith describes himself in the "Prologue": "Short-winded, short-tempered, short-sighted as he may be, soft bellied, weak-bladdered, . . . anemic, arthritic, diabetic, dyspeptic, sclerotic, in dire need of a laxative, . . . *and in perpetual pain.*" As this brief sample of his prose suggests, Word Smith is fond of alliterations—as fond, in fact, as Rabelais, who on occasion alliterated pages at a time. The old fellow's psychiatrist calls Smith's use of the device "an orgy [that] strikes me as wildly excessive and just a little desperate." This verbal tic and a great many others are signs that this inmate of the Valhalla Home for the Aged is as loopy as a scenic railway. He is a mess of aberrations—a sick, talky, vicious, dirty-minded, sadistic, racist, chauvinistic pig with a persecution complex and an aggravated case of paranoia.

It may be instructive to look at a short parade of American comic narrators: (1) the pedantic but witty Diedrich Knickerbocker (1809); (2) the imaginative, self-deceiving Jim Doggett (1841); (3) the drunken Copperhead and political freewheeler Nasby (1861); (4) gently teched but sweet and harmless Jim Baker (1880); (5) bumbling, phobia-ridden "Benchley" of *The New Yorker* (1925); (6) crafty and ornery Jason Compton of *The Sound and the Fury* (1929); (7) Smitty. This sketchy little survey is too incomplete to allow more than a very broad—but we think informative—generalization: The tendency is not to make our humorous storytellers more and more lovable; it is to make them more and more complex.

The obsession that forces Smitty to write his novel is the belief that he has a mission: to give the world a history that evil forces have suppressed—that of a forgotten major baseball organization, the Patriotic League, and more particularly, its fabulous team, the Rupert Mundys of Port Ruppert, New Jersey. The Dies Committee's vile persecutions and fiendish machinations, he is sure, brought about not only the dissolution of the league and the imprisonment of ten of its players but also the purge of every single trace of its glorious history. To make sure of this, no effort has been spared: even the names of the league's cities were changed. Who, except Smitty, ever heard of Asylum, Ohio; Terra Incognita, Wyoming; Kakoola, Wisconsin; and Port Ruppert, New Jersey? See?

To restore the suppressed truth, moving at the pace that suits him, pausing to elaborate whenever he pleases, detouring any time he likes, Smitty gives us his fantastic chronicle.

It seems that there was this third big league, dominated for years by the Mundys. Came World War II. The Port Ruppert stadium was taken over by the government to help with the war. So the homeless Mundy team had to go on an unending road trip. The team wasn't in the best shape for such a heroic odyssey. Decimated by the war and no longer prosperous, this permanent visiting team was a ramshackle crowd that got ramshackler. It included fifty-year-old veterans reactivated after retirement, a refugee from a Japanese league, a one-armed outfielder, a peg-legged catcher, a teen-age genius, an alcoholic ex-con man, a midget pitcher, and so on. Smitty told the wonderful but tragic tale of its past and its final struggles. That was his "great American novel."

It would be pleasant to report that Smitty's opus is to be published, that truth as he tells it is to prevail, and that the author's genius is to be recognized. His pitiful "Epilogue" shows all too clearly that, thanks to the conspiracy of a new persecuting group, the masterpiece will never see print. Twenty-seven publishers have fobbed him off with weak excuses. One letter turned it down because its "treatment of blacks, Jews, and women, not to mention the physically and mentally handicapped, is offensive in the extreme; in a word, sick." Another tells the author:

> I am returning your manuscript. Several people here found portions of it entertaining, but by and large the book seemed to most of us to strain for its effects and to simplify for the sake of facile satiric comment the complexities of American political and cultural life.

As the alliterative sad saga stops, Smitty is sending off a screed to the chairman of the People's Republic of China in a desperate (and surely futile) attempt to get his history published in Peking.

Our knowledge of Roth, like that of Faulkner, has been enriched by a recent study. This is Bernard F. Rodgers's University of Chicago doctoral dissertation, "Stalking Reality: The Fiction of Philip Roth" (1974), for the most part unpublished. One article based upon it, "*The Great American Novel* and 'The Great American Joke,'" published in *Critique*, 16 (December 1974), 12–29, includes and supplements what follows. Rodgers makes a good case for his claim that when Roth decided to join the redfaces and wrote this book, he "employed comic techniques which echo the raucous and ribald quality of nineteenth-century native American humor and twentieth-century popular comedy."

It is impossible for us (or Rodgers) to know how consciously he did this. Writers, since each is unique, create in many ways. Our guess is that even so self-conscious an artist as Roth, though he knows American humor well, when he became playful and outrageous gave little or no thought to "models" or "influences" or "echoes." But we do not know. We can only say, with Rodgers, that in a very individual way he wrote in the styles of old and new schools, and adapted them to serve his purposes.

One kinship is with antebellum Southwestern humor. Its creators had as a chief outlet a magazine for men dealing with sports, the stage and literature. Two installments of Roth's novel came out in *Sports Illustrated* and *Esquire*. Like Roth's, the older humor of *The Spirit of the Times* is masculine, exuberant, vulgar, and full of sheer animal spirits. Both the older comedy and Roth's are characterized by irreverence, profanity, physical discomfort, scatology, and even obscenity. Both here and in the older humor, boasts and tall tales abound. One of many instances: Gil Gamish, legendary pitcher for the Mundys, takes his place alongside Mike, Davy, Mose, and Corpse Maker. "I'M GIL GAMESH!" he would yell, in capital letters. "I'M AN IMMORTAL, WHETHER YOU LIKE IT OR NOT!" Let a strong batter step to the plate, and Gil would become obnoxious:

> "You couldn't lick a stamp. You couldn't beat a drum."
> . . . Then, sneering away, he would lean way back, kick that right leg up sky-high like a chorus girl, and that long left arm would start coming around by way of Biloxi—and next thing you knew it was strike one. He would burn them in just as beautiful and nonchalant as that, three in a row, and then exactly like a barber, call out, "Next!" He did not waste a pitch, unless it was to throw a ball at a batter's head, and he did not consider that a waste.

The legendary Davy Crockett, storytellers claimed, topped his earlier fantastic feats after the world thought he had died at the Alamo. Gil, too, after his death was reported was immortalized in stories that placed him everywhere—riding the rails in Indiana, tending bar in Florida, singing grand opera (for God's sake) in cities with big auditoriums. Roth has him actually turn up toward the end of the book, now a double agent from Russia, as mean and ornery as ever.

Roth, guiding Smitty's pen, proves that he has perfected an art which American storytellers tenderly nourished from the start—that of developing scenes with multitudinous, apt details that almost convince because they seem inevitable. A wide detour—one of many that Smitty takes—brings a leisurely history of the Mosquito Coast League of Nicaragua. Its teams, we learn, are far worse off than the Mundys. They are made up of "native boys," sailors who have jumped ship, unemployed spitballers and "assorted nuts and desperadoes"—fugitives from decent society. The picture of their sordid lifestyle has the ring of absolute truth:

> Carried from village to village on mules, sleeping in filth with the hogs and the chickens, or in hovels with toothless Indians, these men quickly lost whatever dignity they may once have had as ballplayers and human beings; and then, to further compromise themselves and the great game of baseball, they took to drinking a wretched sort of raisin wine between innings, which altered the pace of the game immeasurably. But the water tasted of rats and algae, and center field in the dry season in Guatemala is as hot as center field must be in Hell—catch nine innings in Nicaragua in the summer, and you'll drink anything that isn't an out-and-out poison. Which is just what the water was. They used it only to bathe their burning feet. Indian women hung around the foul lines, and for a penny in the local currency could be hired for an afternoon to wash a player's toes and pour a bucketful of the fetid stuff over his head when he stepped up to bat. Eventually these waterwomen came to share the benches of the players, who fondled and squeezed them practically at will. . . .

Anyone who suspects Smitty is a loon who has dreamed up his "history" surely must waver when he reads this vivid and authoritative passage.

The overall construction of *The Great American Novel* is picaresque—loosely linked episodes, brief tall tales, anecdotes, vignettes, sketches such as Southwestern writers of humor ordinarily (though not exclusively) wrote. As the older group did, Roth—or Smitty—likes a climactic ordering for a tall tale: one of his best uses of it is in his history of Gil's more and more incredible pitching feats. And much of the language reminds a reader who knows Southwestern humor of its phrasings. (This may well be, of course, because of the common influence of oral speech. Transcripts of the tapes that Roth credits, when compared with the book, show that the author joyously glaumed onto many of the salty phrasings of reminiscing ballplayers.)

Smitty, himself an ex-newspaper columnist, is also a great one to write in the fashion of the Phunny Phellows and the Algonquinites. Verbal acrobatics—puns, malapropisms, alliterations, incongruous catalogues, afflicted logic, contorted sentences—dot the pages. In just one of many innumerable plays on words, Smitty says he would "rather be a writer than President." A host of names in addition to that of Word Smith are puns—Base Baal, Spit Baal, Angela Trust and others. Smitty's belief in the world-shaking importance of his scrimy team inevitably brings anticlimactic sequences. Listing scenes of great achievements, he swoops from the Runnymede of the Magna Carta and the Philadelphia of the Declaration of Independence to the Mundy Park of his heroes' triumphs, and on the same page he talks of "notables ranging from Secretary of War Stimson and Governor Edison to the Mayor of Port Ruppert, Boss Stuvwxyz."

Like the writings of the literary comedians and the *New Yorker* crowd, too, this book is stuffed with burlesques and parodies. Victims cover a prodigious range—the Bible, ancient epics, Chaucer, Henry Fielding, classic American fictionists such as Poe, Hawthorne and Twain, Joseph Conrad's "Heart of Darkness," Henry James, and Roth's contemporaries (Bellow, Malamud, stuffy book reviewers, Richard Nixon, and Edward Kennedy). The very first sentence in the "Prologue," "Call me Smitty," shows that Herman Melville will be among the victims; and a high point is a parody of Ernest Hemingway doing a parody of *Moby-Dick*.

So what was new in *The Great American Novel?*

Obviously, there were no spanking new ingredients. Now that Americans have been creating humor for more than two hundred years, precedents can easily be found for all the comic elements in today's writings. But even so, there have been qualitative and quantitative changes.

Southwestern humor in the antebellum period, to be sure, was irreverent, scatological, and obscene; but one must add, *for the times.* The times have changed, especially since World War II, and these elements are now used in a far less restrained fashion. Even readers who aren't shocked by the earlier vulgarity and frankness may well be distressed by much of the humor of the 1972 novel. Rodgers's summary suggests some deviations:

> Midgets, dwarfs, dimwits, cripples, one-armed and one-legged characters swarm through the pages of *The Great American Novel* and typically tasteless—and hilarious—fun is made of their physical maladies. At the same time, prostitution, vaginal odors, sexual perversity, urination, flatulence, and various forms of physical pain and punishment are freely and comically treated in ways designed to offend the squeamish.

Something like what happened to Norman Mailer perhaps happened to Roth:

> Mailer [said Mailer, writing about himself in the third person] never felt more like an American than when he was naturally obscene—all the gifts of the American language came out in the happy play of obscenity. . . . So after years of keeping obscene language off to one corner of his work . . . he had kicked goodbye . . . to the old literary corset of good taste, let-

> ting the sense of language play on obscenity as freely as it
> wished . . . with the happiest beating of wings—it was the
> first time his style seemed at once very American to him and
> very literary in the best way . . .

Both Roth/Smitty's frank language, and the dialogue of his unrestrained jocks, quite possibly seem not only more "American" but also more lifelike to readers in the present uncensored era.

Inventive old-time yarnspinners, like all the best liars, made their most outrageous extravaganzas seem believable by peppering them with concrete details. So did Roth, but in step with today's "tell-all" fictionists, he piled up more naturalistic details. The passage about the Mosquito League quoted above illustrates this tendency; so do numerous others.

Some touches give an aspect of reality to Smitty's wild story in a way that is fashionable and that some critics have called novel. Walter Kerr in 1976 wrote:

> With increasing freedom, and a malicious playfulness, writers
> of fiction—writers who are supposed to imagine their
> characters—have been reaching out into real life, picking up
> people who actually lived, shaking them free of their strictly
> factual accoutrements, and scrambling them together with the
> unreal, imagined figures they *have* invented. They're cross-
> breeding fact and any degree of fantasy they care to apply,
> meshing history and improvisation with a deadpan imper-
> tinence.

He cites as an early example the drama *Travesties* by Tom Stoppard, which has Lenin, James Joyce, and Tristan Tzara meet up with an imagined character. He also notices that following the staging of the Briton's play, the American Nicholas Meyer wrote *The Seven Percent Solution* and *The West End Horrors*, in which the fictitious Sherlock Holmes and Dr. Watson have meetings and adventures with the historical Sigmund Freud, Bernard Shaw, and Sir Arthur Sullivan. And he discusses the bestselling E. L. Doctorow's *Ragtime*, which intermingles Harry Houdini, Evelyn Nesbit, and Stanford White with completely imagined characters. His suggestion is that when the real is shoved up against the imagined, it is shown to be "just as subject to manipulation and hence not really any truer." Fictitious writing, Kerr guesses, is "trotting out its own created legends to show that they have just as much continuing life in them as the vague folk in the history books."

The comment evokes this response: the gambit isn't all that new. Historical-play writers and historical novelists always did something similar. The historical Prince Hal romped with the fictitious Falstaff; the Four Musketeers mingled with Richelieu. Louis XIII, and the Queen of France; the fictitious Pauper changed places with the historic Prince. Even fictitious characters who mingled with more recent historical figures weren't novel. Upton Sinclair's Lanny Budd novels (1940–1949) had their hero meet historical characters active and famous between 1913 and 1945 all over the world. Even our old-time comic figures met real contemporaries: Jack Downing was the pal of several Presidents; Artemus Ward met Abe Lincoln and gave him some good advice.

Smitty starts nothing entirely new, therefore, when he says that he has been a crony and speech polisher for four Presidents and ties his unbelievable "history" to actual history. In his account, Black Jack Pershing and William Howard Taft help General Oakhurst become president of the Patriotic League; Bob Hope cracks jokes before GI's in army bases through the world about the wandering Mundys, and so on. The device isn't new. But the way it is used, and the gilt that it acquires by association, enable it to deliver a modern-day message.

Roth, helpful as usual, has talked about his use—or Smitty's—of factual matter in his all-but-incredible yarn. "The paranoid fantasist Word Smith," Roth says, was created because his amanuensis wanted him to describe "what America is really like to one like *him*." He wanted a narrator "like him," he specified, because Smitty's distorted vision is representative: "His is not so unlike the sort of fantasies with which the national imagination began to be plagued during the last demythologizing decade of disorder, upheaval, assassination and war." What does he mean by "demythologizing?" It is the process by which "venerable institutions and beliefs" in war aims, foreign policies, Camelot and men in high offices—in "what was assumed to be beyond reproach—became the target for blasphemous assault." Baseball, itself a "venerable institution," could, he decided, furnish "a counterhistory, or *countermythology*":

> It was not a matter of demythologizing baseball—there was nothing in that to get fired up about—but of discovering in baseball the means to dramatize *the struggle* between the benign national myth of itself that a great power prefers to perpetuate, and the relentlessly insidious, very nearly demonic reality (like the kind we had known in the sixties) that simply will not give an inch in behalf of that idealized mythology.

In the last pages of his narrative, Smitty has the Dies Committee haul up and try the Mundys for Communist activities, find them guilty, and destroy them. Roth "anchored the book" in these investigations, he explains, "to establish a kind of passageway from the imaginary that seems real to the real that seems imaginary, a continuum between the credible incredible and the incredible credible." The intermingling of the wildly imagined and the factual so characteristic of the old tall tales here achieves "thematic reverberations, . . . depth, . . . overtone, finally . . . meaning."

"Ultimately, all jokes, parables, lies, and in fact all fictions and fables of whatever sort," says G. Legman, "are simply the decorative showcases of their tellers' anxieties, their repressions, and generally of their neuroses . . . being juggled with onstage to beg the audience's applause." Smitty's history is a showcase for a cartoon of America. That editor who turned it down because of its "satiric comment [on] the complexities of American political and cultural life" knew what he was talking about.

With this in mind, a reader can notice how Roth made its ingredients contribute to the book's "reverberations." Smitty is nostalgic—as nostalgic as the postbellum local colorists were; but bygone scenes that he recalls are anything but idyllic. What he believes was baseball's golden age is funny, to be sure; but it is also brutal, ugly, and obscene. Its heroes are dwarfs, cripples, perverts, and freaks. These are Smitty's comic demigods. Their astonishing feats, like those of a mental asylum team in one episode, are "as low as low can be." They enact for our laughter what Saul Bellow in *Herzog* calls "the degraded clowning of this life through which we are speeding."

Laughable gyrations of language also help "demythologize." Players' names recall gods—Astarte, Baal, Demeter, Roland Agni (cf. Agonistes) and lesser deities; but given names—Frenchy, John, Deacon, and the like—ground them and encourage readers to make uncomplimentary contrasts. The profanity, obscenity, and scatology pollute the atmosphere of Smitty's never-never land.

Parodies of great fictional works help the impeachment. Roth ended his self-interview by saying why Smitty, loopy though he was, was on target when he put himself in a class with Hawthorne and Melville. These two also tried to write "the great American novel," and "Smitty's book, like those of his illustrious forebears, attempts to imagine a myth of an ailing America; my own is to some extent an attempt to imagine a book about imagining that American myth."

Philip Roth Reconsidered

Irving Howe*

> . . . the will takes pleasures in begetting its own image.
> —J. V. Cunningham

When Philip Roth published his collection of stories, *Goodbye, Columbus*, in 1959, the book was generously praised and I was among the reviewers who praised it. Whatever modulations of judgment one might want now to propose, it is not hard to see why Roth should have won approval. The work of a newcomer still in his twenties, *Goodbye, Columbus* bristled with a literary self-confidence such as few writers two or three decades older than Roth could command. His stories were immediately recognizable as his own, distinctive in voice, attitude, and subject; they possessed the lucidities of definition, though I would now add, lucidities harsh and grimacing in their over-focus. None of the fiction Roth has since published approaches this first collection in literary interest; yet, by no very surprising turn of events, his reputation has steadily grown these past few years, he now stands close to the center of our culture (if that is anything for him to be pleased about), and he is accorded serious attention both by a number of literary critics and those rabbis and Jewish communal leaders who can hardly wait to repay the animus he has lavished upon them. At least for a moment or two, until the next fashion appears, we are in the presence not only of an interesting writer but also a cultural "case."

I

The stories in *Goodbye, Columbus* are of a special kind. They are neither probings through strategic incident to reach the inner folds of character nor affectionate renderings of regional, class, or ethnic behavior. They are not the work of a writer absorbed in human experience as it is, mirroring his time with self-effacing objectivity. Nor is Roth the kind of writer who takes pleasure in discovering the world's body, yielding himself to the richness of its surfaces and the mysteries of its ultimate course. If one recalls some of the motives that have moved our novelists—a hunger to absorb and render varieties of social experience, a respect for the plenitude of the mind, a sense of awe induced by contemplation of the curve of heroic fate, a passion for moral scrutiny—none of these seems crucially to operate in Roth's work. It is, in fact, a little comic to invoke such high motifs in discussing that work, and not because Roth is a minor writer but because he is a writer who has denied himself, programmatically, the vision of major possibilities.

What one senses nevertheless in the stories of *Goodbye, Columbus* is an enormous thrust of personal and ideological assertiveness. In the clash which, like Jacob with his angel, the writer must undertake with the world around him—and, unlike Jacob, must learn when and how to lose—there can be little doubt that Roth will steadily pin his opponent to the ground. His great need is for a stance of superiority, the pleasure, as Madison Avenue puts it, of always being "on top of it." (Perhaps he should have been a literary critic.) Only rarely do his fictions risk the uncharted regions of imaginative discovery; almost all his work drives a narrative toward cognitive ends fixed in advance. Roth appears indifferent to the Keatsian persuasion that a writer should be "capable of being in uncertainties, mysteries, doubts," since that would require a discipline of patience; nor does he pay much heed to the Coleridgean persuasion that "tragedy depends on a sense of the mind's greatness," since that would mean to acknowledge the powers of *another* mind, to soften his clattering voice, and to ease himself into that receptivity to experience which is one mark of the creative imagination.

For good or bad, both in the stories that succeed and those that fail, *Goodbye, Columbus* rests in the grip of an imperious will prepared to wrench, twist, and claw at its materials in order to leave upon them the scar of its presence—as if the work of fiction were a package that needed constantly to be stamped with a signature of self. With expectations of being misunderstood I am tempted to add that, despite their severe and even notorious criticisms of Jewish life in America, Roth's stories are marked by a quintessentially "Jewish will," the kind that first makes its historical appearance in the autobiography of Solomon Maimon, where the intellectual aspirant sees himself as a solitary antagonist to the world of culture which, in consequence, he must conquer and reduce to acknowledgment.

The will dominating *Goodbye, Columbus* clamors to impose itself—in part through an exclusion of inconvenient perceptions—upon whatever portions of imagined life are being presented. And that is one reason these stories become a little tiresome upon rereading: one grows weary of a writer who keeps nagging and prodding and beating us over the head with the poker of his intentions. What is almost always central in Roth's stories is their "point," their hammering of idea, and once that "point" is clear, usually well before a story's end, the portrayal starts to pale, for not enough autonomous life remains and too much of the matter seems a mere reflex of the will's "begetting."

Even in regard to details of milieu and manners, for which Roth has been frequently praised, the will takes over and distorts. In his title novella, "Goodbye, Columbus," there are some keen notations—the refrigerator in the basement bulging with fruit, the turgidities of the wedding—which help to characterize the newly-rich Patimkins in their suburban home. And there are moments of tenderness—a quality not abundant in Roth's work—during the romance between Neil Klugman, the poor Newark boy, and Brenda Patimkin, the self-assured Radcliffe girl (though nothing she says or does could persuade one that she would ever have been admitted to Radcliffe). Yet if the novella is read with any care at all, it becomes clear that Roth is not precise and certainly not scrupulous enough in his use of social evidence. The Patimkins are easily placed—what could be easier for a Jewish writer than to elicit disdain for middle-class Jews?—but the elements of what is new in their experience are grossly manipulated. Their history is invoked for the passing of adverse judgment, at least part of which seems to me warranted, but their history is not allowed to emerge so as to make them understandable as human beings. Their vulgarity is put on blazing display but little or nothing that might locate or complicate that vulgarity is shown: little of the weight of their past, whether sustaining or sentimental; nothing of the Jewish mania for culture, whether honorable or foolish; nothing of that fearful self-consciousness which the events of the mid-20th century thrust upon the Patimkins of this world. Ripped out of the historical context that might help to define them, the Patimkins are vivid enough, but as lampoon or caricature in a novella that clearly aims for more than lampoon or caricature. (There is, for example, a placing reference to Mrs. Patimkin's membership in Hadassah, employed as a cue for easy laughs in the way watermelons once were for Southern blacks—it is an instance of how a thrust against vulgarity can itself become vulgar, and by no means the only one in Roth's work.)

On the other side of the social spectrum Roth places Aunt Gladys, still poor, fretting absurdly over her nephew's health and, quite as if she were a stand-in for the Mrs. Portnoy yet to come, rattling off one-liners about the fruit in her icebox. Aunt Gladys, we learn, is preparing for a Workmen's Circle picnic; and for a reader with even a little knowledge of Jewish immigrant life, that raises certain expectations, since the Workmen's Circle signifies a socialist and Yiddishist commitment which time, no doubt, has dimmed but which still has left some impact of sensibility on people like Aunt Gladys. But while named, as if to signal familiarity with her background, this aspect of Aunt Gladys's experience is never allowed to color Roth's portrait, never allowed to affect either the ridicule to which she is subjected nor the simplistic fable—so self-serving in its essential softness—of a poor but honorable Jewish boy withstanding suburban-Jewish vulgarity and thereupon left without any moral option in his world.

The price Roth pays for immobilizing the Patimkins into lampoon and Aunt Gladys into vaudeville is that none of the social or moral forces supposedly acting upon Neil Klugman can be dramatically marshaled. And Neil Klugman himself—poor cipher that he is, neither very *klug* nor very *man*—can never engage himself in the risks and temptations that are supposed to constitute his dilemma, if only because Roth is out there running interference, straight-arming all the other characters in behalf of this vapid alter ego. Even so extreme an admirer of Roth's work as Theodore Solotaroff acknowledges the "abstractness that Neil takes on. He . . . is too far along the path he is supposed to be traveling in the story. One could wish that he were more his aunt's nephew, more troubled and attracted by the life of the Patimkins, and more willing to test it and himself."

Now the issue is not, I had better emphasize, whether newly-rich suburban Jews are vulgar—a certain number, perhaps many, surely are—nor whether they are proper targets of satire—everyone is. What I am saying is that in its prefabricated counterpositions "Goodbye, Columbus draws not upon a fresh encounter with the post-war experience of suburban Jews but upon literary hand-me-downs of American-Jewish fiction, popularizing styles of rebellion from an earlier moment and thereby draining them of their rebellious content.

I doubt, in any case, that Roth is really interested in a close and scrupulous observance of social life. He came to the literary scene at a moment when the dominant kind of critical talk was to dismiss "mere realism," as if that were a commodity so easily come by, and to praise "the imagination," as if that were a faculty which could operate apart from a bruising involvement with social existence. And this critical ideology served to reinforce Roth's own temperament as a writer, which is inclined to be impatient, snappish, and dismissive, all qualities hardly disposing him to strive for an objective (objective: to see the object as it is) perception of contemporary life.

Defending himself several years ago against the rather feckless attacks of outraged rabbis, some of whom complained that he did not provide a "balanced portrayal" of Jewish life, Roth wrote that "to confuse a 'balanced portrayal' with a novel is . . . to be led into absurdities."[1] Absurdities, he continued, like supposing a group of 19th-century Russian students sending off a complaint to Dostoevsky that Raskolnikov is not a "typical student." Well, that's amusing, though I think it would be quite possible to show that, in some sense, Dostoevsky *does* present a "balanced portrayal" of Russian life. In any case, Roth in his defense, as in his fiction, makes things a little too easy for himself. For the critical issue is not whether he has given a "balanced portrayal" of the Jews as a whole or even the suburban Jews, but whether his portrayal of the Patimkins as the kind of people they are is characterized by fullness and precision. After all, no fictional portrait is merely idiosyncratic, every novel or story aspires to some element of representativeness or at least reverberation—and indeed, at a crucial point in "Goodbye, Columbus," when Neil Klugman is reflecting upon what his fate would be if he were to marry Brenda, he at least takes the Patimkins to be representative of a way of life. It will not do to say that the Patimkins are "unique," for if they were they could have no interest other than as an oddity. What is at stake here is Roth's faithfulness to *his own materials*, the justice and largesse of his imaginative treatment.

There remains another line of defense against such criticism, which Roth's admirers frequently man: that he writes satire and therefore cannot be expected to hew closely to realistic detail. This is a defense that quite fails to apprehend what the nature of good satire is. To compose a satire is not at all to free oneself from the obligation to social accuracy; it is only to order that accuracy in a particular way. If it can be shown that the targets of the satirist are imprecisely located or that he is shooting wild, the consequences may be more damaging than if the same were shown for a conventional realist. And if it can be shown that the satire is self-serving—poor Neil, poor Alex . . .—then it becomes—well, imagine how absurd *Gulliver's Travels* would seem if we became persuaded that the satiric barrage against mankind allows for one little exception, a young hero troubled by the burdens of being English and resembling Jonathan Swift.

Roth's stories begin, characteristically, with a spectacular array of details in the representation of milieu, speech, and manners and thereby we are led to expect a kind of fiction strong in verisimilitude. But then, at crucial points in the stories, there follow a series of substitutions, elements of incident or speech inserted not because they follow from the logic of the narrative but because they underscore the point Roth wishes to extract from the narrative. In "The Conversion of the Jews" a bright if obnoxious Jewish boy becomes so enraged with the sniffling pieties of his Hebrew-school teacher, Rabbi Bender, that he races out of the classroom and up to the roof, threatening to jump unless the rabbi admits that "God can do anything" and "can make a child without intercourse." The plot may seem a bit fanciful and the story, as Mr. Solotaroff justly remarks, "inflated to get in the message"—but no matter, at least our attention is being held. Then, however, comes the breaking point, when the writer's will crushes his fiction: Ozzie "made them all say they believed in Jesus Christ—first one at a time, then all together." Given the sort of tough-grained Jewish urchin Ozzie is shown to be, this declamation strains our credence; it is Roth who has taken over, shouldering aside his characters and performing on his own, just as it is Roth who ends the story with the maudlin touch of Ozzie crying out, "Mamma. You should never hit anybody about God. . . ." Scratch an Ozzie, and you find a Rabbi Bender.

A richer and more ambitious story, "Eli the Fanatic" suffers from the same kind of flaws. An exotic yeshivah sponsored by a Hasidic sect settles in Woodenton, a comfortable suburb. The local Jews feel hostile, tension follows, and Eli Peck, a vulnerable Woodenton Jew, undergoes a kind of moral conversion in which he identifies or hallucinates himself as a victim in kaftan. It is difficult, if one bears in mind Roth's entire work, to take at face value this solemn espousal of yeshivah Orthodoxy as the positive force in the story; I cannot believe that the yeshivah and all it represents has been brought into play for any reason other than as a stick with which to beat Woodenton. Tzuref, the yeshivah principal, is well-drawn and allowed to speak for his outlook, as Aunt Gladys in "Goodbye, Columbus" is not: which is one reason this story builds up a certain dramatic tension. But again Roth feels obliged to drop a heavy thumb on the scales by making his suburbanities so benighted, indeed, so merely stupid, that the story finally comes apart. Here is a Woodenton Jew speaking:

> Look, I don't even know about this Sunday school business. Sundays I drive my oldest kid all the way to Scarsdale to learn Bible stories . . . and you know what she comes up with? This Abraham in the Bible was going to kill his own *kid* for a sacrifice. She gets nightmares from it, for God's sake. You call that religion? Today a guy like that they'd lock him up.

Now, even a philistine character has certain rights, if not as a philistine then as a character in whose "reality" we are being asked to believe. To write as if this middle-class Jewish suburbanite were unfamiliar with "this Abraham" or shocked by the story of the near-sacrifice of Isaac, is simply preposterous. Roth is putting into the character's mouth, not what he could plausibly say, but what Roth thinks his "real" sentiments are. He is not revealing the character, but "exposing" him. It is a crucial failure in literary tact, one of several in the story that rouse the suspicion Roth is not behaving with good faith toward the objects of his assault.

This kind of tendentiousness mars a number of Roth's fictions, especially those in which a first-person narrator—Neil Klugman, Alex Portnoy—swarms all over the turf of his imaginary world, blotting out the possibility of multiple perspective. It is a weakness of fictions told in the first person that the limits of the narrator's perception tend to become the limits of the work itself. Through an "unreliable" first-person narrator it is, of course, possible to plant bits of crucial evidence that call his version of things into question, but that requires a good deal of technical sophistication and still more, a portion of self-doubt such as our culture has not greatly encouraged these past two decades. There usually follows in such first-person narratives a spilling-out of the narrator which it becomes hard to suppose is not also the spilling-out of the author. Such literary narcissim is especially notable among minor satirists, with whom it frequently takes the form of self-exemptive attacks on the shamefulness of humanity. In some of Mary McCarthy's novels, for example, all the characters are shown as deceitful and venomous, all but a heroine pure in heart and close to the heart of the author. Neither Klugman nor Portnoy is exactly pure in heart, but as a man at ease with our moment, Portnoy has learned that "sincerity" can pay substantial dividends by soliciting admiration for the candor with which it proclaims impurities. And as for those of Roth's stories that avoid the looseness of the first-person narrative, his own authorial voice quickly takes over, becoming all but indistinguishable from a first-person narrator, raucous, self-aggrandizing, and damned sure that the denouement of his story will not escape the grip of his will.

To these strictures I would offer one exception, the Roth story that, oddly, was most attacked by his rabbinical critics: "Defender of the Faith." This seems to me a distinguished performance, the example of what Roth might have made of his talent had he been stricter in his demands upon himself. Roth's description of the story is acute: "It is about one man who uses his own religion, and another's uncertain conscience, for selfish ends; but mostly it is about this other man, the narrator, who because of the ambiguities of being a member of a particular religion, is involved in a taxing, if mistaken, conflict of loyalties." This conflict is at once urgent for those caught up in it and serious in its larger moral implications. Nathan Marx, back from combat duty in Germany, is made First Sergeant of a training company in Missouri; he is a decent, thoughtful fellow whose sense of being Jewish, important though it is to him, he cannot articulate clearly. A few recruits in his company, led by Sheldon Grossbart, attach themselves to Marx, presumably out of common feeling toward the problem of being Jews in an alien setting, but actually because Grossbart means to exploit this sense of solidarity in behalf of private ends—he looks forward to the crucial favor of not being sent overseas to combat. As Roth comments, Grossbart is "a man whose lapses of integrity seem to him so necessary to his survival as to convince him that such lapses are actually committed in the name of integrity." At the end of the story, Sergeant Marx, incensed at the manipulation to which he had been subjected, makes certain that Grossbart is indeed shipped overseas, while he, Marx, braces himself to face the consequences of an act he admits to be "vindictive."

The power of this story derives from presenting a moral entanglement so as to draw out, yet not easily resolve, its inherent difficulties. Unattractive as Grossbart may be, his cunning use of whatever weapons come to hand in order to protect his skin seems entirely real; one would have to be thoroughly locked into self-righteousness not to be drawn a little, however shamefacedly, to Grossbart's urgency. The willingness of Marx to bend the rules in behalf of the Jewish recruits is plausible, perhaps even admirable; after all, he shares their loneliness and vulnerability. Established thereby as a figure of humaneness, Marx commits an act that seems shocking, even to himself, so that he must then try to resist "with all my will an impulse to turn back and seek pardon for my vindictiveness." If it is right to punish Grossbart, Marx also knows the punishment is cruel, a result, perhaps, of the same Jewish uneasiness that had first made him susceptible to Grossbart's designs.

The story does not allow any blunt distribution of moral sympathies, nor can the reader yield his heart to one character. Before the painfulness of the situation, Roth's usual habit of rapid dismissal must melt away. We are left with the texture of reality as, once in a while, a writer can summon it.

Neither before nor after "Defender of the Faith" has Roth written anything approaching it in compositional rigor and moral seriousness. It may, however, have been the presence of this story in *Goodbye, Columbus* that led reviewers, including myself, to assume that this gifted new writer was working in the tradition of Jewish self-criticism and satire—a substantial tradition extending in Yiddish from Mendele to Isaac Bashevis Singer and in English from Abraham Cahan to Malamud and Bellow. In these kinds of writing, the assault upon Jewish philistinism and the mockery of Jewish social pretension are both familiar and unrelenting. Beside Mendele, Roth seems soft; beside Cahan, imprecise. But now, from the vantage point of additional years, I think it clear that Roth, despite his concentration on Jewish settings and his acerbity of tone, has not really been involved in this tradition. For he is one of the first American-Jewish writers who finds that it yields him no sustenance, no norms or values from which to launch his attacks on middle-class complacence.

This deficiency, if deficiency it be, need not be a fatal one for a Jewish writer, provided he can find sustenance elsewhere, in other cultures, other traditions. But I do not see that Roth has—his relation to the mainstream of American culture, in its great sweep of democratic idealism and romanticism, is decidedly meager. There is no lack of critical attitude, or attitudinizing, in Roth's stories, but much of it consists of the frayed remnants of cultural modernism, once revolutionary in significance but now reduced to little more than the commonplace "shock" of middlebrow culture. And there is a parasitic relation to the embattled sentiments and postures of older Jewish writers in America—though without any recognition that, by now, simply to launch attacks on middle-class suburbia is to put oneself at the head of the suburban parade, just as to mock the up-tightness of immigrant Jews is to become the darling of their "liberated" suburban children.

One reason Roth's stories are unsatisfactory is that they come out of a thin personal culture. That he can quote Yeats and Rilke is hardly to the point. When we speak of a writer's personal culture we have in mind the ways in which a tradition, if absorbed into his work, can both release and control his creative energies. A vital culture can yield a writer those details of manners, customs, and morals which give the illusion of reality to his work. More important, *a vital culture talks back, so to say, within the writer's work*, holding in check his eccentricities, notions, and egocentrisms, providing a dialectic between what he has received and what he has willed—one can see this in novelists as various as Tolstoy, Hawthorne, Verga, and Sholem Aleichem.

When we say, consequently, that a writer betrays a thin personal culture we mean, among other possibilities, that he lives at the end of a tradition which can no longer nourish his imagination or that he has, through an act of fiat, chosen to tear himself away from that tradition—many American writers of the late 19th and early 20th centuries, for example, could no longer continue with firm conviction in the line of transcendental idealism which had been so liberating fifty or sixty years earlier. It is, of course, a severe predicament for a writer to find himself in this situation; it forces him into self-consciousness, improvisation, and false starts; but if he is genuinely serious, he will try, like a farmer determined to get what he can from poor soil, to make a usable theme of his dilemmas.

Perhaps this thinness of culture has some connection with that tone of *ressentiment*, that free-floating contempt and animus, which begins to appear in Roth's early stories and grows more noticeable in his later work. Unfocused hostility often derives from unexamined depression, and the latter, which I take to be the ground-note of Roth's sensibility, fully emerges only in the two novels he wrote after *Goodbye, Columbus*. But even in the early stories one begins to hear a grind of exasperation, an assault without precise object, an irritable wish to pull down the creatures of his own imagination which can hardly be explained by anything happening within the stories themselves. If sentimentality is defined as emotion in excess of what a given situation warrants, what are we to say about irritability in excess? As one of Roth's critics, Baruch Hochman, has sharply noticed:

> The energy informing [Roth's] stories is scarcely more than the energy of irritation, an irritation so great that it makes the exposure of inanity seem a meaningful moral act. For Roth does not seem really to be concerned with the substance of the values he shows being eroded. It is not at all clear how Neil Klugman, who is so offended at the Patimkins, stands for anything substantially different from what they stand for—setting aside the fact that he is poorer than they, which he cannot help. His differences with them lie elsewhere than in the moral realm. . . .

At times the note of disgust is sounded in full, as in "Epstein," a nasty joke about a middle-aged man's hapless effort to revive his sexuality. Reading the last paragraphs of this story, arranged as a pratfall for the poor slob Epstein (and how pleasurable it is for "us," the cultivated ones, to sneer at those slobs, with their little box houses, their spreading wives, their mucky kids, their uncreative jobs), one is reminded of D. H. Lawrence's jibe about writers who "do dirt" on their characters.

II

The standard opinion of Roth's critics has been that his two novels, *Letting Go* and *When She Was Good*, add slight luster to his reputation, and there is not much use in arguing against this view. Yet it should be noticed that there are patches of genuine achievement in both books, sometimes a stumbling, gasping honesty. They are not novels that yield much pleasure or grip one despite its absence, but both are marked by tokens of struggle with the materials of American life. And there are moments that come off well—the persistence of the battered divorcee, Martha Reganhart (*Letting Go*), in raising her children decently, the precocious eeriness of little Cynthia Reganhart, the struggle of Lucy (*When She Was Good*) to raise herself above the maudlin stupor of her family. Conventional achievements all of these are, and of a kind novelists have often managed in the past—of a kind, also, they will have to manage in the future if the novel is to survive. But right now, in our present cultural situation, this is hardly the sort of achievement likely to win much attention, as Roth evidently came to see.

Roth is not a "natural" novelist at all, the kind who loves to tell stories, chronicle social life, pile on characters, and if in his early fiction he seems willfully bent on scoring "points," in the novels his will exhausts itself from the sheer need to get on with things. He is an exceedingly joyless writer; even when being very funny. The reviewers of his novels, many of them sympathetic, noticed his need to rub our noses in the muck of squalid daily existence, his mania for annotating at punitive length the bickerings of his characters. Good clean hatred that might burn through, naturalistic determinism with a grandeur of design if not detail, the fury of social rebellion—any of these would be more *interesting* than the vindictive bleakness of Roth's novels.

What, one wonders, does he really have against these unhappy creatures of his? Why does he keep pecking away at them? I think the answer might furnish a key to Roth's work. Perhaps as a leftover from the culture of modernism and perhaps as a consequence of personal temperament, Roth's two novels betray a swelling nausea before the ordinariness of human existence, its seepage of spirit and rotting of flesh. This is a response that any sensitive or even insensitive person is likely to share at some point and to some extent, but it simply does not allow a writer to sustain or provide internal complications of tone in a large-scale work. It starts as a fastidious hesitation before the unseemliness of our minds and unsightliness of our bodies; it ends as a vibration of horror before the sewage of the quotidian. Men grow paunches, women's breasts sag, the breath of the aged reeks, varicose veins bulge. It all seems insufferable, an affront to our most cherished images of self, so much so that ordinary life must be pushed away, a disorder to be despised and assaulted. It is as if, in nagging at his characters, Roth were venting some deep and unmanageable frustration with our common fate.

III

The cruelest thing anyone can do with *Portnoy's Complaint* is to read it twice. An assemblage of gags strung onto the outcry of an analytic patient, the book thrives best on casual responses; it demands little more from the reader than a nightclub performer demands: a rapid exchange of laugh for punch-line, a breath or two of rest, some variations on the first response, and a quick exit. Such might be the most generous way of discussing *Portnoy's Complaint* were it not for the solemn ecstasies the book has elicited, in line with Roth's own feeling that it constitutes a liberating act for himself, his generation, and maybe the whole culture.

The basic structural unit of *Portnoy's Complaint* is the skit, the stand-up comedian's shuffle and patter that come to climax with a smashing one-liner—indeed, it is worth noticing that a good many of our more "advanced" writers during the last two decades have found themselves turning to the skit as a form well-suited to the requirements of "swinging" and their rejection of sustained coherence of form. The controlling tone of the book is a shriek of excess, the jokester's manic wail, although, because it must slide from skit to skit with some pretense of continuity, this tone declines now and again into a whine of self-exculpation or sententiousness. And the controlling sensibility of the book derives from a well-grounded tradition of feeling within immigrant Jewish life: the coarse provincial "worldliness" flourishing in corner candy-stores and garment centers, at cafeterias and pinochle games, a sort of hard, cynical mockery of ideal claims and pretensions, all that remains to people scraped raw by the struggle for success. (This sensibility finds a "sophisticated" analogue in the smart-aleck nastiness of Jules Feiffer's film, *Carnal Knowledge*, which cannot really be understood without some reference to the undersides of Jewish immigrant life, not as these have affected the subject-matter of the film but as they have affected the vision of the people who made it.)

Much of what is funny in Roth's book—the Monkey's monologues, some rhetorical flourishes accompanying Alex's masturbation, Sophie Portnoy's amusement at chancing upon her son's sexual beginnings—rests on the fragile structure of the skit. All the skit requires or can manage is a single broad stroke: shrewd, gross, recognizable, playing on the audience's embarrassment yet not hurting it too much, so that finally its aggression can be passed off as good-fellowship. (We all have Jewish mamas, we're all henpecked husbands, we all pretend to greater sexual prowess than. . . .) The skit stakes everything on brashness and energy, both of which Roth has or simulates in abundance. Among writers of the past Dickens and Celine have used the skit brilliantly, but Dickens always and Celine sometimes understood that in a book of any length the skit—as well as its sole legitimate issue, the caricature—must be put to the service of situations, themes, stories allowing for complication and development. (A lovely example of this point can be seen in the skits that Peter Sellers performs in the movie version of *Lolita*.)

It is on the problem of continuity that Portnoy—or, actually, Roth himself—trips up. For once we are persuaded to see his complaints as more than the stuff of a few minutes of entertainment, once we are led to suppose that they derive from some serious idea or coherent view of existence, the book quickly falls to pieces and its much-admired energy (praised by some critics as if energy were a value regardless of the ends to which it is put) serves mainly to blur its flimsiness. Technically this means that, brief as it is, the book seems half again too long, since there can be very little surprise or development in the second half, only a recapitulation of motifs already torn to shreds in the first.

It is worth looking at a few of the book's incoherences, venial for a skit, fatal for a novel. Alex is allowed the human attribute of a history within the narrative space of the book, presumably so that he can undergo change and growth, but none of the characters set up as his foils, except perhaps the Monkey, is granted a similar privilege. Alex speaks for imposed-upon, vulnerable, twisted, yet self-liberating humanity; the other characters, reduced to a function of his need, an echo of his cry, cannot speak or speak back as autonomous voices but simply go through their paces like straight-men mechanically feeding lines to a comic. Even more than in Roth's earlier work, the result is claustrophobia of voice and vision: *he never shuts up*, this darling Alex, nor does Roth detach himself sufficiently to gain some ironic distance. The psychic afflictions of his character Roth would surely want to pass up, but who can doubt that Portnoy's cry from the heart—enough of Jewish guilt, enough of the burdens of history, enough of inhibition and repression, it is time to "let go" and soar to the horizons of pleasure—speaks in some sense for Roth?

The difficulty that follows from this claustrophobic vision is not whether Mrs. Portnoy can be judged a true rendering, even as caricature, of Jewish mothers—only chuckleheads can suppose that to be a serious question!—but whether characters like Mr. and Mrs. Portnoy have much reality or persuasiveness within the fictional boundaries set by Roth himself. Sophie Portnoy has a little, because there are moments when Alex, or Roth, can't help liking her, and because the conventional lampoon of the Jewish mother is by now so well established in our folklore it has almost become an object of realistic portraiture in its own right. As for Mr. Portnoy, a comparison suggests itself between this constipated *nudnik* whom Alex would pass off as his father and "Mr. Fumfotch" in Daniel Fuchs's novel *Homage to Blenholt*. Fuchs's character is also a henpecked husband, also worn down by the struggle for bread, but he is drawn with an ironic compassion that rises to something better than itself: to an objectivity that transcends either affection or derision. In his last novel Fuchs remarks, while writing about figures somewhat like those in Roth's work, "It was not enough to call them low company and pass on"—and if this can be said about Depression Jews in Brighton Beach, why not also about more or less affluent ones in the Jersey suburbs?

We notice, again, that Portnoy attributes his sexual troubles to the guilt-soaked Jewish tradition as it has been carried down to him by his mother. Perhaps; who knows? But if we are to accept this simplistic determinism, why does it never occur to him, our Assistant Commissioner of Human Opportunity who once supped with John Lindsay in the flesh, that by the same token the intelligence on which he preens himself must also be attributed to the tradition he finds so repugnant—so that his yowl of revulsion against "my people," that they should "stick your suffering heritage up your suffering ass," becomes, let us say, a little ungenerous, even a little dopey.

And we notice, again, that while Portnoy knows that his sexual difficulties stem from his Jewishness, the patrician New England girl with whom he has an affair also turns out to be something of a sexual failure: she will not deliver him from the coils of Jewish guilt through the magic of fellatio. But if both Jewishness and Protestantism have deeply inhibiting effects on sexual performance—and as for Catholicism, well, we know those Irish girls!—what then happens to this crucial flake of Portnoy's wisdom, which the book invites us to take with some seriousness? As for other possible beliefs, from Ethical Culture to Hare Krishna, there can surely be little reason to suppose they will deliver us from the troubles of life which, for all we know, may be lodged in the very nature of things or, at the least, in those constraints of civilization which hardly encircle Jewish loins exclusively.

There is something suspect about Portnoy's complaining. From what he tells us one might reasonably conclude that, in a far from perfect world, he is not making out so badly; the boys on his block, sexual realists that they are, would put it more pungently. Only in Israel does he have serious difficulties, and for that there are simple geographical solutions. What seems really to be bothering Portnoy is a wish to sever his sexuality from his moral sensibilities, to cut it away from his self as historical creature. It's as if he really supposed the super-ego, or *post coitum triste*, were a Jewish invention. This wish—Norman O. Brown as a *yingele* —strikes me as rather foolish, an adolescent fantasy carrying within itself an inherent negation; but it is a fantasy that has accumulated a great deal of power in contemporary culture. And it helps explain, I think, what Roth's true feelings about, or relation to, Jewishness are. *Portnoy's Complaint* is not, as enraged critics have charged, an anti-Semitic book, though it contains plenty of contempt for Jewish life. Nor does Roth write out of traditional Jewish self-hatred, for the true agent of such self-hatred is always indissolubly linked with Jewish past and present, quite as closely as those who find in Jewishness moral or transcendent sanctions. What the book speaks for is a yearning to undo the fate of birth; there is no wish to do the Jews any harm (a little nastiness is something else), nor any desire to engage with them as a fevered antagonist; Portnoy is simply crying out to be left alone, to be released from the claims of distinctiveness and the burdens of the past, so that, out of his own nothingness, he may create himself as a "human being." Who, born a Jew in the 20th century, has been so lofty in spirit never to have shared this fantasy? But who, born a Jew in the 20th century, has been so foolish in mind as to dally with it for more than a moment?

What, in any case, *is Portnoy's Complaint*—a case-history burlesqued, which we are invited to laugh at, or a struggle of an afflicted man to achieve his liberation, which we are invited to cheer on? Dr. Bruno Bettelheim has written a straight-faced essay purporting to be the case notes of Alex's psychoanalyst, Dr. O. Spielvogel, who can barely restrain his impatience with Alex's effort to mask his true problems with "all the clichés of a spoiled Jewish childhood."

> A few times I [Dr. Spielvogel] indicated the wish to say something, but he only talked on the more furiously. . . . This extremely intelligent young Jew does not recognize that what he is trying to do, by reversing the Oedipal situation, is to make fun of me, as he does of everyone, thus asserting his superiority. . . . His overpowering love for his mother is turned into a negative projection, so that what becomes overpowering is the mother's love for him. . . . While consciously he experienced everything she did as destructive, behind it is an incredible wish for more, more, more. . . .

Now this is amusing, though not as amusing as the fact that it often constitutes the line of defense to which Roth's admirers fall back when the book's incoherence is revealed ("after all, it's a patient on the couch, everyone knows you can't take what he says at face value. . . ."). But to see the book in this light, as the mere comic record of a very sick man, is radically to undercut its claims for expressing radical new truths. Roth, never unwary, anticipates the problem by having Portnoy say, "Is this truth I'm delivering up, or is it just plain *kvetching*? Or is *kvetching* for people like me a *form* of truth?" Well there's *kvetching* and *kvetching*. At times it can be a form of truth, but when the gap is so enormous between manifest content and what Dr. Spielvogel *cum* Bettelheim takes to be its inner meaning, then *kvetching* becomes at best an untruth from which the truth must be violently wrenched.

It seems hard to believe that Roth would accept the view that his book consists merely of comic griping; certainly the many readers who saw it as a banner behind which to rally would not accept that view. For, in a curious way, *Portnoy's Complaint* has become a cultural document of some importance. Younger Jews, weary or bored with all the talk about their heritage, have taken the book as a signal for "letting go" of both their past and perhaps themselves, a guide to swinging in good conscience or better yet, without troubling about conscience. For some Gentile readers the book seems to have played an even more important role. After the Second World War, as a consequence of certain unpleasantnesses that occurred during the war, a wave of philo-Semitism swept through our culture. This wave lasted for all of two decades, in the course of which books by Jewish writers were often praised (in truth, overpraised) and a fuss made about Jewish intellectuals, critics, etc. Some literary people found this hard to bear, but they did. Once *Portnoy's Complaint* arrived, however, they could almost be heard breathing a sigh of relief, for it signaled an end to philo-Semitism in American culture, one no longer had to listen to all that talk about Jewish morality, Jewish endurance, Jewish wisdom, Jewish families. Here was Philip Roth himself, a writer who even seemed to know Yiddish, confirming what had always been suspected about those immigrant Jews but had recently not been tactful to say.

The talent that went into *Portnoy's Complaint* and portions of *Goodbye, Columbus* is real enough, but it has been put to the service of a creative vision deeply marred by vulgarity. It is very hard, I will admit, to be explicit about the concept of vulgarity: people either know what one is referring to, as part of the tacit knowledge that goes to make up a coherent culture, or the effort to explain is probably doomed in advance. Nevertheless, let me try. By vulgarity in a work of literature I am not here talking about the presence of certain kinds of words or the rendering of certain kinds of actions. I have in mind, rather, the impulse to submit the rich substance of human experience, sentiment, value, and aspiration to a radically reductive leveling or simplification; the urge to assault the validity of sustained gradings and discriminations of value, so that in some extreme instances the concept of vulgarity is dismissed as up-tight or a mere mask for repressiveness; the wish to pull down the reader in common with the characters of the work, so that he will not be tempted to suppose that any inclinations he has toward the good, the beautiful, or the ideal merit anything more than a Bronx cheer; and finally, a refusal of that disinterestedness of spirit in the depiction and judgment of other people which seems to me the writer's ultimate resource.

That I have here provided an adequate definition of vulgarity in literature I do not for a moment suppose—though I don't know of a better one. It ought, however, to serve our present purposes by helping to make clear, for example, the ways in which a book like *Portnoy's Complaint*, for all its scrim of sophistication, is spiritually linked with the usual sentimental treatment of Jewish life in the work of popular and middlebrow writers. Between *Portnoy's Complaint* and *Two Cents Plain* there is finally no great difference of sensibility.

Perhaps the matter can be clarified by a comparison. Hubert Selby's novel, *Last Exit to Brooklyn*, portrays a segment of urban life—lumpen violence, gang-bangs, rape, sheer debasement—that is utterly appalling, and the language it must record is of a kind that makes Roth seem reticent; yet as I read Selby's book there is no vulgarity in it whatever, for he takes toward his barely human figures a stance of dispassionate objectivity, writing not with "warmth" or "concern" but with a disciplined wish to see things as they are. He does not wrench, he does not patronize, he does not aggrandize. Repugnant as it often is, *Last Exit to Brooklyn* seems to me a pure-spirited book; amusing as it often is, *Portnoy's Complaint* a vulgar book.

IV

About the remainder of Roth's work I have little to say.

Our Gang, purporting to be a satire on Richard Nixon, is a coarse-grained replica of its subject. A flaccid performance, it has some interest through embodying a strong impulse in our culture, the impulse to revert not so much to the pleasures of infantilism as to the silliness of the high-school humor column. About this book I would repeat what Henry James once said of a Trollope novel: "Our great objection . . . is that we seem to be reading a work written for children, a work prepared for minds unable to think, a work below the apprehension of the average man or woman."

The Breast, extravagantly praised by my literary betters, is a work to which, as students would say, "I cannot relate." Well-enough written and reasonably ingenious, it is finally boring—tame, neither shocking nor outrageous, and tasteless in both senses of the word. Discussions will no doubt persist as to its "meaning," but first it might be better to ask whether, as a work of literature, it exists. For simply on the plane of narrative it cannot, or ought not, hold the interest of a reasonably mature reader.

Flaubert once said that a writer must choose between an audience and readers. Evidently Roth has made his choice.

Notes

1. "Writing About Jews," *Commentary*, December 1963.

Roth and Kafka: Two Jews

Morton P. Levitt*

"What have I in common with Jews? I have hardly anything in common with myself and should stand very quietly in a corner, content that I can breathe."

"I am as old as Jewry, as the wandering Jew."
—Franz Kafka, in his diaries and in conversation.

Nowhere in the fictions of Franz Kafka does the word "Jew" appear. Yet we should have little doubt that he is a profoundly Jewish writer, chronicler not of the mores but of the attitudes and isolation of his people, historian in a sense of the Middle European Jewish Predicament in the post-World War I and pre-Hitler era. His is a people between, in a world between. What could be more Jewish than to commemmorate this world without naming it, to make of the Jewish experience in Middle Europe a metaphor for all human life in the modern world.

The fiction of Philip Roth, on the other hand, speaks constantly of Jews, of their conventions and customs, of their social and moral psychological predicaments, speaks of them intently from within, with humor and pain, attesting at all times (even in *When She Was Good*, which never mentions their existence) to their centrality in his American vision of life. And Philip Roth's Jewishness is constantly questioned by some other Jews, who scorn his humor and dismiss his pain. If Kafka were a self-reflexive novelist writing almost directly of his own life, writing of his writing, then Philip Roth might serve as his persona. There is much that we can learn about Roth, I believe, by looking at Kafka and at his view of Kafka.

The Kafka of whom I speak here is not the familiar, humorless, Germanic satirist of bureaucracy and of man's easy fall from humanity; the epithet "Kafkaesque" cannot so easily encapsulate his breadth and paradoxes. My Kafka is rather the friend of Max Brod, "one of the most amusing of men . . . in spite of his shyness," who "laughed quite immoderately as he read aloud the first chapter of *The Trial*.[1] ". . . he was a born playmate," Dora Diamant has said, "always ready for some prank or

*This essay was written specifically for this volume and appears here for the first time by permission of the author.

other.'"² He is no mere outsider, this Kafka, disaffected from life, terrified of his father, fearful of women, of engagement, of making commitments to life. He is himself a capable and humane official in a bureaucracy;³ lawyer-like, he warns of "the lawyer's tricks" in the Letter to his Father—"it's a lawyer's letter," he advises the reader;⁴ even his dreams are certified by analysts as perfectly normal.⁵ He is also a lover of women and loved by them; he may even have fathered an unknown son on the best friend of his absent fiancée.⁶ His presence, in a city filled with intellectuals and artists, compels the attention of men and women alike. " 'When Kafka attended a performance of some kind, there was a hush: Kafka is here! He himself had sneaked in as unobtrusively as possible and would vastly have preferred to flee quickly again from amidst the throng.' . . . It seemed, however, as though some unseen attendant had whispered to the lecturer: 'Be careful about everything you say from now on. For Kafka has just arrived.' "⁷ Near the end of his life, he begins to learn Hebrew and to make plans to emigrate to Palestine.

This is not to claim, obviously, that Kafka's was a joyful life or that his art is notably joyful. The troubled evidence of his journals, of the letters to Felice and Milena and to his father, of the fictions themselves, is undeniable. But his was not the morbid sort of life that one might expect from the public image, and his art is decidedly not a morbid art. The power of Kafka lies precisely in the tensions which dominate both his life and his art: the tensions between comic impulse and satiric vision, between reason and immoderation, between grotesque inventiveness in detail and matter-of-factness in language, between accepting, humane instincts and a refusal to countenance those forces which threaten our humanity and so easily unman his protagonists. Life and art in Kafka are one, impulse for and support of each other; the art flows from the life, the life from the art. And yet they are always in conflict—with each other, within themselves. It is far too easy to view Kafka through a unitarian lens, as being unloved and unloving in art as in life, his life barely human, his art outside the humanist tradition.

Torn by these tensions and nourished by them—in what may be the apotheosis of Jewish European experience—Kafka the Jew develops an art in which far more is suggested than said, an art of shocking yet mundane surfaces and of unarticulated resonances from centuries of isolation and fear, momentary hopes and persistent disappointments.⁸ It is an outsider's art, a survivor's art, an art in which form and function are wonderfully harmonious: its points of view are severely restricted—omniscience is impossible in a world devoid of a knowing center; it is filled with potential metaphors and myths that are never quite realized; its repeated theme is the individual need to assume responsibility for this unfinished, uncertain, threatening yet potential state of affairs. Without needing to mention the name "Jew," the tales of Kafka are almost immediate manifestations of Jewish experience. We have also come to see, in this century, that they may speak as well for human experience in general.[9] Kafka's perception is analogous, in fact, to those of Joyce in *Ulysses* (with Leopold Bloom as our representative hero), of Mann in the Joseph tetralogy (with ancient Jewish history as a measure against which to judge modern man), of Proust in *A la recherche du temps perdu* (with the Dreyfus Affair and its reverberations providing a fulcrum to individual identity). Kafka's perception, however, is more direct, more felt and less intellectually realized, than are those of his Modernist contemporaries. He is, after all, much closer than they are to Jewish experience. It is perhaps for this reason that he seems to speak more forcefully and immediately to us today.

This is the Kafka who might have created Philip Roth as his persona and who, in turn, serves as metaphor for Roth of human and artistic potential. The lives of Roth's heroes—those agonized intellectuals, rarely artists themselves, who narrate lives of unfulfilled potency, those fluent and comic explicators of responsibility and guilt—are manifestations as much of Kafka's image of himself and his world as they are of Roth's fictional perceptions. They are, in a sense, creations of both Roth and Kafka. They attest together to the centrality of Jewish experience and vision in modern fiction and to the persistence of the humanist impulse into our time.

"I am a breast," proclaims the narrator of *The Breast* (hereafter cited as TB), "a mammary gland disconnected from any human form, a mammary gland such as could only appear, one would have thought, in a dream or a Dali painting" (TB, p. 15).[10] But David Kepesh is a professor of comparative literature, and he knows quite well of another potential analogue—or is it source?—of his affliction. " 'I have out-Kafkaed Kafka,' " he comes finally to boast, despairingly. " 'He could only *imagine* a man turning into a cockroach. But look what I have done' " (TB, p. 105). Kepesh, like Roth, has taught and knows his Kafka, and there are echoes of Kafka in both *The Breast* and its companion novel *The Professor of Desire*, as well as in *Portnoy's Complaint* and *My Life as a Man*.[11] Kafka also appears, as character and metaphor, in some of Roth's most revealing essays and essays which blur into fictions.

"I have always wanted you to admire my fasting," says the hunger artist of Kafka's ironic tale and of the title and epigraph of the Roth piece also called "Looking at Kafka" (hereafter cited as LAK). "I am looking, as I write of Kafka," begins Roth in what appears to be his own voice, "at the photograph taken of him at the age of forty (my age)—it is 1924 . . ." (LAK, p. 103).[12] It is also 1973, and Professor Roth (the piece is dedicated to his students) speaks as critic of Kafka the man and of the last years of his life. And then it is "1942. I am nine; my Hebrew school teacher, Dr. Kafka, is fifty-nine" (LAK, p. 114). In a wonderful metamorphosis presaging that of Anne Frank in *The Ghost Writer*, the European Kafka is whisked to the New World, surviving tuberculosis and the concentration camps that engulfed his sisters and friends, is placed will-he, nill-he, in northern New Jersey, to join the long line of elderly scholars of a generation past who eked out a living by teaching Hebrew, badly, to groups of uncomprehending, uncaring adolescents. It is a fate more comic and crueler than that of any of Kafka's protagonists. The boy Philip Roth—he might almost be the young David Kepesh—is of course his star pupil. And so Dr. Kafka becomes the suitor of young Philip's fortyish, stylish, spinsterish Aunt Rhoda. "How do I warn him? And how do I warn Aunt Rhoda (a very great admirer of me and my marks) about his sour breath, his roomer's pallor, his Old World ways so at odds with her up-to-dateness?" (LAK, p. 117). Then, unaccountably, after several strange letters, the courtship breaks off. " 'Poor soul,' says my mother. . . . 'He's *meshugeh*,' admits my father. . . . 'Sex!' " leers "my brother, the Boy Scout" (LAK, pp. 123–24).

Years later, a junior in college, the fictional Roth receives a clipping from the obituary page of the Essex County *Jewish News*. " 'Dr. Franz Kafka,' the notice reads, 'a Hebrew teacher at the Talmud Torah of the Schley Street Synagogue from 1939 to 1948, died on June 3 in the Deborah Tuberculosis Sanitorium in Browns Mills, New Jersey. . . . He was 70 years old. . . . He leaves no survivors.'

"He also leaves no books: no *Trial*, no *Castle* no 'Diaries.' The dead man's papers are claimed by no one, and disappear . . ." (LAK, pp. 125–26). Roth's Kafka, with his "burrower's face" (LAK, p. 104), his "Oedipal timidity, perfectionist madness, and insatiable longings for solitude and spiritual purity" (LAK, p. 105), probably virginal, surely psychoneurotic, Roth's Kafka dies leaving no heirs: unless we count the novelist, Philip Roth, that is.

I am speaking now neither of direct influence between Kafka and Roth, nor of what Helen Weinberg calls "the Kafkan mode" in contemporary fiction, that sense in which Kafka, "more than Proust, Joyce, or Mann," from intuition and experience, helps us to anticipate and to create our world. Roth's connections to Kafka are more immediate than this; they share not simply a generalized "postreligious spiritual awareness," in Weinberg's phrase,[13] but a very precise concern for sexuality and its implications, a very Jewish sense of morality, an insistence on individual responsibility not only for the individual's acts but also, it seems at times, for the state of the world. Roth writes of Kafka so intimately because he perceives in his predecessor's life and art a paradigm for his own protagonists, a metaphor of potential yet unrealized experience.

Still, Roth's view of Kafka shares some of the familiar clichés: he fails as would-be husband with Felice, as lover with Milena, is "chaste" with Dora Diamant. "Certainly a dreamer like Kafka," Roth says, by analogy to "The Burrow," "need never have entered the young girl's body for her tender presence to kindle in him a fantasy of a hidden orifice that promises 'satisfied desire,' 'achieved ambition,' and 'profound slumber,' but that once penetrated and in one's possession, arouses the most terrifying and heartbreaking fears of retribution and loss" (LAK, pp. 111, 113). Written by some psychoanalytic critic (and similar judgments surely have been), such words would seem portentous and foolish. Coming from Roth, who also means them seriously, they retain a certain comic potential—a plaint like Portnoy's, perhaps. Roth's art, too, is marked by tension between the profound and the ridiculous.

Roth's Kafka is impotent not simply as a cliché or joke but because sexuality serves Roth as a sign of broader, usually unrealized human potential. The failures of David Kepesh, Peter Tarnopol and Alex Portnoy— the protagonists in the Kafka-connected novels—are thus not simple cases of sexual dysfunctioning; they are failures of character and will, existential failures. Portnoy claims to be human, to be moral, but he can deal with others only as stereotypes (the Pilgrim, the Monkey, the Emasculating Jewish Mother, he labels them); he ends by making himself into a stereotype as well (Suffering Son/Lover/Jew). His impotence is rather obviously both sexual and moral. Tarnopol, narrator of *My Life as a Man*, is prey to the same perverse (in their minds) appeals as is Portnoy: the appeal of Christian women, of the disabled and crippled, of Kafkaesque self-humiliation, of the moral redemption that may yet arise from perversity. He is a self-styled Romantic artist who can no longer write, a decent and loving man (as seen from his own point of view) who cannot sustain a relationship with a woman. His impotence is less obvious than Portnoy's but more general: he fails as lover, as man and also as artist. As for Kepesh, his real kinship with Gregor Samsa is not in their unlikely, if convincing metamorphoses; it is in the grounds for their change.

Samsa, like all of Kafka's heroes, is incapable of functioning fully as a man (he hates his job, resents his family, is uneasy in his assumption of responsibility) and so is transformed. We may suggest at times—he accepts his condition so readily—that he has chosen it willfully. He certainly never questions its appropriateness. Kepesh protests overmuch, perhaps: what keeps him going after his metamorphosis, his analyst suggests, may be "those old pulpit bromides, 'strength of character' and 'the will to live.' . . . and who am I not to concur in such a heroic estimate of myself?" (TB, pp. 29–30). We may wonder, however, why he became transformed in the first place. *The Breast* offers little background for Kepesh; to divine the source of his failure, we must turn to its companion novel, *The Professor of Desire*.

The Professor of Desire (1977) is, in a sense, the sequel to *The Breast* (1972), although the story it tells is set earlier in time. Again we view David Kepesh, following him this time from childhood through to adulthood: from a Sadean relationship with two Swedish girls in London to a disastrous marriage (as much a prerequisite for a Roth man, it seems, as the first-person narrative—among the factors seducing us to identify Roth with his heroes), from a strange dream of Kafka in Prague to what seems, at last, the possibility of a mature relationship with a woman. His state at the end of the narrative seems more positive than that of any earlier Roth protagonist. We are left to extrapolate—from what we know of him, from what we know of his predecessors—why it is that he, too, eventually falls from his humanity.

There is another sense in which *The Professor of Desire* is a sequel also to Kafka's *Amerika*, a sense in which all of Roth's heroes follow in Karl Rossman's path—as if the Nature Theatre of Oklahoma, to which Karl journeys at the close of this open-ended narrative, has been moved to northern New Jersey. It is no coincidence that Karl is welcomed to America by the phallic sword brandished by the Statue of Liberty: he has been sent off by his parents, remember, for a sexual crime. Under the New World influence, he quickly blurs the nature of the crime and even his complicity; surrounded by sexual symbols, he seems willing to renounce all pleasures—food, sleep and sex, in particular. Yet he awakens at one point into a nightmare of sex; like a child, he closes his eyes and returns to sleep. "The first days of a European in America," he has been told by his Uncle Jacob, "might be likened to a re-birth. . . ."[14] Cut off from his parents and betrayed by his new parent figures,[15] Karl easily regresses to childhood but then fails to reach out again beyond adolescence—hardly the sort of rebirth that America has historically promised. In this land of vast, distorted vistas and petty urban officialdom, of great, often surreal extravagances—a true Kafka land, it would seem—Karl constantly seeks out initiation but never quite achieves it. There is a suggestion, in both Kafka and Roth, that few reach maturity in this fictional New World. For neither, however, does this free the individual of his responsibility for himself.

The dream from which Kepesh awakens and retreats in *The Professor of Desire* (hereafter cited as POD) is a dream of Kafka. Lying alongside loving, supportive, gentile Claire Ovington, in a hotel room in Prague, he dreams of Kafka's whore. In the daytime, he has visited Kafka's phallic gravestone ("a stout, elongated, whitish rock, tapering upward to its pointed glans"—POD, p. 120),[16] has been told of Kafka's modern appeal for his ancient city, now ruled by autocrats (" 'many of us survive almost solely on Kafka. Including people in the street who have never read a word of his. They look at one another when something happens, and they say, "It's Kafka." Meaning, "That's the way it goes here now." Meaning, "What else did you expect?" ' "—POD, p. 115), has confessed the import of his own leaning toward Kafka. It has to do, Kepesh says, " 'in large part with sexual despair. . . . I can only compare the body's utter single-mindedness, its cold indifference and absolute contempt for the well-being of the spirit, to some unyielding, authoritarian regime.' " And, he goes on, " 'I sometimes wonder if *The Castle* isn't in fact linked to Kafka's own erotic blockage—a book engaged at every level with not reaching a climax' " (POD, pp. 117–18). At night, anticlimactically, he views the aged pussy of Kafka's whore.

Kepesh has gone to sleep feeling wonderfully secure in being loved by Claire, more secure perhaps than he has been since adolescence, "absolutely triumphant: capacious indeed" (POD, p. 128). But then he dreams of Kafka's whore. She is an old woman now, and through an interpreter out of his past, the visiting professor questions her dutifully about Kafka's erections, his orgasms, his sexual preferences. (He prefers, perhaps needs, fellation, like so many of Roth's protagonists.) She can remember nothing of his conversation: he was to her simply one more quiet, clean, undemanding young Jewish client. (" 'I didn't come . . . to Prague to talk about nice Jewish boys,' " counters Kepesh—POD, p. 130). For five dollars more he looks at her pussy.

A few days aferwards Kepesh lectures in Bruges on "Hunger Art"—"Kafka's preoccupations with spiritual starvation" (POD, p. 113). He thinks no more of his dream or its implications, thinks his own life has more to do with Chekhov than with Kafka, fails to connect his father ("a burly, hirsute man, with a strong prominent cask of a chest"—POD, p. 9) with Kafka's, or his own life and needs—his aloneness (POD, p. 82), his "effort to ground myself in what is substantial" (POD, p. 7), his " 'wonderful feel for the complexity of things' " which scares people off (POD, p. 84)—with those of his subject. A friend and colleague of his—a self-styled Dionysiac Jewish poet named Ralph Baumgarten—has spoken of his own respect for confessional art: " 'For me the books count—my own included—where the writer incriminates *himself*' " (POD, p. 95). Kepesh, who is close to Roth but not his reliable spokesman, fails to perceive this need. He reveals himself only up to a point. That he is so brutally honest in his narration about aspects of his life tends to obscure his essential dishonesty: he is dishonest with himself most of all, dishonest because he refuses to see beyond the sexual surface of his predicament—to make the sort of metaphoric and moral connections that Kafka should enable him to make—to accept responsibility for himself and for what he has made of his life: to incriminate himself. He is like other Roth heroes in this respect and, up to a point, like Kafka's heroes as well. But he is separate from Kafka and Roth.

At the end of *The Trial*, Joseph K. comes finally to see, if still incompletely, his own complicity in his fate. " 'The verdict is not suddenly arrived at,' " the priest tells him in the cathedral, " 'the proceedings only gradually merge into the verdict.' "[17] It is the defendant, indeed, who makes them merge, who might be said to choose his own verdict and sentence. " 'The Court wants nothing from you. It receives you when you come and it dismisses you when you go.' "[18] At the end, an instant before his execution, K. sees the shadow of a man and wonders, "Who was it? A friend? A good man? Someone who sympathized? Someone who wanted to help? Was it one person only? Or was it mankind?"[19] Even at the end he cannot see fully his own responsibility. But he does see, for almost the first time, his connection to mankind. K. in *The Trial* is, as he claims, guilty of nothing—he is guilty of having lived so meaningless a life, so aloof from mankind, that he is guilty of nothing. In the end, it is not guilt with which Kafka is concerned but responsibility—for oneself, above all, but for mankind too. It is a traditional Jewish concern, rooted in the emphasis on this life, as opposed to an afterlife, which is central to Judaism. It is the theme of the stories of Abraham, Isaac and Jacob, of Joseph and his brothers, of Noah and Lot and of Job and Ecclesiastes. It persists into more modern times as well. "If I am not for myself," Rabbi Hillel writes, "who will be for me? And if I am only for myself, what am I?"

"I have always been drawn," Philip Roth writes, "to a passage that comes near the end of *The Trial*, the chapter where K., in the cathedral, looks up toward the priest with a sudden infusion of hope. . . . 'If the man would only quit his pulpit, it was not impossible that K. could obtain decisive and acceptable counsel from him which might, for instance, point the way, not toward some influential manipulation of the case, but toward a circumvention of it, a breaking away from it altogether, a mode of living completely outside the jurisdiction of the Court. This possibility must exist, K. had of late given much thought to it.'

"As who hasn't of late? Enter Irony when the man in the pulpit turns out to be oneself."[20] No such resolution, Kafka tells us and Roth affirms, can be found looking upward in a cathedral. It is to be found within man alone.

Our immediate reaction to Kafka's fictions—of men becoming insects, of fearful animals expressing terrible human traumas, of men starving themselves for "art" and the lack of some food which can please them, of innocents condemned to wander interminably, of penal colonies, unresponsive bureaucracies and condemning tribunals—is to assume that they are, on their face, anti-humanistic. Man is never seen as constructive in Kafka; he often seems brutalized and degraded. Yet at the core of Kafka's vision is the individual's need to assume responsibility for what he has made of his life. It is this affirmation of human responsibility—with the implicit dignity which it provides for man: the dignity of being responsible for oneself—which, more than his troubled life or his sexual concerns, attracts Roth to Kafka. In Kafka's Prague, Roth had found not simply Kafka but something of himself. In earlier travels to Western Europe, he had never "felt myself to be anything other than an American passing through." In the Jewish quarter of Prague, "one of those dense corners of Jewish Europe which Hitler had emptied of Jews," he feels something more. "I understood that a connection of sorts existed between myself and this place. . . . Looking for Kafka's landmarks, I had, to my surprise, come upon some landmarks that felt to me like my own."[21] They are Jewish landmarks, to be sure, by they have also been made, by Jewish experience and Jewish art, landmarks of the humanist spirit.

Notes

1. Max Brod, *Franz Kafka* (New York: Schocken, 1947), pp. 39–40, 178.

2. Cited in Nahum N. Glatzer, ed., *I Am A Memory Come Alive: Autobiographical Writings by Franz Kafka* (New York: Schocken, 1974), p. 237.

3. See, for example, Gustav Janouch, *Conversations with Kafka* (New York: New Directions, 1971), p. 66. Janouch's father, who worked with Kafka, told of an old worker whose leg had been crushed at a building site and who "was to receive only a paltry pension from us. He brought an action against us which was not in the proper legal form. The old man would certainly have lost his case, if at the last moment a well-known Prague lawyer had not visited him and—without being paid a penny by the old man—had not expertly redrafted the labourer's case. . . . The lawyer, as I learned later, had been instructed, briefed and paid by Kafka, so that, as the legal representative of the Accident Insurance Institution, he might honourably lose the case against the old labourer.' "

4. Glatzer, p. 187.

5. "The absence of guilt in Kafka's dreams may come as a surprise to those who see in Kafka's writings, especially in *The Trial*, a profound, existential concern with men's guilt." Calvin S. Hall and Richard E. Lind, *Dreams, Life and Literature: A Study of Franz Kafka* (Chapel Hill: Univ. of North Carolina Press, 1970), p. 86.

6. Grete Bloch, who functioned as go-between for Kafka and Felice Bauer, claimed that her son, who died in 1915 at the age of seven, was Kafka's (Glatzer, p. 132). Not everyone is willing to believe her claim, *e.g.*, Meno Spann, *Franz Kafka* (Boston: Twayne, 1976), p. 181n.

7. Johannes Urzidil, *There Goes Kafka* (Detroit: Wayne State University Press, 1968), p. 102, citing Kafka's friend Friedrich Thieberger.

8. Isaac Bashevis Singer has spoken often of the fact that, for more than five centuries, none of his ancestors had learned Polish: they knew that they were not welcome in Poland. After World War I, the situation seemed to have changed, and it appeared for the first time that Jews might indeed become part of the nation. So he and his brother, I. J. Singer, learned the language. They can have had little chance to use it; within a decade, they were both in America. Few of their compatriots were so fortunate.

9. "The word Jew does not appear in *The Castle*. Yet, tangibly, Kafka in *The Castle*, straight from his Jewish soul, in a simple story, has said more about the situation of Jewry as a whole today than can be read in a hundred learned treatises. At the same time this specifically Jewish interpretation goes hand in hand with what is common to humanity, without either excluding or disturbing the other." Brod, p. 187.

10. All references are to Philip Roth, *The Breast*, Bantam edition (New York, 1973).

11. ". . . reading *My Life as a Man* is analogous to reading *The Trial* or *The Castle*, and then reading an artistically ordered version of Kafka's *Diaries* or his *Letters to Milena*. In both Tarnopol's fiction and Kafka's we note common characteristics which reflect their author's obsessive concerns. . . . Like Kafka's fictions, Tarnopol's reflect on both their author's biography and the art of writing itself." Bernard F. Rodgers, Jr., *Philip Roth* (Boston: Twayne, 1978), p. 152. See also pp. 124–30.

12. All references are to Philip Roth, " 'I Always Wanted You to Admire My Fasting'; or, Looking at Kafka," *American Review*, 17 (1973). "Looking at Kafka," says Sanford Pinsker, "is a curious hybrid: not quite literary criticism, although Roth has a deep understanding of Kafka's life and art, and not quite an impressionist memoir about himself. Both elements are there, intertwined by a complex fate and each shedding light upon the other." *The Comedy that "Hoits"* (Columbia, Mo.: Univ. of Missouri Press, 1975), p. 80.

13. Helen Weinberg, *The New Novel in America: The Kafkan Mode in Contemporary Fiction* (Ithaca, N.Y.: Cornell University Press, 1970), p. 1. "But more significant than any

internal evidence of Kafka's direct influence is the impress of the Kafkan hero on the minds of American writers who, from the internal evidence of their work, demonstrate that they share his sensibility. These American writers have inevitably transformed the Kafkan vision by using it in a way that coincides with American consciousness and with their own native perceptions" (p. 13).

14. Franz Kafka, *Amerika*, trans. Willa and Edwin Muir (New York: New Directions, 1962), p. 39.

15. Brod tells us, in his afterword to *Amerika* (p. 299), that Kafka originally planned to have Karl find his parents again in the Nature Theatre of Oklahoma. ". . . it was to be the sole work of Kafka that was to end on an optimistic note, with wide-ranging prospects for life. On the other hand Franz seems at other times to have pictured a different, tragic end for his hero . . ." (Brod, p. 137).

16. All references are to Philip Roth, *The Professor of Desire* (New York: Farrar, Straus and Giroux, 1977).

17. Franz Kafka, *The Trial*, trans. Willa and Edwin Muir (New York: Modern Library, 1956), p. 264.

18. *The Trial*, p. 278.

19. *The Trial*, p. 286.

20. Philip Roth, *Reading Myself and Others* (New York: Farrar, Straus and Giroux, 1975), p. 108, from an interview with Joyce Carol Oates entitled "After Eight Books" (1974). The quote from *The Trial* is on p. 266 of that text. "You might even say," Roth adds, "that the business of *choosing* is the primary occupation of any number of my characters." *Reading Myself*, p. 27, from an unmailed response to a hostile critic entitled "Document Dated July 27, 1969."

21. Philip Roth, "In Search of Kafka and Other Answers," *New York Times Book Review* (February 15, 1976), p. 6. " 'In us all it still lives,' " Kafka says of the old ghetto of Prague, " 'the dark corners, the secret alleys, shuttered windows, squallid courtyards, rowdy pubs, and sinister inns. We walk through the broad streets of the newly built town. But our steps and our glances are uncertain. Inside we tremble just as before in the ancient streets of our misery. Our hearts know nothing of the slum clearance which has been achieved. The unhealthy old Jewish town within us is far more real than the new hygienic town around us. With our eyes open we walk through a dream: ourselves only a ghost of a vanished age.' " (Janouch, p. 80).

Philip Roth: The Ambiguities of Desire

Howard Eiland*

In his essay, "The Fate of Pleasure: Wordsworth to Dostoevsky" (1963), Lionel Trilling critically delineates what he takes to be a central tendency of the modern temper—its renunciation of pleasure. In place of Wordsworth's classical conception of pleasure as "the naked and native dignity of man," his conception of a "joy" at once sensuous and transcendent which marries mankind to nature, there arises in the nineteenth century a more demonic and self-regarding principle of spirit. Trilling adduces the poetry of Keats as a turning point in the tradition, for Keats continues the Wordsworthian thematic of pleasure as "elementary" to human life but understands it in a more radically erotic and even voluptuous way. Pushing past the bounds of reason and moderation, the poet discovers "Pleasure . . . turning to Poison as the bee-mouth sips." He finds in the erotic life a perverse and self-negating impulse, a dark intimation, says Trilling, that sexual fulfillment ultimately entails castration. At its most intense, desire turns against itself, or else bursts and comes to seem illusory. The Keatsian ambivalence is understood to anticipate the "morbid idealism" of Dostoevsky, Nietzsche and their respective successors, for whom deliberate *un*pleasure constitutes the vehicle of human dignity, which is to say freedom from all determining natural conditions. The spiritual or, in Schiller's terminology, "sentimental" artist thus comes to view himself as an adversary to every specious good and shallow humanism of material pleasure, particularly as these are embodied in bourgeois society. His characteristic attitude is disgust and rage. Trilling concludes by acknowledging with Freud that there have always been men who commit themselves to ascetic or "unnatural" modes of life in order to summon psychic energies not found in felicity, but that in the culture of the last two centuries the balance between pleasure-seeking instincts and the ego instincts appears to be altered in favor of the latter. That this alteration should be morbid may be better appreciated when we remember that, in *Beyond the Pleasure Principle*, Frued's other name for the ego-instincts is the death-instincts.

*This essay was written specifically for this volume and appears here for the first time by permission of the author.

I suggest that Philip Roth is a late and not altogether willing heir of this tradition of modern unpleasure. Of course, he himself—not about to be out-professored by anyone—is constantly inviting such influence-tracing by his almost obsessive allusions to the modernist canon. (Indeed, in his fiction of the later seventies is to be found some of the most acute aphoristic criticism in English of writers such as Flaubert, Chekhov, Kafka, Colette, and Bellow.) From the beginning of his career, he has been explicitly seeking out one spiritual father or another, and though his publications (up until very recently) have each differed in their manner of presentation, he keeps returning to an established set of themes concerned with authority and individuation. It is as if he were ringing changes on Nietzsche's idea of man as *"das kranke Tier,"* the sick animal—dis-eased by virtue of his self-consciousness and doomed to ever more ingenious attempts at curing himself. Roth makes much of his coming to maturity in the fifties, that decade of earnestness and of drifting, of "conformity" and incipient anti-establishmentarianism. His protagonists thrive on the cultivation of sin and polymorphous perversity, but at the same time their erotic adventures are informed by missionary, redemptive ideals and their transgressions made keener by an exquisite sense of propriety. Faced with temptation, his hero will usually give in—and then use the occasion to test his capacity for conscience. Never wasting, never in line, he synthesizes the stereotypes of pushy Jew and nice Jewish boy. For his parents, and for the women he loves, Roth reserves both his tenderest and his most scabrous outpourings. As he terms Kafka, so is he himself a "family-haunted son," and yet at all junctures he insists on being "on my own." Having hurt his loved ones, he will get a more vivid sense of himself, of human possibilities generally, through the consequent suffering and guilt he experiences. His ambivalence, in other words—his hesitating and pulsating between carnal and spiritual imperatives—is the ambivalence of Stephen Dedalus and Raskolnikov, only in a minor, bluesy key: tragedy verging on farce.

Roth's characteristic preoccupations are already present in his first extended work (which he calls "apprentice work" despite its winning The National Book Award), the novella, *Goodbye, Columbus* (1959). Narrated in a typically detached, almost insouciant style that yet manages an undertone of pathos, the story maps out what is to be the author's distinctive territory: the manners, values, paraphernalia of second-generation, middle class Jewish life in America. Though somewhat weak on characterization—the figure of hand-shaking Ron Patimkin instancing the crassest caricature—the novella nevertheless displays Roth's genius for dialogue and his predilection for the crystallizing lens of memory. At the same time, in the person of the art-loving, streetwise and stone lion-defying little black boy with whom the ambitious protagonist identifies, this first work indicates something of the creeping sentimentality—concomitant to easy cynicism—which will mar certain of the later novels.

The action of *Goodbye, Columbus* puts to work Roth's mastering themes. The summer romance of Neil Klugman and Brenda Patimkin allows a comic-satiric exploration, not just of disillusionment and the obstructions of social class, but of personal self-deception. Sly, vain and spoiled Brenda may claim to love sports and games—she plays at turning Neil into a miler on the track—but in a jam she becomes practical like her father. Foreshadowing more complex portraits of harassed daughters in later works, she screams defiance at her mother while secretly longing to nestle under that formidable lady's wing.

By the same token, Neil dives into the affair without quite realizing at the time that his air of alternate sweetness and testiness works to conceal "that hideous emotion I always felt for her [which] is the underside of love." Beneath the surface of long, fruit-filled summer evenings together, their lust and their conscience will do battle. In the novella's conclusion, which has been criticized (perhaps unfairly) as overly transparent, Roth brings into the open what has all along been at issue: the business of choice. Having been propelled into a relationship about which they each have harbored reservations from the beginning, Neil and Brenda finally acknowledge their incompatibility. As Neil had pushed her into a tentative commitment (or was it really the first stage of their break-up?) by the purchase of the diaphragm, she now precipitates the end by leaving the apparatus at home for her mother to discover. In doing so, she boldly gives notice to her parents of her independent sexuality, even as she covertly acquiesces in her mother's disapproval of her lover and thus maintains her ties to home. Neil is willing enough to let her decide as long as he can score a few points on her coyness, and for all his wounded pride he finds in this losing a strange sensation of winning. Staring at his own reflection at the very end, he ponders the sort of psychological dividedness that haunts virtually all of Roth's protagonists: "Whatever spawned my love for her, had that spawned such lust too? If she had only been slightly *not* Brenda . . . but then would I have loved her?"

The issue of choice and of consequences receives far denser, more elaborate treatment in Roth's second, critically underestimated novel, *Letting Go* (1962). The action of this novel—with its proliferating triangle-relationships, its seedy abortion scene, and its garrulous, conniving old men in rooming houses—recalls the action of John Barth's first two novels, particularly *End of the Road* (1958), though Roth views his material with both more objectivity and more compassion. He thinks of this novel, together with *When She Was Good*, as his most "Jamesian" endeavors, but, in fact, the non-chronological, associative method of narration (proceeding by means of what he calls "blocks of consciousness") and the insistently moral perspective ally them more closely to the fiction of Saul Bellow, who in turn is solidly rooted in the work of Theodore Dreiser. *Letting Go* occupies a place in Roth's career much like that occupied in Bellow's career by *The Adventures of Augie March* (1953). To be sure, Roth is not interested in picaresque or in hearty affirmations of the creaturely, and *his* experiments in narrative voice come later, but in both *Letting Go* and *Augie March* we find the mimetic tendencies of these two major American authors exploited to the full. Certainly no other of Roth's books to date exhibits anything near the breadth of design, the complexity of characterization, the manifold immersion in urban American life—its fierce mobility and enclosedness—that distinguishes *Letting Go*. Despite its chunkiness and occasional repetitiousness (e.g., in the treatment of Libby's hysteria), it looms as the heart of Roth's fictional world.

Its centrality is perhaps most evident in the characters of Gabe Wallach and Paul Herz, who together constitute the first extended development of the "secret sharer" motif adumbrated in the stories of *Goodbye, Columbus*. Although Paul initially appears to embody the "poetic" side of the author and Gabe the professorial side, the reverse is actually the case. (This, of course, is to state things more schematically than the novel really warrants.) Gabe is the man of feeling. Though he comes of "strong stock" and is used to "conscience cracking its whip," he is basically "soft, rich, boyish," a bit of a "smoothy." He is prone to nervousness and indecision, and, like Augie March, he finds the boundaries of his own personality to be "blurry and indefinite." He can be adamant about "his pleasures," and he believes "not only in the pursuit, but the catching by the tail and dragging down into the clover, of happiness." His mistress suggests that he needs nobody and as a result feels obliged all the time. As he gets drawn ineluctably into the labyrinth of other people's lives, and as the specter of happiness recedes, he discovers that "his heart did not know how to respond."

Paul Herz, on the other hand, comes gradually to understand that, "no, he was not a man of feeling; it occurred to him that if he was anything at all it was a man of duty." He characteristically appears "dead serious," as if carrying around "a load on the heart [*Herz*]," and Gabe thinks he finds pleasure "in saying to the world: Woe is me." He is almost aggressively silent, "impossible to get to," and in fact is full of doubts about himself, full of fears. From an early age he has been "a planner," oppressed by "a strong sense of consequence," and he has banked absolutely on "the Will." But having entered defiantly and precipitately into a difficult marriage, he is compelled to look into himself for some saving "resiliency." The climax of the novel—and I believe it is one of the great unacknowledged moments in contemporary American literature—occurs in a dream-like sequence when he travels from Chicago to New York to attend the funeral of a father who has effectively disowned him. Many of the details of the sequence, including the prominent underwater imagery reminiscent of Bellow's *Seize the Day* (1956), are later echoed in Gabe's ruminations on his more ignoble moment of crisis. The scene also recalls the ending of Updike's *Rabbit, Run* (1960), except that where Rabbit

Angstrom runs *away* from a cemetery into the woods, Paul moves halt-
ingly but surely "out into the open" and *toward* the cemetery: for "*in* was
the direction of his life." As if finally penetrating the center of a storm, he
enters the circle of eyes without shame. He *lets go* of the will and feels
himself "under a wider beam":

> Justice, will, order, change—the words whistled by him,
> windless as the day was, like spirits moving off in the opposite
> direction. Dates. Names. Flowers. Sky. Only facts of history
> and of nature had meaning. The rest was invention.

Accepting the father, the father's death and return into the ground, entails acceptance of the world—a world "without admiration, without
pity. Yes. Oh yes!" He *becomes* his father, at least for the moment, and
begins to grasp the meaning of sacrifice, of Abraham and Isaac. What
Roth leaves us with is an appreciation of how dream-like may be our
enacting of a choice, and of how resolution may paradoxically involve
"letting go" (a formerly fashionable term perhaps not so different in
essence from Heidegger's notion of "*Gelassenheit*"). The irony is that at
the end, having secured his marriage in the adoption of a child, Paul still
can't relax.

   Where *Letting Go* most differs from Bellow, and from high modernism generally, is in its portrayal of women. Libby Herz, Martha
Reganhart and Cynthia Reganhart are imagined with a fullness and
critical empathy seemingly unavailable to the more philosophical martyrs
of the spirit. Bellow's Herzog might be speaking for the whole austere
fraternity (Thomas Mann, Kafka, Conrad, Dostoevsky, Nietzsche,
Schopenhauer, Schiller, etc.) when he calls love and interpersonal relationships "a feminine game." In this regard, Roth is closer to Updike, and
indeed to Lawrence and James, in his refined "womanly" involvement
with the strategies and chivalry of the heart. Except, one must immediately add, that no *shikse* but incurs equal amounts of adoration and
wrath from the creator of Portnoy.

   What is likely to remain his fullest portrait of a woman, *When She
Was Good* (1967), proffers both tribute and mockery to the *shikse*.
Tribute for her fortitude in aspiring to wholesomeness, mockery (and
pity) for her erratic self-deceptions about being "good." Of course, it is
not really as a Christian that Lucy is mocked by prose redolent of Gerty
MacDowell, though ostensible lines of consequence run from Daddy
Will's gospel of civilization to Lucy's collapse. It is more her female vulnerability that is at issue. She would be an upright woman to her hard-
working man, but neither she nor Roy proves very good at suffering.
Locked into a bad marriage, they both seek refuge in idealizing, Lucy in a
particularly volatile and melodramatic manner. Lucy shares with Libby
Herz (née DeWitt) an "ethereal and martyred" quality, a susceptibility to
a highly aestheticized form of religion, an intense self-involvement and a

vague faith in change. Together, the two young women remind one less of Isabel Archer than of Sue Bridehead. Where Libby is passionate, Lucy is icily eloquent. In each of them self-reliance struggles in the absence of in-grained self-respect and in the wake of alienation from their respective families. Lucy early on sets her will against the parents and grandparents she considers "weak" and "inferior"; she wins her independence, only to find herself wishing that her family would tell her no. Having secured a hollow freedom, she fervently prays: "make my father a father." But the past she seeks to escape catches up with her. Her own child locks himself away from her, as she once locked out her drunken father. When her mother seems to blame her for the family's misfortunes, something snaps in her mind, and the reader remembers idiot Aunt Ginny who used to cling to Lucy. Amid mounting paranoia Lucy herself clings to "the un-shakeable knowledge that she was right and they were wrong," but she cannot dismiss from her imagination the image of her father innocent. At the end, before she dies of exposure in the snow, with her father's letter frozen to her cheek, an almost orphic voice tells her, as it does Paul Herz and Gabe Wallach, "Nothing ever changes."

The battered family is no less central to the concerns of Roth's fourth and best known novel, *Portnoy's Complaint* (1969). In a short apology en-titled "Document of July 27, 1969," published in *Reading Myself and Others* (1975), Roth compares Alex Portnoy and Lucy Nelson as an-tithetical "soul mates." Both are "enraged offspring," he says, whose pas-sion for freedom plunges them into gruesome bondage. Both, we might add, are victims of a naive idealism of the good life (a faith that, if they are only good enough, the world will bow to them), and their stories par-take equally in a "history of disenchantment." For all his aspiring to be bad and enjoy it, to yield to "desires repugnant to my conscience," Port-noy's most ardent prayer is: "Bless me with manhood." He is obscene, Roth maintains, because he wants to be saved. Speaking for all the "watery-eyed sons of Jewish parents . . . melancholics and wise guys," he wonders when "we can leave off complaining how sick we are—and go out into the air, and live." No less than that of Lucy, his rebellion against authority conceals a "furious narcissism." He is imprisoned by his own rage, and the great irony of the novel (as Roth puts it in "On *Portnoy's Complaint*," in *Reading Myself and Others*) is that "breaking the taboo turns out to be as unmanning in the end as honoring it." He is impotent in Israel, presumably, just because he is finally *there*; his virility requires a sense of sin and adversary status. And yet he can no longer live, he pro-tests, in the self-lacerating world of ghetto humor. Oh, for the normal, in-dustrious life of "the men," playing softball Sunday mornings and watching Jack Benny with their families back in Newark! Is there no means to reconcile desire and duty?

Of course, the comparison with *When She Was Good* discounts the tremendous difference in the style or voice of *Portnoy's Complaint*, whose inspiration was to treat guilt as a comic idea. It may indeed be that the excellences of the novel are mainly rhetorical—a matter of performance and sustained improvisation. The analogy with night-club and vaudeville routines is obvious, and Portnoy further indicates the influence on his prose of a hyperbolized Jewish family life, where words are shown to function less as vehicles of communication than as bombs and bullets. (It is noteworthy that he relapses continually into the accents of his parents, most of all when indicting them.) In the service of his crafted intemperance, he comically exploits the Jewish imagination of catastrophe, making explicit what remained fearfully unspoken in the kitchen or bathroom. As that robust and outraged sabra tells him at the end, he is never entirely straight. Much like Bellow's Bummidge in his play *The Last Analysis* (1964), Portnoy embodies the artist as actor, or bluffer, afloat in his memories, his dreams, and his self-contempt. "Oi, my character!" cries Bummidge; "What am I going to do with my peculiarities?" For all their modulated fury, we notice, neither Portnoy nor Bummidge is entirely innocent of charm ("always a bit of a racket," says Herzog).

Where Portnoy as narrator is least reliable is in his treatment of "the Monkey," Mary Jane Reed. The (occasionally cloying) tenderness of characterization and the vividness of dialogue time and again undercut the rhetorical put-down ("hopelessly neurotic," "Skip the fight. It's boring," etc.). The reader familiar with Roth's earlier work will see beneath the narrator's baffled lust another in the gallery of vulnerable women, will sense her quickness and wit and girlishness as they mask themselves in the hip toughness or the hillbilly drawl, and as they crumble before her desperate need for justification. In fact, the free-wheeling vulgarity of the novel has caused many readers, even one so discerning as Irving Howe, to miss the lyrical undertone which emerges in scenes of family life (his mother dressing on the bed) or during the trip to Vermont, and which works to establish a strange counterpoint of diatribe and commemoration.

The fact remains, however, that in *Portnoy* rhetoric and exhibitionism generally trample mimesis. Scenes and characters are brief, flashy, formulaic. Roth has spoken, in *Reading Myself and Others*, of the appropriately "satyric" direction his career took in the later sixties, involving a deliberate and perverse subversion of his earlier earnestness. In "After Eight Books" (1974), he contrasts the "devoted effort at self-removal . . . necessary for the investigation of self that goes on (in *Letting Go*)" with the "self-pageantry" and the "ego-ridden" character of his comedies. In fact, in *Our Gang* (1971) and *The Great American Novel* (1973), we find the seething playfulness of *Portnoy* carried to calculatedly absurdist extremes, as if the author were relentlessly exorcising his grinning private demons. Both works reflect the fascination with conspiracy that was rampant in American culture during the early seventies, and it is significant that Roth's forays into farcical unrealism should coincide with a kind of political despair. (He comes from a family of New Deal Democrats, which will help explain why his responses to the Viet Nam era, often based on rather naive suppositions about "demythologizing," differ so radically from the responses of his peers like Bellow and Updike.) At least *The Great American Novel*, for all its breezy pastiche, cartoon characterology and anticipation of critical revulsion, can still entertain. The narrator, Word Smith—a lover of literature, liberty, lists, Luke Gofannon (the legendary Patriot Leaguer), and alliteration—knows how to deliver doom on the upbeat. Still, his travestying exposé of ambition and game-playing wearies after 382 pages, and the book strikes us finally as signifying, in terms of Roth's career to date, the furthest usurpation of action by voice.

The most succinct and suggestive of the whimsical spawn of *Portnoy* is *The Breast* (1972). It is written in a mix of Augustan elegance and American vernacular, and though we smile at the deadpan tone, the prevailing mood of the tale is sad and reflective. The metamorphosis of David Kepesh into a six-foot long, talking, writhing human breast completes the equation between desire and disease that is implicit in *Portnoy*. (The novel alludes not only to Kafka, Gogol, and Swift, but to Hans Castorp's researches into "the fever in matter" that is life in *The Magic Mountain*.) Desire is revealed to be essentially regressive, intent on oblivious escape from "the burden of verbalization," the duty of self-consciousness. Trying to explain his extravagant "mammary envy," his primitive identification with "*the* object of infantile veneration," Kepesh thinks to discover in himself "a churning longing to be utterly and blessedly helpless, to be a big brainless bag of tissue, desirable, dumb, passive, immobile, acted upon instead of acting, hanging, *there*, as a breast hangs and is *there*." The breast is his cocoon, in which he will finally be at rest in the mountains of female anatomy. In his "desperation to be cured," he dives inward toward some primeval sea bottom and imagines he has returned "to the earliest hours of my human existence . . . when the breast is me and I am the breast, when all is oneself and oneself is all." The novel implicitly asks, what is a body? It quotes at the end Rilke's "Archaic Torso of Apollo" (a poem about a pre-Hellenic age when Apollo was one with Dionysus) to suggest that the flesh has eyes, the body is a subject. Kepesh himself, despite his "inner turbulence," finds his memory intact and wants to convince the world that he is still a man, "for who but a man has conscience, reason, desire, and remorse?" At the conclusion, he is trying to live his life as usual from a hospital room, only he is *listening* more.

Kepesh's "talent for mimicry" is comparable to that of Portnoy, Word Smith, and Peter Tarnopol, the impersonating narrator of *My Life as a Man* (1974). This latter work, written at a time when the idea of "fictions" was especially fashionable in the academy, is Roth's most self-reflexive and hermeneutical venture, at the same time that it is the most determinedly unpleasurable and "ego-ridden" of his books. The ploy of

multi-layer fictionality—tending toward a "full-length fictional
fugue"—very likely is meant to compensate for naked autobiographical
urgings: "his self is to many a novelist what his own physiognomy is to a
painter of portraits: the closest object at hand demanding scrutiny, a
problem for his art to solve—given the enormous obstacles to truthfulness,
the artistic problem." The strained syntax here is symptomatic of a writer
who, as Sanford Pinsker has said, "finds it hard to strike a balance between satirical aloofness and passionate self-righteousness." The enormous obstacles to truthfulness are not to be entirely overcome: "no matter
how close I come," writes Tarnopol, "I only come close." Everything in
this novel is subject to a deliberate ambiguity of interpretation, a search
for causes, reasons, meanings that ruthlessly diffracts the surface of the
action. Was Lydia/Maureen really raped by her father? Or is it "all
pretense," as Lydia claims? Are Zuckerman's migraines physiologically
grounded, or are they brought on by cowardice in the face of military service, or are they insidiously related to his reading of Virginia Woolf and
Thomas Mann, his romantic conviction in "illness as a necessary catalyst
to imagination?" Like Paul Herz in *Letting Go*, the narrator would make
of his fiction a solitary therapy of "acting out"; he claims that writing is
"really all I trust." But the anxieties of influence bear down on the teacher
of "Creative Writing," polyphony falters, the appearances become entangled, until he can no longer believe in even his own characters: "Tarnopol, as he is called, is beginning to seem as imaginary as my
Zuckerman."

On the other hand, *My Life as a Man* is not finally a Borgesian hall of
mirrors. Its skepticism is less epistemological than moral. Amid the proliferating strategies and slippery texts, it tries to fathom yet another failed
marriage. It tells the story of Zuckerman/Tarnopol's passage from a
regimented and confident late adolescence into the tangle of adult life. It
also seeks, in the service of an ironic feminism, to "demystify" the myth of
male inviolability—the "Prince Charming phenomenon." Like Gabe
Wallach and Alex Portnoy, the narrator is drawn to women whom he
thinks he can redeem. Zuckerman is seduced by Lydia's style, by the sense
that her cool and cozy manner with misery represents "a moral triumph."
By the same token, Tarnopol wants "something taxing in [his] love affairs,
something problematical." Convinced that women are the testing ground
for male virtue, "both" men try to conceal from themselves their own
blazing self-righteousness. What more perfect formula for disaster? The
disjointed scenes of battle between Tarnopol and Maureen are as powerful as their prototypes in Bellow and Mailer, and moreover less given to
caricaturing the hysterical, psychopathic bitch-wife. When Tarnopol
reads from Maureen's diary at the end, wondering if all along he has not
secretly sympathized with this maniacal liar, he realizes that, in a
destructive and "brutally ironic," but also poignant way, she has been his
muse.

Tarnopol's sister tells him, in a literary critical letter, that "you can't make pleasure credible . . . you couldn't create a Kitty and a Levin if your life depended on it." Truth, for him, is what hurts. Almost as if to rise to her challenge, Roth's next novel, *The Professor of Desire* (1977), seeks, among other things, to portray a relatively happy relationship. The title, however (and Roth has always been brilliant at inventing titles: witness Zuckerman's senior thesis title, "Subdued Hysteria: A Study of the Undercurrent of Agony in Some Novels of Virginia Woolf"), the title already suggests that the professor has broached an impossible discipline. As if freed to *feel* by the tortuous self-consciousness of the preceding work, this novel moves in a more fluid, straightforward course ("as understanding grows," writes the narrator, "as familiarity grows, and feeling with it, I begin at last to relinquish some of my suspiciousness"). Constructed more or less conventionally of extended scenes and intervening arias, infused by a muted lyricism and an unwonted modesty, it is Roth's most attractive novel yet. The scene of the parents' visit to Manhattan displays his mastery of *progression d'effet*—of juxtaposition and modulation—and its mingling of the tender and sorrowful and funny is unlike anything else he has done:

> . . . and then, when they are smiling, I will take off my robe and crawl into the bed between them. And before she dies, we will all hold each other through one last night and morning . . . "She cooked for you," he says, his voice trembling, "and then she went away" . . . He carries the frozen food in a shopping bag out to my car. "Here, please, in her memory."

The story concerns the would-be maturation of David Kepesh at a time before his morbid transformation. Having spent a year in London as a "visiting fellow in erotic daredevilry"—a year which sees his matriculation as whoremaster, polygamist, and beginning rapist—he returns home to marry an aristocratic adventuress and *femme fatale* strongly reminiscent of some of Bellow's courtesanlike mistresses. All along he has kept in mind the memory of a young Swedish woman who wears her father's picture around her neck. "How incredibly moving a thing it is, a person's innocence," he thinks, even as he indulges his Portnovian appetite. When his marriage inevitably fails and he finds himself drifting and sinking, he wonders, "How . . . have I come to be on such terrible terms with sensuality?" He finds solace in Chekhov, whose stories he teaches in Desire 341, solace in his humane "pessimism about what he calls 'this business of personal happiness.' " Nevertheless, he is soon drawn into precisely that business, and with calm and beautiful Claire Ovington (the patient ministrant of *The Breast*) he feels that he has "come through" and arrived home. But, as we might have expected, the subsiding of passion spells the end of his happiness—"How much longer before I've had a bellyful of wholesome innocence?"—and the novel concludes, ominous and elegiac, with his mourning the loss of desire.

To his psychiatrist Dr. Klinger, "a specialist in common sense," Kepesh talks confusedly about "This something in me that I turned against . . . before I even understood it, or let it have a life." He likely refers to an instinct for happiness, trust, ordinariness, such as is satisfied for a while with Claire, but the reader may speculate whether or not Roth here is thinking analogously of the mimetic tendencies that gave rise to his first three books and that afterward got progressively squelched. In "After Eight Books," the interviewer Joyce Carol Oates asks about the possibility of "some violent pendulum swing" in his career away from Sheer Playfulness and "back to what you were years ago, in terms of your commitment to 'serious' and even Jamesian writing." Her question now seems prophetic, for in *The Professor of Desire* and *The Ghost Writer* (1979), we find, if not Deadly Seriousness, at least a move back from jerk-off artistry to something like Jamesian representation. To his undergraduate class Kepesh explicitly argues a principle of referentiality, and the revived, 43-year-old Nathan Zuckerman of *The Ghost Writer* chooses for his narrative of father-seeking and martyred wives the context of the realistic *Bildungsroman*, which in truth lies behind everything Roth has written. Of course, the subjective or self-reflexive impulse (which will not listen) is still around, awaiting future transformations, but it is seemingly restrained and regarded with suspicion: Zuckerman refers to "the novelist's dubious wizardry" and exclaims, "If only I could invent as presumptuously as real life!" His presumptuous invention of Anne Frank, which misled certain reviewers, represents an attempt to mediate not only between the written and the unwritten, but between invasion and propriety—an attempt to embrace and re-enter the community. It is an apology, characteristically outrageous, to the Jewish philistines like Judge Wapter who have stung him with their accusations of Jewish anti-Semitism. "What do I know other than what I can imagine?" he asks, and proceeds to re-imagine something of the unimaginable holocaust and the Jewish saint. The pendulum has swung full around, for at this point we remember the story "Eli, the Fanatic" in *Goodbye, Columbus*, in which a character first tries to straddle the conflicting claims of the law and the heart.

Oedipal Politics in *Portnoy's Complaint*

Robert Forrey*

If Freud was correct, the Oedipus complex is the nucleus not only of neurosis but of civilization; that is, it is not only a negative factor creating momentous psychological problems but a positive one also, creating structure, meaning and culture. The French structuralist Jacques Lacan has elaborated and extended Freud's ideas on the Oedipus complex, particularly the central role of language and culture, in the structuring and organization of human experience. Explicating Lacan's theories, which are embedded in a notoriously dense prose, Anika Lemaire writes, "the Oedipus complex is the unconscious articulation of a human world of culture and language; it is the very structure of the unconscious forms of the society . . . [Lacan's] point of view consists simply in seeing the Oedipus complex as the pivot of humanization, as a transition from the natural register of life to a cultural register of group exchange and therefore of laws, symbols and organization."[1] On the crucial role of the father in the Oedipus complex, she says, paraphrasing Lacan, the father is "the representative of the Law and a protagonist in the subject's entry into the order of culture, civilization and language. 'It is in the Name-of-the-Father that we must recognize the symbolic function which identifies his person with the figure of the Law' (*Ecrits*, 16)."[2]

At his father's insistence, the David Schearl of Henry Roth's *Call It Sleep* (1934) went to cheder and studied Hebrew, God's language. It is an indication of how far removed from Jewish religious roots Alexander Portnoy is that his father insists he learn shorthand. After all, because Billy Rose knew shorthand, Bernard Baruch hired him as a secretary. By contrast, learning Hebrew never became an issue; it apparently was a dead, useless language. Even Yiddish was nearly a lost tongue for Portnoy, or so he felt. "Talk Yiddish?" he asks. *"How?* I've got twenty-five words to my name—half of them dirty and the rest mispronounced!"[3] He suffers a similar feeling of linguistic inferiority about his English—he refers deprecatingly at one point to his "five-hundred-word New Jersey vocabulary" (p. 233).

*This essay was written specifically for this volume and appears here for the first time by permission of the author.

266

Portnoy's feelings of linguistic inadequacy are complemented by and inextricably tied up with his feelings of sexual inadequacy, as one might expect, according to Lacanian theory. A (seemingly) small vocabulary and a (seemingly) small penis go hand in hand. Furthermore, consistent with Lacanian theory, it is the mother, Sophie Portnoy, who made the son feel ashamed of the size, and even the existence, of his penis. Never in his whole life had Alex Portnoy felt more humiliated than when his mother chided him as a boy for wanting a bathing-suit with a jock-strap in it. Her words on that occasion were inscribed indelibly in his memory: "For *your* little thing?" (p. 51). Another incident which Portnoy recalled from his childhood is instructive in illustrating the connection between the penis and what Lacan designates as the "Name-of-the-Father." When Portnoy Sr. urinated with the bathroom door open, Sophie scolded him for setting a bad example for his son, whom she referred to in that situation not by name but as "you-know-who." Significantly, when it came to sexuality and the penis, neither father nor son possessed a name. Recollecting the episode, Portnoy bitterly lamented, "If only you-know-who [himself, the son] could have found some inspiration in what's-his-name's [Jake, the father's] coarseness" (p. 50). What it was about his father, "what's-his-name," that Alex wanted most to be proud of and identify with was his masculinity, symbolized by his penis.

When Portnoy in describing to Spielvogel an act of masturbation in adolescence says he grabbed "that battered battering ram to freedom, my adolescent cock" (p. 35), he is simultaneously playing with language and his penis. In the scene from adolescence, as Portnoy recalls it, he was being nagged by his mother about what foods he should and should not eat. To escape from this nagging, he fled to the bathroom and behind the closed door, as was his frequent habit, began masturbating his "battered battering ram," etc. This is linguistic as well as sexual playing because Portnoy's penis in that situation was anything but a means to freedom, for the object of Portnoy's fantasies in adolescence was often his sister, who in turn was a barely disguised substitute—as other young women were later—for his mother, who in that same bathroom when Portnoy was a boy used to try to induce him to urinate by seductively tickling his penis. The sexual desire Portnoy had felt for his mother when he was a child did not disappear when he grew older; it just became more disguised and less conscious. In retreating to the bathroom in adolescence, Portnoy was not getting away from his mother; he was by sexual means attaching himself more closely to her. He was only pretending, playing, he was trying to liberate himself from her when he talked about his cock and freedom. His linguistic model in this act of self-deception was not Yiddish or even American but Anglo-Saxon. The noun "cock" has connotations, stemming from the Old English, lacking in the Yiddish words for penis Portnoy usually uses—schmuck, putz, etc. And the phrase "battered battering ram to freedom" echoes the language ("my head is bloodied but unbowed") and mood of that classic expression of Anglo-Saxon pride and courage in the period of imperial England's decline, Henley's poem "Invictus", which Portnoy had learned by heart in school. It is precisely because Portnoy was so completely in the "fell clutch" of his mother that, with his penis and language, he played games in which he pretended that he was potent, that he was getting away from, or letting go of, his mother. In reality, Portnoy was as impotent as his father was constipated; though the bathroom appeared to be the one place father and son could escape from the mother, it was actually the place where they were most clearly subject to her.

In spite of the sexual and linguistic confusion in *Call It Sleep*, the God of the Old Testament sits on His throne, looming omnipotently over David Schearl's Lower East Side, the creator of the Word and the Law. The God who presides over Portnoy's Newark, if He exists at all (which Portnoy deeply doubts), is a petty, jealous and vindictive God. In referring to Him, Portnoy adopts his mother's linguistic attitude toward his father by calling the Heavenly Father not "what's-his-name" but something very much like it: "None Other." The original kill-joy, None Other is determined that all Jews will grow up to be inhibited, neurotic and miserable, as Alex sees it. As Alex's constipated father told him, this God has a big book in which He annually writes in the names of those who are going to live for another twelve months. If you break the smallest rule, Portnoy concludes, this God will sit down in anger and frustration (like his constipated father on the toilet, he blasphemously suggests) and leave your name out of the book. Such is the meanness and authority of this God—and the control he exerts through words—that if He does not write your name down you do not continue to exist.

Nobody in *Portnoy's Complaint* better bespeaks the bankruptcy of the Law and the Word than the official representative of the God of the Old Testament and spiritual leader for Newark's Reform Jews, Rabbi Warshaw. All of the Rabbi's limitations as a man and a Jew are epitomized, in Roth's characterization of him, in his speech; he is defined in the novel and we see and measure him primarily, perhaps exclusively, through the pretentious and condescending way in which he uses English to say nothing. The overweight and Pall-Mall smoking Rabbi is the American Jew as English gentleman. "This is a man," Portnoy says of him, "who somewhere along the line got the idea that the basic unit of meaning in the English language is the syllable. So no word he pronounces has less than three of them, not even the word God" (p. 73). In contrast to herring-breathed Reb Pankover in *Call It Sleep*, with his unkept clothes and atrocious English (but fluent Hebrew and Yiddish), the role of "Rabbi Syllable," as Roth calls Warshaw, is not to badger, exhort or instruct on God's behalf, but rather to establish through syllabification his own social respectability, in contrast to his uncouth Newark congregation with their Yiddish and East European-inflected American accents. For the effete Rabbi Warshaw, scripture is not Hebrew but "Anglo-oracular" English, perhaps the ultimate antithesis, for an American Jew, from the father's tongue.

In his quest for manhood, Portnoy turns pleadingly to the psychoanalyst Spielvogel, with his heavy foreign accent, as to another Jewish father.

> Doctor Spielvogel, this is my life, my only life, and I'm living it in the middle of a Jewish joke! I am the son in the Jewish joke—*only it ain't no joke!* Please who crippled us like this? Who made us so morbid, and hysterical and weak? . . . Doctor, I can't stand any more being frightened like this over nothing. Bless me with manhood. (p. 37.)

Again, it accords with Lacan's theories that Portnoy's attempt to achieve manhood is quintessentially linguistic, as if talking to a new Jewish father (Spielvogel-Freud), whose authority with words is much greater than his own father's, can make him a man. (And note, too, in the child-like candor, Yiddish-like locutions, and intentionally bad grammar of this appeal, the pains Portray takes to distinguish his speech from that of the phony Jewish father, Rabbi Warshaw.) Instead of continuing his obsessive and futile pursuit of women, i.e. the mother, Portnoy through psychoanalysis in a sense goes to bed with the father. With Freud's *Collected Papers* in one hand and his penis in the other, reading the one and "kneading" the other, to quote Roth's pun, Portnoy looks eagerly for "the sentence, the phrase, the *word* that will liberate me from what I understand are called my fantasies and fixations" (p. 186). A compulsive, determined masturbator, as previously noted, Portnoy plays religiously with his penis; he also plays with words, with English, Yiddish and psychoanalytic words, trying to get them to liberate him from his compulsions, trying to come to some understanding of the meaning of his complaint. Psychoanalytic desiderata—the truths of the secularized Jewish faith—occur to him in the form of punning slogans: "LET MY PETER GO!"; "LET'S PUT THE ID BACK IN YID!"; etc. These slogans are rhetorical therapy, part of the "talking cure" which Portnoy conducts in the form of a monologue with his Jewish father figure—Spielvogel.

Before turning to Spielvogel, Portnoy had tried to find salvation sexually through a number of Gentile women. His feelings for and against them were often related at least in part to language. The only Gentile woman he ever seriously thought about marrying was from that same Iowa family in which language was used gently, if not also somewhat genteely. As young as thirteen Portnoy had felt the irresistible appeal of the well-bred blond shikses, but he understood even then that they lived in an entirely different world, with "grammatical fathers" and mothers named Mary ("Mary! Mother also of Jesus Christ!" he said of the Iowa shikse's mother). Another shikse, a boarding-school type from Connecticut, disqualified herself as a candidate for Mrs. Alexander Portnoy, if Alex is to be believed, because in part she spoke in an intolerable "cutesy-wootsy boarding school argot" (p. 233). Nothing could redeem her in his eyes, not even her great personal sacrifice in finally performing fellatio on him. All of his deeply problematic and ambivalent feelings about Gentile Women came to a head in his relationship with a sexually uninhibited and uninhibiting model he dubbed "the Monkey." He named her this not simply because of her passion for, as he put it, eating his banana, but also, it appears, because he had trouble calling her by her real name, Mary— the mother of Christ again. What in the end convinced Portnoy that he could not find his manhood through the Monkey, in spite of her sexiness, was his discovery that she was barely literate, as she revealed in a note she left for her maid: "dir willa polish the floor by bathrum *pleze* & dont furget the insies of windose mary jane r." Not her promiscuity or predilection for sexual perversity, but such ignorance of the language led Portnoy to the moralistic conclusion: "How unnatural can a relationship be! This woman is ineducable and beyond reclamation" (p. 206). What this rejection of the Monkey may in part signify—and other dimensions of the novel support of this point—is that the Gentile woman, Mary (the mother of Christers) is a hopeless pagan, a slut: the woman who did not get the Word. As inadequate as he, a Jew, felt linguistically, his Gentile paramour was appallingly worse; her illiteracy served to remind him of his inescapably linguistic, Jewish identity.

As a teen-ager in Newark, Portnoy had reluctantly joined some other Jewish boys in a visit to the flat of "Bubbles" Girardi, a loose Italian-American girl. Afraid of being infected or contaminated in the unkosher surroundings, he was appalled by a picture of Christ above the kitchen sink. "What kind of base and brainless schmucks are these people to worship somebody who, number one, never existed, and number two, if he did, looking as he does in that picture, was without a doubt the Pansy of Palestine" (p. 168). In Portnoy's eyes, Christ is the nice Jewish boy become homosexual messiah. By way of settling the question of whether he himself was homosexual, Portnoy answers that, amazing as it sometimes seemed to him (in view of his mother's influence), he was not; he was infected by neither it nor Christianity. We can believe that he sincerely believes he was not, and still be unconvinced that Christ, the prototypical nice Jewish boy, was not a haunting religious and sexual influence in Portnoy's life. It is quite possible that Portnoy's unexplained but deep hostility toward Christ is the result of feeling pressured all his life into becoming a nice Jewish boy or, to put it in a different light, a Jewish son-as-savior. Elsewhere Portnoy had pointed out the tendency of Jewish parents to make their children feel, on the one hand, like "evil little shits," and on the other, like "saviors and sheer perfection" (p. 119). He felt this pressure from within his own family, even after he was a grown man. Weary and feeling on death's doorstep, his father Jake looked to Alex, when the latter was thirty-three, to keep him alive. "Does he actually believe that I somehow have the power to destroy death?" Portnoy asks Spielvogel. "That I am the resurrection and the life? My dad, a real believing Christer! And doesn't even know it!" (p. 118). Jake Portnoy may not have been aware that he wanted his son to be a savior, but the Monkey, the Gentile, knows that's what she wanted, and she goaded him to live up to her expectations. "But—what, what was I supposed to be but *her* Jewish savior?" (p. 153), he asks Spielvogel. But isn't that really his secret forbidden wish, to be a "Christer," that is a Jewish son who transcends the Oedipal politics of the Jewish family, who sexually renounces not only the mother and the debased (Gentile) sexual objects who serve as her substitute, but also renounces sexuality (or at least heterosexualty) itself? Isn't Portnoy afraid that, to get out of the Jewish family, where words were weapons and language somewhat lethal, he would be willing to become anything—a savior, a Christian, a pansy or perhaps, like the ex-Jewish son ascending over the Gentile sink, all three? Until he discovered psychoanalysis, with its putatively therapeutic rhetoric, the Jewish son had only two alternatives: follow in the footsteps of Christ or become permanently trapped in a Jewish joke.

The sexual, religious and linguistic threads of *Portnoy's Complaint* are woven together in the trip Portnoy describes taking at the age of thirty-three to Rome, Greece and Israel. He went to Rome with the Monkey and the two of them went to bed with a whore in Rome, fulfilling one of Portnoy's conscious sexual fantasies, as well as, possibly, one of his unconscious religious ones. The experience proved disappointing to him, and in a recurrence of an old phobia, he became obsessed with the idea that the whore of Rome had infected him. It was in Rome that he saw clearly the futility of having looked for salvation, that is for his manhood, through Gentile women. In Greece, his next stop after Rome, he abandoned the Monkey. Given the Oedipal nature of his problems, it was an appropriate place, he himself reflects, to end the relationship. However, he was under no illusion that his Oedipal drama was Greek rather than Jewish, tragic rather than pathetic. "*Oedipus Rex* is a tragedy, schmuck, not another joke!" (p. 266), he castigates himself. The conclusion Portnoy reached in Europe was that, instead of wasting his life pursuing Gentile women, he wanted to marry a Jewish girl and raise a Jewish family. But to do that he has to feel like a man, like a *Jewish* man, the model of which he fondly remembers as the Jewish fathers who played baseball in Newark: "Because I love those men! Because I want to grow up to be one of those men!" (p. 277).

Possible reflecting the relatively low status of the male in Yiddish culture, the Yiddish language contains a number of demeaning and deprecatory slang words for the penis. Derogatory words like schmuck, putz, shvontz, and schlong can be used to describe the penis or, alternately, a contemptibly hapless or stupid, usually Jewish, male (i.e.

schlemiel). On the subject of emasculated Jewish sons, Portnoy says his mother held up to him as models to follow a number of namby-pambies who did everything to please their Jewish mothers. " 'Do you remember Seymour Schmuck, Alex?' she asks me, or Aaron Putz or Howard Schlong, or some yo-yo I am supposed to have known in grade school twenty-five years ago, and of whom I have no recollection whatsoever" (p. 99). In assigning fictitious names to the boys his mother praises, Portnoy exploits the connotations of Yiddish slang words for penis to underscore the Jewish son's slavish attachment to his mother. What the penis-names Portnoy makes up reveal is the tendency of the Jewish son, in his attempt to please the mother, to become the phallus, which, Lacan reminds us, is the object of her desire. To escape becoming a mama's boy, the son must renounce those sexual feelings for his mother which tend to make him identify with the object of her desire—the phallus. To become a man and accede to the Name-of-the-Father, the son must, under the threat of castration, represented by the father, graduate from being the phallus to having it (he must lose it before he can use it), the distinction between which, Lacan claims, is absolutely crucial. If to please his mother the son persists in being the object of his mother's desire, that is the phallus, then he becomes a schmuck.

When Portnoy had fantasies of becoming a Jewish father, bringing his family up in New Jersey, he imagined them all listening each evening not to the sacred texts of Judaism (the *toroth*) but to those Jewish comics, with or without Yiddish accents, who kept Americans laughing when he was growing up in the thirties and forties: Jack Benny and Mr. Kitzel (of whose Yiddish accent the boy Portnoy could do a flawless and hilarious imitation); Fred Allen and Mrs. Nussbaum; and Phil Harris and Frankie Remly. (Omitted, by oversight no doubt, were Eddie Cantor and the Mad Russian.) The point is even Portnoy's sentimental dream of Jewish marriage and fatherhood unfolds within the context of a Jewish joke—the same Jewish joke in which he felt he had lost his manhood and from which he had pleaded with Spielvogel to liberate him. Nationalized by radio and later extended and further commercialized by popular literature, film and television, the Jewish joke become the cultural code, the linguistic mode in which the complaining Jewish son, blaming most and often all his problems on his Jewish mother, capitalized on—and became further mired in—his feelings of emotional and sexual incompetence.

Portnoy's ultimate complaint is not only against the mother; it is also against language, against the word, the traditional repository of Jewish faith. And against talk, which Michael Gold, writing in the thirties, claimed "has ever been the joy of the Jewish race, great torrents of boundless, exalted talk."[4] Some post-War Jewish-American writers, like Roth, tend to see language and talk as complaint, perhaps a specifically Jewish complaint, which they want to get away from, or at least reduce to its most elemental meaning: pain. Instead of wanting to talk exaltedly, Portnoy at the end of the novel wants simply to howl. "A pure howl," he tells Spielvogel, "without any more words between me and it!" (p. 273). (The antithesis, perhaps, to the excessive syllabification of Rabbi Warshaw.) What all this howling (or is it merely whining?) is about is the Jewish son's lack of tumidity and potency. Unable to assume the role of the father, who possesses the Phallus and the word, Portnoy is driven to cunnilingus—the tongue substituting for the phallus, sex for language. Without the word, without the phallus, the only way the son can relate to the forbidden other, the Mother, and her substitutes, is by using the tongue to complain futilely about, or orally and impotently enter into, her. In behaving like this Portnoy is lacking in culture, in Lacan's sense; he is reduced to an animal, non-linguistic level: "Maybe that's all I really am, a lapper of cunt, the slavish mouth for some woman's hole. Eat! And so be it! Maybe the wisest solution is for me to live on all fours! Crawl through life feasting on pussy, and leave the righting of wrongs and the fathering of families to the upright creatures!" (p. 270). Portnoy's rough beast can not come; his howling complaint is utter wordlessness; his argument, in its various senses, is without issue.

More complex linguistically than it may at first appear, Portnoy's complaint, i.e. the Oedipus complex, nevertheless becomes in Roth's treatment of it, a Jewish joke, a brilliant, elaborate spiel. (It is perhaps a compensation for his complex fate as a Jew that the castrated Portnoy becomes such an accomplished, cunning linguist.) The psychoanalytic dialogue turns into a Jewish monologue; the quest for *the* psychoanalytic *word* that would help resolve the Oedipus complex ends in a howl of frustration and painful laughter. The new Jewish father to whom Portnoy had prayed for deliverance from the Jewish joke his life had become turns out to be an "ungrammatical" father, another creature of the Diaspora and of the doctrine of historical impotency. That Spielvogel is circumscribed by and a victim of the same Jewish joke that Portnoy had prayed for deliverance from is indicated by the fact that the only words the psychoanalyst speaks, the very last words in the novel—"Now vee may perhaps to begin. Yes?"—bear the accent and syntax of a Jewish vaudevillian, and are introduced with the caption "Punchline," thus emphasizing that all that had been said up to that point was a joke, an extended vocal Jewish spiel.

Writing at a time when or in a frame of mind in which it was still possible for an American Jew to be romantic and mythopoeic about the Oedipus complex, Henry Roth called it sleep. Writing in the nineteen-sixties, in a very different frame of mind, Philip Roth reduced that monumental human complex which Freud connected with "the beginnings of religion, ethics, society and art" into a hysterically funny, a specifically, if not exclusively, Jewish complaint: the complaint of the Jewish son to the Jewish father about the Jewish mother. However, Portnoy's fundamental but unspoken complaint is language, that symbolic discourse in the complex structure of which not only meaning but manhood (the Phallus) can be either achieved or, as in Portnoy's case, lost. Roth's novel suggests that language is a Jewish and perhaps ultimately a human complaint. But language is also, structuralists remind us, the precondition of humanity, "the site of possible liberty and truth."[5] Perhaps that is the point which Portnoy, if he is to be more than a cunning linguist, must take seriously.

Notes

1. Anika Lemaire, *Jacques Lacan* (London: Routledge & Kegan Paul, 1977), p. 92.

2. *Lacan*, p. 85. Because of the vital importance which Lacan attributes to the resolution of the Oedipus complex in the acquisition of language and accession of the subject to the symbolic realm, it is worth trying to clarify a complex point in his theory, specifically the notion that "in the quest for the Phallus, the subject moves from being it to having it." (*Lacan*, p. 95.) In the immediate, undifferentiated relationship with the mother, the son is the phallus (by which Lacan means much more than penis), which is the object of the mother's desire. "Originally, the *infans* subject wishes *to be* the Phallus, the object of his mother's desire. This means that in order to ensure himself of his mother's presence and her complete affective support, the child unconsciously seeks to be that which can best gratify her. He seeks to make himself exclusively indispensable. This affective wish is tinged with eroticism, and the multiple phantasies elaborated by the child, who is, in a confused way, awake to his parents' sexual relations, are grouped around the phallic symbol, around the general idea of the 'Father' ": and yet it is the father who "renders the mother-child fusion impossible by his interdiction and marks the child with a fundamental lack of being . . . His true desire and the multiple phantasmatic forms it took are pushed back into the unconscious. This is the primal repression which determines accession to language and which substitutes a symbol and a Law for the Real of existence." (*Lacan*, p. 87.) By accepting the Law of the father the son gives up the mother, as a sexual object, and begins a quest for other objects farther and farther from the original object of his desire. The son gives up the mother but he acquires by way of compensation the whole world—that is the world of discourse and symbolic exchange, all that we designate by the term culture. If the son had not made this transition, language would have for him no referent; words and "reality," the signifier and the signified, would be indistinguishable, which is why schizophrenia is not just a sexual problem; it is also a language problem.

3. *Portnoy's Complaint* (New York: Random House, 1967), p. 224. Subsequent page references will be incorporated into the text of the paper.

4. *Jews Without Money* (New York: Avon Books, 1965), p. 70.

5. "Forward by Antoine Vergote," in *Lacan*, p. xxiii.

INDEX